the summer That saved Baseball

Trent,

Thanks for the cool photo.

Enjoy the "Journey"

4/25/09

the ultimate fans' road trip

the summer that saved Baseball

A 38-DAY JOURNEY TO THIRTY MAJOR LEAGUE BALLPARKS

BRAD NULL & DAVE KAVAL

CUMBERLAND HOUSE • NASHVILLE, TENNESSEE

Published by
CUMBERLAND HOUSE PUBLISHING, INC.
431 Harding Industrial Drive
Nashville, Tennessee 37211
www.CumberlandHouse.com

Cover design by Unlikely Suburban Design, Nashville, Tennessee.

Library of Congress Cataloging-in-Publication Data

Null, Brad, 1975– .
    The summer that saved baseball : a 38-day journey to thirty major league ballparks / Brad Null & Dave Kaval.
        p.   cm.
    ISBN 1-58182-187-5 (pbk. : alk. paper)
    1. Baseball fields—United States. 2. Null, Brad, 1975– .–Journeys—United States. 3. Kaval, Dave, 1975– .—Journeys—United States. I. Kaval, Dave, 1975– . II. Title.
GV879.5.N85 2001
796.357'06'873—dc21

00-065921

Printed in the United States of America

2 3 4 5 6 7 8—05 04 03 02 01

To our fathers for their motivation
and our mothers for their support

contents

The Beginning

At ABOUT 5 P.M. on July 26, 1998, Dave and I, cruising south through Minnesota down I-35, slipped over the state line into Silver Lake, Iowa. The moment passed unbeknownst to anyone outside our black '96 Nissan Pathfinder. But inside, Dave and I were fully aware of the magnitude of the situation. At the moment I wasn't feeling any of the general animosity toward Dave that had characterized much of the last thirty days or so. We were back to the familiar best-friend team that had begun this adventure, and we were now united in our desire to rocket through the corn and reach our destination. Of course, we were just driving through Iowa en route to Kansas City and our thirtieth major league baseball game at our thirtieth major league park in thirty-eight days, a feat we humbly referred to as the Baseball America Tour. Before we finished the Tour, however, we had one penultimate stop. And we had to get there by sunset.

Unfortunately, at that moment we were more than three hundred miles from our goal: The Field of Dreams. And after another three hours passed uneventfully, we would see the sun set on our ambition. A good seventy miles away from our Dyersville, Iowa, destination, the sky darkened. But we pushed on regardless.

Ironically, as the day faded into darkness, Dave and I became even more excited. We would not reach the field in daylight, but we again shared that delusion of grandeur that had become so familiar to us over the course of our trip. We found ourselves hoping, even expecting, that (just like in the movies) they would leave the lights on for us. After all, we had driven twelve thousand miles to get to this point. We had fulfilled 29/30ths of what a select group might label as an American Dream. And en route to that final thirtieth, we were anxious to make it to the lonely baseball field with that famous cornstalk fence.

Of course, cynics might regard the Field of Dreams as a tourist trap and one of the more subtle examples of corporate greed and exploitation of the last twenty years in this country. But we never would have gotten to this point by being cynical. We were approaching the end of a personal quest. Thirty-seven days prior we hadn't known what to expect from this journey. We were just kids looking for a little adventure and some fun along the way. Which we'd had, along with fair servings of exhaustion (mostly because of seemingly endless driving) and frustration (mostly because of each other). But now we were less than one hour from the Field of Dreams, what any unabashed baseball sentimentalist would call a true shrine to the game—fifty-five miles now—and we couldn't help but think that maybe, just maybe, somebody had left the lights on for us.

THIS IS the story of the Baseball America Tour, and while it culminated shortly after that trip through Iowa, it began some six months earlier in January 1998. Dave and I were seniors at Stanford University, and as seniors are wont to do, we invariably found ourselves discussing postgraduation plans. Dave already had a job lined up beginning that fall and was contemplating an extended vacation to Europe or some other exotic locale with his girlfriend (now fiancée), Maria, during his last summer of freedom from the daily grind. I, on the other hand, had yet to make any plans at all concerning that vast span of time after my June graduation.

In the creative throes of a slight beer buzz one rainy January night, we began discussing some of the things that we might like to experience in the years to come (preferably sooner rather than later). In fact, to say that several things were discussed is misleading. As soon as the issue was raised, only one topic received much attention at all. The great American road trip.

Since childhood Dave and I had both harbored a desire to venture on an elaborate cross-country road trip to see each of the major league ballparks. How we could have each come up with the idea independently while living thousands of miles apart is a mystery even to us, although I personally recall hearing something of a suburban legend of people making such trips. There were stories of people who had been to all the parks in their lifetime, even those who had made it to all of the National League parks in one season. But what about all of the parks in a row? Now that would be interesting! Does anybody actually do that? (Yes, actually, it turns out it is quite common.) But we thought it was a great idea. And it was our idea. And I personally was determined to get it done. At least until I passed out that night. When I awoke the next morning the trip had faded into something of a pipe dream.

The trip slipped in and out of our conversations for the next couple of months, one of those plans that would be great as long as someone else did all the work and all you had to do was show up (very much like the plan to write this book, actually). Quite honestly, I think we were both very excited about the idea, but neither of us really believed that the other would follow through with it.

As the days passed, and the trip remained little more than an idea, it seemed obvious that it would never materialize. But at the end of March, Dave and I found ourselves in position to experience another once-in-a-lifetime sports-themed road trip following the Stanford Cardinal basketball team to San Antonio for the Final Four, the NCAA basketball championship series. We both had a great time in the Alamo City and, despite Stanford's loss, consequently decided that the only thing more fun than a four-day road trip would be a forty-day road trip. So we decided then and there to commit to the Baseball America Tour (our pretentious name for our postcollege road trip). Lest we have any doubts, fate played the final hand in our decision in the form of a full two-page baseball pullout in the *San Antonio Express News*. The pullout detailed the full schedules of each of the major league ball clubs for the coming season. We saved that piece of paper and later used it to schedule our trip.

Once the trip was decided upon, all we had to do was plan it, the details of which we managed to avoid for at least another month. In fact, it wasn't until the middle of May that Dave and I sat down to plot the whole thing out. First and foremost, what we needed to do was come up with a schedule. We began by grouping the teams into regions: the West Coast (six teams), the Mountain Zone (two), Texas (two), the South (three), the East (five), Canada (two), and the Midwest (ten). Then we built a large list with each of the teams grouped in these geographical zones and in a rough order in which the zones could be connected. Next to each of the teams was a series of check marks and blanks extending across the page, indicating days that each of the teams would be in town. We were bound to a very narrow window of forty-five days to complete the trip, limited on one end by graduation day and on the other by my brother's wedding. Missing either appointment would have grave consequences. And it was immediately apparent that the trip was going to require some planning, because rarely were all the teams in any particular region, much less adjacent regions, at home on consecutive days.

We initially had a couple of options on how to structure the trip. We could start on the West Coast, hit all of the parks there, then travel by way of Phoenix and Denver to either Kansas City or Texas as a gateway to everything east of the Mississippi. Alternatively, we could start in Dave's hometown of Cleveland, borrow a car, hit the whole Midwest and East Coast, tour the South, and finish out west. Or we could structure the trip so that it would originate in my hometown of Houston. We would then take out the South, followed by the East Coast, Midwest, and the West Coast.

These last two options held the most appeal to us for two reasons. First, we both had to be on the West Coast at the end of the trip; Dave for work in San Francisco, me for the wedding in San Diego. Second, if we started somewhere else, we could drive someone else's (namely a loving parent's) car. Sadly, though, these plans fizzled both because we had no good way of getting the car back to its hometown at the end of the trip and because none of the West Coast teams seemed to be in town during the last couple weeks of our window.

Consequently, we decided to start in the West, quickly finding an easy path from San Francisco to Seattle then back down the coast (Oakland, Anaheim, L.A., and San Diego), across to Phoenix, and up to Denver. From there we had three options: Kansas City, Minnesota, or Arlington. We thought it might be nice to end the trip in my home state of Texas, so we looked north first. Minnesota was ruled out because of an extended road trip that the Twins had coinciding with our schedule. But Kansas City fit well and led us through to St. Louis, Chicago, and the rest of the Midwest before heading east. There we got stuck though and couldn't seem to fit in all of the teams before we would have to head south due to time constraints. Ultimately, it turned out that the only way the trip would work out with Kansas City as our gateway to the East was if we finished the trip by going from Texas to Toronto to Atlanta to New York on consecutive days to end our trip. We decided to look for a better route.

So from Denver we headed to Arlington then Houston and Atlanta. All smooth, even providing us three much-needed rest days to get from Phoenix to Denver, Denver to Arlington, and Houston to Atlanta. But we found ourselves stuck in Atlanta two days before the All-Star break with no way of bagging both of the Florida teams. Finding no other way, we conceded the two extra rest days, giving us a five-day All-Star break, and planned to start in Miami the day after the break and hit Tampa the next day. To make a long story short, the only way we could subsequently fit in the last seventeen parks was to zip from Tampa to Baltimore overnight (1,001 miles), and proceed to New York (for the Mets), Pittsburgh, Cleveland, Detroit, Chicago (for the Sox), St. Louis, Cincinnati, Toronto, Montreal, New York (for the Yanks), Philadelphia, and Boston, all in consecutive days. Then we had to get back to Chicago (for the Cubs) and hit Milwaukee, Minnesota, and Kansas City, all within the next four days. We opted for an off-day to get from Boston to Chicago (over 1,000 miles) and subsequently a double-header the next day with Chicago and Milwaukee, which seemed like a particularly nice touch. Regardless, we were left with nineteen parks in nineteen days to top off the trip. We would necessarily have to make a figure eight through the East and Midwest in order to catch everybody when they were in town, but none of it looked all that challenging, except for the overnight jaunt from Tampa Bay to Baltimore and possible complications from the double-header in Chicago and Milwaukee.

We considered these to be minor inconveniences though, compared to some of the obstacles our other schedules were presenting, and having discovered what we both concluded was a very doable trip, Dave and I each cracked open a beer and celebrated. Seeing on paper how our dream was a definite possibility, it seemed as good as done. It was because of this sense of accomplishment that we were only slightly off-put by the numbers my calculator generated when we tried to devise a rough budget. Despite our

In an effort to score tickets and other comps for the trip, Dave spent a good amount of time on the phone in his one-room, no-frills apartment in Palo Alto.

strongest efforts, we could not develop a methodology that would present us with a budget that was anywhere near a realistic price range. Both Dave and I had very little money to complete the trip and were on shoestring budgets. As a result, we began to employ frantically every element of creativity we could muster in an effort to reduce the bottom line.

First, we decided to be as friendly as possible to most everybody we knew, at least for a couple of weeks, before we informed them that we *would* be sleeping on their floors when we came through town and that a home-cooked meal was not mandatory, but the lack thereof *would* be frowned upon. We also developed a scheme to print T-shirts of our trip, ostensibly to memorialize the occasion, but also to generate more backing for the Brad and Dave "I have a dream" fund (no disrespect intended). Unfortunately, that plan fizzled, and we just managed to sell enough of the shirts at cost to avoid spending more than a hundred dollars apiece on the venture. Nonetheless, it still seemed worth it, knowing that people were walking around in shirts advertising our trip.

We were learning the ways of beggars fast, but not quite fast enough. We had a ways to go from our traditionally self-respecting ways, and it was only about six weeks before the trip was to begin that the great idea to call all of the teams and politely request free tickets came to us. When people actually got back to us with tickets and began throwing in free parking passes and tours of the stadium, we became even bolder, calling the various concessionaires and asking for free memorabilia and food. Dave, a natural salesman, managed to procure enough comps to effectively cut our ball-park budget in half. The free food we had arranged for also enabled us to cut into our overall food budget when we made the strategic decision to test the theory that man cannot live on ballpark food alone. (It turns out that he can.)

At this point, we were starting to realize that our self-indulgent fantasy struck a chord with Middle America. People were actually impressed by our plans, which honored us, but more importantly seemed to us like a perfect opportunity to seize a little publicity and perhaps more free stuff. We became so bold as to contact automobile, sporting goods, and media companies, trying to entice them to sponsor our trip. To no avail. We did, however, get some very enthusiastic rejection letters (one scrawled in longhand by an admiring intern). We also managed to get ourselves on television and into a couple of newspaper articles, which at one point somehow led to death threats—but more on that in due time. After receiving all this aid, one final adjustment to our budget managed to make the project reasonable for a couple of starving students: the realization that the time spent driving into the wee hours of the night would trump most of our originally sizable beer budget. For the record, we would never drink and drive.

So there. The trip was planned. (The whole itinerary is detailed in the following table.) It was affordable, and we were ready. All we needed to pull it off after that was an automobile willing to take on fifteen thousand miles in just over a month (Dave recommended my 1996 Nissan Pathfinder) and whatever voodoo or incantations we could find to ward off rain as we had not left much margin for error in our schedule. I won't ruin the ending for you now by telling you whether we made it or not. (Although I imagine you have figured it out just by the fact that this book was written.)

Itinerary

JUNE

20 Sa	11 A.M.	Leave Sunnyvale, Calif., for San Francisco (45 mi)
	1:05 P.M.	SD v SF + (3) Kaval family
		stay w/Kaval in Sunnyvale (36 mi)
21 Su	8:25 A.M.	Fly to Seattle (800 mi)—pick up by Juno
	1:35 P.M.	Oakland v Seattle + (1) Juno
		stay w/Juno
22 M	6:30 A.M.	Fly to San Jose (800 mi)—pick up by Kaval
	7:05 P.M.	SF v Oakland + (2) Beatty, Fredricsson
		stay w/Fredricsson (181 mi)
23 Tu		Leave Oakland for Anaheim (412 mi)
	7:05 P.M.	LA v Anaheim + (1) Arden
		Leave Anaheim for LA (45 mi)—stay w/Arden

The Beginning

24 W	7:35 P.M.	Anaheim v LA + (1) Arden
		stay w/Arden (37 mi)
25 Th		Leave LA for SD (154 mi)
	2:05 P.M.	Seattle v SD
		Leave SD for Phoenix (362 mi)
		stay w/Knowler
26 F	7:05 P.M.	Seattle v Arizona + (1) Knowler
		stay w/Knowler (9 mi)
27 Sa		Leave Phoenix for Eagle, Colo. (696 mi)
		visit Monument Valley and Valley of the Gods
		stay in motel
28 Su		Leave Eagle for Denver (128 mi)
	1:05 P.M.	Oakland v Colorado
		Leave Denver for Lamar, Colo. (219 mi)
		stay in motel
29 M		Leave Lamar for Weatherford, Tex. (680 mi)
		visit Palo Duro Canyon
		stay w/Mickle
30 Tu	7:35 A.M.	Leave Weatherford for Arlington (51 mi)
		LA v Texas + (2) Null, Williamson
		Leave Arlington for Houston (292 mi)—stay w/Null

JULY

1 W		get car serviced
		pick up Weisner
	7:05 P.M.	Chicago (AL) v Houston + (5) Null, Montz, Weisner
		stay w/Null
2 Th		Leave Houston for Pascagoula, Miss. (490 mi)
		stay in motel
3 F		Leave Pascagoula for Atlanta (410 mi)
	7:40 P.M.	New York (NL) v Atlanta + (1) Weisner
		stay w/Clouse
4 Sa		Fourth of July party in Atlanta
		stay w/Clouse
5 Sun		Leave Atlanta for Panama City (390 mi)—stay in motel
6 M		Panama City (20 mi)
		Watch All-Star warm-up in bar
		stay in motel

7 Tu		Leave Panama City for Boca (630 mi)
		Watch All-Star Game w/Perez
8 W		Boca
		stay w/Perez (30 mi)
9 Th		To Lauderdale (50 mi)
	7:05 P.M.	Atlanta v Florida + (1) Weisner
		stay w/Kaval
10 F		Leave Miami for Tampa (258 mi)
	7:05 P.M.	New York (AL) v Tampa Bay + (1) Weisner
		Leave Tampa for Baltimore (1,001 mi—overnight)
11 Sa		Arrive in Baltimore
	1:10 P.M.	Boston v Baltimore + (1) Weisner
		pick up Kaval (36 mi)
		stay in hotel w/Kaval
12 Su		Leave Baltimore for New York (205 mi)
	1:40 P.M.	Montreal v New York (NL) + (2) Weisner, Kaval
		visit sites of Polo Grounds and Ebbets Field
		drop Weisner
		Leave New York for Harrisburg, Pa. (168 mi)
		stay in hotel w/Kaval
13 M		Leave Harrisburg for Pittsburgh (204 mi)
		visit the site of Forbes Field
	7:05 P.M.	Chicago (NL) v Pittsburgh + (1) Kaval
		Leave Pittsburgh for Cleveland (132 mi)
		stay w/Kaval
14 Tu		Get car serviced; switch cars
		drop Kaval off
	7:05 P.M.	New York (AL) v Cleveland + (3) Kaval
		stay w/Kaval
15 W		Leave Cleveland for Detroit (180 mi)
	7:05 P.M.	New York (AL) v Detroit + (4) Kaval
		Leave Detroit for Chicago (300 mi)
		stay w/Hauler
16 Th	1:05 P.M.	Toronto v Chicago (AL)
		stay w/Hauler (60 mi)
17 F		Leave Chicago for St. Louis (315 mi)
	7:10 P.M.	LA v St. Louis
		Leave St. Louis for Evansville (159 mi)
		stay in motel

18 Sa		Leave Evansville for Louisville (91 mi)
		visit Louisville Slugger Museum
		Leave Louisville for Cincinnati (108 mi)
	7:05 P.M.	San Diego v Cincinnati + (1) Zannoni
		Leave Cincinnati for Cleveland (255 mi—overnight)
		pick up Junior in Cleveland
19 Su		to Toronto (299 mi)
	1:05 P.M.	New York (AL) v Toronto + (1) Junior
		Leave Toronto for Montreal (337 mi)
		stay w/Kivenko
20 M	7:05 P.M.	Philadelphia v Montreal + (3) Junior, Kivenko
		Leave Montreal for Cooperstown (308 mi)
		stay in motel
21 Tu		tour Hall of Fame
		Leave Cooperstown for New York (249 mi)
	7:35 P.M.	Detroit v New York (AL) + (2) Junior, Graham
		stay w/Graham
22 W		Leave New York for Philadelphia (109 mi)
		visit Hoboken, N.J.—birthplace of baseball
	7:35 P.M.	Atlanta v Philadelphia + (1) Junior
		Leave Philadelphia for New York (109 mi)
		stay w/Graham
23 Th		Leave New York for Boston (240 mi)
		pick up Null at airport
	7:05 P.M.	Toronto v Boston + (2) Null, Junior
		Leave Boston for Cooperstown
		stay in hotel w/Null
24 F		Leave Cooperstown for Cleveland (648 mi)
		Switch cars, drop off Junior
		Leave Cleveland for Chicago (355 mi)
		stay in hotel w/Null
25 Sa	12:15	New York (NL) v Chicago (NL) + (1) Null
		Leave Chicago for Milwaukee (92 mi)
	7:05 P.M.	Montreal v Milwaukee + (1) Null
		Leave Milwaukee for Minneapolis (409 mi—overnight)
26 Su		Arrive in Minneapolis
	1:05 P.M.	Texas v Minnesota + (3) Null, Harp, Colvin
		drop off Null
		Leave Minneapolis for Field of Dreams (270 mi)
		sleep on Field

27 M		Visit Field of Dreams
		Leave Field of Dreams for Kansas City (350 mi)
	7:05 P.M.	Anaheim v Kansas City + (5) Ochsner, Schoonover
		stay in motel
28 Tu		Leave Kansas City for Richfield, Utah (1,070 mi)
		stay in motel
29 W		Leave Richfield, Utah, for Las Vegas (290 mi)
		bet on baseball; pick up dad
		stay in hotel w/Null
30 Th		gamble more; Dave flies to San Francisco
		Leave Las Vegas for San Diego (336 mi)

TOTAL: 30 major league ballparks, Hall of Fame, Field of Dreams, Louisville Slugger Museum, four abandoned fields (Ebbets Field, Polo Grounds, Forbes Field, League Park), and a pass through Hoboken, N.J. (birthplace of baseball)

TOTAL RANGE: 34 states and 2 Canadian provinces

TOTAL MILEAGE: 14,455 (9,258+ mi in Pathfinder; 3,597+ mi in Kaval's two cars; 1,600 mi by airplane)

WHERE WE WOULD STAY: 27 nights w/friends or family; 9 in motels; 3 in the car; 1 on the Field of Dreams

BALLGAME HIGHLIGHTS: 5 Yankees games; 1 Astros game; 1 Indians game

ELEMENTS OF THE BALLPARKS TO BE EVALUATED OR NOTED: fans, hot dogs, microbrews, park (overall), sports bars, city, pretzels, restrooms, field, fence, seats, specialty food, peanut guys, entertainment between innings, gimmicks, mascots, underrated and overrated

---

After the trip had been fully planned out, Dave and I were left to wait for it to begin. It seemed like an eternity. Even when graduation came, we almost sleep-walked through the ceremonies, that being the second biggest accomplishment each of us would achieve that summer.

In the days following graduation, time moved even slower. All of our friends moved away, and we were left spending most of our time following up with the baseball teams and piling on more freebies in the process. We also had two interviews with newspaper reporters in the Bay Area, which went very well and resulted in flattering articles that inflated our egos even more before the trip began.

Also, following graduation, Dave and I slowly began the migratory pattern that was to become the norm for us over the next month and a half. I got kicked out of my dorm room the day after graduation and subsequently moved, along with everything I would need for the next six weeks, into Dave's one-room apartment (NOTE: not one bedroom, one room). Two days later, and two days before the official start of the trip, we were evicted again and shuttled to a hotel in Sunnyvale, fifteen miles south of Palo Alto on the San Francisco Peninsula. There we stayed with Dave's family, who had been in town since graduation. They also were eager to send us off on our tour. Finally, on Saturday, June 20, we packed our stuff into my Pathfinder, which was to be our only residence for the next thirty-eight days—in my case possibly even longer—and headed out on the Baseball America Tour.

The narrative spills out below in chronological order: where we went, what we did, and what we thought (when we were thinking). Three main objectives permeate the text: to create an impression of the ballparks (not just what they look like, but what they feel like), to portray a sense of what it felt like to make the trip, and to offer insights into the game in general from the point of view of a couple of guys living baseball to the bone. These themes arise in conjunction with the events and experiences of our tour, and occasionally license is taken to dwell on them. Sometimes the ballparks inspired us to describe in detail a venue's nuances and arguments for greatness. At other parks, our experiences were memorable enough that we generally chronicle our adventure, leaving the discussion of the nuts and bolts of the park to the second half of the chapter. Always, we have tried to relay the most interesting things we have to say about each park (we cannot guarantee nothing has changed since we were there) and about baseball in general.

On one other point of note, since the completion of our tour through Baseball America two summers ago, six of the parks have been retired. In our opinion, the chapters covering these bygone parks are possibly the most important contribution of this book, serving as they do to document the elements of those parks that we found particularly interesting, memorable, and enduring. For the sake of thoroughness, at the end of the narrative, we include reviews of the four parks that premiered by the 2000 season. Two more will open with the beginning of the 2001 season.

And in case you might be wondering why we did it, there wasn't any strong conviction or master plan behind it. It was for the same reason that people do anything. We wanted to put ourselves in interesting situations and have interesting experiences

We did not know how this tour of the ballparks was going to turn out—and that's the whole point. We knew we both had a bond with baseball, a bond with the road, and a pretty strong friendship. Whatever might happen when all three of these were tested would be a whole other story.

This is that story.

WE WOULD like to thank our supplementary authors, Steve Juno and Dave Halsing, plus all of our dedicated readers, our fathers, Maria Fredricsson, Zach Montz, and Peter "Junior" Kaval. Thanks to Don Harp for having friends in high places and to Ron Pitkin and Ed Curtis at Cumberland House for making this book a reality. Plus special thank-yous to Mako Bockholt for her help typing up all of the messy draft revisions to the book, Emma Wilson for making sure Brad's dad got his email, and Ashley and Chris for their sage advice.

We want to thank our family and friends for all their help and support throughout the trip and the course of completing this book, especially our parents, without whose financial support and constant encouragement we may not have survived the trip. We are also particularly indebted to those who traveled with us and helped keep us sane: both of our fathers, Aron Weisner, and Junior.

Finally, we would like to thank all the people who supported our trip and helped us along the way. Without them the adventure would never have been possible: Maggie in the EESOR department at Stanford, Mark Simon at the *San Francisco Chronicle,* Geoff Lepper at the *Palo Alto Daily News,* KPIX in San Francisco, Dr. and Mrs. Juno, Ben Arden and his family, the Fredricssons, Mickayela Beatty, Richard Walfringer and Ogden Entertainment at the Kingdome, the Oakland Coliseum Concessionaires, the Giants, the Athletics, the Angels and our tour guide Mark Hastings, John Ireland, Lon Rosenberg, Tommy Lasorda, Vin Scully, the operations team at Dodger Stadium, Ken Wilson and the Qualcomm concessions, Dayle Boyd, Larry Luccino, John Moores, Heidi Knowler and her family, Aramark Denver and Jim Lawler, Carl Middleman, Jay Williamson, Brad's sister Tracy, Susan Dipuma, Aramark Houston, the sous chef, Milo Hamilton, Frank Smith and the kind folks at SoHo, Ryan, Tom Clouse and his sister Hollie, Dr. Uncle Vince and Aunt Helen Kaval, Jeanette Perez and her family, Kevin Austin, Georgina at Pro Player, the Marlins, Aramark Baltimore, Chris Clatterbuck, Aramark Shea, Aramark Three Rivers, Frank Boslett, Tom Moran, Bill Miller, Dave's Uncle Gene, Dave's Uncle Vince, Bret Thomas, Joe Hauler, SportsService at Busch, Mike Shannon, Jack Buck, Luke Zannoni, the concessionaires at Cinergy, the Blue Jays, Danny and Sharon Kivenko, Isabelle at Le Stade, the Immigration inspector, George Steinbrenner and the Yankees, Jim Graham, the Phillies, the Phillie Phanatic, Jack Lyons and Aramark Boston, Cooperstown, Gary Colvin, Eric Harp, Andy Ochsner, Charles Schoonover, Al Amskamp and the Left and Center Field of Dreams folks, the Kansas City Royals, all the other kids at Stanford and Toyon (Qasim, Ben, Dustin, Court, Alicia, Nick, Vineet, Jenny, Al . . .), everyone who read our email correspondences from the road, and everyone who signed The Map. And a special thanks to Sam Chiu for The Map and publicity, Gaurav Misra for the website (*www.baseballtour.com*), and Major League Baseball and all of the teams for their assistance regarding the content of this book.

We have surely forgotten to mention someone's name here. Please don't hold it against us; we haven't forgotten your kindnesses.

the
summer
That
saved
Baseball

1

3com park

san francisco

June 20, 1998

DAVE WAS my best friend when we left on the baseball trip, and he is my best friend now, but he was most definitely not my best friend from about the tenth day of this thirty-eight-day trip until about six months after the trip was over. But you will read all about that in due time.

By the time the voyage actually started, my excitement and Dave's had been building up for some time, and it had already begun to take on legendary proportions, at least in our own minds. But it wasn't just the two of us who were excited about the trip. Everyone we talked to was eager to hear about it and jealous of our impending adventure. They wanted to know all of the details. They wanted pictures, postcards, and even, albeit on very rare occasions, autographs. And of course, until the trip actually started, all of the talk and hoopla had made the wait seem interminable for Dave and me. But finally, it was over.

As is usually the case, we were totally unprepared when it came time to begin the trip. Thus when we woke up on the morning of the San Francisco Giants game, we were swamped with last-minute preparations. Since it was our first game, we were still not sure what all we wanted to bring to the ballpark to memorialize the experience. After much hand-wringing, we finally opted for . . . everything. We packed a video camera, extra tapes, two 35mm cameras, extra film, layers of clothing, snacks for the road (even though it was only a forty-mile trip), a laptop computer, notebooks for

3

journaling, gloves, and a cell phone. Amid all this hustle and bustle, my expectations were running counter to what I had anticipated. For one thing I realized that this was not going to be some laid-back, free yourself from the grind, summer vacation. Instead, the simple fact that it was to be such a memorable experience (everybody said so) was compelling us to go to great lengths to document it. And this documentation was going to eat significantly into our pursuit of leisure.

Second, I noticed that the certain sensation I had expected to feel running down my spine as we headed off to the ballpark was not there. As much as I had wanted to believe otherwise, we were not on our way to the ballpark to suit up and try our hands against the big boys for the first time. While I had hoped that a decisive moment of new meaning in my life had come, it hadn't. As we closed up the car and began the jaunt to 3Com Park, I fully realized for the first time that I was simply going to the ballpark to watch a ballgame, the same as a half million other people across the continent. Although we had been trying so hard to come out ahead with this trip, pushing ourselves to be more ambitious, make it truly exciting, I was beginning to doubt (before the trip even started) whether there was anything deep to it at all.

I recognized that this would not be that decisive moment in my life. And the craziest thing about it all may be that I've never really considered that to be a bad thing. Although we could not always avoid delusions of grandeur on the trip, from the start both Dave and I saw it as the self-indulgent fantasy that it was. It was *our trip,* our vacation, and we were going to enjoy it—and if all we got out of it was a bit of frivolous notoriety and some great memories, that would be plenty.

Once we finally got everything packed, Dave and I traveled to the ballpark in my car with Dave's parents and his high school–age brother Pete (hereafter known as Junior). I drove, and Dave rode in the passenger seat in his customary role as cheerleader. Junior sat between his parents in the back seat trying to figure out how to operate our cameras. Consequently, we have a lot of footage of the interior of my car.

En route to the ballpark, as if there had not already been enough suspense, we had two final stops to make. The first was in Palo Alto to raid the local newspaper machines of the *Daily News,* which was running a flattering article on us and featured a picture of Dave and me alongside my car, which we had begun calling Black Bessie (we soon stopped though). We were so taken by the article that we stockpiled approximately twenty-five copies of the paper (they were free), of which twenty still languish in my closet.

The second stop before the game was on the Stanford campus, where we were meeting my engineering professor, Sam Chiu, who was to bestow us with the final trapping with which we would begin the Baseball America Tour. The Map. The Map is a two-foot-by-three-foot outline of the United States on white foamboard. The Map folded in the middle, and upon the cover was printed in bold black letters, Baseball

America Tour 1998. The perfectly rendered outline of the United States on the inside was punctuated by bright orange dots pinpointing each of the ballpark cities we were to visit and numerous green lines connecting them, plotting out the path of our trip.

The Map came into being exclusively through the efforts of Professor Chiu, who, the night before the trip, not only came up with the idea that we should carry with us a map that showed the entire route but also constructed it. To be honest, when he first mentioned the idea to me, I wasn't sure that it was a good idea, and it certainly would not have been had I been in charge of the artistry. But The Map, as conceptualized and created by Sam Chiu, was a marvel to behold. The Map laid everything out in one place and would spark many conversations over the course of our trip. Whenever we showed The Map to people, their eyes widened as they realized the scope of the trip, particularly the lines that darted back and forth over the Northeast. The viewing was always followed by scores of questions that Dave loved answering.

How many days? Thirty-eight. Which park is this one? The first. What is your favorite so far? This is the only one so far. Can I come along? Sure.

It was quite a conversation starter.

3com park

SAN DIEGO V SAN FRANCISCO

Game Time: 1:05 p.m.

AFTER SAYING our many thanks to Professor Chiu we headed for Candlestick, I mean 3Com, arriving about an hour before the 1:05 game time. It was a day game, and the sun was out. We parked in the vast 3Com lot and made our first purchase of the trip. Fifteen dollars for parking.

Beating the rush, we easily found a parking place, packed our gear, and headed into the stadium. Everyone, including Dave's mom, wore our Baseball America T-shirts with the Field of Dreams on the front and the route of our trip listed on the back like a concert shirt. I wore my lucky hat, a battered Stanford cap that had faded from Cardinal red to some shade of aged brick, and carried The Map. Dave was loaded down with cameras and journals. The car was locked, and we were off.

Now if you were starting a tour of the baseball parks in America, you might feel, as we did, that there was absolutely no good reason to begin with Candlestick. I assure you, we had tried to find any other way to begin, such as driving to Seattle overnight, watching a game, and driving back over the second night of the trip. But that schedule did not really work out for us, so we began our trip with the softballish task of driving forty miles up the peninsula to see the hometown San Francisco Giants in thoroughly unremarkable

Here we are with Dave's dad about to head into 3Com. Dave is on the left, and Brad's in the center. Brad's hand signal is meant to indicate that this is our first park; Dave's dad is simply giving a gesture we refer to as "the spank."

3Com. We could only hope that for this special occasion we would find some sort of magic there: Perhaps a magic in the city that Joe DiMaggio took with him when he left the San Francisco Seals for the New York Yankees. A magic that Willie Mays brought back twenty years later. A magic that seeped into the cracks of the ballpark's infrastructure during the 1989 Loma Prieta earthquake. Of course, that was a bleak hope.

Dave and I had both been to 3Com numerous times before and had already come to the conclusion that it was not really much of a park, baseball or otherwise. Granted, the name does not help, but even the slightly more classically sounding Candlestick was never much more than an afterthought of the dual-sport stadium era when it was built in 1960. I had seen both baseball and football games at 3Com before, and of the stadiums that have seen their last baseball game in recent years I am glad to see this one go.

In all honesty, my initial reaction to 3Com had not been as harsh as the criticisms above. When I moved to the Bay Area from Houston at age eighteen, I had still only seen about five major league games outdoors, so it was something of a novelty and a genuine thrill for me to take in a ballgame without a roof overhead. As a result, I had enjoyed my first couple of experiences at Candlestick.

Somewhere around the time that they changed the name of the park in 1996, I began to become aware of its many flaws. Chief among them is the weather. During a night game at 3Com, it is simply impossible to get comfortable. The stadium was designed as a perfect wind tunnel, and for good measure it was erected just off the Bay where the winds whip the fiercest. As such it is generally very, very cold anywhere in the stadium. During the day, conditions are only slightly better. The covered sections of the park in the upper half of the field level are as chilly as they are at night, but as soon as you step out of the shade, you are hounded by sunlight and then a suddenly still breeze. (Don't ask me how this is possible; I just know that it happens.) Thus, regardless of your seat, you will be generally uncomfortable and will, for good measure, be cursed by abrupt changes in climate as you move about the ballpark searching for that elusive comfort zone. On top of the park's ironic weather issues in one of the most pleasant areas of the country, the stadium is ugly and offers some of the worst food in all of baseball. Don't get me wrong, I still have had a hot dog every time I have been there.

The new corporate name doesn't help much either. Like many other baseball purists, I am not the biggest fan of the corporate sale of ballpark names. I hold special enmity for the enterprising young business analysts in the Candlestick team that led the trend that has left us with Qualcomm Stadium, Cinergy Field, Pro Player Stadium, and other notorieties—including the sadly departed Poulan Weedeater Independence Bowl. I also firmly believe that companies with aesthetically unpleasant names such as 3Com should be banned from naming anything after themselves for any amount of money. I'll admit, though, four million dollars is a lot to pay for the dubious distinction of having a place like Candlestick named after you, but I take no small pleasure in the fact that 3Com as a company has suffered ever since. Go Cisco!

So this was the big beginning to our trip. On top of all of the above, the simple fact that Willie Mays always preferred New York to San Francisco made me even less enthusiastic about the park (and he never had to eat their food).

The funny thing about our experience, though, was that despite the park's flaws, Dave and I had a great time. The magnitude of our trip really started to kick in, and the excitement we caused was palpable. Others sensed that we were up to something. (The fact that we looked like consummate tourists was a dead giveaway.) Even in the parking lot, people asked us about our shirts and the tour, and we responded by telling them that we were actually doing it. The Map also generated some excitement. As soon as anyone asked a question, we whipped it out and showed them how the whole thing worked. Subsequently, we received volumes of unsolicited advice.

In addition to the excitement surrounding our trip, we had caught another break with the exciting matchup to begin our schedule. In town for the weekend were the San Diego Padres, who, riding an eleven-game winning streak, were building a considerable June advantage in the National League West.

The game lived up to expectations. It was an exciting one, and thirty-nine thousand locals came out to see the hometown boys take on their division leaders. The Giants won a tight one, 5-2, with Rich Aurilia driving in three runs and Ramon Martinez (not the pitcher) going three-for-three in his major league debut. Even the usually less-than-enthusiastic San Francisco fans seemed to be firmly behind their team.

Near the end of the game, the local CBS affiliate, KPIX, came by and taped us watching the last inning. KPIX even had us on their website, which all seemed like a big deal to me. And it must have been a very slow news day, because we were all over the news.

It wasn't all glamour though. In fact, throughout the game we had to put up with a lot of annoying calls on our cell phone from one of the KPIX producers checking on our progress. Dave and I got a little contentious over the matter, especially when I accused him of being more interested in the publicity than the ballgame. Although, to be honest, I have to admit that I thought it was kind of cool being on television.

Ultimately, despite the fact that being at this park was a thoroughly familiar experience, there was something special about it. Even though nothing amazing or spectacular happened, the whole thing will forever stay in my mind. From the moment in the first inning when, on a whim, I decided to keep score in my program, thus sealing my fate to spend the next five weeks squiggling in little boxes in overpriced magazines, to witnessing Ramon Martinez's first major league hit. It was the kind of feeling that you get when you realize you are having a good time and it isn't going to stop any time soon.

As I wrote in my journal at the time: "There's not much good to say about this park. But regardless, it might have been the best ballpark experience I have ever had. I guess the bottom line is that it is all baseball, and I love it. And even though it wasn't a new or exciting experience here, there was something special about this game, and it was a great experience." And I expected to love every game and every park, in spite of the flaws (although I had heard that the Metrodome was unredeemable).

So in any case, despite my criticisms (which should be ignored in general), we had a great time. But the trip hadn't really started yet. By the time we got back to the hotel, we'd only logged eighty-one miles on the odometer. Soon enough though, we'd really be off on the road and things would get a bit more intense. We had to wake up early to go to Seattle the next morning, so we didn't do too much celebrating that night. Not that we had accomplished anything anyway.

As I lay down to go to bed, I felt anxious for the actual trip to start. I was definitely ready. One down, twenty-nine to go.

3com park

CITY: San Francisco, California

TENANT: San Francisco Giants

OPENED: April 12, 1960

CLOSED (to baseball): 1999 (still home to the San Francisco 49ers)

NICKNAME/ALIASES: Candlestick Park, The 'Stick

DESIGN: Multipurpose stadium (baseball and football), circular design, movable seats.

SISTER PARKS: Veterans Stadium in Philadelphia, Three Rivers in Pittsburgh, and Shea Stadium in New York.

FIELD: Grass (1960), Artificial Turf (1971), Grass (1979)

DIMENSIONS (feet): left field—335, left center—365, center field—410, right center—365, right field—328

FENCES (feet): 8

LOCATION/DIRECTIONS: Intersection of Giants Drive and Gilman Avenue. 3Com Park is in the southern portion of San Francisco on Candlestick Point.

CAPACITY: 63,000. Total attendance: 1,690,869 (1998). Average attendance: 20,874 (1998).

PARKING: $10–$15. WARNING: Don't wear nice shoes or pants, most of the parking lot is unpaved and turns quickly to mud.

TICKETS: $10–$22. BEST BANG FOR YOUR BUCK: Good luck. It is almost impossible to pick the best seat in the house at 3Com, as that distinction is liable to be different on any given day. For a day game, we recommend finding a seat in the sun, as the wind tunnels formed by the tiered stands create chills in the shade even in the balmiest of weather. The safest bet may be the upper deck, unless you can get a very good field box seat. As for night games, the general rule of the multisport stadiums applies: the closer, the better. Regardless of game time or season, layered clothing is a necessity, and be prepared to go bare-chested in the upper decks on those hot summer days.

BALLPARK EXPERIENCE: Cold winds and dark concourses welcomed us to 3Com Park. From the exterior, the towering light posts are the most distinctive feature of the park, and the structure has been described (by Dave) as resembling a birthday cake from afar with its eight enormous light standards each two to three times as high as the park itself. It is primarily built with steel-reinforced concrete, which, although it isn't much to look at, was strong enough to withstand the 7.1 Loma Prieta quake during the 1989 World Series. Being a concrete structure, gray is the predominant color. Gray is also the predominant feeling for most visitors unless you happen to be on the first stop of a baseball odyssey.

Seats dominate the interior of 3Com Park. Once the stadium was enclosed in 1971, the view of the bay was eliminated but the predominantly incoming wind effects were dampened or at least altered. There are two tiers to 3Com Park with a huge second deck that juts out over the lower seats. As a result, the upper deck leaves many of those seats cold, dark, and distant from the action. Other idiosyncrasies of the park include temporary bleachers that are removed for football, scoreboards that list a player's hometown, and escalators that whisk fans to the upper reaches of the structure. But these small facets are not enough to save the cold and dreary stadium from the lowest rungs of our list.

FANS: From our experiences living in the Bay Area, it is tempting to label Bay Area fans as bad fans in general. They are fickle at best. Fortunately for the Giants, they are the chosen team in the Bay Area and generally draw much more respectable crowds than their counterparts across the Bay. It seems, however, that sports fans in this town, having been spoiled by the 49ers' success throughout the 1990s, quickly turn on their less successful franchises. This can be seen both in the town's relationship with Barry Bonds and in their newfound penchant for booing their once beloved 49ers. An alternative explanation for the tepidity of San Francisco fans is simply that 3Com is a bad ballpark. Who would come here without a good reason? The 49ers are (uh . . . were) a reason. The muddling overachieving Giants have struggled for that distinction. The much larger crowds at Pac Bell Park since its opening in 2000 support this theory, although the loyalty of those fans has yet to be tested.

FACILITIES: Crowded. In the restrooms, you figure washing your hands gives you about a fifty-fifty shot of actually getting them cleaner. The seats at 3Com are a mixed bag with the newer seats in the box sections wider than the upper reserve. The concourses are typical of multiuse parks in that they are narrow and do not offer a view of the action. This is unfortunate since the long Gordon Biersch lines (see below) can make you miss an inning or two. On top of these lines, the concourses detract from the ambiance of the park since they are removed from the action. The only way to keep up with the play on the field is with the limited number of televisions that dot the concession stands.

FOOD: Two words: Gordon Biersch. If you've ever had even a pleasant experience eating at 3Com, you are undoubtedly familiar with this local microbrew. Their beer (Martzen being the most popular) and garlic fries are the only things worthy of note at this ballpark. Otherwise, nothing good can be said of the concessions at 3Com. The worst part is that the concessionaires don't seem to care. The prices are expectedly exorbitant, and if you plan to economize by sharing a large soda with your friends, bring your own straws, because the concessionaires, as policy, do not stock them. Another warning concerns the Mexican food at the park that is simply not good. Finally of note is another local microbrew, Anchor Steam, the only steamed beer brewed in America. LAST CALL: Alcohol is served until the middle of the eighth inning.

GREAT PLAYERS AND HISTORIC MOMENTS: Yes, Willie Mays played here, but remember that he spent his best years in New York. Other great players include Orlando Cepeda, Felipe Alou, Juan Marichal, Bobby Bonds, and the beloved Willie McCovey. Two World Series have been played at Candlestick, including the aforementioned Quake Series of '89. In both cases, the Giants did not win the title. The Giants won their first National League

Though we weren't fans of 3Com in general, we enjoyed a lively contest at the park as the Giants snapped the Padres' eleven-game winning streak.

pennant in San Francisco in 1962 and went on to lose to the New York Yankees in seven games. In 1989 the Athletics across the Bay managed to sweep the Giants in four games. Fitting for this park though, that by far its most memorable moment came on October 19, 1989, the day that shook the World (Series). All-Star Games in '61 and '84.

BALLPARK HISTORY: In August 1957, Horrace Stoneham, the owner of the New York Giants, announced his decision to move the team to San Francisco. The Giants left the famous Polo Grounds and Coogon's Bluff and ventured across the country along with their cross-town rivals, the Dodgers, to populate the West Coast with major league baseball. After two years at Seals Stadium, the old home of the San Francisco Seals of the Pacific Coast League, the San Francisco Giants moved into the brand-new Candlestick Park on April 12, 1960. Cold weather greeted the new inhabitants and did not let up for forty years. The rumor is that San Francisco mayor John Christopher showed Stoneham the park on a beautiful fall day when the weather was perfect and there wasn't a cloud in the sky. Little did Horrace know that Candlestick Point and most of

San Francisco suffers from tremendous bouts of fog and chilly weather all summer. As Mark Twain said, "The coldest winter I've ever spent was a summer in San Francisco."

FUN FACT: 3Com and the Giants pay homage to the San Francisco Seals who played from 1936 to 1956 in San Francisco by having a seal as their mascot. There is also a less well-know mascot—he makes two or three appearances a year—know as the Crazy Crab. He should be avoided at all costs. The team created the antimascot as a PR stunt to spoof the San Diego Chicken. His outlandish costume and penchant for rooting for the Dodgers have made this antimascot a number-one enemy for Giants fans.

THE ONE THING YOU SHOULD HAVE DONE AT 3COM PARK AND WHY: Venture down to the field boxes behind the bleachers in left field and partake of a few pitches from the only totally obstructed view seats in all of baseball! Then wonder why they could not find a better way to design this debacle of a stadium.

OTHER THINGS TO REMEMBER: In the spirit of San Francisco and Rice-a-Roni, 3Com puts on a cable car race on the Jumbotron. The red cable car always seems to win.

LASTING IMPRESSION: Hope to see a good game at 3Com because the food, facilities, and ambiance won't make up for it.

BAT (Baseball America Tour) Info

FINAL SCORE: Giants 5, Padres 2

OUR SEATS: LRES1, Row 12, Seats 11–12

BALLPARK: 1 of 30

DAY: 1 of 38

MILES TRAVELED: 81 of 81 total

STATES: 1 (1 total)

OUR EXPENSES: $40
food $5
groceries and film for the trip $35
EXPENSES TO DATE: $40

OUR FREEBIES: $125
game tickets $30
food—hot dogs, pretzels, garlic fries, and beer
parking (courtesy of the Kavals) $25
lodging (equivalent) $50
dinner (again the Kavals) $20
FREEBIES TO DATE: $125

2

THE
KINGDOME
seattle

june 21, 1998

O N SUNDAY, we awoke at 7 A.M. for an 8:25 flight to Seattle. The early wake-up was doubly hard for me because, first, I had not been up before 9 A.M. in my four years of college and, second, it had taken me hours to get to sleep the night before. The insomnia was a new thing to me but something I vaguely expected, given the excitement generated by the trip. Ironically, the source of my insomnia had more to do with my life after the trip than with the trip itself. Although the trip had occupied my thoughts for two weeks prior to our actually beginning it, once it had begun, I found myself obsessing over what I was going to do with my life when it was over.

During most of the last six months of college I had been totally relaxed. Live life minute to minute; let the wind take you where it may. When everyone else was mapping out long-term career goals, I remained indecisive. I halfheartedly applied for one job that had a .1 percent acceptance rate, and I refused to consider any alternatives. Needless to say, I did not get that job and was left aimless and alone.

I also broke up with my girlfriend of two years a couple of months before graduation. And not for any good reason. Of course, I eventually begged to get her back, but what would you think of an aimless dreamer whose long-term goal was ending up in Kansas City on July 27?

Subsequently, my only attachments in life were with my SUV Pathfinder and my best friend Dave, who was already getting on my nerves after spending most of a week

13

together. My only obligations were appointments at various baseball diamonds scattered throughout North America over the next month or so.

In any case, there I had been Saturday night, staring at the ceiling, pondering heaven's cruel joke that the earlier you have to get up, the harder it is to get to sleep. Of course, I did eventually fall asleep after I finally became too exhausted to worry about it anymore. And we ended up at the airport the next morning just in time to make our flight.

The flights to and from Seattle were to be the only air travel of the trip. We had debated whether we should fly at all, worrying that it would somehow taint what we were trying to achieve. (I am sure by now you get the general pattern that Dave and I rarely had much better to do than debate trivialities and technicalities.) It was either three hours in the air round trip or a little over twenty hours and two sleepless nights by car. It was a tough decision, but we went with the plane.

We were escorted to the airport by the entire Kaval clan. They all seemed to have slept much better than me, and the entire family bantered on throughout the car ride. In the airport I was still in a daze for lack of sleep, and Dave and his dad guided me toward the check-in gate where Mr. Kaval made fast friends with the flight attendant. By this point, I had known Dave's family for a week, but it was obvious that Dave had gotten his gift of gab from his garrulous father. And sure enough, social tactics that to me had always seemed overbearing returned results. Dave's dad sold our trip to the gate attendant well enough to convince her that we were men of importance. Subsequently, we were rewarded with free first-class upgrades.

As is often the case with unexpected gifts, the first-class experience was bittersweet. Although it was the most luxurious ninety minutes I had spent in the air, all of the excitement about traveling first class continued to keep me awake on the plane when I probably shouldn't have been. It's being another memorable experience as well, we took a lot of video footage outside the plane window, as if the view were better from first class. Dave and I also had to employ all our willpower to refuse the free alcohol at 9 A.M., but we managed. For the good of the trip, we convinced ourselves.

In Seattle we were picked up by our friend Steve. Actually, to say he picked us up is not entirely accurate. He arranged to meet us in the airport, where he was dropping off his visiting girlfriend. To put it politely, Steve is the most dedicated boyfriend on the planet. He does not consider you to be his friend if his girlfriend is in the same state, and to a large degree it was this fact that had forced us to start our trip in San Francisco rather than Seattle. As Steve's girlfriend was not leaving till the twenty-first, Steve would not pick us up or in any other way assist us while she was present. (It was hard enough just getting him to answer the phone.) Therefore, as Steve was the only friend Dave and I had in Seattle, and we were too cheap to pay for a room, we were forced to rearrange our schedule. Despite the scheduling difficulties, we did find Steve in the airport after we arrived, and we promptly headed to the Kingdome.

the Kingdome
OAKLAND V SEATTLE

GAME TIME: 1:35 P.M.

WE HAD a day game in Seattle, so there was no time to sightsee after we got into town. We arrived at the park sufficiently early for our 1:35 P.M. start, took the customary pictures outside the stadium, and headed into the ballgame with our cumbersome array of cameras, The Map, gloves, and notepads—all of which was already becoming annoying.

At the ballpark we received free Mariners T-shirts that read "Dad" on that back. I was confused. I wondered if they were advertising a new mascot that I had never heard of. Perhaps they had swapped their Moose with the Padre Friar, although I imagined I would have seen something about that on *SportsCenter*. Finally though, I figured out that it was Father's Day and felt horribly guilty for having forgotten. I made a note to call my father later and then promptly forgot. In any case, I never doubted that my dad knew that I loved him, even though I kept the shirt for myself.

Coming in, we had not heard much about the Kingdome, and most of what we had heard was not that good: that it had no character, was just like any other dome, etc. This set our expectations low, which ended up being a good thing and ultimately, from our point of view, the stadium, although having little flash to it, was a quality experience.

In particular, this was Dave's first game in a dome, and in spite of all his badmouthing of domes in the past. I sensed that he enjoyed at least the novelty of the experience. In general, people tend to criticize domed stadiums, saying that they're all the same and don't have any sense of individuality, but at the Kingdome I realized that was simply untrue. This dome was vastly different from the Astrodome of my hometown, and in comparison with that cavernous Texas stadium it felt more like an arena. The seats in Seattle were right on top of the field, relative to the Astrodome and all of the other multiuse stadiums of the 1960s and 1970s (the one negative consequence of that being no legroom), and the small park provided for a lively if not a traditional game.

After the whole experience, one could argue that the two domed stadiums I had been to had much more in the way of individual character than the cookie-cutter outdoor stadiums of the 1960s—like Cinergy and Three Rivers. And in some respects, the Astrodome and Kingdome had more character than the cookie-cutter stadiums of the 1990s—Coors Field, Arlington, etc.

We reveled in the beautiful weather outside the Kingdome before we headed in and reveled in the beautiful free food.

Due in large part to the bandbox nature of the stadium, the game that we saw was entertaining despite the lopsided 10-5 score. Having grown up in Houston, I had still never gotten used to American League, offensive-minded home-run ball. And in this park, which some have referred to as a launching pad, it really seemed to be almost a different kind of ballgame. The shallow power alleys and lack of pitching in Seattle led to a lot of balls bouncing off the wall in right field. But at least on this occasion, we were entertained, despite the five errors. To their credit, the Mariners organization used the Kingdome's inherent favoring of the offense to fashion a dazzling display of domed stadium pyrotechnics whenever the home team put one out of the park (which was often).

In Seattle we also became acquainted with the ways of living as ballpark royalty. As mentioned earlier, we had set up a number of perks at ballparks throughout our trip. The first of these was to come in the form of a concessions tour of the Kingdome with Richard Walfringer from Ogden Entertainment. Actually Richard didn't give us a tour so much as he gave us free run of the place. He simply handed us two pieces of paper, each with little boxes listing almost every food available at the Kingdome. At first we were nonplused, until we realized that these slips of paper were vouchers and that they could be redeemed for, not just one of the items on the vouchers, but all of the items on the vouchers. He gave us vouchers for *two* of everything. As our way of thanking him, we impulsively asked Richard to sign the Seattle area of The Map, making him the first person, other than ourselves (and Sam Chiu), to mark it. But he was by no means the last.

As naive ballpark travelers, Dave and I inhaled the free food. Sausages, nachos, specialty sandwiches, and even lattes were no match for us. It added to the experience that we had to trek to specialty stands all over the Kingdome to find each of the foods we wanted, as apparently everything worth eating at the Kingdome has its own specialty stand. Steve tried to help out, but he was no match for the feeding machines Dave and I had become. We were filling up fast by way of our gluttonous spree, and by far the biggest culprit toward that end was a massive Philly cheesesteak. These cheesesteaks were carefully crafted for us with onions, two kinds of peppers, and special sauce by a vendor who referred to himself simply as the "Philly Cheesesteak Man." The cheesesteaks he presented us were so loaded with meat that before we bit into them, Dave whispered, "The guys in Philly better start slaughtering some cows right now." Although not a huge baseball fan, the Philly Cheesesteak Man was intrigued with our trip, our T-shirts, and The Map. (We were of course obliged to ask him to sign it, too. Thus beginning a trend that quickly went out of control.) He also felt obligated to tell us that we had to check out the microbrew festival in Portland, Oregon, in mid-July. We told him it probably wouldn't fit our schedule this year, but we would try later.

Eventually we staggered away from the Philly Cheesesteak Man's booth and the concessions in general, at which point we were in a massive food coma that was compounded later by a home-cooked meal at Steve's house immediately after the game. By the time we stumbled away from that dinner table, we were very sleepy. As I dozed off, it occurred to me that we should send postcards and thank-you notes to all of the people who had helped us so far. I also realized that I had not called my dad to wish him a happy Father's Day. Of course, when I woke up the next morning, these great ideas were not even memories.

The Kingdome

CITY: Seattle, Washington

TENANT: Seattle Mariners

OPENED: March 27, 1976

CLOSED: June 27, 1999

DEMOLISHED: March 26, 2000

NICKNAME/ALIASES: King County Stadium, The Tomb (1980s) due to the stadium's resemblance to a mausoleum, Puget Puke (1980s) due to the stadium's proximity to Puget Sound

DESIGN: Domed multipurpose stadium (baseball and football), circular, movable seats.
SISTER PARK: Tropicana Field in St. Petersburg, Florida.

17

FIELD: artificial turf with mound and base cutouts

DIMENSIONS (feet): left field—331, left center—376, deep left center—389, center field—405, deep right center—380, right center—352, right field—312, apex of dome—250

FENCES (feet): left field—11.5, center field—11.5, right field—23.25

LOCATION: 1250 First Avenue South, Seattle, WA 98134

CAPACITY: 59,166. Total attendance: 2,651,511 (1998). Average attendance: 32,735 (1998).

PARKING: $10–$15

TICKETS: $6–$28. BEST BANG FOR YOUR BUCK: The best seats in the Kingdome were in the lower field box with their "I am practically in the game" feel. And these seats were usually easy to come by, given the stadium's large capacity. NOTE: While the cheap seats in the Kingdome did not feel as far away from the action as they did in many of the other multisport stadiums, they did feel very far *above* the action (see also Shea Stadium).

BALLPARK EXPERIENCE: One word: concrete. The Kingdome was a huge monolith of concrete that you could see from miles away as you approached the Seattle skyline. Compared to the larger domes in Minnesota and Houston, the Kingdome was more like an arena, even from the outside. Symmetry was observed with each side of the concrete structure in complete harmony. This meant that prominent signs were a must to avoid getting lost. The Kingdome did an adequate job with their signage to curb this problem. One nice touch on the exterior was an enormous American flag atop the 250-foot dome. Too bad you couldn't see the flag when they sang the national anthem.

Consistent with the outside, the structure of the inside of the park was again concrete, particularly the roof, which was an inverted concrete sphere. We wondered how it managed to stay up there until we realized that hasn't always been the case (see HISTORIC MOMENTS). The unavoidable concreteness of the roof served additionally to make you feel much more claustrophobic than, for instance, the faux panels of the Astrodome, or the carnival balloon of the Metrodome.

Combined with the tightly clustered seats, the roof gave the Kingdome an almost cozy feel on the inside, much more so than any other domed baseball or football stadium. This made for a great home field advantage in football but provided an unusual aftertaste when applied to baseball. Perhaps the most unusual interior features of the Kingdome were the hanging foul poles, which made it impossible for a ball to go over the foul pole and thus lead to a difficult call for the umpire, unless of course it hits the roof.

FANS: Considering that the first Mariners sellout did not occur until 1990, fourteen years after the park opened, Seattle fans can hardly be labeled die-hard. In the era of Ken

Griffey Jr., Alex Rodriguez, and Edgar Martinez, however, the team started to draw fans, particularly thanks to their spectacular playoff run in 1995 when they beat the Yankees in five games and challenged the Indians in the ALCS. Even throughout the Mariners' subsequent slide (which they were in when we came through town), characterized by atrocious pitching and four-hour games, the fans remained loyal and enthusiastic.

FACILITIES: As with most multisport stadiums, particularly those that manage to draw more than a few fans, the Kingdome was cursed with narrow concourses that made for cramped facilities. We had a difficult time navigating from one concession stand to the next as we scavenged the free food. The worst thing about the Kingdome's facilities was by far the seats, which were dreadfully small and provided the least legroom in the majors. The problem was compounded by the fact that the steps rose so dramatically that you often ran the risk of being kneed in the back of the head by the person sitting behind you.

FOOD: The Kingdome had a fine selection of standard as well as gourmet foods. Building on Seattle's reputation as the coffee capital of America, we found lattes and cappuccinos

The Mariner Moose mascot is one of the best in the big leagues. This time his ATV was stolen by the Athletics' bat boy.

to be ubiquitous. With our food vouchers, we sampled three versions of the American classic: the standard hot dog, the King Dog, and the Polish Dog. The King Dog was the best value and was much larger than the standard fare. The best specialty food at the Kingdome was the West Coast Philly cheesesteak. We like to believe that the infamous Philly Cheesesteak Man, who took great pride in making the best cheesesteak west of the Mississippi, still supplies the Mariners' new park with these culinary masterpieces. We also shouldn't forget some of the best specialty beers in the majors, which included a large assortment of Pyramid and Redhook. LAST CALL: Alcohol was served until the middle of the seventh inning.

GREAT PLAYERS AND HISTORIC MOMENTS: Although the Mariners were awful most of their first fifteen seasons, the Kingdome did manage to serve as home field for a number of future Hall of Famers, such as Randy Johnson, Ken Griffey Jr., and (probably) Alex Rodriguez. Also, although the Kingdome was destined to never see a World Series game, its high point came in 1995 when the Mariners beat the Yankees in the first round of the playoffs to advance to the ALCS and a heartbreaking series against the Indians. Additionally, Dave Kingman of the Oakland A's hit a towering fly ball back on April 11, 1985, that hit a roof support wire and was caught for an out, and both Randy Johnson (1990) and Chris Bosio (1993) tossed no-hitters in the Kingdome. On a final

BAT InFO

FINAL SCORE: Seattle 10, Oakland 5

OUR SEATS: Aisle 109, Row 21, Seats 111–112

BALLPARK: 2 of 30

DAY: 2 of 38

MILES TRAVELED: 800 by plane; 30 by car (911 total)

NEW STATES: 1 (2 total)

OUR EXPENSES: $208
  plane tickets $194
  parking $6
  programs $8
    EXPENSES TO DATE: $248

OUR FREEBIES: $130
  game tickets (courtesy of the Mariners) $30
  ballpark food—multiple Philly cheesesteaks, hot dogs, pretzels, nachos, sundaes, cappuccino, and soda (courtesy of Ogden) $50
  lodging (courtesy of Steve Juno and family) $50
    FREEBIES TO DATE: $255

ignominious note, multiple ceiling tiles fell before a game in 1994, forcing the Mariners to play their last fifteen games of that season on the road. All-Star Game '79.

BALLPARK HISTORY: The Kingdome was conceived and built as a football stadium. Its large capacity made it ill-suited for baseball from the beginning. Nevertheless it opened to baseball in 1977 for the expansion Seattle Mariners but did not generate its first baseball sellout until 1990. The Mariners are the second MLB franchise in Seattle, coming eight years after the expansion Seattle Pilots moved to Milwaukee after one season. The Pilots played baseball at Sick's Stadium, which was an expanded minor league park. The Mariners played all their home games at the Kingdome until the opening of Safeco Field in July 1999. The Kingdome was destroyed on March 26, 2000, to make more room for the Safeco parking lot.

FUN FACT: The Mariners have a popular mascot in the Moose, who is definitely one of the best mascots in baseball (from one who has seen them all). In the Kingdome he rode a scooter (à la the Phillie Phanatic), taking advantage of one of the few inherent benefits of AstroTurf. During the 1995 ALCS, the Moose fell off the wall in left field and broke his leg. In a strange coincidence, the Indians' mascot, Slider, pulled a similar feat in Cleveland the next day. Ken Griffey Jr. is quoted as saying about the series, "These are two teams fighting for large puffy mascots."

THE ONE THING YOU SHOULD HAVE DONE AT THE KINGDOME AND WHY: You should have visited the Royal Brougham trophy case in the Mariners museum. It had some great memorabilia, such as the old home plate from Sick's Stadium (home of the Seattle Pilots). Hopefully, they moved it to the new park.

LASTING IMPRESSION: A lot of concrete did not detract from a lively game in the Kingdome.

3
oakland
coliseum
oakland

WE HAD a ruthless 5 A.M. departure for our flight back to San Francisco on Monday morning. But it actually wasn't as hard to catch as the 8 A.M. on Sunday, which was probably because of the unexpected assist from the food coma that put us out by sundown the night before. It is amazing how easy it is to sleep with every food in the Kingdome in your stomach along with Steve's mom's famous fried chicken.

Already having been swept up by our pseudo-celebrity status, I was half expecting a first-class upgrade when we got to the airport. Dave and I even shamelessly played it up for the flight attendant when I discretely placed our map on the check-in counter as he casually mentioned our trip. The attendant seemed unfazed, and her disinterest shockingly jolted us out of our false sense of importance (although we would reacquire it soon enough).

We were welcomed back to San Jose by Dave's family and proceeded to put down a huge breakfast. Although I had been thinking somewhere around 5 P.M. the day before that I would never be able to eat again, my appetite surprised me. Our plan of glutting ourselves and never having to pay for a meal during the trip was on schedule.

Dave and I spent most of the day reloading my car and preparing for the real road trip that was to begin the next day. Already, although it was still early in the trip, Dave and I were communicating noticeably less than we had over the previous week. It seemed as if everything worth saying had already been said. Dave, on the other hand, was unfazed and rattled on. The experience was akin to having a play-by-play commentator in the background of your life.

After we said good-bye to Dave's family, who were finally heading home to Cleveland, we got squared away at Dave's girlfriend (now fiancée) Maria's house, where we would be spending our final night in the Bay Area. Having a couple of hours to spare before the evening's game in Oakland, I finally got to check my e-mail for the first time since the trip had begun. To my surprise, I had eighteen messages. I realize of course that by today's standard this is not such a staggering figure, but this was 1998! To be honest, we had been half expecting a couple of messages as my e-mail address had for some unknown reason been broadcast on the KPIX news along with our feature story, but we didn't really think more than one or two eccentrics would have any interest in contacting us.

Sixteen of the messages were from people who had seen us on the news two nights prior. (The other two were from girls named Sexy Suzy and the like courteously inviting us to visit their websites.) Almost all of the messages were positive: "Good luck, guys. Wish I could be there with you," etc. But by far the most interesting message came from James Sherry, a true fan who promised to "swerve at [us]" if he ever saw us on the road. It seems that he was not much of a baseball fan and was offended by our shameless pursuit of media attention. We were, to say the least, put on guard by this message.

Nonetheless, we decided to carry on with our tour, despite the obvious peril we were putting ourselves in. So we headed off to the park.

oakland coliseum

SAN FRANCISCO V OAKLAND

Game Time: 7:05 P.M.

LIKE 3COM, the Oakland Coliseum was a stadium that Dave and I had grown thoroughly familiar with during our years in the Bay Area. Also like 3Com and the Kingdome, the Coliseum was a multipurpose ballpark. But despite these anti-qualities and its generally low-key status, I was somewhat excited to be going there. I had always found Oakland a great place to watch a baseball game. The concessions have great food, and the stadium takes full advantage of the Bay Area weather while avoiding the wind tunnel effect of 3Com. Subsequently, as opposed to most of its multipurpose brethren, the Coliseum almost manages to feel like an actual baseball stadium.

In fact, when I first visited the stadium in 1994 there was a very low, almost bleacher look to the outfield stands. The park passed itself off as a baseball stadium very nicely. But then in 1996 the park was remodeled to the extent that a large overhang, comprising three decks towering one hundred feet into the air, was tacked on right behind the outfield. These decks stack higher than the stands around the rest of the park and are additionally set off (1) by the fact that they are completely separated from the regular stands by wide gaps on both sides, and (2) because nobody ever sits there. All in all, another example of corporate greed (this brought upon us by Al Davis), detracting from the game of baseball. Nonetheless, I was excited for the ballgame. So was Dave.

Maria was meeting us at the game, which added a little bit to the experience for Dave since he would be saying good-bye to her and the Bay Area at least for a while. He was particularly excited that she was coming to the game with us so that he could show her a good time before he left. Maria wasn't raised in a baseball family, and I'm sure she was not entirely thrilled when Dave told her that he was going to be spending his last few months of freedom traveling around the country and watching baseball games while she sat alone at home. So Dave wanted to do whatever he could to make it up to her before we left.

Our friend Kyla also made the trip, unwilling to pass up the free food and a brush with greatness. It was good having her along, too, as I had found myself realizing more and more that a big part of the excitement of the trip had been sharing it with friends. As a matter of fact, if it weren't for everybody else's awe of the trip, I probably would never have been half as impressed with myself. For Kyla's part, being the true friend that she was, she never let on how excited she was by the experience. But I could tell.

When we got to the Coliseum, long before game time, a crowd was already starting to form. Clearly the fact that the cross-town rival Giants were in town had generated a much larger and more enthusiastic crowd than this neglected stadium was used to. Excited about that proposition, we picked up our comp tickets at the window and headed in. Upon entering the stadium our level of celebrity continued to increase, and consequently, the delusions of grandeur returned after seeing ourselves on television two nights earlier. Foremost in contributing to our sense of self-importance was the fact that, shortly after we arrived at the Coliseum and got situated in our seats, the *head* of concessions for the Coliseum, John McCarty, stopped by. Of course, we had previously made arrangements for the meeting, but we weren't sure he would actually show, at least not in person. Particularly given the first-class snub we had received earlier that morning.

But John did show up, and as Richard Walfringer had done in Seattle, he gave us a couple of coupons for hot dogs and sodas. We were plenty grateful—and then he took us on a mini-tour of the ballpark's concessions. (NOTE: the Oakland Coliseum has by far the largest selection of beers in the major leagues.) Finally, he introduced us to the sta-

Kyla and Brad pose in front of the Oakland Coliseum. She was one of our many friends who briefly joined us for a game as we trekked from ballpark to ballpark.

tion manager at the concession directly behind our seats and informed him that we were to be comped the entire night. He made a special effort to point out to us that this included free beer.

Dave and I were speechless. Finally, we had achieved the holy grail of every recent college graduate: free beer. Free beer was just below taking batting practice on our wish list of things to get out of the trip. Immediately, we ordered two Pyramids, not certain the dream would last, and thanked John profusely. We began another long slide into a food coma, but we were ready for the game.

Throughout the game, our many trappings and Dave's loud excitement about the trip (and the beer) gave us away to everyone around us. The attention heaped upon us was even more exaggerated than at the two previous parks. I was startled by it all. I had never expected such attention because I've never been the kind to notice what the guy next to me is doing, and so I didn't figure too many people at the ballparks would catch on to what we were doing or even care. But I found that the pace of baseball games seems to loosen up everybody's concentration. You probably know the feeling of casually taking in the game when the guys behind you get into a heated debate about the best shortstop in A's history, or what would happen if . . . Either you've turned around and helped someone out on such occasions, or somebody has turned around and butted into your conversation. In any case, the people sitting close to us always seemed to know what we were up to, whether they were eavesdropping or not. Since baseball is one of the most social spectator sports, once you strike up a conversation with someone, everyone starts asking questions. At one point, Dave was having a conversation with at least six people concerning the route of the trip while I was having some disc jockeys sign The Map.

Given all of this attention, it was in Oakland that the ritual of signing Sam's map really took off. There must have been twenty-five people who put their John Hancocks on Oakland alone, which dwarfed our previous high of two in Seattle. Practically everyone we met ended up signing it. By the end of the day, The Map was becoming quite crowded with signatures. We were worried that we would run out of room in the eastern states where so many teams are so close together.

Part of the reason we spent a lot of time socializing at the Coliseum was that there was much more interest off the field than on, and the excitement around the Bay Area series between the A's and Giants contributed to the electricity in the stands. Unfortunately, the game itself did not live up to the billing. No pitching. No defense. It was a three-and-a-half-hour 12-8 slop-fest, with the visiting team winning for the first time on our short trip. Dave and I were disheartened by this fact because we were always hoping to see the hometown team pull it out. Kyla, however, being an avid Giants fan, had no qualms in reveling in her team's success. Maria, having trouble disguising her disinterest in the outcome of the game, at least tried to sympathize with the Oakland faithful. Despite the outcome, I continue to think that Oakland is a great stadium. The fans, the view of the game, and the food—particularly their specialty sausages and the Pyramid Hefeweisen Ale—were great.

As for the beer, Dave and I started to get a little carried away, it being our first chance to consume free frosty beverages, which made up for the missed opportunity on the plane to Seattle. But I think the fact that Dave's girlfriend was around forced us to behave ourselves. Of course, we promised each other that the next such opportunity would not be treated so lightly.

By the end of the evening, we were feeling real good about our trip (a common theme over these pages thus far). A photographer from the *San Francisco Chronicle* approached us before the game, and we agreed to have our photo taken. A couple of people we didn't know offered, actually almost insisted, that we stay with them when we were in their neck of the woods during the trip. And though I had always envisioned Dave as the talker, and had generally kept myself immersed in the two games before this one, in Oakland I was genuinely interested in discussing baseball and the trip with everybody. Maybe it was the poor quality of the play on the field that started it all, but it got me worrying that the trip might be breaking down my introverted personality. If it did though, I determined that I would find times throughout the trip to enjoy the games and the beer.

When we got back home, Dave and I began to ponder exactly how we were going to pull this thing off. In only our third park, I had soiled my lucky baseball cap with beer and managed to get lost on the freeway just thirty miles from my home of the last four years. We adopted the catch phrase that we were "just a couple of screw-ups." We were doing this trip, impressing some people with our exploits, even getting some free stuff and publicity out of the whole matter, and basically we were bungling through every step of the way.

oakland coliseum

CITY: Oakland, California

TENANT: Oakland Athletics

OPENED: April 17, 1968; Remodeled, renovated, and expanded in the 1996 season

NICKNAME/ALIASES: Oakland-Alameda County Stadium, The Net, Network Associates Coliseum (NOTE: When we were there on the trip, it was known by everyone as the Oakland Coliseum. Now it has acquired this ridiculous name. Since our trip predates the name, we don't feel compelled to use it.)

DESIGN: Multipurpose stadium, circular design, movable seats. SISTER PARKS: 3Com in San Francisco, Qualcomm in San Diego, Shea Stadium in New York, Busch Stadium in St. Louis, some design elements of Dodger Stadium in Los Angeles.

FIELD: Grass. NOTE: Oakland is considered to have one of the best fields in baseball, but it looked the same as all of the other natural grass parks to us.

DIMENSIONS (feet): left field—330, left center—362, center field—400, right center—362, right field—330

FENCES (feet): 8

LOCATION: 700 Coliseum Way Oakland, CA 94621. The stadium is in South Oakland off of Interstate 880, which runs just east of the San Francisco Bay. The BART train also runs right by the stadium (Coliseum–Oakland Airport Stop) and is a good way to avoid traffic hassles getting to the ballpark from several directions. Check their website at *www.bart.org* for stations and train times.

CAPACITY: 43,662. Total attendance: 1,232,343 (1998). Average attendance: 15,214 (1998).

PARKING: $10 at a spacious lot. This combined with the fact that attendance is usually low makes it pretty easy to get into and out of the stadium. Watch out for the overflow football seats that are inexplicably stored in the middle of the parking lot.

TICKETS: $5–$24. BEST BANG FOR YOUR BUCK: Hands down, the best bet is the Dollar Days every Wednesday night. Oakland opens up their upper reserve and bleacher tickets for a dollar apiece. This is one of the best deals in baseball, far surpassing the Cincinnati

The Oakland Coliseum was one of our most social ballpark experiences. We must have spoken with a hundred people and added twenty-five autographs to The Map.

daily $3 special. Otherwise, great tickets are readily available to most series (except against the Giants). $25 will get you field box seats and probably Jason Giambi's autograph as well. Remember that, due to the multisport aspect of the stadium, Oakland has an expansive foul territory and the action is relatively distant, even in field boxes. So the general rule applies: the closer the better.

BALLPARK EXPERIENCE: The Coliseum's most striking exterior features are the numerous light standards that tower over the field. Since the park is sunken and has many trees and shrubs around its perimeter, the light standards are even more pronounced. Alas, the major $200 million renovation in 1996 changed the complexion of the park for the worse. Gone was the open center field that allowed fans to see the inside of the stadium as they approached the park. Now, a massive concrete structure greets you as you stroll across the overpass from the BART station. This new monolith and the ramps and concrete that dominate the other sides of the park make for a rather cold exterior and bitterness at Al Davis from Athletics fans who remember the days prior to the renovation when the exterior and interior were in better symmetry.

The Oakland Coliseum's interior is far better than its bland outside. The new green seats give that retro nostalgic feeling à la Camden or Jacobs Field. The circular stadium's large foul territory, although pushing fans a little too far from the action, has a certain pleasant appeal given the lushness of the immaculately groomed field. Before the renovations, the park resembled Dodger Stadium in its view of the California hills. Now, it has become a closer cousin to other enclosed multipurpose parks, such as Busch Stadium in St. Louis and Qualcomm in San Diego. On the plus side, the concourses in the Coliseum are sufficiently wide and allow for good viewing of the action on the field. This unifies the concourse, the seats, and the field, which gives fans a constant awareness of the game and is one of the most appealing aspects of the park.

FANS: The A's are the forgotten team of the Bay Area. The sad fact is that unlike the overflowing metropolis of New York, this metropolitan area really cannot seem to support two franchises in one sport. Al Davis is the only person who ever seems to have figured this out (and then even he keeps changing his mind). In short, the fans that do come out to support the A's are a die-hard, enthusiastic, working-class crowd and are some of the most intelligent and committed fans in baseball. Trouble is that there are not enough of them. The stadium is consistently empty, and Oakland has fought off continued attempts to move the team.

FACILITIES: The Coliseum has ample new facilities, apparently the only upside of the recent renovation. Restrooms are numerous, large, and clean. The stadium's seats are wide and angled toward the action of the battery. With the wider concourses, concessions are larger and offer diverse choices from descriptively named stands such as The American Grill and The Doghouse.

FOOD: Oakland is known throughout baseball for its food choices. Both selection and quality were near the best of any park we visited. There are stands for pizza, Mexican, deli favorites, specialty sausages, and traditional ballpark fare. Most fans will find something in the wide selection to enjoy. On the hot dog front, Oakland has a broad selection. The Tommy Boy dog is served with full-sized pickles, relish, mustard, ketchup, onions, and peppers. It is quite a hot dog and a two-handed affair. Oakland also has the Chicago-style Polish dog, which is larger and covered in relish, good for big appetites. The specialty food in Oakland is the world-famous super nachos (if not one of the many sausages), virtually a four-person meal. The nachos are piled six inches high with guacamole, sour cream, and salsa. Oakland also has the widest array of beer choices in the majors, including all of the macrobrews, Heineken, and specialty beers, such as Sam Adams and Pyramid. LAST CALL: Alcohol is served until the bottom of the seventh inning.

GREAT PLAYERS AND HISTORIC MOMENTS: The Oakland Athletics have fielded some of the greatest baseball teams of all time at the Oakland Coliseum. Legends such as Reggie

Jackson, Jim "Catfish" Hunter, and Rollie Fingers led the Athletics to three consecutive World Series from 1972 to 1974. Their colorful owner from 1960 to 1981, Charles O. Finley—who was behind the yellow-and-green uniforms, an experiment with orange baseballs, and the move to Oakland—was always at the center of the Athletics' success. Finley, like the legendary Bill Veeck, loved promotions and controversy. His exploits included walking a mule named Charley O about the field and advocating night World Series games in an effort to boost fan interest. In the 1980s such legends as Mark McGwire, Dennis Eckersley, Jose Canseco, and Dave Stewart led the Athletics to a Bay Area World Series championship over the Giants in 1989. All-Star Game '87.

BALLPARK HISTORY: The Oakland Coliseum was built in 1966 to house the Oakland Raiders. Just two years later, the park and city lured the Kansas City Athletics to California. Numerous World Series in the mid-1970s were highlights for the ballpark. The look of the Coliseum was unchanged until 1996, when the city renovated the venue as part of the agreement to bring the Raiders back to Oakland. The cost for the renovation, initially estimated at under $100 million, ended up over $200 million. Also, due to delays with the renovation, the Athletics were forced to play six games in Las Vegas at Cashman Field at the beginning of the 1996 season.

BAT INFO

FINAL SCORE: San Francisco 12, Oakland 8

OUR SEATS: Section 210, Row 13, Seats 11–12

BALLPARK: 3 of 30

DAY: 3 of 38

MILES TRAVELED: 800 by plane; 181 by car— we were all over the Bay Area (1,892 total)

NEW STATES: 0 (2 total)

OUR EXPENSES: $37
parking $6
program $8
gas $23
　　EXPENSES TO DATE: $285

OUR FREEBIES: $172
breakfast (courtesy of the Kavals) $12
game tickets (courtesy of the A's) $40
food—2 specialty sausages, jumbo nachos, pretzels, soda, and several Pyramid beers (courtesy of Ogden) $70
lodging (courtesy of Maria Fredricsson and family) $50
　　FREEBIES TO DATE: $427

FUN FACT: The Athletics' official mascot is Stomper the Elephant. Back in Philadelphia, rival manager John McGraw of the New York Giants once dubbed the Athletics the white elephants. Connie Mack, the great Athletics manager, placed the elephant on the jersey to spite McGraw. Today all Oakland jerseys still sport the elephant on their arms.

THE ONE THING YOU HAVE TO DO AT THE COLISEUM AND WHY: Find the Banjoman, the Athletics' informal mascot and one of the biggest fans in baseball. Decorated head to toe in Athletics garb and sporting a yellow cape, he wanders the stadium with his banjo and generates a frenzy of activity. Watch out if you have visiting-team paraphernalia, because the Banjoman will seek you out and make you root for the A's. NOTE: Although not confirmed, the Banjoman also doubles as the 49er's Banjoman.

OTHER THINGS TO REMEMBER: The Oakland Jumbotron puts in a good day's work. Three marriage proposals, six birthdays, and a shout out to "keep it real" are a typical day's work.

LASTING IMPRESSIONS: A fine park that was remodeled out of its premier status. Thanks again, Al Davis.

4
edison
international
field
Anaheim

So HERE we were, day four of thirty-eight, and the road part of the trip finally began. Four hundred miles down to Anaheim starting at 8 A.M. with our finally getting to eat up some pavement. This was another occasion that Dave and I felt compelled to proclaim ceremoniously as a turning point in the trip, although it was actually just routine business. The long stretch of Interstate 5 from the Bay Area to southern California had been well trodden by Dave and me in our four years at Stanford. Between us, we had made the trek at least thirty times for everything from Stanford football games to summer internships to appearances on *The Price Is Right*. Given the familiarity of this stretch of road, we placed another asterisk in our journals and pushed back our celebration of the beginning of the "real road trip" to when we actually left the state on June 25 and began traveling over unfamiliar highways.

Just being on the road, although there was nothing monumental or new about the trip down to southern California, gave us an exhilarating sense of freedom and beginning. For the first time, we were really on our own, not counting the insomnia-filled plane rides to and from Seattle, and we really fed off of each other's enthusiasm. We left our once and future home of the Bay Area in the rearview mirror. We were free at last.

I think what so excited us about the road trip experience was the relaxed pace that comes with being on the open road, especially when you have someone to help with the driving. I was thrilled just knowing that for the next five hours there would be nothing in our future but driving. No interviews, no packing, no unpacking (we had already moved four times in the Bay Area in the last week), no socializing. Just me and Dave—and the cell phone.

I have yet to highlight the role of the cell phone, because it was not until we were on the road that I became aware of just how much of a nuisance it had become. Somebody calls about our plans in St. Louis. We have to call and make sure everything is squared away in L.A. Dave's mom calls to make sure we are all right. We have to call Dave's mom to make sure we are all right. My mom calls, jealous that we call Dave's mom more than her. We have to call my mom to assure her that it is not because Dave's mom is more important. My dad calls to make sure we are all right as well as to compare notes on the last park and get a sneak preview of our commentary. So the phone saga carried on like that for the next few weeks until we just stopped taking incoming calls and gave up on trying to call people as well. Although the cell phone does not come up that much in the coming pages, you can trust that I was no less annoyed with its "convenience."

Another accessory that finally rose to a new level of importance once we got on the road was the video camera. It had long been our plan to shoot some footage during the trip that would ultimately become a documentary (still pending), and given all of the downtime once we were on the road, the video camera became the default tool for addressing our boredom, especially by me. Looking back, I am not sure why I thought that the trees along the side of the road in California looked any different from those in Georgia. Or for that matter why the sunset through a dirty windshield outside of San Diego needed to be recorded alongside the setting of that same sun as we left St. Louis. But I've got it all on tape, all ten hours of it.

It was with these newfound friends—the cell phone and the video camera—that we journeyed into L.A. just after 3 P.M. to pick up our friend Ben. A classmate from Stanford, Ben was graciously letting us sleep on the floor of his parents' house while we were in town, and he was to accompany us to that night's game and the next. He was a couple of years younger than us and consequently a bit more wide-eyed about the whole Baseball America experience than we were. He was thrilled to be a part of the trip, and his enthusiasm would shine throughout the two days that we spent with him.

We met Ben at his house without a hitch and headed on to Edison International Field. The three of us arrived at the park around 4:30 for our first guided stadium tour of the trip, an experience that our naive minds were simply thrilled about.

edison International Field

··

LOS ANGELES V ANAHEIM

GAME TIME: 7:05 P.M.

DRIVING BY Disneyland on our approach to Edison Field, I began to suspect that "the Ed," as the Angels' stadium was known, would be unlike any other park I had visited before. The Disney Company had recently acquired the team, and I could only imagine what they had done with it. Additionally, although Dave had been to the stadium years earlier, neither of us had heard much about it since the recent makeover. Upon inspection, my expectations were borne out. An accurate and concise description of the park could be made with the use of a single adjective: Disney-esque.

Although I had never been to the ballpark, it was obvious that Disney's off-season makeover had entailed some wholesale changes. It had even been renamed—from Anaheim Stadium to Edison International Field. Dave was kidding in the car about being excited to see his first "international" baseball field. I think he was hoping the signs would be in different languages. I was just hoping I could find the restroom.

The other changes were controversial, to say the least. Not that any of it was necessarily either good or bad. But Disney baseball is just not like traditional baseball. So the Disney team, true to their core competency, built at Edison the one thing they are good at building: an amusement park. Consequently, the impression you get at Edison is that Disney has stopped at nothing in its fervent effort to entertain patrons with nonstop music, geysers in center field, home-run fireworks, and numerous between-inning games. It's like somebody told the company brass that Americans found baseball to be a little on the slow side, so they threw every diverting gimmick that the company could come up with into this park in some form or another. Not that there are animated movies and roller coasters at the park. But it feels like there should be.

Without a doubt, baseball purists would be annoyed at watching a game in Anaheim. I am surprised that there have not been more diatribes in the press from the likes of George Will and Bob Costas on how Disney has ruined baseball. But it is not surprising. Disney, being the media titan that it is, probably has contracts with those two somewhere down the line. But they don't own me yet, so I can be as subjective as I want about the experience.

Watching your first game at Edison, you get the feeling, unless you are twelve years old, that all of the park's gimmicks and diversions would eventually become irksome. But given that the Angels aren't your team, and you never expect to make it out here more than a handful of times, the experience is somewhat . . . . entertaining.

Beyond the thrill of being in an unfamiliar ballpark, particularly this one that felt like a new toy, our experience at Edison was coupled with two other unique opportunities. First, we were given a tour of the facility by Mark Hastings, from the Edison operations office, who not only gave us the tour but a goodie bag of leftover souvenirs from previous ballpark promotions that included a cozy and a thermos. Worth particular note were a couple of high-quality Angels caps. Immediately we removed our "lucky" caps, which we had intended to wear throughout the trip, to show some solidarity with the home team—a practice we repeated numerous times over the course of the trip.

The tour showed Edison to be, as expected, given the recent renovation, very luxurious. It even had that new-car smell. The offices and concourses were very nice, with an architecture that fittingly relied heavily upon a motif of baseball-bat wood, a nice touch, but one we found to be pervasive throughout the newer ballparks on our tour. The topper of the tour was the opportunity to walk onto the playing field, an honor we did not take lightly. And this being my first time on a major league ball field, wouldn't you know that those reliable delusions of grandeur started flaring up again. Getting way ahead of ourselves, Dave and I started whispering about what the odds might be that they would let us hop into the cage for a few cuts.

Of course the odds were nil, and the delusions were only slightly shattered when we were warned not to get too close to the players or the field itself. In fact, they wouldn't even let us play a little harmless game of catch. But we took full advantage of the moment regardless. Just to reach down and touch the grass was like nothing else we had experienced before. It seemed about the smoothest and softest surface I'd ever felt. No wonder the big leaguers are such great fielders. My first instinct (after wanting to hit

After a long day's drive from San Francisco, we were excited to see a crosstown matchup between the Angels and the Dodgers with our friend Ben (we made him hold the sign).

and catch) was to lie down on the grass, but I resisted the urge out of respect for the players. I did, however, take perverse joy in casually spitting on a major league field. Dave and I stood there and gawked for about fifteen minutes before they lured us from the field with the promise of more exciting things to see. We acquiesced, but I told Dave that we should right the injustice of not being able to throw or take batting practice when we visited future parks.

Before we were hauled off of the field, we were introduced to John Ireland, the local "Man in the Stands" for the game telecast on KCAL. He was another passerby who became more excited about our trip than we were and insisted on interviewing us during the game. So we made plans for him to come by our seats later for the chat. Of course, when he did come by, he decided that our second-deck seats were not suitable to our stature, or for the camera angles, and so he spirited us to the field boxes. Once we were situated in much better seats, we had the interview, which proved to be a fun experience. John asked the usual questions. We explained the trip, showed off The Map, and made a couple of witty comebacks when he asked us how drunk we must have been while we were planning the trip. It was all old hat to us by now, it being the fourth interview we'd done so far.

The most immediate consequence of the interview was that we missed a whole inning of play in which apparently some interesting things happened, so that was kind of disappointing. Afterward though, it made us pretty famous with the people sitting around us at the game, even more so than in Oakland, which I was sure made Dave happy, because his greatest thrill always seemed to be talking to people about . . . whatever he talked to all those people about.

On the whole, the game was pretty good, even though I missed the best part and Dave pretty much missed the whole thing while fraternizing with his new friends. The Angels pulled off a come-from-behind victory with a strong effort from the bullpen. We were also fortunate enough to see the Angels' new closer and fast fan favorite, Shige-toshi Hasegawa, shut the door on the cross-town Dodgers. As he mowed down opposing hitters, the Disney control center kept blaring their witty takeoff on a popular Will Smith song, "Getting Shiggy with It."

We were exhausted by game's end, but despite the fact that three hours of nonstop entertainment had just ended, I had my favorite experience at Edison after the game was over. En route to our car, we stopped just outside the main gate, where the Angels had designed a brick baseball diamond lit with yellow lights. Dave and I played catch there, standing between the bases that light up at night.

I'd played catch a million times, but the fact that we had already immersed ourselves into this world of baseball over the past few days had built up a need to do something on a baseball diamond. Since they hadn't let us toss on the green one inside, we settled for the concrete one outside. It was a fine game of catch. Our friend Ben, not wanting to be left out of the festivities, videotaped the whole catch excursion with a uniquely nauseating vertigo, follow-the-ball camera style that was different from Dave's unintentionally nauseating shaky-cam technique.

After about ten minutes of making passersby dodge our errant throws on the crowded pavilion in the midst of night, we headed back to Ben's place. On the way, Dave and I noted that it was almost scary how enthusiastic people were becoming about our trip. It was as if this summer vacation that we had planned on a whim was striking a chord not just with our friends and hometown locals, but with people around the nation. Ben was just excited about being on television.

edison international field

CITY: Anaheim, California

TENANT: Anaheim Angels

OPENED: April 19, 1966

NICKNAME/ALIASES: Big A (1966), Bigger A (1980), Big Ed (1998)

DESIGN: Baseball only, asymmetrical design, no movable seats. The formerly multipurpose stadium was remodeled into the Camden style prior to the 1998 season. SISTER PARKS: Yankee Stadium (when it was built); the new park borrows design elements from Camden.

FIELD: Grass

DIMENSIONS (feet): left field—330, left center—365, deep left center—395, center field—406, deep right center—395, right center—365, right field—330

FENCES (feet): left field to right center—8, center field to right—18

LOCATION/DIRECTIONS: 2000 Gene Autry Way, Anaheim, CA 92806. BOUNDED BY: Left field (N), Katella Ave. Third base (W), 2000 State College Blvd. then Interstate 5. First base (S), Orangewood Ave. Right field (E), Freeway then Santa Ana River. Center field (NE), Amtrak railroad station.

CAPACITY: 45,050. Total attendance: 2,519,280 (1998). Average attendance: 31,102 (1998).

PARKING: $10. The park is surrounded by 12,500 parking spaces and finding a spot and subsequently gaining access to the stadium is usually not a problem.

TICKETS: $6–$19.50. BEST BANG FOR YOUR BUCK: The lower-deck seats provide a great view of the action, and given the small foul territory, the upper-deck box seats also afford a surprisingly close look. Beware of the upper reserve, which hangs considerably back from the foul lines. The bleachers are a nice new addition and are lively, especially when the Dodgers come to town.

BALLPARK EXPERIENCE: When Edison was completely renovated after the 1997 season, the outfield was again opened up, new green seats were added, and a large fountain complex appeared in left center field. The changes are a huge improvement. The park now resembles the original Anaheim Stadium of the mid-sixties but with all the latest amenities, such as expanded concessions, luxury boxes, and an asymmetrical design. The entrance to Edison Field is especially unique with two large plastic Angels baseball hats and a large awning supported by enormous baseball bats providing some respite from the sun. Dave is of the opinion that this whole design is reminiscent of Ebbets Field and its famous rotunda of baseball bat chandeliers, baseball stitched marble floors, and stained-glass windows. (Dave is also of the opinion that all things baseball are reminiscent of Ebbets Field.)

Edison Field's interior is spacious and open with large concourses with unobstructed views of the field and an eclectic outfield. The outfield from left to right features a small bleacher section, both home and visitor bullpens, a traditional Fenway-esque light

We were entertained by Edison Field's Disney-esque feel, complete with geysers in center field, home-run fireworks, and numerous between-inning games.

standard, three large flagpoles, a Disneyland fountain, an AstroTurf batter's eye, an eighteen-foot wall with secondary bleachers, and a huge electronic scoreboard. The rest of the stands are somewhat traditional, with a plethora of newly added luxury boxes between the lower and upper decks. Overall, Edison provides a hodgepodge of Camden-like design elements that give fans everything they need to enjoy baseball in Orange County.

FANS: Anaheim as a franchise has never had a glory period to develop the nostalgia that makes a great fan base. Runs at the playoffs in 1983 and 1995 both ended in disappointment. The Angels have the additional disadvantage of being the L.A. area's second favorite team, which is not as crippling as having the same distinction in the Bay Area (see Oakland), unless you are the Clippers. In fact, the Angels have pushed, with middling success, to establish themselves as Orange County's team, not a second-rate L.A. squad. Despite these setbacks and lack of history, the fans at our game were good spirited and in general excited about baseball, particularly when their team is winning.

FACILITIES: The structure is spotless, and, significantly, restrooms are plentiful. Concourses are wide and allow easy navigation, intermittent views of the field—which helped us see the game as we toured the park—and house numerous concession stands. Stadium seats are wide and angled for views of the action, especially in the lower deck. On our tour, we learned that even the old steel has been gutted and repainted so that no part of the park seems old, and the place passes itself off well as a new park.

FOOD: In our impression, Disney seems to focus more on specialty foods than standard fare. While all the basic hot dogs and peanuts are there, there is an almost expected focus on foods more suited to an amusement park than a ballpark; in particular, many vendors sell candy, such as cotton candy and red vines. To our disappointment, Anaheim only offers a basic dog, which is average at best. The most popular specialty food is a barbecue sandwich that is covered in sauce but lacks the size of a great BBQ sandwich. The King nachos are probably the best food item at the place, with their generous supply of synthetic cheese (at least double the ballpark average). Sadly, on our trip we could find no specialty beers at all in the Ed, only Bud and Miller. LAST CALL: Alcohol is served until the middle of the seventh inning.

GREAT PLAYERS AND HISTORIC MOMENTS: The Angels' greatest players have been Nolan Ryan, Reggie Jackson, and Don Baylor. On an interesting note, Baylor won the MVP as the team's *designated hitter* in 1979. Unfortunately, the team itself has rarely been above average and has contended very few times. In 1982, their greatest World Series hopes were dashed in a 3-2 ALCS loss to Milwaukee. A World Series game has never been played at the park. On a final note, on the last day of the season of 1984, Mike Witt pitched a perfect game. All-Star Games in '67 and '89.

BALLPARK HISTORY: Anaheim Stadium was built over a two-year span, from 1964 to 1966, and opened in 1966. A traditional three-level baseball-only stadium reminiscent of Yankee Stadium, it was one of the last parks built before Shea and Atlanta's Fulton County kicked off the cookie-cutter multipurpose phenomenon. In 1979 the park was enclosed to accommodate the Los Angeles Rams—thus making it akin to the cookie-cutter parks. This design prevailed until the Rams left after the 1994 season. The renovations in 1998 have created a Camden-style park with the most recent amenities.

FUN FACTS: The old three-story A with the halo, originally behind center field, is now in the parking lot behind right field. (NOTE: the Halo didn't move; the park did.)

THE ONE THING YOU HAVE TO DO AT EDISON INTERNATIONAL AND WHY: Watch the scoreboard. The Anaheim scoreboard and music controllers must have learned the ropes in a hockey arena. At our game, they were constantly running different cartoons and dance-along songs. The "rally monkey," which is a picture of a monkey jumping up and down, is especially entertaining and is the subject of numerous ESPN *SportsCenter* highlights.

OTHER THINGS TO REMEMBER: There are only cotton candy, peanuts, and souvenir roving salesmen. Do not expect the "beer man" to show up in your section anytime soon.

LASTING IMPRESSION: Edison Field is the newest attraction at Disneyland with the flair of a classic ballpark.

BAT Info

FINAL SCORE: Anaheim 6, Los Angeles 4

OUR SEATS: Section 418, Row C, Seats 13–14

BALLPARK: 4 of 30

DAY: 4 of 38

MILES TRAVELED: 457 (2,349 total)

NEW STATES: 0 (2 total)

OUR EXPENSES: $52
Taco Bell in Coalinga $8
programs $6
ballpark food—hot dogs, nachos, and cola (we tended to skimp when it was on our own dime) $18
gas $20
EXPENSES TO DATE: $337

OUR FREEBIES: $83
parking $6
game tickets (courtesy of the Angels) $27
lodging (courtesy of Ben Arden and family) $50
FREEBIES TO DATE: $510

5

Dodger stadium

Los Angeles

WEDNESDAY WAS probably the most casual day of the tour. Having already made the trip down to southern California, we were able to get to sleep fairly early (it's amazing how exhausted you get spending half of your day in a car and the other half in a ball-park; it's almost like work . . . almost). We also got to sleep because we only had a ten-mile trip ahead of us to get to Dodger Stadium.

By the time we began to stir around 11 A.M., Ben was at work and his house was pretty much deserted. Soon though, Ben's mom got back home and politely offered us breakfast. She had already been very generous to us; his whole family had been, in fact. It had been somewhat difficult the night before, after coming back from the Angels game, to convince her that we really didn't need anything to eat. So the next morning, when she started trying to feed us again, Dave and I, feeling that we had taken too much from Ben's family already, politely excused ourselves for the afternoon.

Ben's family lives on the north side of Los Angeles, somewhere between L.A. proper and what is commonly referred to as "the Valley," popular as the pulse of both the American shopping mall scene and the adult film industry. We didn't really have any-where to go, but Ben's mother pointed us toward a Bank of America where there had been a highly publicized shootout just a few years prior. Dave and I were intrigued, so we started off in that direction.

When we got to the scene of the crime, we were somewhat disappointed not to find any bullet holes or police lines in or around the bank. We had, after all, heard that there were tanks and heavy artillery involved in this shootout. But to our dissatisfaction, this bank was even open for business. Despite the anticlimax though, we did hang around long enough to stage our own raid on the bank, pretending as James Earl Jones would put it, that our fingers were guns, and we got some pretty good *Cops*-style video of that. I think we also managed to disconcert a few of the locals who may or may not have been reminded of the heist we were trying to reenact.

When we tired of our childish exploits, we realized we were quite hungry. Although we had been trying, we could never quite make it through the day on one enormous ballpark meal. So Dave and I decide to go in style and treated ourselves to the most expensive meal that we would pay for on the entire trip. We went to Sizzler.

It is beyond logic to explain why, in the midst of our endless food coma of ballpark gluttony, Dave and I decided to partake of the lowest-quality lunch buffet available in the country. In all honesty, it seemed like a good idea at the time, and subsequently it caused more indigestion than all of the ballpark hot dogs on the trip. After logging a couple of good hours at the Sizzler, we headed off and cruised the Valley. Being unoccupied on a summer afternoon, we took it upon ourselves to put on a little Tom Petty and cruise Ventura Boulevard. Dave also videotaped, in one tedious take, our half-hour drive up and down and up Ventura Boulevard. Don't ask me why, when we had so many other tourist opportunities available to us in southern California, we chose this use of our time. Again, it seemed like a good idea at the time.

Having gotten our Tom Petty associations out of the way, we headed back to Ben's, picked up the kid, and prepared to set off for the ballpark.

Dodger stadium

ANAHEIM V LOS ANGELES

Game Time: 7:35 p.m.

WE SHOWED up at Dodger Stadium, still traveling with our gracious host, young Benjamin, at about 5:30. Before we could get in though, we ventured on a comical journey up and down the many tiers of the stadium trying to find the operations offices. A little piece of advice, if you are meeting someone from a ball club or a stadium before a game, make sure you ask them in advance where you should meet and how to get there. Baseball stadiums are very large, and more often than not, the many personnel in the parking lot and at the gates don't really know where anything is.

Eventually, we found the Dodgers offices, and upon our arrival we were instantly greeted like celebrities. This was our initial exposure to what would become two defining elements of our experience at Dodger Stadium. First, we realized that everybody at

Here we are with Ben just before going on the field at Dodger Stadium, just one of the many perks that Lon Rosenberg and the Dodgers provided us at the park.

that stadium recognized us because they had seen us on television the night before. This made us instant celebrities in a town that knows how to kiss up to celebrities. And second, the people who work at and attend ballgames at Dodger Stadium are extremely generous and outgoing. If I stopped to think about it, I might have wondered how sincere all the attention was, this being L.A., but I realized that if they stopped to think about it, they wouldn't be able to come up with any good reason to treat us so well either. They might even have realized that it was totally unfair that we not only got to go on this amazing trip, but we were also treated royally throughout. In any case I decided that it was best not to think about it. Dave and I were even a little afraid to mention it to each other, and we rarely did until the trip was over.

Dodger Stadium was the first park in which we were received by both the operations people and the concessionaires, although we had been treated by one or the other in each of the last three parks. As far as the Dodgers organization goes, they, along with the people at Aramark there, were very kind. I recommend that you contact both parties if you undertake a trip similar to ours. On our tours through the ballpark we went onto the field, into the press box—the works, generally an even more exciting experience than our inaugural tour in Anaheim. We even met Tommy Lasorda and Vin Scully. Although Vin was a little preoccupied with his cappuccino, Tommy was a real character. When we were introduced to him, he noticed Ben was without a Dodger hat. He immediately commanded at least a half a dozen people to search for a Dodger cap until they put one on his head.

Throughout these travels the hero of the Dodgers organization from our perspective, and not just because he introduced us to Lasorda and Scully, was Lon Rosenberg, the head of concessions at Aramark. Not only his enthusiasm for our trip and us, but also his enthusiasm for his job, for the ballpark, for the Dodgers, and for baseball was quite contagious. I was so enthralled by him that I asked him to sign a T-shirt on which I planned to keep a memory of the very special experiences of our trip.

Contributing to the excitement of our experience at Dodger Stadium was the simple fact that it is a great ballpark. The general rule if you're not from southern California is that everyone hates the Dodgers, but nobody hates Dodger Stadium. It is simply not possible. Although it doesn't quite engender that same sense of awe that you would get upon arriving at Fenway Park, Dodger Stadium has a definite history and nostalgia. But given its unassuming nature—there is no monstrous green wall in left field or ivy on the outfield wall—the park is rarely overhyped and so it often comes as a pleasant surprise to first-time visitors.

There are countless little things about the ballpark that are quite unique: the murals on the outside, the tiered parking lot, the openness of the outfield stands that allows you to see a large portion of the park as you walk through the stadium parking lot. The stadium's interior is also simply tasteful and pleasant. Dodger Stadium can accurately be described as the exact opposite of Edison Field in Anaheim. The park is pretty much there for baseball and baseball only. It is a classic baseball-only park, and the management doesn't concern itself with the dot race or the cap dance or any other frivolities, which is quite the opposite of the amusement park approach that the Disney folks take in Anaheim down the interstate. Where Edison is rigged with every gimmick you can imagine, the Dodger philosophy is to provide you with a quality team and a quality stadium where you can simply enjoy the game. The Dodger brass obviously feels the need to respect your intelligence as baseball fans above all else. Aggregated, all of these aspects make Dodger Stadium one of the elite parks in baseball, although its lack of flash often leads to its being taken for granted, particularly by repeat visitors.

In line with its classic baseball feel, Dodger Stadium is traditionally a pitcher's park and generally yields characteristic National League ballgames. The game we saw with Ben fit that mold perfectly and was an all-around exciting contest. It was a rematch of the game we had seen the night before in Anaheim, so we were expecting a lively crowd given the cross-town rivalry. We were not disappointed. Thanks to interleague play, this was the third cross-town rivalry of our trip already, and the opportunity for such experiences make it almost worth having to put up with games like the Astros versus the White Sox.

The game was great, with the Dodgers winning in eleven innings. It was a little disconcerting to notice that even in a rivalry like this, with the game tied in the ninth inning, about half the crowd had already gone. Its being the consummate city of titillation, attention spans in Los Angeles are even shorter than the rumors would lead you to believe.

The fans who stayed throughout the game though were die-hards on both sides. We were a little surprised that the fan support for the Angels outnumbered that of the Dodgers, but it made sense given that the under-appreciated Angels were having a much better year than their attention-grabbing cross-town rivals. The Angels fans at both games we saw were obviously glad to make that fact known. In any case, on this night the Dodger faithful were rewarded when Matt Luke came home with the winning run. Our enthusiasm at this event was heightened by the fact that our new friend "Loco Rob," one of the many overly friendly characters in L.A., had just introduced us to Luke's aunt. Despite Rob's manic enthusiasm, which bordered on hostility, he seemed to have befriended everyone in the stadium within shouting distance. He also somehow convinced me to give him the shirt off my back (NOTE: not the one Lon had signed).

In total, although we had already tasted free food, free beer, major league grass, and fifteen seconds of fame, Dodger Stadium was the first stadium where the whole experience really came together. Subsequently, by the time we left, I had about thirty minutes of video footage of meeting people and touring the park. Tommy Lasorda, Vin Scully, Loco Rob, the famous Peanut Guy of *Tonight Show* fame; all were immortalized on my camera. Loco Rob was just one of the many overzealous friends we made. Throughout the ballgame, people would walk by our seats and whisper about "those guys on television." I imagine this happens often in Los Angeles, and it had a heightened effect for us as we ended up in seats on the last row of the lower deck where everybody walking through the concourse had a good look at us. What really convinced us that we had hit the big time though was that we were approached for our autographs by two enamored college students. We also met another guy who had done a stadium tour similar to ours five years earlier when there had only been twenty-eight parks. We shared stories—he obviously had more than us at this point in our trip—and talking to him was like peeking into the future. It was amazing how vivid his memories of that trip were, and he drilled it into our heads that this would definitely be a high point of our respective lives.

On an absurdist note, Dave and I got into a row about the ballpark etiquette associated with the singing of "Take Me Out to the Ballgame" in a park you are only visiting. Although Dave was usually off talking to someone during the seventh-inning stretch and missed it altogether, when he was around we would get into a debate about the song. Although the lyrics are "root, root, root for the home team," he and I had always said "Indians" and "Astros" respectively, those being our childhood and subsequently lifelong home teams. On the trip though, we had begun to root for the home teams, necessitating a change in our approach to the lyrics. I had begun to sing the original lyrics. Dave, however, insisted on singing the home team's name. I told him that it was very fickle and not in the spirit of the song to change the lyrics every day. He told me that I was a self-righteous screw-up. If you stop to think about it, obviously it's the stupidest argument

The classic design, traditionalist approach, and legacy of historic moments make Dodger Stadium one of the best parks in the major leagues.

you've ever heard of, but you start to argue about a lot of stupid things when you spend every moment together for this long. And it was going to get worse before it got better.

Dodger Stadium

CITY: Los Angeles, California

TENANT: Los Angeles Dodgers

OPENED: April 10, 1962

NICKNAME/ALIASES: Chavez Ravine (official name of the park when used by the Los Angeles Angels, 1962–65), Taj O'Malley (obscure), O'Malley's Golden Gulch (obscure)

DESIGN: Baseball-only stadium, immovable triangle-shaped stands with a large amount of foul territory. Although the park is a contemporary of Shea Stadium in New York, Candlestick Park in San Francisco, and a plethora of other multipurpose stadiums, Dodger Stadium's classically simple baseball-only design has remained unique.

FIELD: Grass

DIMENSIONS (feet): left field—330, left center—385, center field—410, right center—385, right field—330

FENCES (feet): left center field to right center field—8, foul poles to bullpens in corners—3.83

LOCATION: 1000 Elysian Park Avenue, Los Angeles, CA 90012. Dodger Stadium is on the northern edge of downtown Los Angeles off of Highway 110. As a result, it is easily accessible by all of the major freeways that run through downtown L.A.: Highway 110, I-5, I-10, and Highway 101.

CAPACITY: 56,000. Total attendance: 3,098,042 (1998). Average attendance: 38,247 (1998).

PARKING: $7. WARNING: There is plenty of parking, so don't get sucked in by an empty space once you get onto the grounds. Since the stadium is built on the side of a hill, the parking lot is multitiered behind home plate, which is where most of the seats are located. So know where you are sitting when you get to the ballpark. If you are in the upper deck, and you park in the outfield, you have a long hike ahead of you.

TICKETS: $4–$17. BEST BANG FOR YOUR BUCK: You can't beat $17 field boxes; some parks charge that much for the bleacher seats. Beware though, the field boxes could sell out for popular games with rivals old (the Giants) and new (the Angels). Regardless, the stadium rarely reaches capacity, and even the cheap seats in the upper deck and outfield offer a nice view and pleasant breeze.

BALLPARK EXPERIENCE: Dodger Stadium is a unique baseball-only ballpark built in the early 1960s. From the outside, the stadium is surrounded by an enormous parking lot and built into the side of a hill. The first- and third-base sides of the park are covered in alternating red, blue, and yellow murals of old Dodger greats like Jackie Robinson, Don Drysdale, and Sandy Koufax. Large light standards tower above the sides of the park and the consistent jagged '60s roof design that surrounds the park. Since the park is sunken, it seems unassuming from Elysian Park Avenue, which runs behind home plate. From the outfield side of the park, however, you can see inside the park and the massive four levels of multicolored seats. At night, this view is quite remarkable.

The interior of Dodger Stadium creates a perfect harmony of field, fans, and surrounding hillside. It has four color-coordinated levels: yellow, red, blue, and red as you go up. Dodger Stadium does a great job of making a very large fifty-six-thousand-seat stadium feel intimate. The layers of seats and open concourses tie the field and fans in the stands together. Moreover, from almost everywhere in the stadium you can see the golden hills and trees of the surrounding topography. While the design is simple, it is functional and gains points for its understated simplicity. Dodger Stadium has many of the same characteristics often attributed to old Ebbets Field in Brooklyn: a simple design and harmony in its proportions. Everything in the park is laid out in perfect proportion, including the jagged awning above the bleachers, which has angles that perfectly match those of the adjacent scoreboard in right field. This simple yet unique character makes Dodger Stadium one of the best parks in all of baseball.

FANS: In our experience, Dodger fans are supportive, and their attendance numbers are always near the top of the National League. And why shouldn't fans be supportive? L.A. is a huge market, and the team's owners always dip into their deep pockets if they see a chance to win. Nonetheless, the attendance stats are somewhat deceptive as Dodger fans are notorious for having the earliest curfews in the major leagues. Rarely do half of those who walk through the turnstiles stay for the last pitch. The half that do stay truly bleed Dodger Blue and are among the most loyal and intelligent fans in baseball. Overall, the atmosphere is excellent, at least until the seventh inning.

FACILITIES: Dodger Stadium has a reputation as the cleanest ballpark in the major leagues. At least that is what the guy in operations claimed, and we would believe it. Cleanliness and order are in fact defining characteristics of the stadium that stick with you as you walk away. Everything from the pristine corridors and restrooms to the perfect symmetry of the outfield wall and the color-coded seating is immaculate. It's almost too clean, if you know what I mean, given that the ballpark has been around for forty years. Additionally, everything is easily accessible, and lines are usually not much of a problem.

FOOD: The stadium is known for its standard fare, especially the Dodger Dog. It's all reasonably priced with a few gimmicks thrown in, such as temperature-sensitive drink cups that change color while you drink. The folks at the ballpark would also like to push the Gummy Glove, their unique take on the Gummy Bear, which looks and tastes exactly as the name suggests. On the hot dog front, the Dodger Dog is a baseball classic. Always fresh and warm, it is a must for any dog connoisseur. Farmer John's franks are the only ones served, and this quality makes a substantial difference. The Super Dodger Dog is even better for those with a bigger appetite, like Dave and me.

Specialty food includes the teriyaki bowl and the sushi plate. Both are available on the club level. You've probably heard murmurs about the sushi bar from people outside, since it is such a novelty, but compared to the selection, quality, and lower prices of sushi bars throughout southern California, our sources have told us that it should not be a top priority. Specialty beers are not readily offered throughout the park. As in Anaheim, Budweiser and Miller seem to be the only options. Only the restaurant in right field has an expanded selection of beers. LAST CALL: Alcohol is served until the middle of the eighth inning.

GREAT PLAYERS AND HISTORIC MOMENTS: Since it opened, Dodger Stadium has been blessed with a continuous stream of baseball immortals and magical moments. In its first year, the stadium saw Duke Snider's last at-bat, Maury Wills's MVP season, and Don Drysdale's Cy Young performance. In fact, Dodger Stadium holds an unprecedented and unequaled claim to Cy Young winners, having residents take home the award in each of its first five seasons (Drysdale, followed by Sandy Koufax in '63, '65, and '66, and the Los Angeles Angels pitcher Dean Chance in 1964). This proves ever more impressive when you realize that they awarded only one Cy Young award for all of the major leagues until 1966, when they began awarding one for each league. Not only great players but also great teams and great managers have called Dodger Stadium home. In only thirty-eight years, Dodger Stadium has hosted the World Series nine times, and all of those teams were led by one of two Hall of Fame managers: Walter Alston and Tommy Lasorda. Most notably, one of the most memorable baseball moments of all time came at Dodger Stadium in game one of the 1988 World Series, when Kirk Gibson hobbled off the Dodger bench to deliver a pinch-hit game-winning home run in the bottom of the ninth inning. All-Star Game in '80.

BALLPARK HISTORY: The spectacular site of Dodger Stadium (built into a ravine) was purchased when then owner Walter O'Malley took a helicopter expedition to survey possible locations for a new stadium. Upon seeing the empty lot at Chavez Ravine across the highway from downtown Los Angeles, O'Malley requested the site. The city supervisor he was with immediately said "no problem," and the rest is history. Dodger Stadium is one of baseball's only privately financed stadiums. It was the first since Yankee Stadium in 1923. Recently, Pacific Bell Park in San Francisco has joined that tradition.

Also, until Denver's Coors Field was built in 1995, Dodger Stadium and Chicago's Wrigley Field were the only National League parks built exclusively for baseball. The California Angels shared Dodger Stadium from April 17, 1962, until September 22, 1965. Prior to coming to Dodger Stadium, the Dodgers played three seasons at the L.A. Coliseum, which was one of the most ill-suited stadiums for baseball with a large net in left field and scores of empty seats.

FUN FACT: Dodger Stadium and Yankee Stadium are now the only two baseball parks in America (since the demise of the Astrodome and Tiger Stadium) that are named after their primary tenants. And isn't that a sad commentary on the state of the game?

THE ONE THING YOU HAVE TO DO AT DODGER STADIUM AND WHY: Eat a Dodger Dog (actually we prefer the Super Dodger Dog). Not because they are the best in baseball; they aren't. But because everyone who knows you've been to Dodger Stadium will ask you about the Dodger Dog, and you should have an educated response.

OTHER THINGS TO REMEMBER: The Chavez Ravine parking lot is almost a park in itself. Either before or after the game, take a little extra time to drive around the stadium, stopping at every turn and taking in the view of the stadium or the skyline; there are at least two distinct breathtaking views of the city that the parking lot offers (you also get a pretty nice view from the upper deck). Also, at the base of the parking lot, there are numerous hills that many young families have used for impromptu hikes. There is a nice photo op in front of the large THINK BLUE sign that is easily seen from most seats in the park.

LASTING IMPRESSIONS: Dodger Stadium is a true classic that creates the perfect harmony of field, stadium, and surroundings.

BAT INFO

FINAL SCORE: Dodgers 4, Angels 3
   (11 innings)

OUR SEATS: Aisle 113, Row V, Seats 11–12

BALLPARK: 5 of 30

DAY: 5 of 38

MILES TRAVELED: 37 (2,386 total)

NEW STATES: 0 (2 total)

OUR EXPENSES: $14
  Sizzler $14
   EXPENSES TO DATE: $351

OUR FREEBIES: $184
  game tickets and parking (courtesy of the Dodgers) $44
  programs and memorabilia (courtesy of the Dodgers) $30
  ballpark food—Dodger Dogs, peanuts, pretzels, nachos, Gummy Gloves, sodas, and ice cream (courtesy of Aramark) $60
  lodging (equivalent, courtesy of Ben Arden and family) $50
   FREEBIES TO DATE: $694

6

qualcomm
stadium
san Diego

June 25, 1998

Brad, Dave, wake up. Your car alarm is going off and the car door is wide open."

That was my nightmare. It was also the reality at 4 A.M. Thursday morning when Ben's father jolted us awake with those words. We flew out the front door (Dave carrying one of his minibats) in that way that you hurry to the scene of the crime, as if getting there sooner will somehow reverse the certain and horrific thing that has just happened to you.

As we approached Ben's front door, we could hear the alarm whirring and chirping, which ironically gave me some sense of relief knowing that the car was still alive. But when I opened the front door, my heart sank. It was true. There sat my car, directly in front of me where we had left it, the same as it had been the night before except that the passenger door was wide open, which to me meant that everything we had left in the car (video camera, computer, CDs, clothes, memorabilia) was surely gone.

I steeled myself to see an empty space on the passenger seat where I had left the video camera and cell phone the night before, and as I came through the fence to Ben's house, there on the seat . . . were the video camera and cell phone. Right behind it was my case of one hundred CDs. Tucked behind the driver's seat, my laptop was still in place. I scanned the entire car until I got back to the video camera and cell phone just two feet in front of me. Nothing had been taken.

We were ecstatic to realize that all of our valuables were still safe. But at the same time I was terribly confused as to how this could be. How could somebody have gone to all of the trouble to pry open the car door and not take the extra half-second needed to grab all of the valuables he had assuredly been salivating over a moment before. Obviously, the alarm had scared off the would-be thief. And I was thankful that the unknown culprit was not a seasoned pro, or else Dave and I would have certainly been lighter a few thousand dollars' worth of valuables. Many of which weren't ours to lose.

Feeling blessed that nothing was missing, Dave and I grabbed a few of the most valuable items and took them inside with us (and we would make this a habit for the rest of the trip). We locked the car and fell back to a peaceful sleep much earlier than we expected.

In the morning we said our thanks and good-byes to the Arden clan and headed off for a day game in San Diego. Along the way, we continued to cycle through our memories, thinking of various objects we had brought with us and accounting for their whereabouts. We were skeptical that we had been so fortunate to escape such a potentially disastrous experience unscathed. It wasn't until we got to Qualcomm that we noticed that the door that had been pried open now no longer locked. This caused us some concern given the recent blow to our faith in humanity. We would be leaving the car unattended in the middle of a huge, apparently unprotected lot for the next five hours. How many bandits were there in San Diego waiting to get the next crack at our stuff? We fretted over it for a few minutes, then, realizing that we were already taking most everything of real value into the park with us, decided not to worry about it. We grabbed all of our traditional gear plus the laptop, hid the large stash of CDs out of view,

Outside of Qualcomm Stadium, one of the premier multipurpose parks in the country, we proudly displayed our plethora of gear.

locked up the rest of the car, pressed the alarm button (which provided only psychological protection at this point), and headed into the ballpark.

qualcomm stadium

....

SEATTLE V SAN DIEGO

Game Time: 2:05 P.M.

OUR CONCERN for the car was alleviated by the fact that we were able to park very close to the front of the lot, given that we had arrived for this 2:05 game about two and a half hours early. We had plans to meet Dayle Boyd of the Padres before the game, who was going to take us on a tour and hopefully get us onto the field. Dayle was the first person we had talked with when we began contacting teams to get free tickets and special attention. She had been the first because of the fortunate coincidence that my mother had been the interior designer for Padres owner John Moores when he lived in Houston. As a result, we had an "in," so to speak. Through my mother's contacts, we got Dayle's name and spoke with her to see what the Padres could do for us. She got back to us, assuring us that she could get us tickets and would be glad to show us around the park. At the time, we had been delighted and used her promise as leverage when trying to convince other teams to match the offer. This proved to be an effective technique. But since our red-carpet experience in Los Angeles, we were sure that whatever came of this San Diego trip would feel like a letdown in comparison. We were wrong.

If we had felt important in L.A., we felt presidential in San Diego. Among other things, we went on the field and were given a personal tour of the entire stadium by Ken Wilson, the head of merchandise and concessions. We met Tony Gwynn, visited the owner's box where we met Padres owner John Moores, and, oh yes, we had front-row seats. Actually, to call these seats front row would be misleading. A more accurate description might be to call them subzero-level seats. In Qualcomm, as in many of the other behemoth multisport arenas (the Astrodome, Pro Player, Three Rivers), temporary stands have been added in front of the field boxes that, to accommodate two very different ball fields, were fixed a considerable distance from the baseball diamond. Thus, at least a handful of deep-pocketed fans could get that "right on top of the action" feel that all of the new ballparks were advertising.

In most of these cases, seats have been added only behind home plate, but Qualcomm also inserted small sections, holding about forty people each, along the foul lines, just beyond the dugouts. It was in one of these sections that we were seated. In particular, our section, just beyond the Padres dugout and even with the first-base box, was known locally as Wally's World, for Padres first baseman Wally Joyner, who spent most of his time that season just fifteen feet away.

Our seats were right on top of the action and arguably the best seats in the house, but easily the most awe-inspiring thing about them was that to get to your seat, you had to be escorted out of the regular field boxes onto the field. They even placed a small footstool between the stands and field for you as you entered and left so you would not be too inconvenienced by the step. The whole procedure was such an ordeal, in fact, that you could only go to and from the seats between innings. Other not-to-be overlooked amenities of our VIP seating arrangements included free food and drink—including shrimp cocktail and specialty beers, served by very attentive and attractive waitresses—and a great view into the Padres dugout. Dave must have taken two rolls of film of players apparently up to no good in the dugout.

The seats were, as you might suspect, amazing and afforded us the opportunity to get the most out of our experience in San Diego. Additionally, the tours and experiences before the game contributed to our unique perspective on Qualcomm Stadium. Foremost in forming this perspective was the great food we glutted on throughout the ballpark. Not only do they have the biggest hot dog in the majors at Qualcomm—one-half pound—but the fish tacos, not the first thing you think of when you think of baseball, were incredible. These were just two of the many edibles that were thrust upon us by Ken Wilson, the head of food and merchandise at the park. For added entertainment value, he even insisted on videotaping us taking a bite out of each of the different foods we tried. He was quite a character, and his enthusiasm for his job showed in the quality of food he provided throughout the park.

Our experiences with Dayle Boyd also helped to memorialize our trip to San Diego. She provided us with several great opportunities, such as walking onto the field and standing only a few feet from my idol, Ken Caminiti, although being too intimidated and respectful to talk to him; meeting Tony Gwynn in the tunnel behind the locker rooms and getting him to sign The Map and my shirt; and just being in an owner's box, even though they look a lot like any other luxury box but with more famous people and better food.

I might as well confess that Dave and I managed to get wrapped up in this feeling of celebrity in San Diego. And given all of this spoiling, it was easy to overlook Jack Murphy's, er, Qualcomm's inherent shortcomings. And hey, if you had an experience like ours, wouldn't you? After all, Qualcomm's flaws are pretty boring when you come to think of them.

They are really no different from those of any of the twelve other multiuse stadiums discussed in this book. Basically, Qualcomm, being primarily a football facility—and a very good one at that—is very large for a baseball stadium. The fact that our visit was only a few months after the Super Bowl had been held there highlighted this fact. As a baseball stadium then, there are a few things to be desired, especially when considering the feeling of intimacy being pushed at the newer stadiums. Already mentioned, the biggest drawback of the multisport stadiums tends to be that many of the seats are too far from the action. Qualcomm is not immune to this even though it has seen the addition of the temporary sections behind home plate and next to the dugouts in which we were fortunate enough to find seats. As in its sister stadiums, Qualcomm's twenty thousand or so fans who weren't lucky enough to land the best five thousand seats might as well forget about watching the rotation on the ball coming out of the pitcher's hand and enjoy the highlights.

Despite this obvious obstacle to creating a baseball atmosphere in a football stadium (see Pro Player), the Padres and Qualcomm staff have definitely done well with what they have had to work with. They make it easy to find a nice seat in the sun, grab a fish taco and a Corona, and forget about the fact that you can't tell who is batting or what that last pitch was. Like they say, as long as you've got nice weather, you've got a nice ballgame.

And speaking of the game, the one we saw in San Diego was an enjoyable one, even though the Mariners did not really seem all there (probably distracted by the weather like everyone else). It ended as a 6-0 shutout with the crowd firmly behind the Padres, and why not with them some twenty-five games over .500.

Waxing philosophical during the game, I realized that there are two kinds of ballgames you can enjoy. One is obviously the classic ballgame: great execution, one-run leads, sacrifice bunts, double switches, extra innings, and the like. We had seen that the night before in L.A. The other is the kind of game we saw in San Diego, where one team just comes out and demands the victory, with the crowd totally behind them. With fans like this, you have to root for the home team, because everybody has fun when they win.

The team and the town were great. And to our surprise, the fans everywhere had really been amazing. Despite all the talk of baseball's being the number-three sport in America, our experiences on the trip had given us no indication of that. Everywhere we had been, the fans had been great, even in Seattle with a team thirteen games under .500. Sure, football and basketball sell themselves great on television and in department stores, but baseball is the sport that people love. Because of that, I felt like I could understand why people were so interested in our trip. Not only do fans live vicariously through the players on the field; they also live through other fans. At least it seemed that way to me.

In any case, San Diego was a high point on the trip. In my journal after the game I wrote, "We continue on the trip, and I continue to be reinforced by my feeling that there is no bad place to watch a ballgame. Originally, I wanted to compare the ballparks with regard to several of the amenities and such, but more and more I am feeling like I just really want to let myself fall in love with baseball and appreciate the little things that each of the parks has to offer. Although I am told I should reserve judgment until I see some of the stadiums in the Midwest (which are apparently unredeemable)." My blissful state did not last long.

Qualcomm stadium

CITY: San Diego, California

TENANT: San Diego Padres

OPENED: April 19, 1966

NICKNAME/ALIASES: San Diego Stadium (1969–80), Jack Murphy Stadium (1980–97), The Q

DESIGN: Multipurpose stadium (baseball and football), circular symmetrical design, movable seats. Recently remodeled in 1997. SISTER PARKS: Oakland Coliseum, 3Com in San Francisco, Shea Stadium in New York, and Busch Stadium in St. Louis.

FIELD: Grass

DIMENSIONS (feet): left field—327, left center—370, center field—405, right center—370, right field—330

FENCES (feet): left field to right center—8.5, center field—8.5, right field—17.5 (scoreboard in front)

LOCATION/DIRECTIONS: 9449 Friars Road, San Diego, CA 92108. The stadium is between I-15, I-805, and I-8, a former swampland near the San Diego River. The park is not easy to see from the road, so beware.

CAPACITY: 67,544. Total attendance: 2,555,874 (1998). Average attendance: 31,554 (1998).

PARKING: $6 and plentiful

TICKETS: $5–$24. BEST BANG FOR YOUR BUCK: For a multipurpose stadium, Qualcomm provides a fantastic selection of seats. As long as you avoid the second deck of the outfield and the last rows of the upper deck, views are adequate. The lower box seats at the field level either on the first-base or third-base sides give good sightlines and an intimate feel for a multipurpose park (the foul territory down the foul lines is quite small).

BALLPARK EXPERIENCE: Qualcomm Stadium was built in the late sixties as a traditional multiuse stadium for the San Diego Chargers and a baseball expansion team. The exterior of the park is mostly concrete with numerous circular ramps to lead fans to the upper levels. The ramps are quite distinctive but generally resemble a parking structure. The stadium is fully enclosed and circular in design to accommodate both sports. The concrete exterior is made of thin concrete supports as opposed to the massive concrete walls that adorn other parks, such as SkyDome and Veterans Stadium, which gives the park an open feel from the outside despite the fact that it is fully enclosed.

The interior of Qualcomm Stadium looks more like a football stadium than a baseball park. The enclosed setting, large second deck, and rectangular shape are better suited for the NFL than MLB. In spite of these shortcomings, Qualcomm in our estimation makes every effort to cater to its baseball fans. We were surprised that the lower box seats were so close to the action at a multipurpose venue. The palm trees just beyond the outfield fence give the interior some character and make it stand out from

We enjoyed more red-carpet treatment in San Diego, which included a sampling of their fantastic food options and a trip to the owner's box—from which this picture was taken.

the many other multiuse stadiums (Cinergy, Three Rivers), but on the whole the palms felt pretty contrived to us. The park serves its multirole purpose as well as it can while adding some unique touches.

FANS: San Diego has only a recent history with major league baseball. As an expansion team in 1969, the Padres posted some of the lowest attendance records of all time. Only with Ray Kroc's purchase of the club in 1974 did fan support increase and a winning tradition begin. Since the mid-'70s the Padres have managed to attract a loyal base of fans who have a distinctive southern California flair. Dark tans, sunglasses, and surfboards on cars characterized the fans we saw at the park.

FACILITIES: The structure is well maintained especially after the renovations in 1997. The exterior concourses are wide and offer many concession facilities and picnic tables filled with families. Seats are wide but not angled to face the action along the first- and third-base sides.

FOOD: San Diego has the widest selection and best-quality food in the major leagues. The park is set up with concessions in mind. All the exterior concourses are dotted with specialty stands from Rubio's Famous Mexican to Randy Jones BBQ. Sampling all the foods would take an entire season. By far the most exotic food is the Baja Fish Taco from Rubio's. Known throughout southern California for their fish tacos, Rubio's has their entire selection of food at Qualcomm. Moreover, Qualcomm has the largest in-seat concession service in MLB. This allows fans to stay seated while a waiter or waitress takes your order and returns with food. This menu is as vast as the concession booths and even features shrimp cocktail, a Kaval and Null favorite.

Adding to its reputation, Qualcomm boasts the largest hot dog in the major leagues, the infamous half-pound Randy Jones BBQ special. To see thirty or forty of these suckers grilling up at a time is quite a sight. It is not the best dog in the majors, but it is something of a badge of honor (like the Dodger Dog). Qualcomm also offers the Buffalo Dog, which is made with bison meat and is a nice healthy break from the standard beef dog (note our admittedly suspect definition of healthy). As for beer, Budweiser and Miller are prevalent, but some specialty beers, such as Corona, which goes great with the fish tacos, do crop up. LAST CALL: Alcohol is served until the end of the eighth inning.

GREAT PLAYERS AND HISTORIC MOMENTS: As an expansion team in 1969, the Padres struggled to a 52-110 record. Successive bad seasons nearly sent the team packing to Washington, D.C. Only the last-minute purchase of the club by Ray Kroc, the man who made McDonald's a household name, saved baseball in San Diego. Several good seasons and the emergence of stars like Randy Jones, who won the Cy Young in 1976, helped generate interest in the club. Other great players like Dave Winfield, Rollie Fingers, and Gaylord Perry all played with the Padres in the late 1970s. Appearances in the World Series in 1984 (a loss to the Detroit Tigers) and in 1998 (a sweep by the New York Yankees) are the only two National League pennants for the Padres. All-Star Games in '78 and '92.

BALLPARK HISTORY: Jack Murphy, the sports editor of the *San Diego Union,* succeeded in garnering support for a multipurpose stadium in the mid-1960s. After passing a $27 million referendum in 1965, construction began. In honor of the sportswriter, the park was renamed Jack Murphy Stadium in 1980 and then, in honor of a pile of cash, renamed Qualcomm Stadium in 1997. Renovations included moving in the fences in 1982, adding seats in right and right-center in 1983 for the Chargers, and fully enclosing the park in 1997.

San Diego approved a plan to build a new downtown ballpark in 1998 with a mix of private and public money. The new ballpark will feature an asymmetrical, natural-grass playing field, and varied wall heights. An existing downtown landmark, the

---

BAT Info

FINAL SCORE: Padres 6, Mariners 0

OUR SEATS: Section—First, Row 1, Seats 5–6

BALLPARK: 6 of 30

DAY: 6 of 38

MILES TRAVELED: 516 (2,902 total)

NEW STATES: 1 (Arizona by nightfall; 3 total)

OUR EXPENSES: $54
  parking $6
  Burger King $7
  gas (twice) $41
    EXPENSES TO DATE: $405

OUR FREEBIES: $260
  game tickets (courtesy of the Padres) $60 (very nice seats)
  programs and memorabilia (courtesy of the Padres) $80
  ballpark food—fish tacos, pizza, buffalo dogs, hot dogs, shrimp cocktail, peanuts, pretzels, sushi and beer (courtesy of Volume Services and the Padres) $70
  lodging (equivalent, courtesy of Heidi Knowler and family) $50
    FREEBIES TO DATE: $954

Western Metal Supply Building, will be renovated and incorporated just like the B&O Building in Baltimore. The structure will be a part of the left-field wall, including the left-field foul pole. The new park is scheduled to be ready for baseball on July 4, 2002.

FUN FACT: Ivy was grown on the center-field fence in the early 1980s.

THE ONE THING YOU HAVE TO DO AT QUALCOMM STADIUM AND WHY: Have a fish taco. They are damn good.

LASTING IMPRESSION: Qualcomm Stadium is the premier multipurpose stadium in the country with superb facilities, great food, and a relatively good compromise between baseball and football.

7

Bank
one
Ballpark
phoenix

june 26, 1998

IT WAS hot.

In Oakland we had worn blue jeans, and they came in handy as it got a bit nippy that night. But since leaving northern California, it had been hot. Even San Diego had been somewhat hot, the city with the greatest weather in the country year-round. It was the summer of El Niño, but we had no idea what was ahead. And then came Phoenix.

I had been to southern Arizona before. I knew it was in the desert. I knew it was 100 degrees there from March to September, day and night. But to this point, I had always managed to convince myself that it wasn't as bad as Houston (no humidity). As it turned out though, that is just a bald-faced lie. It is worse. They say the desert is not so bad, because you don't sweat so much. And maybe that's true, maybe *you* don't sweat so much. But I do.

The horrible thing about the lack of humidity is that as soon as the sweat begins to seep out of your pores, it begins to evaporate. It felt like rolling around in cactus needles, and there were plenty of saguaro to go around. But damn the wide-open spaces of Arizona, and how I wish I could just sweat and feel the intermittent chill when the breeze hits my sweaty body just right. It was not to be. When the sweat came, there was no breeze. When the breeze came, the sweat was gone. And by the way, it doesn't get cold at night in the desert in late June.

Maybe the heat was getting to us, because as Dave and I were driving across the state border, we got into a surreal conversation. I said something like, "It sucks that we are going to have to get the car fixed."

Dave replied, "It does suck."

"I guess you should pay for the repairs."

"I think you should."

And like that, we were no longer friends. And let me say, it sucks when your best friend is not only no longer your best friend, but no longer your friend at all. And maybe you're even anti-friends.

And it sucks more when you still have to spend the next thirty-two days together.

So we didn't talk to each other for the rest of the night, which lasted until 2 A.M. when we arrived in Phoenix.

Early the next morning, we took the car to a shop. It turned out the damage wasn't that severe, only about eighty dollars' worth. So Dave and I both offered to pay for it, and we were friends again. It had been a tense twelve hours though, and our relationship would never fully recover.

In Phoenix we were staying with our friend Heidi and her family. She had lived in Phoenix her whole life and seemed oblivious to the unfortunate weather. I don't know if she noticed the sting of the dry heat, but she never did any of the flinching and howling that I did when I was walking between air-conditioned places. Nonetheless, she seemed to have precious few landmarks to show us, so we highlighted our day by making a trip to the drugstore to stock up on supplies: film, soda, chips, beer. We looked at some other things outside the car window, not daring to roll it down, and then headed off for the ballgame.

Bank one Ballpark

· ·

SEATTLE V ARIZONA

Game Time: 7:05 P.M.

Bank One Ballpark, the Bob. The newest park in the majors and the first retractable-roof stadium I'd ever been to. The approach to Bank One was unique. It is in downtown Phoenix, but you don't get that sense of awe stumbling across it that you get when you look up and see the Green Monster as you are walking around Boston. Instead it looks like a big Costco warehouse stuck amid a bundle of new-age adobe-style office buildings and painted beige to blend in with the rest of the city.

This made it rather complicated to take our customary picture in front of the park as you could hardly tell where the front of the ballpark was. Dave and I had dreamed of a

As we relaxed under the night sky inside air-conditioned Bank One Ballpark, we felt none of the effects of the oppressive 100-degree weather outside.

day when we could sit back and see a montage of snapshots of ourselves in front of every ballpark. We had even thought of unique ways to display such a photo collection from wall-mounted 8x10s to a pocket-sized wallet version. But to achieve that goal, we had to come up with some way to photograph ourselves outside of Bank One, which from the outside more closely resembled a headquarters for its namesake, and convince people it was a ballpark. After much debate and tons of sweating, we snapped some shots in front of the corner of the warehouse with the large Bank One logo on it and proceeded inside.

Although unspectacular on the outside, the interior of the Bob is something entirely different. Being from Houston, I had always wondered what it would be like if you could play baseball on real grass under a blue sky in a nasty summer climate. And I must say, it was an awesome feeling. When we got there, the roof was closed, which is to be expected in 100-degree heat. And I was not about to complain. Just seeing the lush green grass was good enough for me. But then, just before game time they snuck the roof open (it opens in a record five minutes with nary a peep), and we could see the blue sky to boot. The most impressive part of the experience by far was the realization that it was 100 degrees outside, but a pleasant and controlled 70 degrees where we were. The most remarkable feat of engineering I had ever witnessed.

Beyond this marvel, Bank One is a pretty nice ballpark all around. Despite the unaesthetic exterior, Bank One is quite accurately described as a member of the new wave of stadiums (which includes Camden Yards, Coors Field, and every park built since 1992) and was the first of these that we had seen on our trip. Like most of its sister parks, the Bob is built with a lot of brick and green steel (on the inside at least) and has a very intimate feel.

Also in line with the custom among modern ballparks, sparked inadvertently by the warehouse in Baltimore, Bank One has a gimmick. The Costco look and retractable roof over grass things were not enough, so the masterminds in Phoenix decided to put a swimming pool behind the center field fence. The pool has gotten a lot of press, positive and negative, but the bottom line is that it is the worst feature of any ballpark in America. Worse, the pool exemplifies a deeper problem in the development of modern ballpark style. In short, there isn't one. Teams want to hearken back to the nostalgia of old parks like Fenway, but at the same time they want to add a lot of gimmicks and amenities. They cannot choose a ballpark style, and they end up getting lost without one. Dayle Boyd in San Diego summed up this kind of philosophy when she was talking about what the Padres had done with Qualcomm. They wanted a tradition-oriented game but also felt like they needed to provide some extra entertainment value, which would draw in families and children. So they scattered some random touches, like the palm trees behind the outfield wall, as a kind of shorthand signature that this was their park.

The result of this fence-sitting actually fares worse than the carnival feel of a place like Edison Field in Anaheim, where the whole game is established as an amusement park ride from the moment you drive onto the grounds. The folks in Bank One, among others (see Qualcomm, Turner Field, and Enron), are trying to split it down the middle, but you can't draw on the nostalgia of a Fenway Park and then put a pool in center field. Give the pool to the people at Disney; they would know what to do with it.

We might have been more excited about the pool idea if they had given us tickets to watch the game from the pool, but unfortunately, no such perks were provided at Bank One. Of course, we never expected that our experiences at successive parks could continue to top each other as they had so far, and it was in Phoenix that the bubble finally burst. There would be no close encounter with the magically grown indoor grass nor with any of the players or shiny new facilities in Phoenix. We were, however, scheduled to meet with the concessionaires for some free samples before the ballgame, and given our newfound stature we were expecting a little something special.

But wouldn't you know, as soon as you get comfortable being a celebrity, you find yourself among people with no idea who you are and an entirely different opinion as to your level of importance. And so the concessions guy stood us up. Probably forgot all about us. It was a bitter jolt of reality for us.

Nevertheless, we enjoyed the relatively low-key game at Bank One. Despite my carping, they must be doing something right at the Bob, because regardless of their record they managed to fill the house.

Although our celebrity status had died down a great bit since our California heyday, we made several friends in Phoenix. In particular, we were sitting near some employees of the team who were very nice and very interested in the trip and in helping us out when we visited other cities. In general, the fans were enthusiastic, thanks in part to the fact that the D-backs set a team record with five home runs in the game. Everyone went crazy when Devon White hit a seventh-inning grand slam to put Arizona ahead for good, and Dave and I were shocked that we were able to pull the home team to victory for the sixth time in seven games, especially in Phoenix, given that the Diamondbacks had by far the worst record in baseball. On one low note, the fans did show that they were a little green dealing with baseball protocol, as evidenced by their yelling at the people in front of them, namely us, to sit down with two strikes and two outs in the ninth inning.

As for the game on the whole, it was another sloppy and exciting slugfest à la our Kingdome experience. It led me to the distinct conclusion that, although Alex Rodriguez may be a great hitter, he really needed to work on his glove work. Twice in this game A-Rod let double-play tosses at second bounce off his glove, and twice awestruck ump Jim Quick gave him the out. We booed. We booed loudly and were ecstatic to see Diamondbacks manager Buck Showalter get himself tossed arguing those calls. I would have expected nothing less.

After the game, we tried to see the city a little, although it was still very hot. We stopped off at the Taste of Phoenix Festival and sat down for a little dessert and a beer. It was good to finally relax and splurge a little. I think we had got to a point in the trip where we had been a little too frugal (see the car repair episode), so Dave and I bought each other beers and called it therapy. We headed back to Heidi's house and sat out by the pool with a six-pack. I saw the first two shooting stars of my life, which was exciting. I made the same wish twice.

Relaxing under the stars was a celebration of getting through the first week. It had been a little rough, but we felt like we were figuring out how this whole thing was going to work out, finding our routine. Of course, we were wrong.

Bank one Ballpark

CITY: Phoenix, Arizona

TENANT: Arizona Diamondbacks

OPENED: March 31, 1998

NICKNAME/ALIASES: The Bob

DESIGN: Baseball only, retractable-roof dome, asymmetrical interior design, no movable seats. SISTER PARKS: Enron Field in Houston, Safeco in Seattle.

The inside of Bank One, pictured here with the roof open, was a lot like many of the newer Camden Yards–era parks, such as Jacobs Field and Coors Field.

FIELD: Zoysia blend of grass know as DeAnza. Although the grass was specially developed for the new park to allow for real grass in a dome setting with high temperature changes, it looked the same to us.

DIMENSIONS (feet): left field—330, left center—374, deep left center—413, center field—407, deep right center—413, right center—374, right field—334

FENCES (feet): 8

LOCATION/DIRECTIONS: 401 E. Jefferson Street. BOUNDED BY: Seventh St. to the east, Fourth St. to the west, Jefferson St. to the north, and the Southern Pacific railroad tracks to the south.

CAPACITY: 49,075. Total attendance: 3,610,290 (1998). Average attendance: 44,571 (1998).

PARKING: $10. The park is in an urban setting and not surrounded by parking spots.

The crowd in Phoenix really got into it as the Diamondbacks hit a record five home runs to down the Mariners, 13-8.

TICKETS: $4–$55. BEST BANG FOR YOUR BUCK: We found that lower-deck seats provide good sightlines and ambiance. The next-best choice are the bleachers in right, which are a good bargain and have some of the liveliest fans.

BALLPARK EXPERIENCE: Bank One Ballpark may be the most unusual baseball stadium in the world. The design for the outside of the park, although borrowed from the warehouse district that surrounds it, causes the stadium to look like a cross between an arena, an office building, and an airport hangar. The interior, however, heavily references the many new ballpark designs like Camden in Baltimore and Jacobs in Cleveland. The big difference is that Bank One Ballpark has a huge roof that opens and closes with the sun. To our surprise, they open the roof for night games even in July, unless there is rain. This makes for a traditional ballpark feel on the inside.

There are some shortcomings of the enclosed design, however. For instance, the park ends abruptly in center field, where the engineers seem to have suddenly run out of room. They have squished a diamond-shaped field in a rectangular box with some creative engineering. Finally, Bank One features a rotunda dedicated to Arizona history at its main entrance. All these great interior features almost make up for the utilitarian exterior. Almost.

FANS: For a recent expansion team, Arizona fans have flocked to the game. Possibly due to the history of spring training in the Cactus Leagues or the novelty of a convertible dome, fans have filled the Bob from day one. Having a deep-pockets owner and stars like Randy Johnson, Luis Gonzalez, Matt Williams, and Steve Finley could also make the difference. The fans at our game were energetic, but that may have been because of all the Diamondback offense (see above).

FACILITIES: The structure is brand-new and superb. Wide concourses, plenty of restrooms, good-sized seats, and clean surroundings all are hallmarks of the park. The park does a good job of preventing walk-through traffic from disrupting sightlines. You are not allowed to move down the aisles in the lower box section when play is on. While annoying to fans that make five trips to the restroom, it is a nice touch for people who are into the game.

FOOD: Arizona has a wide selection of food but lacked the specialty foods of many other parks. There are numerous chains represented at the stadium, including McDonald's, Blimpie's sandwiches, Little Caesar's pizza, and Garcia's Mexican food. One nice touch is a farmer's market, Fielder's Choice, which offers a selection of fresh fruits and vegetables. There is a sports bar, Friday's Front Row Sports Grill, in the left-field corner, and the upper concourse houses two six-thousand-square-foot Miller Lite beer gardens that overlook the playing field. These areas were crowded during our game and had an energetic feel. Their Mexican restaurants served the best and most authentic options with real enchiladas, chimichangas, and flautas on the menu. One last noteworthy event was our first run-in with sauerkraut. This topping is a favorite of ours, and we heaped it all over the bratwurst. LAST CALL: Alcohol is served until the middle of the eighth inning.

GREAT PLAYERS AND HISTORIC MOMENTS: Arizona's owner Jerry Colangelo decided to spend some serious cash to finance his young team. Since its inception in 1998, Arizona has had one of the highest payrolls in professional baseball. Luring players such as Randy Johnson, Matt Williams, and Curt Shilling has made the Diamondbacks a playoff contender since 1999. In 1999 the team posted over one hundred wins. This completed the biggest turnaround in MLB history, going from sixty-five wins to the century mark from 1998 to 1999. (This just edged the thirty-four-and-a-half-game turnaround by the 1902–3 New York Giants.) The party, however, was short-lived as the upstart New York Mets beat the Diamondbacks in four games in the NLCS.

BALLPARK HISTORY: Bank One's claim to fame is that it is the first retractable-roof stadium with a natural-grass field. Toronto's SkyDome was the first retractable dome and was an engineering marvel when built in the mid-1980s. The vast expanse of concrete and symmetrical interior, however, made the SkyDome style feel woefully outdated when the Camden era began. In response to this reality and the unbearable weather, the Bob was constructed to create an intimate old-style park with the convenience of a roof. Ground was broken for the park on November 16, 1995. Construction took twenty-eight months and cost $354 million. Since its completion in 1998, three other parks (Enron in Houston, Safeco in Seattle, and Miller Park in Milwaukee) have imitated the new-age retractable roof design.

FUN FACT: The park is on final approach to Phoenix Airport, and planes fly during the entire game, especially Southwest Airlines (see Shea Stadium).

THE ONE THING YOU HAVE TO DO AT BANK ONE BALLPARK AND WHY: Arrive early enough to see the roof open. It is an amazing sight to see it roll back so quickly and open the park up to the sky. The roof has an east and a west side, which operate either in unison or independently. Either side of the roof can be opened to any position to maximize sunlight on the turf and minimize it on the interior steel and concrete. This is important because it is so damn hot.

LASTING IMPRESSION: While ugly from the exterior, the inside provides a great environment to play baseball in the 110-degree heat.

BAT INFO

FINAL SCORE: Diamondbacks 13, Mariners 8

OUR SEATS: Section 132, Row 12, Seats 16–17

BALLPARK: 7 of 30

DAY: 7 of 38

MILES TRAVELED: 20 (2,922 total)

NEW STATES: 0 (Arizona had been the night before; 3 total)

OUR EXPENSES: $104
 trip supplies $32
 parking $10
 programs $7
 ballpark food: hot dogs, pretzels, beer $30
 drinks afterward $25
 EXPENSES TO DATE: $509

OUR FREEBIES: $95
 game tickets (courtesy of the Diamondbacks) $45
 lodging (equivalent, courtesy of Heidi Knowler and family) $50
 FREEBIES TO DATE: $1,049

8

coors
field
Denver

SEVEN PARKS in seven days. Just like that. It didn't feel like much of an accomplishment. On Saturday we were crossing two more parks—albeit national parks—off our list: Monument Valley and the Valley of the Gods.

Monument Valley is where John Ford shot his well-respected westerns in the '30s, '40s, and '50s. *Stagecoach, The Searchers,* stuff like that. We went through it. Saw some big rocks in funny shapes. Took a lot of pictures that we might show to our kids someday. "Hey kids, look a these . . . big rocks . . . funny shapes."

We wanted to enjoy our off-day. It was a bit of the country that at least I had never seen. And I certainly did not want to travel a good fifteen thousand miles over most of the important parts of North America having seen nothing of note save for patches of grass and dirt surrounded by brick and steel. So we stopped at the official rest stop of Monument Valley and walked out on the plateau amid the fifty-cent blurry telescopes. "Hey look, it's a really big, blurry rock . . . in a funny shape." We looked to the east: funny-shaped rocks. To the north: funny-shaped rocks. Even a few not-so-funny-shaped rocks to the west. I got a postcard and about fifteen minutes of video.

We finally stumbled out of Monument Valley. Of course, in conspiracy with Kodak, the coolest rocks are at the end of the park so you will keep taking pictures because, "Hey, look, that rock is funnier-looking than the last one."

Then we stumbled into the Valley of the Gods. That morning neither Dave nor I had any clue what the Valley of the Gods was, and driving north along U.S. Route 163, we hadn't any idea we were anywhere near it until I saw a speck on the map that proclaimed we were just a few miles east of the pretentiously monikered valley. Lucky for us there was a little gray line that ran right through the valley, and seeing as how gray meant paved road, and we were only two hours behind schedule, we bit on it.

So just in case you are not entirely familiar with the road atlas and how it works, a good rule of thumb is never to drive on anything that is not at the very least a solid red line. Because gray may mean paved, but they don't tell you what with. Consequently, approaching the valley, we made it about seventy-five feet in before we decided our only practicable course of action would be to pick the car up and carry it back off that godforsaken road. We did manage to get out of the valley without any major vehicle damage, a good thing, being five hundred miles from civilization, and we found an alternate path that took us up on a ridge overlooking the Valley of the Gods (all of which begs the question, since when do the gods live in a valley anyway?).

The view from up there was quite majestic, so much so that I burned another four rolls of film and thirty minutes of video. Again, we might as well throw in a nonbaseball-related sightseeing tip: The view usually gets better as you go up.

But even more therapeutic than the view was the silence. Dave and I actually started coming out of the cynical stupor we had gotten ourselves into after fighting over money and tiring of telling people and their families about how this trip was our childhood dream, how we were getting along great, and how we most look forward to making it to Fenway Park, but a pleasant homecoming would also be nice, and . . .

At midnight, we were still driving across Utah, trying to get close enough to Denver to make the Sunday afternoon game. We didn't realize until the off-day how much we needed it, and in classic revisionist history form, we imagined we were just like major league ball players enjoying a much deserved day of rest after a hard week's work. We imagined ourselves as players from earlier in the century as they barnstormed around the country on the team bus. Of course, we weren't players and the only baseball we played was catch in numerous fast-food parking lots. But the dream of how it must have been to be a ballplayer in 1907 had a romantic appeal to it, and Dave and I would speak to many fans about how our daily grind embodied the true spirit of baseball. As baseball is an everyday sport and our trip was also an everyday affair, in that there were very few of these rest days, there was a kind of pace to the trip that somehow mimicked the game. Of course, the cynic in me was never sure whether this justification was sincere or just a PR stunt. But once we got into the flow of the trip, the experience of "living" baseball became palpable. Ironically though, it was not until the time for reflection afforded by our first off-day that the feeling really set in.

At Coors Field, Dave's hunt for the elusive mascot autograph turned into an obsession.

We ended up spending the night two hundred miles from Denver in Eagle, Colorado. I never did find out if that is the home of Eagle Brand Snack Chips. But I tell people it is anyway. Having gotten nowhere near Denver by the wee hours the night before, we were forced to wake up mind-numbingly early Sunday morning. But once the sun rose, the landscape kept us awake. It was an amazing view heading into Denver in the morning. The night before it had gotten dark before we made it into the Rockies. But heading into Denver, we saw the mountains through a breaking dawn as we descended toward the city and Coors Field.

coors field

OAKLAND V COLORADO

Game Time: 1:05 P.M.

COORS FIELD, like Bank One in Phoenix, is tucked away in downtown Denver. So coming in, it doesn't scream out at you from miles down the approaching freeways like most of the ballparks built over the last eighty years do. You have to rely on your maps to tell you that you are going in the right direction until—there it is. Unlike Bank One though, Coors is such a beautiful place from the outside that this characteristic of the park immediately gives you a cozy and nostalgic impression before you ever step inside, which is, of course, what the architects of these new ballparks were going for in mimicking Wrigley and Fenway.

But whether the urban ballpark captures that nostalgia or not, the major drawback of having the park hidden among the city streets is that first-time visitors from out of town, such as us, never know when they are actually close enough to the ballpark to park the car. These ballparks never have a lot of parking on-site. So there are two options: Pull into a lot when you start seeing people trying to wave you in, but then you run the risk of paying some guy twenty dollars to park in his driveway in the suburbs. Or drive until you actually see the stadium, at which point you are right next to it, all the parking for miles is full, and you will never get out.

After numerous experiences like this on our trip, we learned the clever trick of driving toward the park until you see, not just one car pulling into a lot (that guy is probably a sucker just like you), but a whole line of cars waiting to get into a lot. Then pull into the lot right next to that one. Amazingly, no one else seems to have figured this trick out.

Being tucked away downtown isn't the only thing that Coors has in common with renaissance parks old and new (such as Fenway and Camden). It also sports the much-imitated red brick and green steel of both of those aforementioned parks. Having been to Camden once before, I immediately noticed the resemblance of this park to that one. Although Coors still came across as a very beautiful ballpark, the entire design was reminiscent of Camden excepting, of course, the absence of a huge warehouse in right field.

The one immediately noticeable difference between Coors and the rest of the new wave of major league ballparks, however, is that Coors is a bit bigger, or at least it feels that way. The stadium seats 50,351 fans, only about 2,500 more than Camden, but it is a noticeable difference, particularly in the form of the massive center-field bleachers (nicknamed the Rockpile). Apparently, as the story goes, the original plan was for Coors to have a capacity of only 43,800, but after the 1993 season that averaged about 72,000 fans in Mile High Stadium (home to the Denver Broncos), the higher-ups with the Rockies realized that adding another 6,500 seats in center field would basically be like printing money. And the fact that the Rockies still manage to sell the stadium out a good chunk of the time (and have among the highest average attendance in baseball) goes to show that this plan worked.

Unfortunately, though, the Rockpile is the one element of the ballpark that doesn't really fit in with the rest of the design. It's not quite as jarring to the eye as the monolithic center-field expansion in Oakland, but it feels even more out of place given that it is anathema to the inherent goal of the new wave of ballparks to have a certain quaint and cozy feel. And no, the cute nickname doesn't really help much to make it seem any more intimate.

Aside from the Rockpile though, Coors Field really is a nice park if not very remarkable. I may not be the most ardent supporter of some of the new wave of déjà vu ballparks (you will soon catch onto the theme of Arlington reminds you of Coors reminds you of Camden, which reminds you of everything good about the old ballparks), but the part about Camden tapping into everything that was good about baseball stadiums before the multisport monoliths is true. And Coors manages to capture much of that same intimacy, even if it loses a few points on originality.

It almost goes without mentioning that the sightlines are great, and the seats are right on top of the action with the obvious exceptions of the Rockpile and the seats that top a mile in altitude. Also, the grass is very green (at least as green as it is at any of these other parks), and the facilities are all clean and new and offer most anything you could ask for at a ballgame. As we discovered over the following month, these characteristics pretty much hold for every park built after 1992.

For our game, I should start by saying that we weren't expecting much in the way of hospitality from our trip to Denver. Being stood up by the concessionaires in Phoenix and the fact that we had barely managed to finagle free tickets to this game in Denver had humbled us a bit. But when we got to Coors Field we were greeted out of the blue by a small band of people from Aramark, their concession company, and from the operations team. Apparently our new best friend from Los Angeles, Lon Rosenberg, had come through on his promise to talk us up to his peers at the Aramark offices of other ballparks. (Aramark served nine of the ballparks we visited on our trip: Los Angeles, Denver, Houston, Atlanta, Baltimore, New York [Shea], Three Rivers, Montreal, and Boston. We got the royal treatment at most all of them.) Did I mention that Lon is a swell guy?

In Denver, though, we weren't just greeted by one Aramark executive, we were greeted by a whole swarm of ballpark personnel, all of whom seemed very excited to meet us. For some reason, our visit was the highlight of their week, and subsequently our crowd of tour guides, which fluctuated between two and eight throughout the ballgame, led us off on an eventful tour of the stadium that lasted through the seventh-inning stretch.

Our tour's first stop was the Coors Field brewery. It was there that we made a remarkable discovery: Coors actually makes good beers. The beers at the brewery are microbrews, and you can only find them at the park. But they were easily good enough to replace everything Coors offers in stores. The brewery is also notable for its architecture. It is housed within a turn-of-the-century building that had been incorporated into the design of the ballpark, à la the warehouse at Camden. And just as the B&O Building gives Camden an instant history, the brewery's old-brick facade does a great job adding a past to the new ballpark in Denver.

After we left the brewery, we headed around the park to sample some of the foodstuffs. And the food was good, everything from the one-third-pound hot dogs overflowing with sauerkraut to the thick Bavarian pretzels. My particular favorite was the Rocky Mountain oysters. You may already know what Rocky Mountain oysters are, or you found out what they were before you ever tried them (and subsequently never did). But I had no idea what a Rocky Mountain oyster was until I bit into my first. But when I tasted it, I immediately became aware of two things: first, it was not an oyster and, second, it was one of the best things I had ever eaten. Unfamiliar with what I was eating, I asked one of the five or six guides (a lot of them were obviously tagging along for the great food) what they were. The frankest reply was, "Bull's balls." I know, you're freaked out by the image now, and you can't imagine eating such a thing: sliced, pressed, and deep-fried. But I still insist that it is the best food I have ever had at a base-ball park. Ever.

After we had rolled through most of the menu, and it is a lengthy menu (fortu-nately for us, our stomachs were growing rapidly in a defensive effort to outwit the per-nicious specter of food coma), we were taken on a complete tour of the ballpark. Among the leaders of our expedition was an old acquaintance of Dave's from high school in Cleveland, Carl Middleman, who was now an Aramark manager at Coors. It was an unexpected coincidence, to say the least.

Although Dave and Carl had apparently not been close in high school, you would have thought they had been best friends to look at them jabbering away at each other. But then Dave could carry on a conversation with a shoe for a good half-hour, so I didn't make much of it. Perhaps it was this newfound bond of friendship, perhaps it was simply carrying out Lon's orders, but whatever it was, Carl and the rest of the guys in Denver seemed inspired by our visit. They gave us an amazing tour. In short, we saw just about everything but the locker rooms. The field, nice. The stadium club, nice. The underbelly of the stadium, nice. The food court on the upper deck with a view of downtown (home of the ever popular Rocky Mountain oyster stand), nice. But Dave and I were most impressed with our visit to the Coors Field security booth, or "eye in the sky," where they monitor the numerous surveillance cameras around the park, making sure everything is in order. During our visit we witnessed the guys in the booth leading a stadium-wide pursuit for some underage drinkers, tracking them from camera to camera. These bandits got away, but shortly thereafter we were treated to a highlight reel of the young stadium's best covert footage, which was the equivalent of a PSA about public intoxication intercut with an ongoing pursuit of "concealed weapons" among well-endowed women. Our lesson from this: Even at the ballpark, big brother is watching.

The game was good fun too, another very American League–style slugfest, which was to be expected in the American League air of Denver. We saw the first couple of innings and the last couple of innings from right behind the backstop, about a hop step from the visiting dugout, while we caught most of the rest of the game on closed-circuit television as we were traversing the corridors, passing through the buffet or stopping in the brewery for a refill. If this had happened to us four or five days earlier, I probably would have flipped out about missing the ballgame, like I did in Anaheim when we missed an inning, but fortunately, the L.A. and San Diego experiences had conditioned me to the possibility that some things, on occasion, might be more important than baseball, namely food and beer.

As a result, I quickly learned to be ready and willing to see some more sights at any moment. And sure enough, every time we sat down, our escort would get a buzz on the walkie-talkie from the higher-ups recommending what new amenity they still needed to show us. It was great treatment, although I'll admit Dave and I were quick to take it for granted, given the spoiling we had received in both L.A. and San Diego just days prior. And in retrospect I don't know who had more fun during these exploits, us or our gaggle of guides.

In capsule, though the A's pulled ahead three times, the Rockies came back every time and won 11-10 with a four-run outburst in the seventh. This was the third time we had seen the A's, and in three games they had scored twenty-three runs and lost all three. As for Coors Field, it lived up to its reputation as a launching pad, demonstrating the park's only true flaw.

If you are not familiar with what I am talking about, the story is simply that the thin air in Denver diminishes gravity and wind resistance by about 10 percent, resulting in an unavoidable offensive bonanza. It's unfortunate, really, because Denver is otherwise a great baseball city. Sadly, though, it is simply not possible to play baseball the way the game was meant to be played in Colorado. And being something of a baseball purist myself, it is somewhat off-putting seeing baseball scores that look more like football scores.

In the ballpark's defense, there is nothing they could do to prevent this short of designing a high-altitude ball, one that travels only 90 percent as far and breaks 10 percent more on the curve. Short of that step though, balls will continue to go 10 percent farther in Colorado, and measures to push the fences 10 percent farther back will remain fruitless because exponentially more balls will continue to fall into the yawning power alleys and chasms between outfielders and infielders. And Darryl Kile curve balls will continue to resemble Darryl Hannah curve balls. And everyone will continually be out of breath. In short, it's Little League all over again in Denver, and you and I will continue to rue the lost significance of the one-run eighth-inning lead.

But the people of Denver will continue to embrace this brand of baseball, much as American League fans have for several years now. And they will probably keep coming out in droves for these four-hour slugfests. Oh well, if they don't mind, why should we?

coors Field

CITY: Denver, Colorado

TENANT: Colorado Rockies

OPENED: April 26, 1995

DESIGN: Baseball-only stadium; asymmetrical design, no movable seats. SISTER PARKS: Camden Yards in Baltimore, the Ballpark in Arlington, Pacific Bell Park in San Francisco, and Jacobs Field in Cleveland.

FIELD: Bluegrass with strains of rye; although again it just looked like grass to us.

DIMENSIONS (feet): left field—347, left center—390, center field—415, right center—375, right field—350

FENCES: Left to center field—8, right field—17 (out-of-town scoreboard)

The scoreboard at Coors Field is a lot more attractive than the Rockpile (at right in this picture), but neither measured up to the Rocky Mountain oysters in making this ballpark a memorable stop.

LOCATION: Main entrance is on Twentieth and Blake Streets. BOUNDED BY: First base (SE): Blake St. Third base (SW): 20th St. Left field (NW): Union Pacific Railroad tracks. Right field (NE): Park Ave.

CAPACITY: 50,381. Total attendance: 3,792,683 (1998). Average attendance: 46,823 (1998).

PARKING: $6-$15 at small lots throughout the largely industrial area surrounding the stadium; this is the fate of a downtown ballpark.

TICKETS: $4–$30. BEST BANG FOR YOUR BUCK: All the seats are close to the action with the lower box, as we discovered, especially well suited for viewing the action. Even though it is inexpensive, the seats in the Rockpile are too far from home plate, and you will end up spending the entire game watching pitchers warm up in the adjacent bullpens.

BALLPARK EXPERIENCE: Coors Field is a stunning sight from the exterior. A hand-laid brick facade is surrounded by green steel supports in the Camden style. At the corner of Twentieth and Blake, a small clock tower denotes the main entrance. The exterior architecture is symmetrical along the first- (Blake St.) and third-base (Twentieth St.) lines with the warehouse-style brick facade spanning both distances. The best elements of the design are ones that make the park blend into its Colorado surroundings, such as the existing building made into a brewery, natural sandstone from a Colorado quarry, and structural steel that reflects the site's rail yard heritage.

Coors Field boasts possibly the best interior design in major league baseball. Three levels of green seats extend around the entire stadium except for the bleacher section in center and left fields. Center field is dominated by the Rockpile, which encloses the stadium to fans seated in the lower sections. Nice views outside the park are still offered on the club and upper levels. The wide lower-level concourses at Coors extend 360 degrees around the stadium. It is possible to walk entirely around the park and not miss the action. There are also upper-level concourses behind the upper deck with an assortment of concessions and facilities including the Rocky Mountain oyster stand and a view of the Rocky Mountains. Coors's exterior facade, integration with its surroundings, and unique touches all contribute to a memorable ballpark experience. The major drawback is that the park is so derivative of Camden Yards.

FANS: The fans in Denver are great, maybe the best in baseball. Since the team came to town they have been drawing sellout crowds even in cavernous Mile High Stadium, and these fans aren't just here to see a nice ballpark. They are here to support their team, and they have been here through good years and bad. And they are loud.

FACILITIES: The structure is clean and well maintained. Wide concourses give plenty of room for restrooms and concession facilities. There are forty-three permanent concession stands as well as eight permanent and nine portable novelty shops at Coors Field. We were told that this ranks as one of the highest total concessions counts in MLB. The seats are wide and angled for action between the pitcher and batter, especially along the first- and third-base lines.

FOOD: We were overwhelmed by the great selection and high quality of food at Coors Field. They even offer beers other than Coors. The centerpiece of the food selection at Coors Field is the Rocky Mountain oysters, deep-fried and served with fries and specialty sauce (see above). Coors Field takes pride in having many healthy alternatives to the fat-filled ballpark favorites. They feature a chicken sandwich, garden burger, chef salad, and veggie wrap—not your average ballpark food. But for purists, Dave and I were excited to learn that Coors has the largest basic dog of any park. The Rocky Dog is a full one-third pound and can be dressed with every condiment imaginable. LAST CALL: Alcohol is served until the middle of the seventh inning.

GREAT PLAYERS AND HISTORIC MOMENTS: When you think Denver, don't even try to think of great pitchers; it's a physical impossibility. See Darryl Kile. But hitters. They're a dime a dozen here. Which makes it hard to distinguish the great players from those who are merely altitude assisted. (For the record, Larry Walker v. Dante Bichette). Of course there is the occasional story of the nonslugger who comes to Denver and becomes a slugger, leaves Denver and somehow stays a slugger. See Andres Galarraga.

As for historic moments, the most historic thing about Coors Field is that Mark McGwire and some other guys have hit some balls a very, very long way out of the park. A World Series game has never been played at Coors Field. On October 1, 1995, the Rockies became the fastest expansion team in history to reach the postseason and the National League's first wild-card team. The new club lost in four games to the eventual World Champion Atlanta Braves. All-Star Game '98.

BALLPARK HISTORY: On August 14, 1990, voters from the six-county district of metro Denver passed a 0.1 percent sales tax to finance the construction of a baseball facility. This vote took place before the franchise was awarded to Denver and helped the city secure the team. The park, later named Coors Field, was opened in 1995 after the expansion Colorado Rockies spent their first two seasons at Mile High Stadium. It was the first new park built for a National League club since Le Stade Olympique was opened in 1977. Its baseball-only design is similar to Camden Yards and Jacobs Field. The same architect, HOK Sport of Kansas City, designed all of these parks.

FUN FACT: The twentieth row at the top of the upper deck is painted purple. These are the "mile high" seats, as they are exactly 5,280 feet above sea level. Granted it is kind of a cheap thrill sitting in seats that are exactly 5,280 feet from sea level. But the view is nice.

THE ONE THING YOU HAVE TO DO AT COORS FIELD AND WHY: If you're man enough, go for the Rocky Mountain oysters and give the microbrews a try.

OTHER THINGS TO REMEMBER: We can't reiterate enough the park's hitter-friendly nature (nine runs were scored in the seventh inning alone at our game). If you yearn for a pitcher's duel, don't go.

LASTING IMPRESSION: Everything they say about Coors Field is true. It's a great ballpark with great fans, if not the greatest place to see a baseball game the way it was meant to be played.

BAT Info

FINAL SCORE: Rockies 11, A's 10

OUR SEATS: Section 126, Row 28, Seats 5–6

BALLPARK: 8 of 30

DAY: 9 of 38

MILES TRAVELED: 729 on day 8 + 347 on day 9 (3,998 total)

NEW STATES: 2 (Utah, Colorado; 5 total)

OUR EXPENSES: $301
car repair $90
McDonald's $8
gas and supplies $39
lodging (in Eagle, Colo.) $70
breakfast $4
parking $8
gas $42
lodging (in Lamar, Colo.) $40
  EXPENSES TO DATE: $810

OUR FREEBIES: $105
game tickets (courtesy of the Rockies) $30
ballpark food—dogs, Rocky Mountain oysters, Rocky dog, beers, nachos, more beers, pretzels, ice cream, etc. (courtesy of Aramark) $60
programs and memorabilia $15
  FREEBIES TO DATE: $1,154

9

The Ballpark in Arlington
Arlington

AFTER THE afternoon game in Denver, Dave and I followed what was fast becoming our habit and got out of town quickly. But given our break-of-dawn wake-up that morning, the fact that we had already driven several hundred miles from Eagle, Colorado, and our tiring activities at Coors Field in the 90-degree heat, we were tired and couldn't seem to go more than a couple of hours.

We spent the night in Lamar, Colorado. A small town about two hundred miles out of Denver, most notable as the birthplace of Houston Astros pitcher Scott Elarton. Needless to say, it was not the craziest night we had ever spent. We picked up burgers at Sonic. Dave dropped our tater tots, which he had been hyping up for an hour, all over the ground. We watched *Booty Call* in our room. All in all, about par for the course in Lamar I would imagine.

In the morning (after sleeping in entirely too late) we got on the road for Arlington. We had another off-day to make the nine-hundred-mile trip into the heart of Texas. I was excited to finally be heading home. I thought maybe there, with more close friends around, we could put off a few of the inane conversations for a while. I think even Dave was getting a little sick of talking about Ebbets Field. Of course he would never admit it.

81

When we crossed the state line into Texas, after a brief ride through the Oklahoma panhandle, I had a sudden feeling of calm. Near Amarillo we stopped and visited Palo Duro Canyon. Like the national parks we had blown through the prior two days, it was very colorful and beautiful and, as usual, we burned a lot of film there. The craziest thing about the canyon was that I had lived in Texas for eighteen years and had never heard of the thing until the day before, when my mother mentioned that we would be driving right by it. It's a pity, too, because it's probably the nicest landscape in the state. Too bad it's about four hundred miles from civilization.

By the time we began to approach the Dallas–Fort Worth area, it was closing in on midnight. We were about fifty miles from our destination when we had a scare on the freeway. We were anxious to get some sleep, so we were going about 90, trying to make it to Weatherford, Texas, about forty miles from Arlington, where we would be spending the night. Traveling at that speed, we were basically passing what little company we had on the highway. But then, just after midnight, we were rudely awakened when an eighteen-wheeler flew by us. Looking at the speedometer, we confirmed that we were doing 90. So this guy must have been well over 100. And not just that, he wasn't alone. There were more in the rearview. A whole pack of eighteen-wheelers, burning fast on our tail. It was like the Hell's Angels in semis. After a couple more eighteen-wheelers overtook us, we began to realize that our best chance of surviving this barrage was to either get off the road or keep up with the flow of traffic. Of course, stopping was out of the question. So before we got rammed by a several-ton truck, we found ourselves cruising down the freeway at about 110 miles per hour. We didn't even realize these trucks could go that fast. We wondered if they had some sort of permit for this. Had we

We were happy to have fellow travelers along again to break up the tension that periodically built up between us. Pictured here with Dave are Brad's dad and Jay Williamson, who is demonstrating the correct way to eat a turkey leg.

gotten ourselves caught in a professional big-rig race? In any case, we came out of it all alive. And we shaved about thirty minutes off our time.

We stayed the night in Weatherford with some of my dad's friends, the Mickles, who lived on a ranch and private golf course in this rural town. Given that it was about one o'clock in the morning when we got to Weatherford, everybody was asleep when we got to the door, and expecting this to be the case we had been instructed to just go upstairs to the guest room and go to sleep. So that's what we did. The only problem with the whole plan was that our directions had been somewhat vague, and we weren't at all sure that we were in the right house. But we figured with the amount of noise we were making, if we weren't, somebody would let us know before morning. Fortunately that nudge from the cop with a flashlight never came.

The end of the day marked the end of the national-park tourist stretch of our trip, and with it the end of the leisurely pace and touristy feel of the last few days. We only had three parks to visit in the next nine days, which might seem like a laid-back stretch, but we weren't too sure about that. We would be meeting up with a few of our crazier friends—Tom, Zach, and Aron (but we just called him Ron)—over the course of the next few days, so we were expecting it to be anything but boring.

Waking up the next day, I suddenly realized that I had absolutely no idea what day of the week it was. Apparently, when you're on semi-permanent vacation, days of the week lose all meaning. But for whatever reason, losing my conception of time was forcing me to question my sanity. So I racked my brain to determine what day it was. I figured it might be Monday or Friday, because we had seen a day game the day before, and they like to play those on Sundays and Thursdays. Then I remembered that it hadn't been the day before, but two days before that we had seen that game. And subsequently realizing that we had seen eight parks with two off-days and had started the trip on a Saturday, I walked through the math in my head to finally figure out that this was Tuesday.

In any case, on Tuesday we woke up none too early, according to our new modus operandi of driving all night, sleeping all day, and catching a ballgame in the evening. Fortunately, since we were so close to Arlington on this Tuesday, we were afforded the opportunity to play nine holes of golf at the local course, which our hosts owned. And even though I am a horrible golfer, and it was hot as Hades, it was a fun time. Dave and I had the bright idea to wear our brand-new black golfing shirts from San Diego for the excursion, which it turns out, was by all accounts a stupid idea. The two of us, both big sweaters, were drenched after the front nine. We had an opportunity to keep playing, but after about two hours of swinging metal sticks and baking in the sun, we called no joy and packed up for the ballpark.

I had been excited about this game for a while, as I would be meeting up with one of my best friends from high school, Jay Williamson, for the first time in four years. My dad was also meeting us, so it was already starting to feel like home after a very long time on the road.

The Ballpark in Arlington

LOS ANGELES V TEXAS

Game Time: 7:35 P.M.

We were meeting my dad and Jay at the Marriott Hotel in Arlington, which was about a stone's throw away from the Ballpark. As we approached the hotel, about three hours before game time, we got a sneak peak at the Ballpark. In stark contrast with the last two parks we had seen, the Ballpark stood unaccompanied, except by the hotel and some Little League fields, off the side of a highway in a very pastoral setting. This sort of isolation on the side of a freeway isn't really a unique characteristic; most of the cookie-cutter parks of the '60s are situated that way. But the Ballpark's disposition was unique in that, unlike those unsightly monoliths, this was a beautiful and enchanting green-steeled structure surrounded by an arched facade of red brick and concrete etched in bas-relief. Additionally, the grassy lawn surrounding the stadium provided a relaxing rural feel. And the whole effect really made it feel like we were approaching a castle somewhere in the European countryside, a castle adjacent to a Little League diamond and a small pond. All in all, it was definitely the most beautiful thing I had seen on the trip, although there was one minor drawback.

By the time we rolled into Arlington, I had begun to fear that the cookie-cutter ballparks of the '60s—Candlestick, Riverfront, and Atlanta's Fulton County—were being replaced by a new kind of cookie-cutter ballpark of the new millennium, the likes of Camden, Coors, and Jacobs Field. Certainly the newer models were all beautiful and undoubtedly an improvement over their monolithic concrete forbearers, but I feared a certain hollowness and facsimile quality to them at some level. And wouldn't you know, as we approached the beautiful Ballpark in Arlington, it kind of reminded me of something.

The Ballpark in Arlington—bonus points for the most stately name in all of baseball—is unmistakably among the new-era, neo-nostalgic major league ballparks. And it was the third of these such parks that we had seen in the last five days. In each park the same reddish brick, the same green steel, the same new-car smell, plethora of amenities, glut of luxury suites, great sightlines, and forty thousand seats full every night. I hadn't even made it to the two most renowned among the throwback parks—Camden and Jacobs—but already I was sick of the trend. Was this the future of baseball, in every town forty thousand seats and exactly forty thousand fans to sit in them? Sure I

The Ballpark in Arlington's unique pastoral setting contributes to one of the most beautiful exteriors in all of baseball.

respected that each park was unique: Camden had a warehouse, Bank One a roof, Coors a warehouse, and in Arlington . . . a riverboat?

About the game, I'll confess that I don't actually remember that much. Although the heat had been modestly uncomfortable up to this point in the trip, in Arlington it was simply unbearable to the point of causing delirium. And contributing to our feelings of lightheadedness in this sultry weather was the fact that we had had several beers each at the Marriott before we hopped over. When we finally did get to the park, we were already drenched in sweat from the walk over. And soon after finding our seats, we found ourselves thoroughly exhausted. Subsequently, we didn't venture about the park too much. And thankfully, Arlington is one of those parks where the beer comes to you. Unfortunately, the boring game we witnessed did little to keep us awake. The only excitement lasted through Darren Dreifort's four perfect innings. Outside of that, the players seemed as exhausted as we were. It was our second home loss too, so we took that pretty hard as well.

In all honesty, I was thankful for the low-key experience we had in Arlington: no tours, no rush of strangers that we had to keep sharing our experiences with, no free food that we would feel compelled to eat. Just an opportunity to sit back and watch a ballgame with some friends. Although granted, with Dave around, I could not truly escape the trip. As I have mentioned before, Dave is a constant talker, and he spent much of the ballgame talking my dad's ear off about all of our experiences from the bandits in Studio City to the Rocky Mountain oysters in Denver.

Having my dad and Jay around really helped keep the harmony between Dave and me, though, more so than when we had been with Ben in L.A. or Heidi in Phoenix. In Arlington I managed to put my dad on Dave duty, where he diligently and with interest listened to my partner's stories. Dave's stories were always interesting . . . the first time.

With them in a corner bantering on, I spent some quality time catching up with my best friend from years past. And while our conversation invariably turned to baseball and the trip, we also managed to cover the other important topics of school, family, women, and life's ambitions. It was a conversation I'd been through a thousand different times with a hundred different people, but it was always unique. Particularly here with a good friend who had changed so much in four years yet seemed so familiar. Particularly in the context of this intensely baseball-centric life I was leading, this experience served to keep me grounded particularly well.

A parting note on the ballpark, although you can't easily distinguish between it and many others at a glance, it is still a great place for a game. As I mentioned, there were a lot of resemblances between this park and the other new ones (Camden, Bank One, at least on the inside). And it definitely concerns me that the new parks are turning into a whole new brand of cookie-cutter. Obviously, for the sake of our trip, it would have been cool if all the parks had a very distinct flavor, but can you fault the owners? They just want to build a park that works, and this design is fail-proof. Since Camden and Jacobs have been popular, everyone is trying to emulate that. I wasn't complaining in Arlington because I had enjoyed all of these parks, but I did find myself wondering how far this can go before all of these parks start running together like the lifeless facsimiles of thirty years ago.

All in all, I would have thought that the Ballpark was the nicest park I'd been to if it weren't for the weather. We were sweating when we got there in the 98-degree weather, and we were sweating when we left. Ironically, those offices in center field turned out to be the one main black mark against this stadium (other than the no air-conditioning thing). The offices, which were ostensibly added to prevent gusts of wind from swirling into the ballpark and creating a 3Com effect, ended up preventing any sort of breeze from coming through the ballpark at all. Thus, an uncomfortably hot day becomes an unbearably hot day. I guess that's just a lesson from the ballpark gods. Even if you find a way to put offices or apartments in your stadium without creating an eyesore, their presence is still going to haunt you one way or another. In any case, with or without a breeze, outdoor baseball in Texas in late June with forty thousand people burning at 98.6 degrees is unpleasant at best. Our experience in Arlington was the best argument you could have for a domed stadium. And we were about to head off to the birthplace of the domed stadium. My hometown.

The Ballpark in Arlington

CITY: Arlington, Texas

TENANT: Texas Rangers

OPENED: April 1, 1994

NICKNAME/ALIASES: The Ballpark, The Ballpark at Arlington

DESIGN: baseball-only stadium, asymmetrical design, no movable seats. SISTER PARKS: Camden Yards in Baltimore, Coors Field in Denver, and Jacobs Field in Cleveland.

FIELD: Bermuda Tifway 419 grass, although once again the grass looked the same to us.

DIMENSIONS (feet): left field—334, left center—388, center field—400, deep right center—407, right center—381, right field—325

FENCES (feet): left field—14, center to right field—8

LOCATION/DIRECTIONS: 1000 Ballpark Way, Arlington, TX

CAPACITY: 49,178. Total attendance: 2,927,399 (1998). Average attendance: 36,141 (1998).

PARKING: $6–$10. There are ten color-coded lots on the north side of the park, which are named for different Texas historical figures (e.g., Davy Crockett, Stephen F. Austin) from the Republic of Texas era (1830s and 1840s). There is also valet parking for $20.

TICKETS: $5–$35. BEST BANG FOR YOUR BUCK: Due to the hodgepodge of interior designs, there are many different types of seats at the Ballpark in Arlington. The lower-deck seats are close to the action and have good sightlines, especially toward the foul poles. One should be careful about the seats under the overhang behind home plate and near the concourses. These seats in which we actually sat have poor views of the scoreboard and you feel distant from the action.

BALLPARK EXPERIENCE: The Ballpark has a majesty from the exterior that few architectural feats can equal. It is Dave's learned opinion that the huge Roman arches supported by smaller arches give the park a European feel and resemble the Coliseum in Rome and Ebbets Field in Brooklyn (at least he's been to the Coliseum). The many stone reliefs that depict Texas history are a nice addition. The brick-and-granite-stone facade looks brand-new and is connected at each of its four corners with small towers. The towers denote the main entrances and are capped with green cupolas. The park is surrounded by fields and ponds instead of the more common parking spaces. This gives the park a rural feel that is unequaled in any stadium.

The interior of the Ballpark is a hodgepodge design with themes from many different parks. Center field is dominated by an office complex within the park. The white steel complex, in sharp contrast to the green steel around it, takes up from left center to right center field and completely encloses the stadium. From left center all the way around to the right-field foul pole, the design is identical to Camden or Coors with

A hodgepodge of designs, including an office complex with a white-picket facade topped by huge billboards and dual-deck bleachers reminiscent of Tiger Stadium, make up the interior of the Ballpark in Arlington.

88

green seats, concrete, and green steel. Right field is dedicated to Tiger Stadium with two levels of seats in the traditional turn-of-the-century double-decker design. Although it has some interesting touches, the interior is too busy and contrasts with the stately exterior; this disjoint is the park's biggest flaw.

FANS: The fans in Arlington mean well but it's hard to exert much energy in support of your team, given the heat. Additionally, the Rangers' numerous playoff losses to the Yankees have made rooting for them a challenge over the past several seasons.

FACILITIES: We found the seats wide and angled toward the action. Restrooms are spacious and clean. The concourses are far away from the action, and it requires a hike to reach the concessions and restrooms. Because the bulk of the concessionaires are outside the actual seating structure, except for those in the highest level, fans walk down ramps to ground level to reach restrooms, hot dog stands, etc. This allows for very wide concourses but also leads to congestion on the stairs down to the concourse, particularly in the high traffic times between innings. Evidently this design was partially due to the hot Texas summers because wider concourses allowed the air to circulate and keep the temperature down.

FOOD: The Ballpark in Arlington has a wide assortment of standard food. Specialty foods include many Mexican options and famous turkey legs, which take at least two innings to eat and are very good. The carved sandwiches are also a nice option for those less inclined to eat half a turkey. TGI Fridays operates an air-conditioned sports bar in the home run porch. If you cannot handle the heat (few can), spend some innings at the sports bar and cool off. LAST CALL: Alcohol is served until the seventh inning in the stands and until the eighth inning at the concession facilities.

GREAT PLAYERS AND HISTORIC MOMENTS: Once again, with the new ballpark, not much room for history. They've got the best catcher in the game, Ivan Rodriguez, but that's about all. As for historic moments, they've managed to lose a few playoff games to the Yankees, too. A World Series has never been played at the Ballpark. All-Star Game '95.

BALLPARK HISTORY: The Rangers, displaced from Washington, played their first twenty-two years at Arlington Stadium (a.k.a. Turnpike Stadium due to its location near the Texas Turnpike), which was situated across the street from the current park. One small note on the old park, like the Toronto SkyDome where the sacrilegious "OK Blue Jay" is played instead of "Take Me out to the Ballgame," the seventh-inning stretch at the old Arlington Stadium featured the song "Cotton Eye Joe" (see SkyDome). The team moved to the new ballpark in 1994 and aced the "Cotton Eye Joe" song. The Ballpark cost $191 million and was financed with a mix of public (70 percent) and private (30 percent) money.

FUN FACT: There is a brick walk that is eighteen to seventy feet wide on the north and west portions of the park. It is divided into panels chronicling every year the team has been in Texas (since 1972).

THE ONE THING YOU HAVE TO DO AT THE BALLPARK AT ARLINGTON AND WHY: Chase home-run balls into the batter's eye. Every time a ball gets hit out into the lawn in dead center, about five guys go racing after it. Of course we were too tired to get out of our seats, but it looked like fun.

OTHER THINGS TO REMEMBER: Watch your step in the upper deck. The first home game at the Ballpark had a near fatality as a fan leaned over the first-row railing and fell from the top deck into the lower box area. Luckily, the person lived and the railings were raised, but be sure to keep your balance in the second deck, especially given the tendency for heat-induced lightheadedness in this park.

LASTING IMPRESSION: A beautiful exterior set apart from its surroundings in the hot Texas heat.

BAT Info

FINAL SCORE: Dodgers 4, Rangers 1

OUR SEATS: Section 130, Row 34, Seat 15

BALLPARK: 9 of 30

DAY: 11 of 38

MILES TRAVELED: 680 on day 10 + 343 on day 11 (5021 total)

NEW STATES: 2 (Oklahoma, Texas; 7 total)

OUR EXPENSES: $138
lunch $8
Palo Duro Canyon pass $6
McDonald's (again) $8
more film $16
gas $37
lunch $14
programs $8
ballpark food—hot dogs, turkey
legs, soda, and Icees $24
gas $17
    EXPENSES TO DATE: $948

OUR FREEBIES: $170
lodging (courtesy of the Mickles) $50
drinks (courtesy of my dad) $30
game tickets (courtesy of the
Rangers) $40
lodging (my parents' house in Houston)
$50
    FREEBIES TO DATE: $1,324

10

day 12

The Astrodome

Houston

july 1, 1998

THE ARLINGTON game had been our most low-key ballpark experience to date. No tour or anything, and we didn't spend much time talking to the locals. It was good to have the opportunity to just sit and watch a game though. Too bad it wasn't a very good game.

Directly after the game I said my good-byes to my old friend Jay (I'd see him in another four years I figured), and we took off for Houston. We had been tired when we left Arlington, and Dave and I both being sick and tired of the steering wheel of my car, we nominated my dad to drive. He did yeoman's work getting us the entire way home, pulling into the driveway a shade before 4 A.M. We were exhausted when we finally got into Houston. The drive was mostly uneventful (Dave and I slept most of the way), with the exception of the startling sighting of a thirty-foot-high statue of Sam Houston peering at us from the side of Interstate 45. It was lit up like a beacon. I asked my dad if it was new. He said it had been there all my life. I wondered why I had never noticed it before.

After we woke up on Wednesday (?), we had a pretty hectic day. I spent the morning visiting with my mom and sister and trying to ignore Dave's recitation for them of his entire collection of trip stories. In the afternoon we met up with our friend Zach, who had hitched a ride down from Austin to go to this game with us, and another friend, Ron, who had flown out from Oakland and was going to travel with us all the way to New York (just looking for a free ride I guess). We all met my dad at his office for a buffet lunch. Don't ask me why we undertook this suicidal mission given our routine ballpark diet.

Afterward, we spent a couple of hours bouncing around the city before we headed off to the Dome.

The Astrodome

CHICAGO (AL) V HOUSTON

Game Time: 7:05 P.M.

THE ASTRODOME. As a kid growing up in Houston I had loved the Astrodome. For about the first fourteen years of my life, the Astrodome was the only major league ballpark I had ever known. I must have seen two hundred games there before I saw one anywhere else.

I might even go so far as to attribute a great deal of my personality to the Astrodome. The ballpark, because of its imposing and understated nature, tends to come across as a bit reserved. It is the kind of park where you could sit and read the paper between innings and not have to worry about missing anything; where there is ample legroom, but not because the engineers designed it that way, just because nobody else is there. Whether they actually sold tickets for the seats in front of or behind you was always a mystery, but you expected that even if they did, those people would probably go find some other seats when they got to the park so that they could have a little more room to themselves as well. Comfort was the goal.

Not that being at the Astrodome was an isolating experience. There was still always someone a couple of rows over with an educated opinion on exactly how good Dickie Thon could have been if not for his unfortunate accident, and if you looked hard enough you could probably even find someone who knew whatever happened to Glenn Davis. But you didn't have to talk to them if you didn't want to. And you didn't have to hear them either, or feel their kid's feet banging against the back of your chair.

The Astrodome has always been, in my mind, the embodiment of the perfect space to watch a baseball game if you just wanted to be there and watch some baseball with twenty thousand of your closest friends in an arena that seats sixty thousand.

Needless to say, the Astrodome has always gotten a pretty bad rap. And I figured after this trip that my impression of it would fade compared to all of the other great new ballparks, such as the last three we had seen: Arlington, Coors, and Bank One. But it was turning out that the trip was not only helping me to appreciate the parks I had never been to but also the ones I had seen countless times.

In particular, the Arlington experience and general saunalike nature of the previous week made me particularly appreciative of the Dome's air conditioning, especially given that the heat was even worse, and always is, in Houston. I wished that all of those so-called baseball purists who consistently rail against how the Astrodome ruined baseball could have been with us on our trip through Texas. It would have been humorous to see their forced justifications for how our experience in Arlington was more pleasant than the cool 71-degree breeze that hit our faces when we entered the Astrodome.

Not only did I appreciate the Dome for the respite from the heat that it provided, but also for the fact that, although it could never be confused with the "Friendly Confines," it had undoubtedly saved major league baseball in Houston numerous times over the years. If you live in Houston and you love baseball, you have to love the Dome, because you know that, without it, the Astros never would have managed half of the mediocre attendance they have attracted over their mediocre history and the team would have been long gone by now. Granted, a retractable roof and natural grass would be better, but that hadn't been an option for the last thirty-five years.

As for our experience in the Dome on this occasion, I think everyone in our party— Dave, Ron, Zach, my teenage sister Tracy, and me—would agree that it was one of the best baseball experiences of our collective lives. We got to the game a little over two hours early, and with this being an Aramark park (see Lon Rosenberg and Dodger Stadium), we knew that we were going to be treated well. We just didn't know how well.

To start our visit to the Dome, we had the usual tour, venturing to SkyBox seats in the top deck of the stadium—which are possibly the most remote perches in the history of baseball, checking out Lefty's Pub behind the left-field foul pole, and venturing down

Houston was a great homecoming for Brad. We were joined at the Astrodome by Ron (far left), our new travel companion for the next two weeks, Brad's sister Tracy, and our friend Zach (who was behind the camera for this photo).

to the luxury suites on the clubhouse level, right behind the backstop. They were all things I had seen before, but it was an exciting experience in any case because we were an excitable group.

After the tour, we were taken to Aramark's VIP seats behind the first-base dugout and introduced to our waitress for the evening, who was instructed to bring us anything we wanted (shades of San Diego). I don't have to tell you how much food and drink five eighteen- to twenty-two-year-olds can go through. But that's not all.

In the fourth inning, a radio commentator interviewed us, and then we were escorted to the press box to meet renowned Astros broadcaster Milo Hamilton. You probably don't know Milo by name, but if you've ever been to Cooperstown (he's a member of the baseball Hall of Fame), you've probably heard him. Hamilton is the broadcaster on all the clips of Hank Aaron's 715th home run. Not only did we meet him, we were escorted to his private luxury suite and treated to a full buffet.

This experience was also reminiscent of the San Diego trip, except this time it was like being in the owner's box without the owner. In fact, we were the *only ones* there.

While we were up there, we also met the sous chef of the luxury suites. I don't even know what a sous chef is! At the time, we thought he said "sauce chef," which was very impressive to us. But sous chef is just as cool. All of these perks had been arranged by the Aramark guys at the Astrodome, who somehow managed to outdo the royal treatment Lon had shown us in L.A. (NOTE: In deference to Aramark, I stress that the Astros organization and Astrodome had nothing to do with our reception in Houston. They were somewhat aloof, even when I informed them that my dad was a twenty-year season-ticket holder.)

The fact that we were treated so well by the Aramark people shouldn't have an impact on our opinion of the stadium. But it did. It certainly improved my bias, even though I had been there hundreds of times before and was already one of the Astrodome's biggest fans.

The Dome doesn't have any real catchy amenities like the new parks. Certainly, when it was built, it was amazing: a domed stadium, AstroTurf (once considered a feat of engineering), and the largest scoreboard you can imagine, spanning the outfield. In these days, the people who run the place are just trying to keep up with the Joneses. To my way of thinking, they do a good job. There were a lot of food options, good barbecue, a couple of bars, great sightlines (if not seats right on top of the action), and very informative scoreboards. Nothing flashy though.

Sadly, the need for flashiness and buzz in today's ballparks was probably the reason why we saw our smallest crowd of the trip so far: twenty-nine thousand. (But that mark of desolation would get shattered somewhere in the Midwest.) It's also the reason that you and I will never see another baseball game at the Dome. Houston premiered a new ball park in the 2000 season. (See pages 303–5 for some comments on Enron Field.)

But speaking of games, which always seem to end up as something of an after-thought in these chapters, this one was very exciting. My beloved Astros whipped up on the White Sox, 10-4. I went crazy when Jeff Bagwell hit a late-inning home run. It was great having my family with me, too. My parents arrived after the game started and kept a low profile most of the time, although I detected a little envy when the rest of us headed to the luxury suites. Our entourage was easily the largest of the trip. With my family, Zach, and Ron, who was just getting settled in for a two-week stint on the Baseball America Tour, we took advantage of the free food with which we were so graciously provided.

The one low note of the evening came when we returned to our field box seats from Milo's box to find that our waitress had left, meaning that we weren't able to express our gratitude. I asked Dad to give her something when he came back later in the week, but it wasn't the same.

In all, though I had thought that we would have a leisurely stay at home, it was about the busiest twenty-eight hours of the entire trip. Understandably, my family wanted to take care of us, which made me feel a lot better about the decision to make this trip and the indecision that lingered over my life after this trip. I finally got the impression that my dad was proud of me and what I, with Dave's help, was accomplishing on this trip. Even if that was basically just watching a lot of baseball. I had the feeling that if I could navigate to all of the parks and not strangle Dave in the process, then the decisions ahead weren't going to be much harder.

The Astrodome

CITY: Houston, Texas

TENANT: Houston Astros (MLB), Houston Oilers (NFL, 1965–96)

OPENED: April 12, 1965

CLOSED (TO BASEBALL): October 9, 1999

NICKNAME/ALIASES: The Dome, the Eighth Wonder of the World, Harris County Domed Stadium

DESIGN: Multipurpose domed stadium (accommodates baseball, football, rodeo, tractor pulls, even an NBA All-Star Game), circular design, movable seats. SISTER PARKS: none.

FIELD: Tifway 419 Bermuda grass (1965), AstroTurf (1966–   )

DIMENSIONS (feet): left field—325, left center—375, center field—400, right center—375, right field—325, apex of dome—208

This photo of a Jeff Bagwell home run was taken from broadcaster Milo Hamilton's luxury box. The experience of being there was one of our many perks at the Astrodome.

FENCES (feet): left field—14, center to right field—8

LOCATION: 8400 Kirby Drive, Houston, TX. BOUNDED BY: Center field (E): Fannin St. Third base (N): Old Spanish Trail. Home plate (W): Kirby Dr. First base (S): South Loop Freeway/I-610.

CAPACITY: 54,815 (baseball). Total attendance: 2,458,451 (1998). Average attendance: 30,351 (1998).

PARKING: $10-$15. The Astrodome lot is huge (over 30,000 spots) and totally encompasses the ballpark. For convenience, there are numerous gates entering the lot from every direction.

TICKETS: From $6 to $23. BEST BANG FOR YOUR BUCK: Other than the ceiling 208 feet up, not much in the way of layout distinguishes the structure of the Astrodome from the other multipurpose behemoths built in the 1960s. This being the case, if you really want to see the action, you want to get as close as possible. The deceptively close seats, and at a nice price, are those curving around the outfield foul poles in the mezzanine. They are right on the field and often sparsely populated.

BALLPARK EXPERIENCE: From the outside, the Astrodome is a perfectly symmetrical dome. It is eighteen stories along the sides of the stadium with a 208-foot dome. The park has a 1960s feel with angled exterior panels reminiscent of the bleacher deck at Dodger Stadium. Unlike the Kingdome, which was dominated by concrete, the Astrodome—due to its white paint job—has less of a concrete feel to it. The white paint and the many windows at the higher levels give the Astrodome a human touch.

Obviously, being the large multisport venue that it was designed to be, the Astrodome has certain limitations. *Intimate* will never be a word used to describe this park, but a great deal of effort was expended to improve the experience at the ballpark, and the effort has not gone unnoticed. The interior is composed of red and yellow seats that are a perfect match with the old-school Astros' uniforms. There are numerous movable seats, like Cinergy Field or Three Rivers. Fortunately, the Astrodome has wide concourses—an unusual feature in this type of park—that offer a good view of the field as you walk around, with the exception of parts of the lower deck behind the dugouts.

One highlight of our Dome experience was the scoreboards. The Dome had the best out-of-town scoreboards in baseball, with inning-by-inning results from the other ballparks in plain view along the outfield wall. The original stadium had the largest scoreboard in baseball, spanning the top level from foul pole to foul pole through the outfield. The scoreboard included the home run spectacular, which was an assortment of spinning wheels, cartoons, and other bells and whistles that went off when an Astros player hit a home run. The scoreboard and home-run spectacular were removed in 1989 to add seats for the football team that has since skipped town.

FANS: The fan support of the original Colt .45s was average at best. Once the Colt .45s moved into the new Astrodome and eliminated the dog-sized mosquitoes, attendance shot up over two million for several years. Astros fans have had little to root for over many years but have always supported their team. At our game, the fans were lively, especially when the fireworks were shot off to celebrate the home runs of the Astros.

FACILITIES: The Astrodome (along with Busch Stadium in St. Louis) established itself among the best ballparks of its era. The biggest knock against the stadium in years past, beyond the dome itself and the turf, has been the seats. Although the seats are among the most comfortable in baseball—plush, cushioned seats, an oft undiscussed luxury available because of the much derided ceiling overhead—they are arranged in a rainbow color scheme. Red seats in the field boxes, orange in the mezzanine, and blue, gray, yellow, red, and orange seats all the way up to the rafters. This color scheme matched the Astros original and somewhat scorned rainbow-colored uniforms. Those uniforms got the boot in 1986 after the playoff loss to the New York Mets. The seats stay as a reminder of that fashion-senseless era.

FOOD: The food at the Astrodome is generally good across the board. Your best bets are Luther's barbeque chopped-beef sandwich with a Shiner Bock (local microbrew). Also worth mentioning, the Astrodome has an above-average standard dog that is served with a wider than usual assortment of condiments. LAST CALL: Alcohol is served until the middle of the seventh inning.

GREAT PLAYERS AND HISTORIC MOMENTS: Originally the Astros were known as the Houston Colt .45's. Along with the New York Mets, they were the first expansion teams in the National League since the league expanded from eight teams to twelve in 1962. The Astros struggled below .500 until 1969, when further expansion led to their first pennant run. The team finished 81-81 for their first .500 season. The club's first division title occurred in 1980, capped by a 7-1 victory over the Dodgers in a one-game playoff. The fabulous pitching staff led by Nolan Ryan, J. R. Richard, and Joe Niekro was instrumental to the success. The Astros subsequently lost the league championship series to the Phillies. The only other league championship series came in 1986, thanks to the great pitching of Cy Young award winner Mike Scott. The New York Mets, their expansion counterpart, defeated the Astros in a six-game series topped off by a sixteen-inning marathon. All-Star Games '68 and '86.

BALLPARK HISTORY: The Astrodome was the first modern park to have a roof over the playing field. The park replaced the temporary Colt Stadium, which featured the largest mosquitoes in baseball. The Dome opened in 1965 and ushered in a new era in baseball park design, which was copied in Minnesota, Seattle, and Montreal. Up until retractable domes were built in Seattle and Arizona, the Astrodome was the standard for domed stadiums throughout the world. More than a stadium, the park was an architectural feat that was dubbed the Eighth Wonder of the World. Remodeled in 1989 primarily for football, the park added more sky boxes, removed the home-run extravaganza scoreboard, and placed numerous Jumbotrons and electronic scoreboards throughout the facility.

FUN FACTS: Although the Dome is vilified for necessitating artificial turf, the original plan was to have a glass roof and real grass on the field. Just prior to the Astrodome's inaugural season, it was discovered that the glare from the glass panels made it almost impossible to track pop-ups, so a translucent acrylic was applied to each of the 4,796 panels in the roof. As might be expected, the grass died from a lack of sunlight. Although the groundskeepers replaced the grass several times that year, they eventually gave up trying. The Astros played most of their season on dead grass painted green. The next season a new turf was introduced to solve the Astrodome's particular problem, hence the name AstroTurf. Baseball has never been the same since.

THE ONE THING YOU SHOULD HAVE DONE AT THE ASTRODOME AND WHY: Get a tour of the park, which includes a trip to the top. Taking the elevator to the top level, some twenty stories above the field, the tour gives you a feel for how large the dome truly is and how amazing it was when constructed in 1965.

LASTING IMPRESSION: A modern engineering and sports marvel that did its best to host baseball.

BAT INFO

FINAL SCORE: Astros 10, White Sox 4

OUR SEATS: Aisle 263, Row D, Seats 1–2

BALLPARK: 10 of 30

DAY: 12 of 38

MILES TRAVELED: 40 (5,061 total)

NEW STATES: 0 (7 total)

OUR EXPENSES: $20
   drinks $20
      EXPENSES TO DATE: $968

OUR FREEBIES: $285
   lunch (courtesy of my parents) $70
   game tickets, programs and memorabilia
      (courtesy of Aramark) $85
   ballpark food: hot dogs, Luther's BarBQ,
      pretzels, nachos, some seafood, and
      lots of Shiner
      (courtesy of Aramark and Milo
      Hamilton) $80
   lodging (courtesy of my parents) $50
      FREEBIES TO DATE: $1,609

11

Turner Field

Atlanta

I LEFT home the next morning with no idea when I would make it back. It had been a short homecoming but a busy one, and my parents took great care of us. Even going home wasn't very relaxing, given the context of the trip. The experience was quite the opposite, in fact, with so many more people to see in so little time. Nevertheless, we were on the road again, and the superstar treatment at the Dome generated delusions of grandeur again.

Ron was traveling with us now, which shifted the dynamic of my relationship with Dave. Immediately he became the buffer between us: part my best friend, part Dave's best friend, part group psychologist. He handled the role well and effectively diffused the tension that had been simmering between us since southern California. The tension built itself primarily out of the fact that we were getting very annoyed about each other's peccadilloes. Traveling with someone for fourteen days feels like being married to them for fourteen years.

The only real dilemma we faced in adding Ron to the trip was figuring out where to put him. The car had been full to the gills when it was just Dave and me, and now we had to find a way to pile Ron's stuff into the car and still have enough room for another person. The solution was to jettison unessential gear, so naturally a lot of my stuff got left behind, namely memorabilia from the first ten parks and my guitar, which had not been used on the trip although I was always meaning to break it out. Additionally, on our way out of town, we had to drop Zach off at the bus station, so we had an especially cozy trip into downtown Houston.

Shortly after lunch, which we ate in Beaumont, Texas, at the recommendable Luby's Cafeteria, we drove into Louisiana and subsequently Mississippi, two states I had spent very little time in despite their close proximity to my home state. We were taking I-10 straight through Louisiana, and it was pretty much all bayou (swamp). Finding ourselves intrigued by all of the little lean-tos that we saw every few miles along the freeway off overgrown roads that spurred at right angles off of the highway, we pulled off just outside of Grosse Tete, Louisiana, and got out of the car to soak it all in. After taking a few pictures of ourselves in front of some of the most authentic-looking residences, the kind with driveways of rickety bridges that obviously couldn't hold the weight of a car, we left pretty fast, worried that the locals might suspect we were up to something. On our way out though, we did manage to snap some pictures of Ron next to the Grosse Tete city limits sign. *Grosse Tete* means something like "large head" in French, and Ron's being so endowed, we all found this to be a riot.

After Louisiana, we also zipped through Biloxi, Mississippi. We had intended to spend the night there, so we walked into one of the seaside casinos to do a little gambling, but we walked right out as soon as we realized that sports betting was illegal in the state. There being no sports books where we could sit and watch all manner of baseball games, we quickly lost interest in gambling, seeing as how baseball was the only thing that was really on our minds at the time. Spooky, huh? Consequently we returned to the road.

We spent the night in Pascagoula, Mississippi, where they gave us chips for free drinks at the only bar in town. Actually, Dave and Ron got the chips as I was hiding in the back of the car so that we could save five dollars on the room. It didn't matter much in any case, because the bar had closed a half-hour before we got into town. Needing some sort of stress reduction though, we happened into a convenience store and picked up some Red Dog and Kodiak, which we enjoyed outside our motel room. It was a stereotypical southern recreation, and we took to it swimmingly. I had also been getting a serious urge to play some ball, so I hectored Ron into a game of catch in the parking lot. The catch was good but left me yearning for more. In any case, I found myself thankful to have Ron with us for another reason: he can be cajoled into anything.

As for the next day's plans, we'd apparently been set up with tickets and lodging by a bar owner in Atlanta, Frank Smith. Frank had read about us in the *San Francisco Chronicle* while he was on vacation in the Bay Area and for some reason took an interest in our trip. He had contacted Mark Simon, who had written the article, and offered any assistance he could. Mark called us a couple of days before we were to be in Atlanta and told us about Frank. We thought he sounded kind of crazy, but having no tickets to the game yet nor any place to stay in town, we eagerly accepted the offer and promised to get in touch with Frank.

We weren't sure how the lodging setup was supposed to work, but we didn't imagine we would mind sleeping in the bar. Our friend Tom from Tennessee was also coming down to meet us, but probably not until after the ballgame. None of the details had really been hammered out, and since we were going to be in Atlanta for a couple of days, the whole thing was liable to get pretty crazy.

The next afternoon, we made an unscheduled visit to a ballpark in Mobile, Alabama, Hank Aaron Stadium where the Mobile Bay Bears play. No games on the schedule there though, but we were able to wander into the park and take a look around at what was a very classy minor league stadium.

In the afternoon, while we were cruising toward Atlanta, we got in touch with our brand-new friend Frank on the cell phone. The phone conversation was brief, but he seemed entirely too excited to see us although not quite crazy. He was getting us tickets after all, so we made plans to stop by his bar before the game and have a few drinks. While on the one hand, we were eager to see why he was excited, we were at the same time worried about why someone would care about us and what we were doing. When we did show up, Frank and all the other guys at the bar, the SoHo, were very excited to meet us and hear about our trip. We were taken aback by the treatment at first. After all, nobody in Pascagoula had cared who we were. But then we got comfortable with our roles as celebrities once again and started unreeling the stories for our new friends. We took particular joy in pointing out that Ron was only a part-timer on our tour, and he took some lighthearted ribbing from the entire company.

Eventually, we had to leave. Turner Field was an Aramark ballpark, after all, so we had people expecting us. We took the tickets that Frank had finagled for us, expressed our gratitude again at his inordinate kindnesses, promised to stop by after the game, and took off for the ballpark.

Turner Field
....

NEW YORK (NL) V ATLANTA

Game Time: 7:40 P.M.

As I mentioned in the Arlington and Denver chapters, I was apprehensive about the new breed of ballparks. Well before we came to Atlanta, I was afraid that the new parks were turning into cookie cutters with no discernible individual style or character, much like the wave of multipurpose stadiums of the 1960s and '70s had developed. Although each of the newer parks we had been to had held at least a slight aura of individuality, I feared that by the end of the trip they would lose all individual character and just start running together. In Atlanta, my fears were realized.

Turner Field was originally built for the 1996 Summer Olympics as a part of the Olympic Stadium and then afterward was overhauled in a multimillion-dollar remodeling job to become a baseball stadium. Throughout this process, it was designed to end up among the elite new breed of ballparks. It's got all the amenities of the other ballparks: beautiful grass, great sightlines, countless food courts, a restaurant in center field, and numerous diversions for the kids. But there is something missing from this ballpark, and consequently it is rarely mentioned in the same breath as Camden, Jacobs, Coors, and the like.

Although Turner Field has a rap for being the lowliest of the new-breed ballparks, rarely do you hear reasons why this is so. Why don't people get that waft of nostalgia when they walk into this ballpark? I don't know for certain why people don't accord Turner that same general awe with which they approach its sister parks, but I've got an idea: It's the blue seats.

Everybody hates blue seats in baseball stadiums. The only thing considered less appealing, less inviting, less nostalgic than blue seats, are rainbow-colored seats (see the Astrodome). I know it seems petty, but it's true. And it is considered especially unforgivable to have blue seats in a new ballpark because you should have known better. How could you follow the Camden blueprint to the letter but mess up on this one oh-so-critical detail? The seats are supposed to be green.

My real problem with the park is that, blue seats or no, it's got no character to speak of. Although we saw an exciting game between the Braves and their division rivals, the Mets, the general level of excitement in the park was just above that of a wake. Even when Andruw Jones nailed the tying run at the plate in the eighth inning to help the Braves hold on to a 3-2 win, there was little response from the crowd. Despite the excitement on the field, our experience at Turner was the first where the crowd's apparent apathy actually caused the game to become less interesting. Although forty-eight thousand fans had come out to the park to see the game, a fair number left early in this one-run ballgame, and the rest seemed to either be napping or hanging out amid all of the diversionary games in the area known as Scout's Alley. I'm not sure why nobody seemed to care much about the game. Maybe the proliferation of children's games has turned the place into a second-rate amusement park. Or maybe Atlanta fans have become spoiled by their team's success and couldn't find the energy to cheer for their team this early in the season. Even though the fans obviously understood baseball etiquette and stood up for the last out, it came across as mere routine with little emotion behind it.

Being from a town that has little history of continued success, I do not understand the feeling of taking a winning team for granted. In Houston, the closest we came was

We took in the game at Turner Field with our friend Ron. Our initial excitement soon wore off after tasting their hot dogs and pork barbecue.

watching the Houston Oilers win the wildcard berth in the playoffs what seemed like twenty years in a row, only to bow out before the conference championship every year. Apparently the fans in Atlanta have built up a complete intolerance of losing. And I could have sworn when we saw them give up their first run in the top of the sixth, a few people left the stadium in disgust. Whether that was actually the case, or they were just getting up to have some of the worst pork BBQ I have ever tasted, remains to be seen, but there was most definitely a number of people who had better things to do than watch the last third of a 3-2 game. It was like L.A. all over again.

Maybe the fans are the reason for the ballpark's general lack of character. On the other hand, maybe it's because the food is so bad. I feel bad saying so, because the Aramark people there treated us very well, but the food at Turner Field just wasn't very good. In their favor, the restaurant in center field, the Chop Shop, had a nice layout and was very popular. We got a particularly good view of the first few innings from our table on the balcony just above the center-field wall. But most of the food we had there, especially the foot-long hot dog and the pork barbeque, left something to be desired. They do, however, deserve points for being among the first parks to offer beer in a half-yard cup—this one with a lip in the shape of a tomahawk.

In any case, beyond the better sightlines and real grass, Turner Field offers little more than Veteran's Stadium in Philadelphia.

After the game, I was still troubled by the apparent apathy of Braves fans, so we discussed it with Frank back at the Soho. His surprising take on it was that Braves fans aren't very good fans because nobody in Atlanta is actually a Braves fan. Apparently, a great many of the residents of Atlanta are transplants, and many of them, including most of the people we met during our visit, are die-hard Yankees or Red Sox or Cubs fans. Frank thought that Atlanta was a great sports town, because there are great fans from all over the country there, but it doesn't really support its own teams. Ironically, the Braves are supposedly America's team, but they are not necessarily Atlanta's team.

There is invariably, of course, always an exception, and in this case it was a man who we met in the parking lot after the game. We were out observing a remaining piece of the wall from Fulton County Stadium (the Braves' old yard) about twenty feet wide, which was apparently the span that Hank Aaron's 715th home run soared over into the Braves' bullpen. This guy couldn't stop talking about baseball and history and the Braves and how he was there when Aaron hit that shot. He was such an authentic baseball fan that he almost single-handedly made up for the apathy that the rest of his town showed toward their team . . . almost.

Turner Field

CITY: Atlanta, Georgia

TENANT: Atlanta Braves

OPENED: March 29, 1997

NICKNAME/ALIASES: The Ted, due to the Braves' owner and namesake, Ted Turner

DESIGN: Baseball-only stadium, asymmetrical design, no movable seats. SISTER PARKS: Camden Yards in Baltimore, Coors Field in Denver, Jacobs Field in Cleveland, and New Comiskey Park in Chicago.

FIELD: Bermuda Grass, although we couldn't see any difference

DIMENSIONS (feet): left field—335, left center—380, center field—401, right center—390, right field—330

FENCES (feet): 8

LOCATION: 755 Hank Aaron Dr., Atlanta, GA 30302. BOUNDED BY: Left field (N by NW): Georgia Ave. Third base (W by SW): Pollard Blvd. and Interstate 75–85. First base (S by SE): Bill Lucas Dr. Right field (E by NE): Hank Aaron Dr. (Capitol Ave.).

CAPACITY: 49,831. Total attendance: 3,360,860 (1998). Average attendance: 41,492 (1998).

PARKING: $10. More spaces were added in 1998 and the old location of Fulton County Stadium across the street is now a large parking lot.

TICKETS: $5–$35. BEST BANG FOR YOUR BUCK: While the dugout level does provide in-seat concession service, the high price tag doesn't make this a good deal. Try the field and terrace pavilion or the upper level for good views of the action as well as picturesque views of Atlanta.

BALLPARK EXPERIENCE: Turner Field combines some of what is good about the new wave of ballparks with a lot of what is bad about the old 1980s generation of parks. Although a baseball-only park, the facility was originally part of the Olympic Stadium. This meant that the architects were a little more constrained about adopting all of the new design features. For instance, the park has a symmetrical outfield with a blue wall that is almost identical to new Comiskey in Chicago. The park also keeps a low profile without the characteristic light standards that are hallmarks of the Camden-era parks.

These shortcomings are unfortunate because many of the other aspects of the park are superb, including state-of-the-art facilities, wide concourses, and the grand entry plaza. The plaza is one of the most unique features of Turner Field. The large area is like a mini carnival, and part of the plaza is free to the public. This area is always lively and full of fans but takes attention away from the action on the field.

Except for the Coke section in upper left field, the interior of the park is very uniform and symmetrical. One thing that is blatantly apparent on the inside is the plethora of activities aside from baseball in the park. Like Edison in Anaheim, the Braves have many entertainment venues like Rookie Card, where fans can have their image inserted into a baseball card, and Power Alley, where fans can test their hitting skills. If that weren't enough, Scout's Alley near the west is an educational-entertainment area that is designed to teach fans how to be a scout. Overall, the park leaves much to be desired, which is sad considering it is only four years old.

FANS: In spite of Atlanta's history of hosting the Summer Olympics and many other sporting events, we found that the city's fans are some of the worst in baseball. Lulled into a false sense of invulnerability in the 1990s, the fans have failed to support their team even though Atlanta has had one stellar season after another. The 1998–2000 playoff games saw many seats go unoccupied in the forty-nine-thousand-seat Turner Field. This is consistent with the disinterested fans we saw on our trip.

FACILITIES: Concourses behind the infield stands are surprisingly narrow for a new park but widen out in the outfield and in Scout's Alley. Restrooms are numerous and clean. There are a great number of concession booths even though the food is not so good. Our seats were angled toward the action.

FOOD: Atlanta has a wide selection of food that is mostly subpar. Definitely avoid the pork barbeque and the Tomahawk Ale, which is the local specialty beer. Neither is worth the time or money. The Tomahawk Ale is served in a nice souvenir half-yard with a tomahawk-shaped spout at the top. But don't feel like you have to drink thirty-two ounces of their godforsaken brew just to take home this souvenir. You can fill it with

Bud. But if you are, like us, a die-hard experimentalist, save yourself the embarrassment of having to dump out about three-eighths of a yard of it and order a regular glass. Better yet, simply ask for a taste.

Overall, your best bet might be the novelty Taste of the Majors stand, which serves food reminiscent of the visiting team's hometown. Atlanta gets points for starting this trend, along with that of the open-air center-field restaurant. We passed on the Taste of the Majors (didn't make much sense seeing as how we were going to be in the visiting team's city in ten days), but it was definitely the most popular stand at the park and apparently always is (more validation for our opinions of the food). As far as hot dogs go, Atlanta has a terrible standard hot dog. We would not recommend it. The bun was falling apart and the dog was cold. LAST CALL: Alcohol is served until the middle of the seventh inning.

GREAT PLAYERS AND HISTORIC MOMENTS: Unbeknownst to most baseball fans, the Braves are the oldest continuously operating professional sports franchise in America. They have

The end of the game in Atlanta marked the beginning of our five-day break. And by this point we were ready for a little celebration of our accomplishments to date. Plus we were approaching the Fourth of July.

After running into a fan who had been in the ballpark when Hank Aaron hit his 715th home run, eclipsing Babe Ruth's record, we all paid homage to the spot where the ball landed on the old grounds of Fulton County Stadium.

moved several times, uprooting themselves after eighty-two years in Boston to go to Milwaukee in 1953 and then moving to Atlanta in 1966. Turner Field is just a blip on the one-hundred-year history of the club. Great players to call Turner home include Chipper Jones, Andres Galarraga, Tom Glavine, and Greg Maddux. The only true historic moment was that the 1999 World Series was played at Turner, where the Yankees swept the Braves to take the Team of the '90s moniker.

BALLPARK HISTORY: The 1996 Olympic Games gave the Atlanta Braves an opportunity to build a new ballpark. The former home of the Braves and Atlanta Falcons was Fulton County Stadium, which was built in 1966 and helped kick off the multipurpose trend in Pittsburgh, Cincinnati, and Philadelphia. The success of the new classic parks in Baltimore and Cleveland prompted the Braves to consider constructing a similar facility. At the same time, an Olympic Stadium was required for the 1996 Summer Games in Atlanta. In the spirit of partnership and cost savings, the Braves and the Atlanta Committee for the Olympic Games agreed to build a multipurpose stadium for the Olympics and baseball. It had two major parts, the southwest end that would become a section of Turner Field and the northeast side that was comprised of temporary bleachers for the Olympics. The resulting Olympic stadium was a little unorthodox but served its purpose. After the Summer Olympics, the bleacher section was razed and the rest of Turner Field completed. (NOTE: This took less than eight months.)

FUN FACT: Coca-Cola Skyfield, at the end of the upper-level concourse overlooking left field, has games for children and an area where warm fans can cool off under a light mist. There is also a large Coke bottle made up of bats, balls, gloves, and other baseball gear.

THE ONE THING YOU HAVE TO DO AT TURNER FIELD AND WHY: Go check out the wall where Hank Aaron hit his 715th home run to surpass Babe Ruth. It is in the parking lot where Fulton County Stadium once stood. Maybe that old guy will still be there (see above). There are also bases painted onto the parking lot, where the original bases of Fulton County were, so you can stand at the plate and imagine yourself hitting it right over the wall where Aaron did. It's not quite the same on asphalt, but it will still send a chill down your spine.

OTHER THINGS TO REMEMBER: Watch out for the after-game concerts and music sessions that are held in the entry plaza. These can make exiting the park a nightmare unless you want to wait around another hour and listen to some amateur rappers.

LASTING IMPRESSION: Turner Field's many drawbacks make it more like a park built in 1987 than 1997.

BAT INFO

FINAL SCORE: Braves 3, Mets 2

OUR SEATS: Aisle 107, Row 23, Seats 2–3

BALLPARK: 11 of 30

DAY: 14 of 38

MILES TRAVELED: 490 on day 13; 409 on day 14 (5,960 total)

NEW STATES: 4 (Louisiana, Mississippi, Alabama, Georgia; 11 total)

OUR EXPENSES: $174
  Luby's $16
  drinks $10
  gas $35
  lodging (in Pascagoula, MS) $38
  Burger King $8
  programs $10
  drinks (Buckhead) $30
  gas $17
    EXPENSES TO DATE: $1,132

OUR FREEBIES: $172
  drinks (courtesy of Frank Smith) $20
  game tickets (courtesy of Frank Smith) $42
  ballpark food—hot dogs, pork barbecue, pretzels, nachos, and Tomahawk Ale (courtesy of Aramark) $60
  lodging (courtesy of Hollie Clouse) $50
    FREEBIES TO DATE: $1,781

The Break

JULY 4–8, 1998

Days 15–19

INDEPENDENCE DAY was the beginning of our midtrip break. We had made it through eleven parks, but I don't think either Dave or I had expected to be as worn out as we were. Fourteen days into the trip, six thousand miles down. We had five days off then nineteen parks in nineteen days. We didn't know how to get ready for the experience. We decided to relax and have a good time; this was, after all, our summer vacation.

In Atlanta we got off to a good start. After our subdued yet tiring (by virtue of El Niño) experience at the ballpark on Friday night, we met up with some friends from Tennessee, Tom and Ryan. Our new best friend Frank had directed us to the local bar district, Buckhead, as the place to be, so we headed that way. When we got there, we realized why everybody at the game was napping and leaving early: They had to get ready for their big night out. Buckhead was a zoo. When we got there at about 11 P.M., every bar was packed, and we just managed to find parking a half mile away. The crowds, however, kept getting bigger. We bounced through a half-dozen bars and dance clubs. Even though we were half-delirious from the heat when we got there, along with a few thousand others, we managed to continue bouncing around until 4 A.M. And even then no one seemed eager to kick us out. But we had to leave due simply to the fact that at least Dave and I were completely exhausted. Ron too, even though he had only been with us for three days, was feeling the effects of our nonstop "drive, drive, drive, be entertained, drive, be entertained" lifestyle. I caught him a couple of times bouncing around the dance floor from what seemed to be pure momentum. Dave, our designated driver, fell asleep on the bar in one place. And I remember at least once taking a seat against a pillar in the middle of a dance floor because it seemed like a good idea at the time. Only Tom and Ryan seemed ready to go all night. Tom, who could have a good time on a city bus, led us from bar to bar, making new friends and getting free beers. Ryan was simply a wild man. He was completely uninhibited, and his direct way with women served to spark both a lot of interesting conversations and provoke some narrowly avoided confrontations with protective boyfriends and law enforcement officials.

Don't ask how we made it home safely. Rather than overabuse Frank's hospitality, we stayed at Tom's sister's place on the north side of Atlanta. Ryan's vocal nature proved useful for the drive home, as it managed to keep Dave awake long enough to get us there. I, on the other hand, passed out as soon as we got in the car. I woke up the next day on a sofa. Dave was curled up on the rug, and Ron was sitting at the kitchen table. Needless to say, we all slept soundly.

Independence Day. After having so much fun the night before, we decided to stay in Atlanta another day. That afternoon we slept in very late, hit the requisite Fourth of July barbeque, and headed back to Buckhead, meeting up with our new friend Frank and several hundred of his closest friends.

Frank was one of those unexpected gifts you are given in an unknown circumstance. Two thousand miles from home. You don't know anybody in town. You don't know where to go. On our arrival, we hadn't had any idea what to expect from the town or from Frank, but we never would have expected the amazing reception we got.

Our experiences with Frank were the illogical conclusion of a dilemma Dave and I had been facing throughout the trip. Invariably, we encountered people who seemed too excited and eager to help us with things like tickets, food, beer, or a place to stay. It took us long enough to contrive a few reasons as to why the ball clubs, concessionaires, and people who ran the ballparks should be interested in us—in short so that we would say nice things about them in the book that we assured them we were going to write. Try as we might though, we couldn't come up with one thing that people in Frank's position might have to gain from us or by offering us free beer and food and taking us all around the town. But Frank did those things anyway. So our ultimate concern was then, what could he possibly want from us?

In the end, we realized that all Frank wanted was to have a good time. And I assume that what he knew of us gave him the impression that we were the kind of guys that he liked to hang around with. When you get a little notoriety, people make judgments, good or bad, about you based on that one thing. So while the guy who saw us on television in San Francisco wanted to swerve at us, Frank seemed to think that it would be great to meet us and spend some time with us. Just like you'd like to hang out with Tony Gwynn.

As a result, Frank, having far too high an opinion of us, treated us much better than we ever deserved, which followed a general trend over the whole trip. And he was a lot of fun. If anything, Frank was a little bit too much fun for us to keep up with. So when we went out with him on the Fourth, although he had a good ten or more years on all of us, he outlasted us by a few drinks, and I'm sure it would have been more if they hadn't finally shut down the bars shortly before dawn.

And being with Frank we were also immediately welcomed into Frank's large circle of friends. So not only did we make a bunch of new friends, we had groupies as well (the most memorable of whom Ron nicknamed Naughty Nadia). It was this consummate experience with Frank in Atlanta that really brought all of those oft-mentioned feelings of self-importance and delusions of grandeur to a head. We had been celebrities before this, but only ballpark celebrities. Nobody outside of a baseball stadium could have picked us out of a lineup or cared who we were (except for a random encounter at a McDonald's in Yuma, Arizona). But within Frank's sphere of influence, which seemed to be the entire city of Atlanta, we were famous, beloved, storied, legendary. For one night at least. So we spent yet another night being unexpectedly bombarded with free drinks, and for the second morning in a row I awoke not sure where I was or how I got there.

In any case, I suppose it would only be fair to make a feeble attempt to show our gratitude to Frank by making a shameless plug for his establishment, the SoHo Restaurant and Bar in Atlanta. We never actually ate there, but the beer and the people are very nice. Trust us.

Although Atlanta had been fun, on Sunday we decided to push on to Florida. Tom and Ryan went back to Tennessee, having enlivened our experiences in numerous ways. We said good-bye to Frank and many of his friends at a pool party the next day at which we scored another free meal.

The second night of our break, we anchored in Panama City, Florida, a noted beach resort in the state's panhandle. The parties were continuing through the end of the holiday weekend, but since we were utterly exhausted from our previous two nights' celebrations, we crashed pretty early. The three of us saw a movie instead, *Armageddon*, which was a refreshing change of place. It seemed to be a continuation of our natural reaction over the five-day break to dwell on alternative forms of entertainment, picnics, clubs, bars, movies, beaches.

Beaches. We had planned to continue the alternative entertainment at the beach on Monday, but the famously beautiful Panama City Beach was depressingly green with algae. And why wouldn't it be on the biggest holiday weekend of the year? Continuing in our naturally developed roles of evaluating each of our experiences over the last couple of weeks, Dave and I decided we would not recommend the beach here. It was already third on our list of beaches we had hit on the trip (we were including the bayous in Louisiana).

We didn't worry about it too much. When all else fails, there's always baseball. So we hopped to a local fish shack and watched the All-Star home-run derby played in Denver's Coors Field. Of course the sight of those guys making it all look so easy inspired us to go out and hit a batting cage for a while. Despite our poor showing, I quite honestly consider this to be the highlight of the trip to that point, right up there with playing catch in front of Edison Field.

Afterward, we went back to the motel for another mellow evening, where another baseball-inspired habit (this one not so good) crept back into play. This time it was the tobacco. In our strange little world, dipping tobacco always seemed to slide into the frame when there wasn't much motivation to do much else. And the tobacco also always seemed to have the side effects of upsetting my stomach, numbing my lip, and when combined with beer, making Ron turn into a giant grizzly, bearing a striking resemblance to the one on the cover of the Kodiak tin.

Maybe we'd been on the road too long.

By the fourth day of our break, Dave and I were beginning to lose touch with reality. It was as if the continuous stream of baseball parks had provided the bearings for the trip, and now we were floundering without an obvious objective. Our conversations were drifting into dangerous territory: relationships and our futures. And Ron, our guardian angel, wasn't helping us. I noted the following in my journal: "We spend a lot of time talking about deeper issues. Not that they're necessarily deeper than baseball, but more universal. We talk about life and our futures. This is really a turning point for everybody, and our spending so much time together, we have what is an unavoidable opportunity to understand the way others look at the universe."

Pretty scary, huh? We could only hope that we would get back to the ballparks before it was too late. The fact that it was the day of the All-Star Game did little to save us from falling over this emotional precipice. We saw the game on a little fuzzy television in an Applebee's somewhere in the middle of Florida. Not terribly inspiring. I tried to keep my mind occupied imagining the monumental drive up to Baltimore we were to make in three days. Through the night with the sun coming up along the eastern seaboard, it seemed like it would be an amazing experience and so inspiring as to keep us off such saccharine topics of discussion as the meaning of life.

Our last off-day before the iron-man stretch was spent with Jeanette Perez, who showed us the south Florida scene. Jeanette also took us home to meet her dad, who was a huge baseball fan. Cool. Dodgers fan. Oh.

Despite his allegiances, we had a great time talking to him about the game. What was amazing was that we could go on with him for a half-hour and talk about facets of baseball that hadn't really been brought up earlier during the trip. Just when I thought everything that there was to say about baseball had been said, we'd realize some other reason why we loved baseball that had never occurred to us before. Like the perverse joy of debating the benefits of the hit-and-run with a complete stranger. Which leads to a deeper question of why is that fun? Still in the philosophical mind-set our break had given us, but with my thoughts beginning to focus back on baseball, I wrote in my journal: "You have to love baseball. It is a truly democratic sport. Anyone can make it. All you need is an ounce of talent and a ton of determination. I've seen so many examples from my life of people busting their butts to make it. People no better than me. Sitting there in that living room, talking so much about the sport that I loved. I was struck again with that awful feeling. Where did I go wrong?"

I found myself wondering if the real reason I had come on this trip was because it was the next best thing to being on the field. Like so many other people, I accepted the fact that I didn't have whatever it takes to make it as a ball player. Years later I realized that being a successful ball player wasn't just about talent; it was about heart, love, and determination—the same things required in accomplishing any goal. In Florida I struggled again, wondering if I had given up on the dream because all the players on the field loved the game that much more than me. Had I made a mistake?

I pondered that question throughout trip. Eventually I moved on. For better or worse, baseball was not going to be my life (assuming it was my decision to make in the first place), and I couldn't change that by spending thirty-eight days in the ballparks, refusing to grow up.

BAT INFO

MILES TRAVELED: 1,085 (7,045 total)

NEW STATES: 1 (Florida; 12 total)

OUR EXPENSES: $377
food, hotel rooms, and entertainment over the break (Atlanta, Panama City Beach, and Boca Raton)
EXPENSES TO DATE: $1,509

OUR FREEBIES: $220
drinks (courtesy of Frank)
lodging (courtesy of Hollie Clouse and Jeanette Perez)
free meals
FREEBIES TO DATE: $2,001

12

pro
player
stadium
Miami

I T WAS time for another game. We left Jeanette's place in Boca Raton, about a half-hour north of Miami, and spent most of the afternoon with Dave's retired Aunt Helen and Uncle Vince in Fort Lauderdale. They live in a high-rise off of the beach and were the type of peaceful older folk who seem to experience no greater thrill than giving their nephew and his friends a few sandwiches and some sage advice. They were also very interested in the trip and helping us out. But in contrast to Mr. Perez and most everyone else we had met in the last three weeks, they really seemed more interested in us as people rather than as people on a baseball trip, which was definitely a weird experience for us. We talked about life, the past, the future, and in contrast to most of the last few weeks where Dave and I had been doing all of the talking (actually mostly Dave), here we mostly listened.

We left for the game plenty early, driving down A1A, the beachfront avenue immortalized by Vanilla Ice, on our way out of Fort Lauderdale.

We had left a ticket for Jeanette or her father, but they didn't show up. So it was just going to be the three of us again.

Pro Player stadium

....

ATLANTA V FLORIDA

GAME TIME: 7:05 P.M.

THE OVERWHELMING impression you get approaching Pro Player Stadium is that this may be the most beautiful and grand stadium you have ever seen. The most beautiful and grand *football* stadium. We had thought Qualcomm well-suited to the pigskin, but it wasn't the shrine to football that Pro Player is.

Pro Player is overwhelming evidence of the fact that great football stadiums do not make great baseball stadiums or even necessarily adequate baseball stadiums. In fact, the essential qualities of a great football stadium—grandness of scale, symmetry, rectangularity (all of which Pro Player has nailed)—are exactly opposite of those qualities most admired in the great baseball parks today—coziness, quirkiness, and nonrectangularity. This is not to say that there will never be another two-sport stadium. I'm sure there will be, but you can see the difficulty inherent in trying to meet the demands of an ever pickier fan base. Worse though than Pro Player's un-baseball feel is the stadium's name. As names go, about the best thing Pro Player Stadium (nee Joe Robbie) has going for it as a baseball park is Cinergy Field in Cincinnati. Without Cinergy, Pro Player would have the worst corporate sellout name in all baseball.

Of course, the Marlins aren't the only team that suffers from stadium envy. But among those teams, the Marlins may be in the direst position. As even the most casual fan is probably aware, the Marlins won the World Series in 1997, in only their fifth year of existence. Much fanfare was made about how they rose to prominence so fast. But much faster, the team was broken up and sold off for parts. The Marlins' payroll plummeted from $54 million to $19 million, and the team quickly entrenched themselves among the worst teams in baseball for the foreseeable future.

Various parties have been blamed for the Marlins' inability to stay among the league's elite teams, chief among whom is the team's owner at the time, Wayne Huizenga of Blockbuster fame. The one group that has rarely been blamed, however, is the fans. It used to be public opinion that when a good team does not get the expected fan support, the onus of blame was upon the fans who did not appreciate a winner. In this golden age of baseball parks, however, all blame for failing to attract fans to games is generally laid on the ballpark or the ownership that could not generate an irresistible ad campaign. It is as if fans are seen now as mindless and as if baseball is not a sport to be appreciated by knowledgeable followers but an amusement that can only compete with the other amusements through the sheer force of construction. This theory will

116

probably hold as conventional wisdom for as long as Camden Yards continues to sell out despite pitiful seasons by the Orioles.

Returning to south Florida, when the Marlins won the World Series in 1997, the stands remained close to empty well into September. Huizenga was hemorrhaging money trying to buy a team that would put fans in the seats, but it didn't work. So, despite the team's success that season, Huizenga decided his ambition was hopeless and sold off the team.

My purpose here is to stick up for Pro Player (and even Huizenga). True, it is not the greatest ballpark, but it is not at all a bad place to watch a baseball game. It is *Miami*, for crying out loud. No matter how nice the ballpark may be, you cannot save baseball in your town if nobody cares to begin with. That being the case, sometimes you have to accept the fact that regardless of the size of the market, if the city doesn't want a ball club, maybe it shouldn't have one.

The above rant should clue you into the fact that Pro Player is one of those parks that nobody likes, at least as a baseball park. So obviously, we weren't too thrilled to be starting the second half of the tour with it—a situation much like our condition in San Francisco. In fact, we were somewhat disgruntled that our most hype-able moments were coming at less than stellar venues. This stadium is after all known as Underwear Stadium in some circles. (Although we'll grant that those circles could quite possibly consist entirely of the one kid we met at the ballpark.)

To make matters worse, Dave was very apprehensive about coming to this stadium at all. He had had nothing but a deep enmity for the Marlins ever since the aforementioned bought team had beaten his Indians in the '97 Series, and things only got worse

After five days off, we were ready for some baseball in Miami. And we were still making cryptic hand gestures to indicate how many ballparks we had seen to this point.

when our tour of the park began in the Marlins trophy room. Fortunately, the tour picked up quickly thereafter when we were escorted onto the playing field. (Being on a ball field always had a way of picking up both of our spirits.) Afterward, we were treated to some hot dogs and Cuban sandwiches by the Marlins concessionaires, at which point Dave's enmity quickly melted away, if only temporarily.

All in all, our experience of the park was positive. Given the singular agenda that the architects had in building Pro Player as a football stadium, it is actually surprising to notice how good a job has been done in nestling a baseball diamond into the center of it. Granted, you can't go thirty seconds without being reminded of whose ballpark this really is (and the answer is apparently *not* Joe Robbie), but the place treats the Marlins fairly well. The color scheme doesn't work. But who really cares. There are sixty thousand unused seats circling the outfield. And the seats aren't all pointing in the right direction. But how often do you get such a great view of the left fielder anyway. To its favor, the seats are surprisingly close to the action, if only because every seat in use is a good one. And more important, the one general drawback of playing baseball in such a cavernous football arena is not noticeable here, that being the lack of atmosphere. This park most definitely has atmosphere. Granted, not quite twenty thousand people tend to show up for the games, but you can't blame these twenty thousand for the indifference of everyone else in their city. Like the loyal following of a neglected team (see the Brewers), they are as enthusiastic as any crowd in any ballpark and more enthusiastic than most of the forty-thousand-plus crowds we'd seen at all of the newer stadiums. In particular, we were privileged to be a party to the "Let's go El Niño" cheers that the Marlin's self-appointed head fan put up in the field boxes down the left field line whenever Edgar Renteria came up to the plate. (I wonder what cheer he's got going now that Renteria is gone and El Niño is over.)

Having already mentioned the Marlins' string of futility since their World Series title, our hopes of pulling out a hometown victory here and upping our record to 10-2 with the mighty Braves in town were dim. True to their reputation, the Marlins were bad, and this display of futility actually deepened my respect for their few avid fans who managed to enjoy themselves despite the AAA-grade show on the field and made the game enjoyable for us as well. We met some interesting people, saw our names on the Jumbotron, and got our picture taken out on the ball field. We even had another full-service tour, but we were already starting to take those in a very businesslike manner. At an optimistic twenty-five thousand attendance, it was easily the smallest crowd we had seen, and about half the fans were for Atlanta. But the Marlins fans went crazy for every hit, walk, strike, whatever, even mustering up some general excitement when they got the go-ahead run to the plate in the eighth inning.

In truly respectable and loyal fashion, the fans we talked to never seemed aware that this was supposedly a horrible stadium, nor did they mind the uncomfortable heat (which kept getting worse for us all summer). The fans were thrilled to be keeping close with Atlanta. We were pleasantly surprised, too. And even though their Marlins lost, the fans cheered until the last out.

In the end though, it is depressing to watch an organization like the Marlins that can buy a championship team and then throw it away. You feel sorry for the fans who just want something to hold on to, to be proud of. The folks in Miami seemed as soberly knowledgeable as any around the country as to the cold hard truths of the economics of baseball. But they didn't hold it against anybody (except possibly Huizenga). It makes you just feel horrible for these people thinking that perhaps the basic underlying truth of the whole matter is that this town will never muster enough support for a competitive ball club again. And maybe they shouldn't have one. Florida is evidence that baseball definitely has problems, and I don't know who is going to solve them. The popular solution is obvious. They could drop one of those fancy new cookie-cutter parks in here, and people would come out to the new ballpark just as they do everywhere else. Not of course because they really like the ballpark, because they wouldn't have any idea what makes a good ballpark having never been to a baseball game before, but because everybody else is doing it. Either that will happen, we'll have another Comerica on our hands, or the ball club will just move to some other city that promises to build a new park.

pro player stadium

CITY: Miami, Florida

TENANT: Florida Marlins

OPENED: August 16, 1987, first baseball game: April 5, 1993

NICKNAME/ALIASES: Joe Robbie Stadium (1987–August 26, 1996), Underwear Stadium. (Luckily, the park will soon have a new name. The stadium's agreement with Pro Player has been terminated and a new sponsor name is in the works.)

DESIGN: Multipurpose stadium (initially football only). Rectangular design, movable seats. SISTER PARK: Ericsson Field in Carolina (football only).

FIELD: Tifway 419 Bermuda (a.k.a. grass)

DIMENSIONS (feet): left field—330, left center—385, center field—404, right center—385, right field—345

FENCES: left-center scoreboard—33, center and right field—8

Although a great venue for football, Pro Player Stadium left much to be desired as a baseball park, but you wouldn't know that from the fervor of the Marlins fans who shared the stadium with us.

LOCATION: 2269 N.W. 199th Street, Miami, FL

CAPACITY/ATTENDANCE: 47,662 (baseball). Total attendance: 1,730,384 (1998). Average attendance: 21,362 (1998).

PARKING: $7. Parking for all baseball games is $7. Evidently there is a valet service for club seat holders and executive suite holders at Gates A, C, and G.

TICKETS: $7–$45. BEST BANG FOR YOUR BUCK: The second-deck seats (mezzanine reserved) are distant from the action and the $4.50 upgrade to the lower deck is well worth it.

BALLPARK EXPERIENCE: We do not exaggerate: Pro Player is a great football stadium. Make no mistake about it; this is not one of those mid-1960s stadiums built specifically for the purpose of supporting two professional teams in two different sports. This is most unmistakably a football stadium. An utterly beautiful football stadium. From the sheer awe inspired by its size as you drive up to the beautiful symmetry of the spires on each of the eight corners of its beautifully symmetrical octagonal frame, Pro Player is a perfect football stadium. The entire color scheme of the park is Dolphins teal and orange, right down to the seats on the inside that fit perfectly around the rectangular dimensions of a football field and perfectly match the uniforms of the home team and the finishing touch of the Miami Dolphins banners that hang everywhere in the stadium. Even the huge tarps that drape about thirty thousand seats that run around the upper decks and the outfield—thirty thousand seats that are filled with screaming fans for Dolphins games but are a stone's throw from anything with a pulse when the Marlins are in the building—fit in with the whole orange-and-teal motif. All in all it is such a great football stadium that it is almost depressing to realize that you are not here to watch a football game. Another problem is that the park does not blend in with its surroundings like many new baseball venues and has no feeling of intimacy.

One interesting aspect of the park are the lights, with each side of the rectangle illuminated by two standards that are angled toward the field at 45 degrees. The light standards are much smaller (very narrow) than the older light mechanisms at the many 1960s ballparks (3Com, Dodger Stadium, Busch Stadium) but produce more light. There is a manually operated out-of-town scoreboard on the left field wall that has a teal color that is slightly off from the darker teal featured other places in the park. All of these features point once again to the true purpose of the park: football.

FANS: There is a long tradition of baseball in southern Florida that has created a solid group of fans. From the action of spring training to the influx of baseball-loving Cuban Americans, southern Florida has long been home to baseball. Yet it took until April 1993 for Florida to field a professional baseball team. The first year was a huge success with the new team drawing over three million fans. The 1994 strike hurt attendance a lot and only with the purchase of the team by Wayne Huizenga and the subsequent World Series championship in 1997 did fans begin to come back—but not enough to support the team's huge payroll. The subsequent dismantling of the Series team in 1998 saw fans leave and created a backlash in southern Florida. Although good fans remain who know baseball and their team, it has yet to be proven that professional baseball can attract a large enough support base to be profitable in south Florida.

FACILITIES: Pro Player Stadium has a modern assortment of restrooms, wide concourses, and newer seats. The park is designed to handle large crowds with numerous concession stands. But the low attendance of most baseball games forces the concessionaires to close many of the outfield food stands, which requires fans in the cheap seats to hike to the infield to buy food.

FOOD: We did not know what to expect as far as food was concerned at Pro Player. The park has a wide variety of uniquely southern Florida food, which was a nice surprise since we didn't know there was southern Florida food. The Cuban sandwich was the best item that we sampled: a classic submarine sandwich with layers of meat, cheese, and special sauce. It is enough to fill you up for an entire day, and Ron had a tough time finishing it. In the southern Florida food theme, Pro Player has some fine dessert selections from a wide assortment of ice cream treats (the malt is especially good) to Mrs. Field's Cookies. LAST CALL: Alcohol is served until the middle of the eighth inning.

GREAT PLAYERS AND HISTORIC MOMENTS: In their short history the Marlins have been able to field some solid baseball players and even win a World Series. Four games of the historic 1997 World Series were played at Pro Player Stadium. The Series was topped off by a dramatic come-from-behind win against the Cleveland Indians who led 2-1 entering the bottom of the ninth. After tying it up in the ninth off Jose Mesa, Edgar Renteria's two-out single in the bottom of the eleventh scored Craig Counsell to give the Marlins the world championship. (Dave refuses to admit this happened.) Great performances on the 1997 club included the superb pitching of Kevin Brown and Livan Hernandez, the hitting of Renteria and Gary Sheffield, and the managing of Jimmy Leyland.

BALLPARK HISTORY: Pro Player Stadium (then known as Joe Robbie Stadium) was built for the Miami Dolphins in the mid-1980s and marked the beginning of the new ballpark-stadium boom of the late '80s and '90s. Financing for these parks was based largely upon the licensing of executive suites and club seats on a ten-year basis and enabled teams to fund parks with private money. In the case of Pro Player, Joe Robbie financed the park's construction with his own money—$115 million. The park was used only for the Miami Dolphins until the Marlins began playing baseball in 1993.

BAT INFO

FINAL SCORE: Braves 6, Marlins 4

OUR SEATS: Section 106, Row 17, Seat 5

BALLPARK: 12 of 30

DAY: 20 of 38

MILES TRAVELED: 50 (7,095 total)

NEW STATES: 0 (12 total)

OUR EXPENSES: $14
programs and parking $14
EXPENSES TO DATE: $1,523

OUR FREEBIES: $141
lunch (courtesy of the Kavals) $10
game tickets (courtesy of the
  Marlins) $36
ballpark food—hot dogs, pretzels, nachos
  and beer (courtesy of FineHost Corp.)
  $45
lodging (courtesy of the Kavals) $50
FREEBIES TO DATE: $2,142

FUN FACT: The Marlins have a collection of stuffed Marlins that were donated to the club over the past several years. They are displayed in the Marlins front office. Some are the size of two people.

THE ONE THING YOU HAVE TO DO AT PRO PLAYER PARK AND WHY: Watch the pitchers warm up in the bullpen. The seats along the first- and third-base lines have some of the closest proximity to bullpens of any seats in baseball and nobody is ever sitting there.

LASTING IMPRESSION: Along with Qualcomm in San Diego, Pro Player is one of the premier football stadiums in major league baseball.

13
Tropicana Field
Tampa Bay

July 10, 1998

ON THURSDAY night, we bypassed the somewhat legendary Miami nightlife for our mission. We needed to get as much sleep as we could because we couldn't be certain we were going to get any during the thousand-mile drive from Tampa to Baltimore the following night. Also, we were still a little hung-over from the previous six nights of debauchery. By way of A1A, we headed out of town and across the Everglades by traversing the Alligator Alley freeway en route to Tampa.

For those of you, like me, not terribly well informed on Florida geography, the Tampa Bay area consists of the twin cities of Tampa and St. Petersburg. Tampa is the big sister, having the bay named after it and all, and everyone tends to assume this is where all the action is. But the ballpark is in St. Petersburg—just so you don't make the same mistake I did a hundred or so times telling people that the Tropicana Dome was in Tampa.

Tropicana Field

· ·

NEW YORK (AL) V TAMPA BAY

GAME TIME: 7:05 P.M.

SO HERE we were at the end of the third week. Another unpopular stadium, another Florida team already out of the race, another visiting league power. The only reason I was at all optimistic about this experience was that it hadn't been all bad the night before.

My one lasting memory of driving into St. Petersburg was seeing the Tropicana dome on the horizon. The tilt of its roof makes it look like a crashed UFO, and you can't help but stare at it to verify it's just an illusion. It's not. In general, I would tend to think that a piece of architecture that really defines a city would be some sort of a success. In this case, however, I might be inclined to make an exception.

Nonetheless, the stadium's inane exterior might be the best thing it has going for it, because the interior architecture was something of a jumbled mess. Although we were informed that everything was still being renovated, we could see little evidence that any work was in progress. Regardless, a lot of the concourses were crowded, and the inside seemed to be modeled after the Kingdome with a predominant theme of claustrophobia. And throughout the stadium there was so much wiring hanging from the roof that it looked like the circus had just left town . . . in a hurry.

Most of Tropicana's problems can be chalked up to one thing: bad timing. Tropicana was built in 1990, just one year before Comiskey and two years before Camden. The art of building a ballpark at that time was very complicated. There was no generally accepted definition of a great ballpark then as there is now. Some people preferred the classic look of Fenway or Wrigley, but most thought these were too old and run-down. Some preferred the fancy newness of SkyDome with its still-marvelous retractable dome. And some favored the classic baseball feel of a Dodger Stadium. But none of these parks was universally accepted as the perfect ballpark, nor were they easily copied models. And even if you could replicate them, none of them were proved to draw crowds. The truth was that nobody really knew what drew fans to the ballpark. The myth at the time was that the one thing that drew the fans was a good team. So people building ballparks in Chicago, Baltimore, and Tampa Bay all looked for one thing that would make their park unique. In Chicago it was basically rebuilding the old ballpark with a glossier finish. In Baltimore it was hearkening back to the ballparks of yore. And in Tampa Bay it was building a dome with a crooked roof. Of course, in the end, everybody in the country learned that the only way to make a ballpark was to channel the cozy brick-and-green-steel structures of olden days. The days of the domed stadium were history. To build a domed stadium, to play on artificial turf, was suicidal with respect to your public relations and, more important, your pocketbook. Like I said, bad timing.

So the first thing we did when we got to Tropicana was to introduce ourselves to the unfortunate souls charged with the job of turning this brand-new second-rate stadium into a place that people wanted to see a baseball game. Here we are with our brand-new (read: very bad) ball club and our modern (read: not like all the great new nostalgic ballparks you've heard about and seen) ballpark. Come watch us play.

It's heartbreaking.

As you can see, Tropicana looks more like a UFO than a sporting venue.

We really had to feel sorry for them and the whole area, which had invested millions of dollars in a new, apparently modern, domed stadium only to find it outdated by the time it opened. The only consolation in this whole fiasco is that in the midst of this sudden realization that their ballpark was a preternatural dinosaur, Tampa Bay somehow managed to land a baseball team to play in the stadium. Unfortunately, the numbers in St. Petersburg don't bode well for the drawing power of the young club and its ballpark, and whereas its sister team in expansion, the Arizona Diamondbacks, has been able to leverage the popularity of its ballpark by buying itself a winning team, the Devil Rays seem destined for mediocrity—just like the Marlins—until a new ballpark can pull them out of the hole. That or a miracle.

But once again, much like the case in Miami, I was impressed with the enjoyable experience of this ballpark. The ballpark sports a ton of attractions. From perhaps the most diverse choice of concessions at their food court (not the best food mind you, but many options and pretty short lines too) to a colorful viewing deck in the outfield that the stadium people were trying to develop into some sort of dance club–sports bar with a tropical theme (Tropicana, get it?). I wonder whatever happened with that idea. In any case, you have to give them points for trying.

Also, as in Miami, I was impressed by the fans. Even though this was a rookie franchise, they really supported their team (although *more* than half the people there this time were Yankees fans). I did notice one peculiar thing about the fans while I was in Florida though: They are very excitable when it comes to gimmicky stunts. They seem more interested in the dot race in these parts than anywhere else in the country. My theory is that they are so used to minor league ball and spring training, they haven't

For some strange reason, none of our photos inside Tropicana Field came out. This is the main entrance to the ballpark. Just beyond the doors is a five-story rotunda à la Ebbets Field.

learned how to take baseball seriously. But then again, who says you should? Where has all the suffering got Red Sox fans?

Once again, we saw the home team lose. Although it was through no impressive showing on the part of the supposedly invincible Yankees. The Rays demonstrated their true expansion colors more than once by failing to execute on a number of easy plays and clutch situations, basically throwing away the game, and possibly intimidated by the 60-20 Yankees.

In the interests of full disclosure, I should note that my impressions of the Devil Rays are based on less than nine innings of experience, as we had to leave in the eighth inning when we learned that the Baltimore game the next day had been moved up to 1:10 in the afternoon from 7:05 P.M. We were already sweating a tough overnight drive, but now we had roughly fifteen hours instead of twenty-one to cover almost one thousand miles. If you do the math you realize that meant we had to average 67 mph door-to-door, including stops and city traffic. All thanks for this new challenge were due to ESPN and their celebratory opening of the first ESPNZone sports bar on Saturday afternoon in Baltimore. We were sure the thing was going to be a great sports bar and all, but at the time, we were a little more focused on something else.

Before we close the book on Florida though, I want to express our gratitude to all of the people who treated us so well while we were at Pro Player and Tropicana. All of the nice things we said about these parks (if you look closely you can see them) probably would not have been made possible without Margo with the Marlins, Georgina with Fine Host in Miami, and Kevin Austin with Volume Services in Tampa, and the many people whom they work with every day. Throughout our trip, from the West Coast to

Atlanta, everyone who took care of us at the ballparks seemed to love their jobs, especially the part where they got the opportunity to show off their stadiums and their wares. But we hadn't expected such enthusiasm in Florida, particularly Tropicana, having heard such lukewarm reviews of the place. But Kevin seemed to not only love his job but to take a certain pride in it and in the ballpark that he felt personally responsible for, although I would never hold him accountable for this mistake. In fact, the whole state of Florida was very hospitable and, even though the baseball fans are few and far between, every one of those fans adds to the game experience. They never would have done anything to us like the Orioles and ESPN were doing. I don't care if we *were* on *SportsCenter*.

Tropicana Field

CITY: St. Petersburg, Florida

TENANT: Tampa Bay Devil Rays

OPENED: March 3, 1990; first Devil Ray's game: March 31, 1998

NICKNAME/ALIASES: Thunderdome (due to the NHL Tampa Bay Lightning who occupied the facility from 1993 to 1996)

DESIGN: Multipurpose domed stadium (baseball, hockey, basketball, football, figure skating, soccer, tennis, weightlifting, Ping Pong, gymnastics, and monster truck racing), circular design, movable seats. SISTER PARKS: Built in the same era as new Comiskey and SkyDome. It has no true sister park but resembles the Kingdome and SkyDome in its heavy use of concrete.

FIELD: AstroTurf with dirt infield (1998–99); Fieldturf with dirt infield (2000–).

DIMENSIONS (feet): Left field—315, left center—370, center field—404, right center—370, right field—322, roof—225

FENCES (feet): 9.5

LOCATION: One Tropicana Dr., St. Petersburg, FL 33705

CAPACITY: 45,000 (baseball). Total attendance: 2,506,293 (1998). Average attendance: 30,941 (1998).

PARKING: $8. There are more than seven thousand parking spots adjacent to the field plus numerous smaller independent operators at around $5 per space.

TICKETS: $8–$160. BEST BANG FOR YOUR BUCK: While the best deal is The Beach ($10) and the lively atmosphere, you cannot go wrong with lower reserved. The small layout of the park means these seats offer exciting action at a good price. Also, the $160 price tag for the home-plate box seats is not a misprint. Those seats provide in-seat television and Internet access. As a fan, you can change to any camera in the stadium and pull up real-time stats online. We never had the experience, but it doesn't seem worth it to us.

BALLPARK EXPERIENCE: Other than Le Stade Olympique, Tropicana Field was the strangest ballpark in which we saw a professional baseball game. Initially designed to lure the White Sox out of Chicago, the dome was built in 1990 with no real tenants. This was a bad idea. Thus the park was designed to accommodate any game from hockey to monster truck races. This reality gives it an ill-suited setup for baseball. Its exterior is a slanted dome held up by numerous cables. From afar, the park resembles a large flying saucer. At night, this effect is magnified by strange lights on its exterior.

On the inside, the park resembles an arena and/or the Kingdome in Seattle. The slanted roof is an unusual feature with the higher side near the outfield. Many other

The rotunda at Tropicana Field does not have chandeliers made of baseball bats like the one at Ebbets Field, but it does have an interesting devil rays sculpture.

eclectic features fill the inside of the park, including the Batter's Eye restaurant in center field (see FUN FACTS), the Beach area in left field (see THE ONE THING YOU HAVE TO DO), and the food court area beyond the outfield. The one overwhelming feeling inside the park when we were there was that it was unfinished. Many parts of the initial design had been scaled back and even left partially done due to a lack of money. This included numerous ceiling panels, escalators, and the club section. (NOTE: The club was on a different floor from the club seats and thus no one used it.) As far as the current state of the park, we hear some headway has been made in this arena, although apparently not much.

FANS: Although the Devil Rays are only a handful of years old, Tampa–St. Petersburg fans have a deep history with baseball. More spring training games have been played in St. Petersburg than any other city. Teams such as the St. Louis Browns, New York Yankees, Boston Braves, and St. Louis Cardinals all called St. Petersburg their Grapefruit League home. Many players also call Tampa their hometown from Al Lopez (Hall of Fame catcher for the Cleveland Indians and Chicago White Sox) to Wade Boggs to Dwight Gooden. And the fans there seem excited about professional baseball, although Tropicana has apparently scared some of them away. Their first-year attendance numbers, just over 2.5 million fans, were above average on the whole but somewhat disappointing for a new club.

FACILITIES: Tropicana Field has newer facilities, but many of them were not completed when we were there (e.g., ceiling panels, murals, club level). The concourses were wide and spacious in the outfield but far narrower behind the baselines. Overall, first-class intent and design with lackluster execution.

FOOD: To our surprise and joy, Tropicana has a fantastic assortment of food. It was second only to San Diego in terms of selection. The unique food court behind center field features an Outback Steakhouse, a brewery restaurant, Columbia's Classic Café, and a cigar bar. Standing in line for these choices, however, feels more like taking your kids to a shopping mall than a baseball park. Once again, as in Miami, the Cuban sandwich is the best specialty food. LAST CALL: Alcohol is served until the middle of the eighth inning.

GREAT PLAYERS AND HISTORIC MOMENTS: Hmm . . . yeah. I guess Wade Boggs got his three-thousandth hit here. You remember him. The great Devil Rays third baseman. (NOTE: Wade was born and raised in Tampa.)

BALLPARK HISTORY: Tampa Bay finally received a professional team in 1998 after numerous years of campaigning and attempts to lure teams from other cities. The city decided in 1989 to build a domed stadium, against the advice of MLB, to lure a major league team. The White Sox and Giants both seemed headed to Tampa Bay, and a group of investors from the area even called a press conference in 1992 announcing that the Giants were coming. Obviously, the Giants didn't move, and Tampa was left without a team. But persistence paid off, and Tampa Bay was granted a squad on March 9, 1995. A local group led by Vincent Naimoli established themselves as the new owners. The newly named Tampa Bay Devil Rays started play March 31, 1998, at the newly renamed Florida Suncoast Dome (Tropicana Field). The dome was mostly used for smaller events like soccer games, ice skating, and monster truck races from 1990 to 1993. The Tampa Bay Lightning of the NHL played hockey in the dome from 1993 to 1996.

FUN FACT: The Batter's Eye restaurant in center field is tinted with a greenish glass so that it can be directly behind center field, and batters can still see the ball out of the pitcher's hand. An interesting idea, except that this also makes the restaurant a little dark and dreary, not quite comparable to the center-field hot spots in Atlanta and Houston's new field.

THE ONE THING YOU HAVE TO DO AT TROPICANA FIELD AND WHY: Take a picture of yourself out front and tell your friends you were on the set of *Men in Black* when the spaceship landed. Or check out the upper-deck pseudo-resort-type area (the Beach) complete with palm trees.

OTHER THINGS TO REMEMBER: Dave would be upset if we failed to mention that Tropicana has a five-story rotunda just inside the main gate entrance. It doesn't have chandeliers

BAT INFO

FINAL SCORE: Yankees 8, Devil Rays 4

OUR SEATS: Section 304, Row D,
    Seats 5–6

BALLPARK: 13 of 30

DAY: 21 of 38

MILES TRAVELED: 258 (7,353 total)

NEW STATES: 0 (12 total)

OUR EXPENSES: $25
    parking $5
    gas $20
    EXPENSES TO DATE: $1,548

OUR FREEBIES: $102
    breakfast at Irelands (courtesy of the
        Kavals) $12
    game tickets (courtesy of the Devil Rays)
        $30
    programs, memorabilia, and ballpark
        food—hot dogs, sandwiches, pretzels,
        beer, etc. (courtesy of Volume Services)
        $60
    FREEBIES TO DATE: $2,244

made of baseball bats and marble floors with baseball stitching (as at the old Ebbets Field) but it does have some model Devil Rays attached to the wall by little metal rods.

LASTING IMPRESSION: Tampa Bay feels like it would be a great place to watch a game if they could just keep the dome from getting in the way.

14

camden yards

Baltimore

DUE TO the change of game time in Baltimore, we were compelled to leave our seats at Tropicana Field in the beginning of the eighth inning. Honestly, we feared that fifteen minutes in traffic would force us to miss the beginning of the game at Camden. We saw our host Kevin again after the game and thanked him for showing us a great time. He knew of our plans for the evening, and his people prepared some sandwiches for us for the long road ahead. His being, along with Lon, one of the two nicest guys we had met throughout our trip, we almost felt guilty taking anything more from him, but we still had a pretty high opinion of ourselves.

Once we got on the road, we all had a huge adrenaline rush given the obstacle in front of us: one thousand miles of rural southern nightscape. Ron took the first shift behind the wheel. I volunteered for the second shift and was faced with the task of trying to catch some sleep before my 2 A.M. wake-up call. Needless to say, I could manage absolutely no sleep and eventually gave in to the inevitability of an all-night drive on zero rest.

Ron got us out of Florida smoothly. Being the middle of the night, we had very little to do in the way of sightseeing, although we did take note of the Disney World signs we passed on the freeway. After Florida came Georgia, and not surprisingly our second trip through the Peach State was much quicker and significantly less eventful than the first. We took the ninety-six miles along I-95 in about eighty minutes.

Feeding off the energy of zipping through two states, Ron turned to Dave, who was riding shotgun, and calmly stated, "I am going all the way."

"What?" Dave replied with the fear of God in his voice. There was certainly no way to have Ron drive the full 1,001 miles and survive. We didn't test the hypothesis, as Dave feigned a restroom break to drag me out of the backseat to drive.

I took over behind the wheel somewhere near the South Carolina border. But my being behind the wheel did little to make my only visit to South Carolina a memorable one, and I remember only a few brief attempts to train my eyes out the passenger window to the east to spy a bit of the Atlantic Ocean that the map claimed was just abreast of us. It being pitch dark, I'll never know if I saw any ocean at all or just some distant trees billowing in the wind, masquerading as waves. In any case, around 4 A.M. my coherence was suffering. Ron and Dave apparently found the car ride quite relaxing and quickly fell into a slumber as soon as I got behind the wheel. Thus I was left to meander down the highway pretty much by myself.

It had been the plan that there would be at least two bodies awake at any time to prevent potential catastrophes, such as my trying to find the way through the coal-black night of South Carolina by myself, but my earlier inability to sleep had apparently thrown off our entire schedule. In any case, Dave's slumber did not last long since, about fifteen minutes after I took over the wheel, I spent as much time on the shoulder as I did in either of the two main lanes. Thereafter, Dave and I drifted into a pattern of falling asleep every ten minutes and then both grabbing at the wheel five seconds later, as soon as we felt the bump, bump, bump of the shoulder again. After about two hours of this, Ron, who had not slept as soundly as he had hoped, decided to save my suspension and reassumed the wheel.

Ron drove the rest of the way, impervious to any need for sleep. This was in stark contrast to Dave and me, who I was told later talked in our sleep about ballparks and hot dogs. Finally, around eight or nine in the morning, after we were well into Virginia and the smell of baseball was ripe in the air, Dave and I regained a certain level of coherence.

When we stopped for gas and a quick breakfast-like snack, there was some confusion over who was to pay for the next tank of gas. Ron insisted that Dave had paid for the last tank around 4 A.M. in one of the Carolinas, and Dave insisted that he had done nothing of the sort. A quick search of the car turned up no receipt and raised the suspicion that no one had paid for the gas and that the Carolina authorities were probably looking for three half-asleep perps driving a car that happened to bear my license plate. Ron and Dave were somewhat amused by this; I was a little upset at the prospect of arrest. Fortunately, my anxiety was unnecessary as nothing ever came of our delinquency—at least nothing has yet.

As we got closer and closer to Camden, I spent most of my time tracking mile markers and the time, making sure we were on schedule. Invariably I would yell out from the backseat, "Ron, you've got to get up to eighty." At which point Ron would increase his speed. Then we would see another of the not-entirely-accurate mile markers, and I would tell Ron he could slow down a little. Eventually, he disregarded me and just drove ninety the whole way.

Finally, after 1,001 miles and fourteen hours and five minutes, we rolled into a parking garage two blocks from Camden, sixty-seven minutes ahead of schedule. Without Ron, it was very likely that Dave and I would have awakened around 11 A.M. that Saturday morning in a ditch somewhere in the Carolinas, the trip thus far having already stolen from us that collegiate resolve that wards off sleep. But Ron still had it, and it was truly an inspired effort on his part to get us through what was easily the most difficult obstacle of our entire journey.

In more ways than one, Ron was an integral part of the trip, and it would not be an exaggeration to say that Dave and I might never have finished the trip, at least not together, had it not been for Ron. When he joined us, Dave and I were barely speaking to each other, we were both still upset about the car repair incident and increasingly annoyed by each other's idiosyncrasies. But Ron—with the help of Zach, Tom, Ryan, Frank, Jeanette, and the others along the way—really lightened things up and helped us realize, whenever we started to forget, that this was supposed to be fun. For that, and the fact that we woke up that Saturday morning two states removed from South Carolina, Dave and I will always be grateful to Ron. Even though we thought him a coward for chickening out on his original inclination to go the full thirty in thirty-eight with us.

Tired but elated that the 1,001-mile drive ended successfully, we posed with Ron in front of Eutaw Street at Camden Yards. Brad seems a bit dejected here because this picture was taken just after he dropped a foul ball.

camden yards

· ·

BOSTON V BALTIMORE

GAME TIME: 1:15 P.M.

WE SHOWED up at Camden dead beat but with a running-on-empty high that makes you feel like you can face a full day although you know that the feeling can and will vanish at any moment. We somehow stuck with the plan and met our friend Chris Clatterbuck in front of the Babe Ruth statue precisely half an hour before the game, even though none of us had ever seen the statue. (We pulled off a similar feat a week later at Yankee Stadium.) Oh yeah, and one other thing, we hadn't yet procured tickets for the day's sold-out game. We didn't expect that to be a serious problem though. You can always find tickets for a ballgame, right?

In any case, we had more pressing engagements. The nice people from Aramark had offered to host us at their Camden Club before the game, that being the members-only club on the second story of the famous B&O Warehouse in right field at the park. We were of course expecting our invitation to mean free food, free drinks, whatever, at the club, like we'd been treated to everywhere else. But really all it meant was free access to the cigar smoke, the overpriced fare, and the restroom with the urinals overlooking right field (which was admittedly pretty cool). We had also not bothered looking for tickets before showing up at the club, being sure that they would have a few waiting for us when we got there. After all, Lon had told them about us. As it turned out, there are some times when you cannot get tickets to a baseball game. Who knew?

Not only can regular people not get tickets to a ballgame, *we* could not get tickets. And we were famous. But this game being one big ESPN party in honor of the opening of the first in a now-lengthy chain of ESPNZone restaurants, a lineup of A-list celebrities was out for this game—Michael Jordan, Adam Sandler, and some other famous people who took the free tickets we wanted. We figured this was a major PR gaffe on somebody's part. And I am sure that, reading this now, someone's feeling a little embarrassed (or else laughing out loud).

So we sat ticketless in the Camden Club, watching the first three innings of the game from the tiny windows of the warehouse and making frequent trips to the restroom just because that was so cool. By the fourth inning the Aramark guys—who had been trying to find us some spare tickets just to get into the game—gave up that futile plan, and we resorted to Plan B. Plan B was to just walk through the gate like we owned the place and hope we didn't get caught.

We were escorted by a very official-looking fellow from Aramark down to a crossover bridge, which passes over the esplanade behind the right field fence connecting the warehouse and the stadium. As we walked across to the stadium, it was looking like we were home-free. There didn't seem to be a checkpoint at all, and we could already see the bustling fans less than twenty feet away. But then a gray-haired fellow about 5'8" 140 trained his eyes on us. We thought we could take him.

As we approached, we let our credentialed friend do the talking for us. We stood behind him trying to look as important as a bunch of disheveled college kids with matching T-shirts and bags under their eyes could look. Throughout their conversation we kept our focus on the gatekeeper's expression. At first he seemed understanding and sympathetic to what our ally was telling him. But after he had heard the whole story, his expression suddenly changed as if he appeared on the verge of reciting the mantra he was supposed to give to all sad souls with a sob story about why he should let them in. "Sorry, no tickets, no entry."

Just then Dave jumped in with our trusty map, using the ploy that he had perfected over the last three weeks. "Excuse me, sir, would you please sign our map?" At which point, he opened the map and pointed toward the relatively virgin section of the map surrounding Baltimore.

The unsuspecting victim glanced at The Map, taken aback by its scale and the sheer quantity of signatures that were already scattered across it coast to coast. "What's this map for, son?"

"Well, sir, we are in the middle of a trip to see all of the major league ballparks. We started in San Francisco three weeks ago. We've got two weeks left, and now we're in Baltimore."

"Well, that's very impressive." He signed The Map. At that point, we were all still just standing there on the wrong side of the gate. The gatekeeper then looked up at us again, and as if he just realized that he'd forgotten the most common of courtesies, he opened the gate and stepped aside. "If you guys are going to all that trouble, I'm not going to be the one to stop you."

And just like that, we were inside Camden Yards. Like true VIPs, we had accomplished something neither Michael Jordan nor Adam Sandler had that day. We had gained access to the most exclusive baseball park in North America *without* tickets. And suddenly Dave was my best friend all over again.

We were finally here, in the oft-mentioned park that started the renaissance in stadium building. The park that made it cool to build new ballparks. I'll admit, it had always seemed a little overhyped to me. The whole new wave of stadiums did. And even though I had been here once before, I needed to come back and check it out for myself, fearing that the last time maybe I was just an unsuspecting victim of the hype myself.

The B&O Warehouse in right field gives Camden Yards a historic feel. The ballpark's warehouse "feature" and irregular outfield initiated a new era in field design by imitating the classic ballparks of yesteryear. The resulting Camden style has been an influence on every ballpark built since 1992.

After further examination though, I must confess that the hype was justified. Camden Yards is a great park. In chapters before (see the Astrodome) and pages to come (see County Stadium), I have taken it upon myself to expound at length upon why this new wave of ballparks might not be such a good thing. And after our trips through Coors, Arlington, and Bank One, I was becoming perhaps the biggest ballpark cynic about this new-wave mess, thinking that they were, in their attempts to transcend the 1960s cookie-cutter stadiums, a little cookie cutter in their own way. And being back at Camden confirmed all of those suspicions, as there is very little about those parks or Pac Bell or Enron or any of the other parks that are popping up nowadays— except maybe the occasional retractable roof—that cannot be traced directly to Camden. But somehow, even though those facsimiles of Camden had lost a little respect in my eyes as a result of the similarities, Camden still shone in my mind as truly distinct, and not just because of the warehouse in right field. Maybe it is just knowing the fact that Camden was the first that gives it that truly special and unique feeling. In comparison, all the other new stadiums, even though they have replicated the Camden model beautifully on all counts, are lesser imitations of this.

On second thought, maybe it is the warehouse. Comparing the warehouse to the center-field arches in Arlington or the Rockpile at Coors or the pool at Bank One, the warehouse is the only one that has an organic feeling of being part of the ballpark. The warehouse is to Camden as the monster is to Fenway or the ivy is to Wrigley. Yeah, to a certain degree they are all gimmicks. They didn't have to build Fenway on that absurdly small plot of land, you know. But likewise, they all seem inspired by the same sorts of aesthetic reasons. "Wouldn't it be cool if we just left the warehouse there?" And none were banking on an ensuing economic fortune. In contrast, the pool in Arizona, the hill in Houston, even the bay in San Francisco, all seem like contrivances. As if to say, "this will be *our* warehouse."

Maybe I'm wrong, but I'm definitely not alone in seeing Camden as a rung above all of its successors. After all something has to be special about this ballpark to keep sellout crowds coming back for more than eight years to see the disappointing Orioles, the team that has proved itself as the exception to the rule that you can always buy a winner. Maybe George Steinbrenner's job is harder than it looks, after all.

Surprisingly, we stayed awake the whole game. Ron jinxed Scott Erickson's perfect game in the fifth when he turned to me and said, "Is he throwing a perfect game?" Of course the next batter got a hit. Despite that, the Orioles won, and the park had a lot of energy. Even though we were officially awake throughout the game, we were all a little loopy after the previous evening's occurrences. As a result, my firsthand memories of the park aren't very specific. We got a lot of pictures and video though, so we watched that later to confirm our suspicions that we had actually been there.

On a final note, although I am not eager to discuss it, I dropped a foul ball in the eighth inning. We were sitting in the club level in some abandoned seats that an Aramark scout had found for us and a polite usher led us to, still ticketless. We were directly behind home plate and just above the top of the screen that protects fans from being pelted by foul tips. After we had been in the seats about two innings, and just after a nice man sitting behind us had brought us all beers, a line drive screamed straight back at us over the screen.

The ball was actually a little above me and to my left, just between Dave and me. Reflexively, I moved in front of the ball and stuck my hands up. The ball hit right where my palms were connected and bounced out before I knew what had happened. I was roundly booed, unjustly I think, and even heckled. In any case, it made me feel miserable to miss that opportunity.

My spirits were cheered up slightly when a lady behind us expressed her gratitude for my protecting her and her daughter from the ball. They had apparently been somewhat terrified by the whole experience, their lives flashing before their eyes. I didn't tell her that the safety of others had never crossed my mind, that all I was looking for was a souvenir. I was thankful, however, that my failure was not seen as such in everybody's eyes, although it sure was in the eyes of that guy three rows up who kept heckling me. I wondered what he would have done in my spot? Probably that whole life-flashing-before-his-eyes thing. In any case, I never would have heckled him. It also upset me that another guy a few rows in front of us made an easy play on the ball that bounced out of my hands, and then he gloated about it. I vowed that if I ever made a gimme play like that, I would not show the ball around to all of my friends like I had accomplished something. Instead I would give the ball to some kid who would surely appreciate it. Of course I was just jealous. But with good justification.

My only solace came in knowing that I wasn't the screw-up of the day for that, because Ron ripped his pants twice. Dave also bought me a souvenir Orioles baseball and signed something maudlin on it like "you're still the best ball player I know." I was appreciative of the effort from my new best friend, but I was still a little bitter. That wasn't the ball I wanted.

camden yards

CITY: Baltimore, Maryland

TENANT: Baltimore Orioles

OPENED: April 6, 1992

NICKNAME/ALIASES: Oriole Park at Camden Yards (the official name that no one uses). (NOTE: The name of the park was a compromise between Donald Schaefer, the governor of Maryland, and Eli Jacobs, the owner of the Orioles. Schaefer wanted the park to be called Camden Yards, while Jacobs wanted the park to go by Oriole Park. They combined the names into Oriole Park at Camden Yards. Schaefer gets the last laugh because everyone calls the park just plain Camden Yards.)

DESIGN: Baseball-only stadium, asymmetrical design, no movable seats. SISTER PARKS: Coors Field in Denver, Pacific Bell Park, The Ballpark in Arlington, Comerica Park in Detroit, and Jacobs Field in Cleveland.

FIELD: Maryland Bluegrass (by now you get the picture that there are a lot of ways to say grass).

DIMENSIONS (feet): left field—333, left center—364, deep left center—410, center field—400, right center—373, right field—318

FENCES (feet): 7. There is a twenty-five-foot wall-scoreboard in right field.

LOCATION/DIRECTIONS: First base (S by SE): Martin Luther King Blvd. Third base (W by SW): Russell St. Left field (N by NW): Camden St. Right field (E by NE): Howard St.

CAPACITY: 48,262. Total attendance: 3,684,650 (1998). Average attendance: 45,490 (1998).

PARKING: $10. Camden Yards is an urban ballpark and fans must hunt for parking, which is constantly denoted by parking attendants in orange with orange flags. There are four thousand spots on site, but these are quickly taken.

TICKETS: $9–$35. BEST BANG FOR YOUR BUCK: The terrace boxes along the third-base line are great seats. Although over $20, the seats afford beautiful views of the B&O Warehouse, the city, and the field. For a more money-conscious seat, go for the bleachers. For $9 you are close to the action and in the middle of the best fans.

BALLPARK EXPERIENCE: Camden Yards is the paradigm of modern baseball park design. All of the new parks from Coors Field in Denver to Pacific Bell Park in San Francisco have copied the basic structure of this great park. The key elements to the Camden style are a red-brick-and-limestone exterior supported with green steel. This style also connotes intimacy with no more than fifty thousand seats positioned as close to the action as possible. This leaves very little foul territory but superb views of the action. The Camden style also is one with its surroundings. In Baltimore, the famous red-brick Baltimore & Ohio Building in right and center field attaches the park to the city and its past. Other key elements of the Camden style are the towering light standards, green seats, and general asymmetry of design that places the deepest portion of the field in left or right center instead of dead center. Asymmetry was a conscious reaction to the circular behemoths of the 1960s and '70s like Veterans Stadium in Philadelphia and Busch Stadium in St. Louis that all resembled each other. The Camden-style parks all have a uniqueness to them that ironically makes them all blend together in some way. That is the danger of Camden style. Since it is so successful and a fan favorite, the teams risk creating a whole new era of cookie-cutter parks.

With respect to Camden more specifically, the interior of the park features wide concourses with views of the action. There is a large club level with private restaurants and bars behind the midlevel seats. The third level is quite steep but enables fans to be much closer to the action than the wider multipurpose parks. The concourses for the top deck surround the exterior of the park and are above the classic brick-and-limestone roman arches. Great views of downtown Baltimore and the surrounding neighborhoods are abundant. Eutaw Street between the park and the B&O Warehouse is a dynamic avenue of vendors and fans. The street brings the city and the park together in a way no suburban park can match. Finally, there are unique but much copied dual-deck bullpens in left center field. All these features combine to make this the ideal ballpark. Truly a classic.

FANS: The fans are lively. Baltimore seems to have the most festive atmosphere in all of baseball. It makes sense when you realize that if you took the team seriously here you'd quickly give in to depression realizing how much money they keep paying for lineups that can't win. But the fans keep coming back. We don't know how many of them are repeat customers, because the park draws more tourists than any in baseball, but die-hards and tourists alike seem to show a lot of enthusiasm at this park.

FACILITIES: Even though Camden Yards is the oldest of the new-age parks, it still feels new. The restrooms, concession services, shops, restaurants, and exterior are all in great shape. The B&O Building was gutted in the park construction and now features shops, offices (including the Orioles), and the Camden Club. There is even a restroom with a view of the field (see ONE THING TO DO AT CAMDEN).

FOOD: Camden Yards does a fabulous job serving up a wide variety of truly great ball-park food. We discovered that some of the best food is on Eutaw Street, which is between the B&O Warehouse and the park. A classic wrought-iron fence separates the street from the park, and lively vendors are all over the street, including Boog Powell's BBQ. Boog's BBQ sandwich is a classic with tender meat heaped high on a toasted bun. This is a Don't Miss. LAST CALL: Alcohol is served until the middle of the seventh inning.

GREAT PLAYERS AND HISTORIC MOMENTS: Unfortunately, having the most popular ballpark in the major leagues, along with the newfound wealth inherent in that achievement, does not guarantee success. The Orioles have had thoroughly mixed results at their new ballpark, ranging from poor playoff performances (see 1996 and the Jeffrey Schultz incident) to poor performances all around (see most other years). Undisputedly, the most memorable and historic moment Camden Yards has witnessed to date has been Cal Ripken's 2,131st game, which broke Lou Gehrig's "unbreakable" record. The images of those banners unfurled in the warehouse windows remain with us still. Beyond that though, the park has little more at its disposal in attempts to fondly ingrain itself in our memories. It was deprived of Ripken's three-thousandth hit. In fact, other than the pos-sible exception of Ken Griffey Jr. swinging for and eventually succeeding in becoming the first to hit a ball off the warehouse in the 1993 All-Star home run derby, the sta-dium's second most memorable moment might be Ripken's long-awaited day of rest in 1998 after consecutive game number 2,632. All Star game '93.

BALLPARK HISTORY: Camden Yards was a turning point in baseball park design as well as construction. The park, the brainchild of William Donald Schaefer, the governor of Maryland, was initially conceived in the late 1980s as a means to gentrify downtown Baltimore. Success with the inner harbor and the aquarium and science center public works projects inspired the governor to act on his vision of a new baseball-only park. The park was financed using public money, and construction started in June 1989. It

We were stuck on Eutaw Street and in the B&O Warehouse (at right) for several innings before the Aramark folks and Dave's fancy talking got us into the sold-out ballpark.

took thirty-three months to complete at a cost of $110 million. Design elements of the park were steel, rather than concrete trusses, a roman arched brick facade, a sunroof over the gentle slope of the upper deck, an asymmetrical playing field, and natural grass turf. The inspiration for the park was many of the major league parks built in the early 1900s. These included Ebbets Field in Brooklyn, Shibe Park in Philadelphia, Fenway Park in Boston, Crosley Field in Cincinnati, Forbes Fields in Pittsburgh, Wrigley Field in Chicago, and the Polo Grounds in New York. Camden Yards was the first of a new wave of retro-style parks that are all built in the Camden style (see BALLPARK EXPERIENCE above). Cleveland and Arlington followed suit in 1994. Especially in Cleveland and Denver, the parks' generally urban settings served to revitalize stagnant inner cities and bring suburban families back downtown.

FUN FACT: As we alluded to before, the Baltimore & Ohio Warehouse in right field was originally to be torn down when plans were being made for the ballpark. But one unheralded architect had the idea that they should just leave it there, thinking that it would provide a bit of color and uniqueness and would hearken back to the old parks like Fenway that were built with their trademark characteristics like the Green Monster out of necessity. It was, of course, not necessary at all to leave the warehouse there. They had the authority to tear it down, but it stayed and has been credited as the most notable and memorable characteristic of the ballpark. More than any other attribute, that unassuming warehouse sparked the new wave of baseball stadiums, and ironically, its symbolism has been the one aspect ignored by almost all of the newer ballparks (see the pool at Bank One). The B&O Warehouse is also the longest building (1,016 feet long) on the East Coast.

THE ONE THING YOU HAVE TO DO AT CAMDEN YARDS AND WHY: Go to the restroom in the B&O Building. The restroom on the fourth floor in the Camden Club has a beautiful view of the ball field. It definitely had the best view of any restroom we had ever been in.

OTHER THINGS TO REMEMBER: Be sure to arrive early to the game (thirty minutes prior to the first pitch) to see the excitement of Eutaw Street. Street vendors, scalpers, and fans all congregate in this area before the game. There is a playoff energy to the area year-round.

LASTING IMPRESSION: An instant classic that perfectly melds the modern amenities with the ambiance and character of the old parks.

BAT Info

FINAL SCORE: Orioles 2, Red Sox 1

OUR SEATS: Section 244, Row EE, Seats 5–6

BALLPARK: 14 of 30

DAY: 22 of 38

MILES TRAVELED: 1,037 (8,390 total)

NEW STATES: 4 (South Carolina, North Carolina, Virginia, Maryland; 16 total)

OUR EXPENSES: $83
parking $20
programs $8
gas (of course it should have been more) $55
EXPENSES TO DATE: $1,631

OUR FREEBIES: $120
ballpark food—hot dogs, pretzels, beer, etc. (courtesy of Aramark) $50
dinner and hotel room in Baltimore (courtesy of Mr. Kaval) $70
FREEBIES TO DATE: $2,364

15

shea stadium
New York

AFTER THE game in Baltimore, we said good-bye to our friend Chris, who had to head back to D.C. and his summer job. We went so far as to drop him off at the train station because we wanted to be nice, although it probably took us longer to find the place by car then it would have taken Chris by foot. Then we headed to the airport Marriott where we met up with Dave's dad, who had flown in from Cleveland and was going to travel with us until we got back there. This meant we were going to be traveling with four, at least for the next twenty-four hours. That was going to be cozy, but Mr. Kaval was setting us up with hotel rooms, so I wasn't going to complain. By the time we left the ballpark, finding a comfortable bed was the only thing on my mind.

Back at the hotel, Mr. Kaval was waiting for us with keys to our room. My memories from that point are pretty blurry. I remember getting to the hotel, saying hello to Mr. Kaval, and passing out in the room. Maybe we got up later and had dinner, maybe we didn't. But the next thing I knew, we were on the road to New York the following morning. Crammed in the back of my car, I had surprisingly little trouble dozing off.

Ultimately, something woke me up. It always does. Dave's dad had only been with us for two waking hours when we zipped through Delaware (in eleven minutes), but already I was noticing a disturbing trend. While Ron and I drifted in and out of consciousness in the backseat, Dave and his dad bantered interminably in the front. It is generally considered a healthy sign when a father and son have so much to talk about, particularly in light of the many noteworthy experiences we had been through over the past three weeks. But there was something unnatural to me about the way that Dave and his dad carried on. It wasn't what you would expect in the way of father and son catching up on old times. "Oh yeah, Dad, and guess what happened to us in Atlanta," because they just kept rapping away, burning through topics from politics to pop music. By now I was, of course, aware of Dave's love for the spoken word. And it was suddenly *painfully* clear where he got that trait from. In all honesty, it wouldn't have been so annoying except for the fact that I just really wanted to get some sleep.

shea stadium

MONTREAL V NEW YORK METS

GAME TIME: 1:40 P.M.

WE ROLLED into New York City on the south side of Brooklyn by way of New Jersey, bypassing Manhattan altogether. This was Dave's dad's idea, and since he was driving, we all went along. The traffic was relatively heavy through Brooklyn, at least for a Sunday afternoon, but we were in no way pressed for time, so we made it to the Flushing Meadow part of Queens (home of Shea Stadium) about two hours before game time.

Although Sunday is traditionally the biggest day of the week for baseball crowds, we weren't expecting too big a showing for this matchup between the underperforming Mets and the lowly Expos. So when we got to the park we were surprised to see thousands of people lined up to get in. Navigating our way through the crowds to pick up our tickets, it finally dawned on us what all the commotion was about. It was Beanie Baby day.

In the annals of baseball history, 1998 will forever go down as the year of the Beanie Baby. This side of Mark McGwire and Sammy Sosa, and just that side of the Baseball America Tour (that's us), Beanie Babies were the most significant factor in increased attendance around the major leagues. Also-ran teams that were averaging under twenty thousand fans a game in their second-rate stadiums were selling out on random Tuesdays thanks to the Beanie Babies. And here at Shea, this was already the third Beanie Baby promotion they had run during the year, and reportedly this one was shaping up to be relatively tame. At the others, mothers, fathers, and children alike had pulled fists and weapons in crowds more dangerous than a mosh pit at a Metallica concert to claim the last of the limited-edition Beanie Babies being handed out.

The crowds we saw were somewhat behaved, given that most of the die-hards had planned ahead and shown up plenty early so as to avoid any major violence. We waited out the fifteen-minute line to get in, but despite our sweet-talking and invocation of The Map, we couldn't convince the carefully supervised gate attendants to pass us a couple of Beanie Babies to add to our souvenir collection. It's probably better off that way. There surely would have been a pint-sized riot had we gotten our hands on some of the precious commodities.

Inside the stadium we got the same sort of treatment from the Aramark guys that we had grown accustomed to. Free hats, free food, and a tour. Our tour was led by a twenty-something Aramark assistant whose disposition was peculiar because he seemed to hold a relatively important job, at least within Shea Aramark, but he carried it out with the reluctance of a college intern. Of all the people we had met, he seemed one of the most genuine. Genuinely interested in us. Genuinely disinterested in our trip.

This particularly seemed to bother Dave, who for the first time in weeks came across someone who didn't care about the rotunda at Ebbets Field or any field for that matter. In fact, our guide didn't even seem like much of a baseball fan at all and spent most of the time complaining about how he was missing the World Cup Finals. This complaint surprised us, especially given that it was the first time all summer Dave or I had even heard about the World Cup. It was already the finals, and Dave and I hadn't a clue until that point that they were even playing a World Cup that year.

By now you can tell that our enthusiasm for these stadium tours was not at the high pitch it had been at in California. By the time we reached New York, the stadiums were all starting to look alike, and we felt like we had seen it all. But we did have at least one new and notable experience on the Shea tour. This happened when the press box elevator suddenly opened to reveal Mr. Met himself. We got on, rode up next to him, and got off, as if it were no big deal. The whole experience smacked of a *SportsCenter* commercial.

By and large, the tour and the stadium itself were rather unremarkable. The grand circularity of the place reminded me of the Astrodome and Candlestick and all the other behemoth parks of the 1960s, although it seemed larger than its sister parks. This perception arises from the reality that rather than expanding horizontally as most of its contemporaries do, Shea seems to expand endlessly vertically. The obvious benefit of this design is that none of the seats end up in the region where binoculars would be required just to make out second base, as is the case in the cavernous expanses of Veterans and Cinergy. The tradeoff, though, is that the seating tiers rise so steeply that almost everyone in the stadium has to lean forward to see home plate.

In all fairness though, I'll confess that I remember very little of the characteristics of Shea Stadium. It was our fifteenth park, the midpoint of the trip, and by that point everything was running together, (Dave maintains that I fell asleep for an inning.) Generally, though I had managed to keep track of a lot of ballpark characteristics from parks up till Shea, to some degree, all the concrete corridors of all the parks after the midpoint

We ran into Mr. Met, the Mets' mascot, in an elevator at Shea. The encounter was eerily reminiscent to us of a SportsCenter *ad.*

still blur together in my mind somewhat. The seats, the fields, the games were becoming harder to distinguish from each another, as I was slowly starting to realize that those weren't necessarily the most important characteristics of the stadiums. I already considered myself an expert on ballpark structures, designs, facilities, and food. Subsequently, over the rest of the trip, I was noticing and appreciating generally those few things about the parks that really distinguished them.

At Shea, these distinguishing characteristics were the food and the people. As for the food, the most noteworthy thing about Shea was that there were no specialty foods. Instead, at Shea, they consider their specialty to be serving top-notch ballpark staples. The hot dogs, pretzels, lemonade, even the Bud Lite; in New York it's all special. Although there is a certain amount of attitude behind this, to a large part it's true. They've got good food. And it's always refreshing when you know there is no espresso in the stadium.

The other thing about Shea was that, predictably, the people there were New Yorkers. Although we had been concerned that the whole Beanie Baby thing was going to dilute the true New Yorker attitude in our crowd, our fears were unfounded. Granted, the crowd seemed a little below the mean on the New York heckler average, but still, the people we met knew New York, and they knew about the Mets, the Yankees, the Dodgers, and the Giants. All told, this group might have even been better that the typical New York crowd. The same zealous fans but a little better behaved and a little less inebriated due to the behavioral impact of the watchful eyes of their kids.

The game itself was another competitive National League contest. Both teams played very good ball. I say this without shame having only seconds ago admitted that I have no distinct recollection of what happened on the playing field. I do, however, have a scorecard. And I remember clearly and most importantly that we had no foul ball opportunities and therefore no shame.

shea stadium

CITY: Flushing, New York (Queens Borough of New York City)

TENANT: New York Mets, New York Jets (1964–83)

OPENED: April 17, 1964

DESIGN: Multipurpose stadium, circular design, movable seats. SISTER PARKS: Candlestick Park, Veterans Stadium, Three Rivers Stadium, Riverfront Stadium, Fulton County Stadium, Busch Stadium.

FIELD: Grass

DIMENSIONS (feet): left field—338, left center—378, center field—410, right center—378, right field—345

FENCES (feet): 8

LOCATION: 123-01 Roosevelt Ave., Flushing, NY 11368. BOUNDED BY: Home plate (W): Grand Central Pkwy. First base (S): Roosevelt Ave. Third base (N): Whitestone Expressway–Interstate 678 and Flushing Bay. Center field (E): 126th St.

CAPACITY: 55,775 (baseball). Total attendance: 2,287,948 (1998). Average attendance: 28,246 (1998).

PARKING: $7

TICKETS: $12–37. BEST BANG FOR YOUR BUCK: Even though we had tickets from the team, seats in general at Shea are expensive like everything else in the New York City area. We suggest going all out for the $26 loge seats with railings separating each group of seats that give you a clublike feel even if you don't know anyone around you.

BALLPARK EXPERIENCE: Shea Stadium is among the multipurposoids built in the late 1950s and through the 1960s in the trend that began with Candlestick Park in San Francisco. We were told by our tour guide that Shea pioneered movable seats by placing them on tracks that ran with a motorized engine. This way the park could be converted for the Jets and back for the Mets more quickly than other parks. Ironically though, Shea is one of two of the original multipurpose stadiums, the other being Busch Stadium in St. Louis, that has since closed its doors to football. The Mets, however, have done little with this fact, and the circular design continues to prevent a good arrangement of seats around the diamond shape of the baseball field.

In the way of originality, unlike many of its sister parks, Shea Stadium is not enclosed. Rather than being multitiered, the outfield at Shea is in a bleacher format. Thus, from above, the stadium looks like a giant letter C. This gives the park an open feel and adds a little charm to the standard looking giant. It also affords views of the parking lot and of planes on final approach to LaGuardia Airport. (NOTE: the planners of the park did not realize that the location was on final approach to LaGuardia. They visited Flushing during the winter when planes do not fly over the park. Their oversight makes Shea Stadium one of the loudest parks in the major leagues.)

The park's huge size and the fact that it is engulfed by parking lots also overshadow this slightly open feel and give the park that suburban monster feel characteristic of parks of its era. Adding to the large feeling, the huge scoreboard in right field is one of the largest in baseball measuring 86' high by 175' wide, although it is somewhat dated in its styling. While oversized and lacking the charm of smaller parks, Shea, through sheer New York atmosphere, does manage to differentiate itself from many of its sister parks and provide a memorable experience.

FANS: New York fans have the worst reputation in baseball. Heckling, fighting, and drinking are usually synonymous with the general image of New York fans. And while this reputation was built at Yankee Stadium, Mets fans generally tend to exhibit many of the same tendencies, especially on hot muggy summer days. On this particular occasion though, thanks to the Beanie Babies perhaps, we saw far more families and casual fans at Mets games than you would ever see in the Bronx. Mets fans are sometimes labeled fickle and are often caught bandwagoning the Yankees' success. There are, however, many Mets fans who take great pride in being Mets and not Yankees fans. We sat next to a couple in the upper deck. These true Mets fans are easy to spot, given their proclivity for spontaneously lambasting the Yankees and everything about the Bronx Bombers.

FACILITIES: The facilities at Shea Stadium reflect the park's age. While our seats were wide and angled toward the action, the restrooms, concessions, and concourses were old and dirty. One other shortcoming were the wide ramps that shuttle fans to the upper reaches of the park. These ramps are too wide for the smaller baseball crowds and give the park a hollow feeling. You can avoid this by taking the elevators. Maybe, like us, you will meet Mr. Met.

FOOD: As mentioned above, the food at Shea is pretty standard but above average. They have everything you would expect, from cotton candy to peanuts, all at the quality you are accustomed to or slightly above. If you had to label a specialty at Shea, it would be the ice cream. The hot humid summers in New York mean a wider selection of ice cream than most parks. Ice cream vendors were always traversing the park selling cold treats to hot fans, including two weary travelers halfway through their tour. LAST CALL: Alcohol is served until the middle of the seventh inning.

GREAT PLAYERS AND HISTORIC MOMENTS: An All-Star Game was played in Shea's inaugural year of 1964, and since then three World Series have been played at the stadium (a fourth was played after our tour). By far the most notable was in 1969 when the "Miracle" Mets beat the heavily favored Baltimore Orioles in five games. Only slightly less notable, though, is the famous Red Sox–Mets Series of 1986. The sixth game at Shea Stadium was one of the greatest games in World Series history. With the Sox ahead three games to two, Boston got two runs in the top of the tenth to take a 5-3 lead. In the bottom of the tenth, two quick outs for the Mets left them on the brink of elimination. It was so grave that the scoreboard at Shea Stadium briefly posted "CONGRATULATIONS RED SOX." But then the magic began with consecutive singles by Gary Carter, Kevin Mitchell, and Ray Knight. Then Mookie Wilson's infamous grounder went through Bill Buckner's legs, which won the game and ultimately the series for the Mets.

Shea was one of the original multipurpose parks but is not enclosed like its sister parks. This means it has kept its great view of aircraft en route to LaGuardia Airport.

Other great players who have called Shea Stadium home include Tom Seaver, Nolan Ryan, and Gary Carter.

BALLPARK HISTORY: Before the Brooklyn Dodgers left New York for the West Coast in 1957, Walter O'Malley, the Dodgers' owner, petitioned the city to build a domed stadium in Flatbush near the old Ebbets Field. The city refused but did offer O'Malley a new stadium in Flushing. He didn't bite, but nonetheless, this was the first spark of what later became Shea Stadium. After the Dodgers and Giants left town, the mayor of New York appointed a prominent lawyer, William A. Shea, to head a committee to find a new baseball team. He not only got a new team for New York but that new stadium in Flushing as well. The stadium was completed in 1964 and dedicated with two bottles of water, one from the Harlem River to represent the Polo Grounds and one from the Gowanus Canal to represent Ebbets Field. Soon after completion the park was officially named in honor of Shea, who brought National League baseball back to New York. The park underwent a small renovation in 1983 when the New York Jets, unhappy with the park, moved to the Meadowlands in New Jersey. The changes consisted of mostly new paint (blue this time) and new seats. Plans were also drawn up to expand the stadium (it was designed to be able to increase capacity to ninety thousand by filling in the outfield with the same three-deck setup) and place a dome over its top, but concerns about

BAT INFO

FINAL SCORE: Mets 5, Expos 2

OUR SEATS: Section 1, Row D, Seats 9–10

BALLPARK: 15 of 30

DAY: 23 of 38

MILES TRAVELED: 430 (8,820 total)

NEW STATES: 4 (Delaware, New Jersey, New York, Pennsylvania; 20 total)

OUR EXPENSES: $48
tolls $6
parking $8
programs $6
Wendy's $8
gas $20
EXPENSES TO DATE: $1,679

OUR FREEBIES: $170
game tickets $40
ballpark food—hot dogs, peanuts, soda, and vanilla ice cream in Mets souvenir cups (courtesy of Aramark) $60
hotel room (courtesy of Mr. Kaval) $70
FREEBIES TO DATE: $2,534

the structural integrity of such a building scrapped these ideas. Ever since, there have been murmurings about building a new Queens ballpark adjacent to Shea Stadium, possibly with a retractable roof, by some time in 2003.

FUN FACT: The giant Red Apple that symbolizes New York's nickname rises out of a large top hat in right center field whenever a Mets player hits a home run.

THE ONE THING YOU HAVE TO DO AT SHEA STADIUM AND WHY: Go to the top of the upper deck. The park is the tallest in the majors, and you will realize how huge the thing is by how long it takes to reach the top. There are also great views of the borough of Queens from there.

LASTING IMPRESSION: An old, ugly park with some New York charm that keeps baseball fun in Queens.

ebbets field and the polo grounds

THE METS game wrapped up by four o'clock, but our day of baseball was not over. We still had on our agenda an homage to the olden days of baseball in the form of a trip to the old sites of Ebbets Field in Brooklyn and the Polo Grounds in Manhattan. Dave and I were especially excited about this prospect, in light of our trip and the streak of nineteen parks in nineteen days that we were in the midst of. We considered the streak to be getting us in touch with baseball's past, and so we figured something special would happen when we stepped on the hallowed grounds of these shrines to baseball's glory. Of course, both of these sites are housing projects now, the fact of which detracts a little from the luster. But we were getting goosebumps anyway.

It's a little sad to look at the ground where Jackie Robinson broke the color barrier or where Willie Mays made his famous over-the-shoulder catch and not even be able to imagine it, because there's a twelve-story building in the way. It's an even worse commentary on our national pastime to be advised that you shouldn't walk around the site of Ebbets Field with a camera in hand, because too many people there are all too eager to take it from you.

We had been to half of the major league ballparks now. But none of them had been in neighborhoods comparable to those that stood on the grounds of these old parks. Nonetheless, I felt confident (some would say naively so) walking around these neighborhoods. I expected that any malcontents we encountered on these hallowed grounds would have at least some respect for the game and for the heritage of these particular apartment projects.

As it turned out, we were ignored at the site of Ebbets Field in Brooklyn. We found the address where the ballpark had once stood and located in its place the Ebbets Field

Apartments. Despite the awesome name, it didn't seem like the kind of place where people pay premium prices to have the honor of saying they live in the Ebbets Field Apartments. It took us a little longer to find the stone plaque on the brick wall at the front left corner of the complex that reads, "THIS IS THE FORMER SITE OF EBBETS FIELD." Carved into the stone above the block text is a baseball with the year 1962 etched inside, the year they tore the place down. I wondered if people stopped caring for the neighborhood immediately afterward or three years earlier when the Dodgers left town. Walking around the apartment complex, we were noticed briefly by bystanders, if only for the color of our skin. We were obviously not the first to make the pilgrimage to this old-time baseball mecca, although there couldn't have been too many more, because we were quickly disregarded by the locals. Against the advice of others, we took a walking tour around the few blocks that Ebbets once stood on and came across the Jackie Robinson Elementary School, which spans most of what used to be Ebbets' left and center fields. On the wall of the school's hardtop playground is a breath-taking mural of Jackie's exploits. It seemed to be the most inspirational aspect of the neighborhood by far. I wondered how many kids on this playground had been influenced by that mural, and I hoped that there was at least one.

With Ebbets out of the way, we headed off to north Manhattan to see if we could find the Polo Grounds. As opposed to Ebbets, where we had an address and the information that there was a plaque there somewhere, with the Polo Grounds we didn't know where to start and if there was even anything left of the old ballpark at all. So we made our way onto the island and snaked through the various neighborhood streets that crossed through what our research indicated was once the ground of the

Dave's beloved rotunda at Ebbets Field in Brooklyn was razed in 1962. All that remains of the park is this small engraved concrete stone.

New York Giants. The neighborhood seemed in similar shape to the one where Ebbets once stood.

The most remarkable thing I noticed about the neighborhood, however, had nothing to do with the relative poverty of its residents. That was expected after our Ebbets experience. It was rather the basic geographical fact that from some parts of the neighborhood you could see Yankee Stadium right across the Harlem River. I had seen photos before that showed the close proximity of the two ball fields, but they never seemed this close. It was just so baffling to me that a situation that so blatantly defied the laws of baseball economics existed and flourished for so many years.

The driving around north Harlem continued for a while with no signs of the ballpark presenting themselves to us, so we stopped the car as near as we could to where we calculated home plate had once been. And wouldn't you know that as soon as we stepped out of the car we stood almost face to face with a sign welcoming us to the Polo Grounds Towers. Somehow we had driven by it twice without noticing a thing.

The sign inspired us to further venture into the complex through its open gate and look for even more. Dave's dad was not entirely excited about this, but having become aware of our general disregard for our own safety, he let us go without much complaint.

Wandering around the grounds of the Polo Grounds Towers, it was obvious that visitors inside the gate were somewhat rarer than those who had just decided to take a picture by the sign out front and drive away. It was immediately obvious to everyone we saw that we didn't belong here. But after we held up the video camera and pointed to our shirts with the unmistakable depiction of a baseball field, most of our encounters turned helpful and silently pointed deeper into the complex, as if we didn't speak the

We stumbled across this plaque memorializing the old ballpark known as the Polo Grounds deep inside the Polo Grounds Towers apartment project.

same language. Receiving this guidance, Ron, Dave, and I became more excited about what we might find, and sure enough near the center of the complex we came upon a plaque just to the left of the entrance to one of the towers. The marker commemorated the spot where home plate had stood. We were ecstatic and took turns standing next to that spot and looking out toward the field as if we were about to hit one over the 440-foot monster in center field, even though we weren't sure in which direction center field actually was.

After finding the plaque, which we were sure had been seen by very few who didn't actually live in the Polo Grounds Towers, we stumbled around the rest of the complex, looking for what I am not sure, maybe a commemoration to that memorable outfield wall, maybe for some painted bases to run around, like those we had seen at Fulton County. As far as the ballpark goes, we didn't find anything else of note, but we did run into a group of eight locals who were about our age and were particularly interested in what we were doing in their neighborhood. They were obviously used to being in control of their province, and I sensed in Dave a slight worry that all of that advice about wandering around the neighborhood that we had cavalierly disregarded probably wasn't so bad after all. When we told them about our trip, however, their interrogative tone lightened. True to my original assumption, the locals really did respect the sanctity of the ballpark and our trip. They even invited us to get their none-too-friendly dog on video. They were not, however, very excited when I pointed the camera in their general direction.

In the end, maybe my disappointment about these historic neighborhoods was unfounded. In the socioeconomic state that we live in, if it weren't the grounds of these former ball fields that housed the projects, then the projects would most certainly have made their name elsewhere. They wouldn't have been named after old ball fields for sure, and they may or may not have had a local elementary school named after Jackie Robinson. But the only substantial difference would have been that I would have never seen them, and that one less kid would have had the opportunity to be inspired by Jackie Robinson.

At the end of the day we dropped Ron off. It was a little sad to see him go. He had been a great spark to motivate Dave and me when we had gotten a little sick of being around each other. And after his departure the trip dynamic was destined to change again. We were traveling with Dave's dad through Detroit, which meant that we were going to be living on his dime and in luxurious style compared to what we were accustomed. It also meant though, that I was going to be twice as likely to grow tired of the Kaval family garrulousness.

16

Three Rivers stadium

pittsburgh

O N SUNDAY evening we headed out of New York. Not wanting to pay an arm and a leg to stay there through the night and realizing we would be back in a week, we decided to get out of town and into Pennsylvania. We spent a quiet night in Harrisburg, 168 miles outside of New York and 204 miles from our next stop in Pittsburgh, and then awoke early for a busy schedule on Monday.

Pennsylvania is always depicted as a steel state, which had long ago given me a vision of rusted metal structures everywhere. Subsequently, as we drove through, I was startled to find, hidden between Pittsburgh and Philadelphia, a lush countryside complete with rolling hills, quaint houses, and trees that already hinted of their autumn colorings despite the raging heat of summer. The entire scene forced a sense of serenity on me. We seemed to have crossed some sort of border into the peaceful, relaxed Midwest. It was a part of the country that I had heretofore spent very little time in but nonetheless spoke to me as the home of a simpler kind of life.

Given this sense of serenity, I felt somewhat unfazed by our hectic schedule for the first time since we had hit the road. I also seemed to have finally recovered from the sleep deprivation the drive had dragged me through. Dave and I both were finally getting into that groove of driving all night, rolling into a new city in the afternoon, learning what we could about the area, and then catching a ballgame that evening. I was even oblivious to the continuous chatter between Dave and his dad, optimistic that things would go smoothly over the rest of the trip for the first time since San Diego. Temporarily relinquishing financial, navigational, and transportation concerns, I even felt a little like I was on vacation.

On our way to Three Rivers, we had another bonus trip, a guided tour of the site of yet another demolished former major league park. This time it was Forbes Field, the site of Bill Mazeroski's famous home-run shot to win the 1960 World Series.

On this historical tour, we were honored with accompaniment and commentary from local baseball historian Frank Boslett. Frank was a small bespectacled man, the kind of guy who had obviously loved sports from an early age. He reminded me of Dave in his zeal for spectatorship and ballpark trivia. He was particularly passionate about Pittsburgh sports, and he knew everything about Forbes Field.

The site itself was a little more pleasant to visit than the two ruins we had visited in New York. The actual home plate of the stadium is preserved under glass inside an administrative building of the University of Pittsburgh, which expanded over the grounds of the stadium after it was demolished in 1970. Part of the outfield wall still winds through the university courtyard surrounding the library. The brick wall is still draped with ivy, although not as thickly as at Wrigley, and even the intermittent yellow distance markers have been preserved. It is these markers that do the most to give a feel for what Forbes was all about. The numbers 457, 436, 416 make it quite obvious that this was not a home-run hitter's park, and witnessing these dimensions it becomes abundantly clear why nobody is going to break any triples records anytime soon.

In what was once the left center field portion of the wall, a plaque hangs to commemorate Mazeroski's historic shot. And somehow knowing that it traveled some 400 feet, a gaping chasm by modern standards, manages to make that feat somehow more impressive.

Despite all of these mementos, though, it was still hard to imagine a lot about the old park. There were just too many obstructions. Standing at home plate, inside the university building, and looking out toward the playing field, you are confronted by a huge wall that shatters your imagination. I imagined that these few symbols of the old park, the plate, and the wall best served as shorthand reminders of the essence of the park for those who had been there before, like the man who could still see Aaron's shot leaving Fulton County. I wondered if in thirty years Dave and I might make another trip, this time visiting the remains of the thirty parks we had seen the first time through. And if we did, would all of those experiences come rushing back?

In the end, of the ballpark remnants we had seen, I preferred our visit to the totally unhistorical Fulton County Stadium where the old baselines are painted on the parking lot and the section of the fence still stands where Aaron hit number 715. Not to slight

Forbes, we appreciated the tour, particularly seeing it through the eyes of someone who had seen Babe Ruth leave his mark on the place. I knew he could still see the glimmer in the Babe's eye. I wished I could.

After the tour of Forbes, we took leave of Frank and were escorted to Three Rivers by Tom Moran, Dave's dad's contact who had set us up with the Forbes experience. He had contacts at Three Rivers also, so he took us over there to visit the Steelers' offices in the underbelly of the stadium. For those who don't know, the Pittsburgh Steelers also play at Three Rivers.

There we mostly sat in the waiting room and looked at a lot of Steelers memorabilia from their four Super Bowl titles. It was 2 P.M. when we got to the park and 2:05 when we finished with the Steelers waiting room. And so, given another three hours until we were expected by the stadium's baseball personnel, we promptly left and took Tom home to his high-rise apartment, which was just across the river from the park. Since it was a prime location, he invited us up and gave us an overhead view of not just Three Rivers but also the sites where they were building the new side-by-side baseball and football facilities for the Pirates and Steelers.

Three Rivers Stadium

CHICAGO (NL) V PITTSBURGH

Game Time: 7:05 P.M.

As our trip to Three Rivers neared, I flashed back to the only other time I had been to the park, nine years earlier. My dad and I were making a trip to North Carolina, and as was the norm, we turned the trip into an excuse to watch the Astros. So we traveled to Carolina by way of Pittsburgh, where our beloved Astros were playing a midweek series. Dad and I arrived late on a Tuesday night, and the trip from the airport to our motel was totally unnoteworthy, with our passing by a series of nondescript residential communities, office buildings, and factories that I presumed were steel mills. The next day we had planned to tour around the city before our evening game, with our first stop being any restaurant. We must have driven around for hours looking for food to no avail. We went without breakfast. Then we decided to head closer to the park, check out the sights, get some lunch maybe, and head to the ballpark around six o'clock. In short order, though, we could find nothing of interest in the town, no landmarks, no restaurants. We showed up at the ballpark at four, walked around and around the parking lot, where there were at least a couple of cool statues, and zipped through the gates an hour and a half later when they finally opened. We shoved down three hot dogs apiece, which were actually quite good, and took our seats to await the game, finding nothing else of interest to check out at the ballpark that day. The Astros won the game, during which we did get to meet Glenn Davis's sister, who was sitting just behind us and also had shown up somewhat early and found apparently nothing to do in Pittsburgh either. It was probably the worst baseball trip experience I had ever had. And with such memories, I headed to the stadium with Dave and his dad.

Compared to my earlier trip to Pittsburgh, this one had already proved much more eventful by way of the Forbes excursion alone. Once inside the park, we were treated similarly to more such experiences. We had a tour of the park (once again by the concessionaires and not the team or stadium operators), which again seemed to fly by because, like most multipurpose stadiums, this one had very few eye-catching amenities such as the newer parks boasted.

The most striking characteristic of the park in my eyes was its devotion to the Steelers. Even during baseball season the decorum was split almost right down the middle between Pirates signs and banners and Steelers paraphernalia. Thus Three Rivers gave the distinct impression that it was first and foremost a football stadium, which goes along with the preconceived notion that this was first and foremost a football town.

But while the sightseeing part of our tour was uneventful, the food tasting was memorable. By far the best thing the stadium had going for it was the AstroTurf . . . er . . . the food, specifically the Quaker Steak and Lube hot wings, which came in a variety of styles. They were among the best wings I have ever had, rivaling anything coming out of Chicago, and consequently were one of the best ballpark foods we had on the trip. This being the Midwest, too, the beer was always cold and domestic, which added to the experience.

We kept expecting the Steelers to arrive and play a game at Three Rivers since the park felt so much more like their home rather than the Pirates'.

The food almost swayed me into being a fan of the stadium until my opinions were overpowered by the turf. Three Rivers planted turf in the 1970s when it proved to be much cheaper and easier to maintain than grass. And although many of the other ballparks have gone back to grass after the pursuant public uproar over this slight to the good name of baseball, the folks in Pittsburgh, like the ever popular decision-makers in Cincinnati, have stuck with turf. You can't blame them really, the extra handful of fans that grass might draw out to the otherwise unspectacular ballpark certainly wouldn't spend enough to make economic sense of expensively resodding the field several times a year as they do in St. Louis and Kansas City.

Other than the supreme sin of AstroTurf outdoors, I didn't mind the stadium at all. If you get a good seat (and there are plenty available) the sightlines are fine, and it has the best legroom in the major leagues (particularly important to me). It actually felt more inviting and in much better shape than Shea, and this would have become a highlight of the park if some of the locals had joined us. Although I might have expected to feel a letdown going from forty thousand and more screaming fans at both Camden and Shea to the less vocal bunch of twelve thousand we encountered in Pittsburgh, it was actually quite refreshing. Reminiscent of the crowds in Miami and Houston, this one had been drawn to the park by baseball, not by hype or Beanie Babies. That being the case, the experience felt true to the sport. And it was exciting for once to see more people in the stands than in line to get food. Even though I would not have blamed them for going back for more of those spicy ranch buffalo wings.

Given that the Pirates were the home team, we were surprised by how exciting the game was, although Dave was apparently more excited over meeting the Pirates' Parrot mascot before the game. The Pirates weren't as bad as they had been made out to be, and this bunch of no-names really took it to the Cubbies. They were the best $9 million ball club I had ever seen, which is not saying much. But at the very least they had consistently outperformed the big-dollar Orioles for the last few years. Oddly, the scattering of what had seemed to us to be very knowledgeable fans that the Pirates drew was quite muted. We were rooting for the Pirates more than anybody else in the stadium. I chalked it up as quiet desperation given the team's hopeless situation. I couldn't take it out on them; they deserved credit just for showing up.

All in all, the stadium would be fine if they just got rid of the turf, but that is a moot point anyway. Three Rivers—just behind 3Com, the Kingdome, and the Astrodome—is among the stadiums that we saw on our trip whose baseball days were numbered. And having seen the plans for the new park, I am sure they will latch into the Camden buzz and draw twenty-something thousand on a regular basis. That would bring a better team, which would undoubtedly make most of these jaded fans happy. But I wonder if any of them, like me, worry about the fact that baseball parks are turning less into a place to watch baseball and more into simply a place to be. Will baseball be forever lost to those who don't understand the infield fly rule and don't care?

Three Rivers stadium

CITY: Pittsburgh, Pennsylvania

TENANT: Pittsburgh Pirates, Pittsburgh Steelers of the National Football League

OPENED: July 16, 1970

NICKNAME/ALIASES: none

DESIGN: Multipurpose stadium (initially football only), circular design, movable seats. SISTER PARKS: Shea Stadium, Candlestick Park, Fulton County Stadium, Veterans Stadium, and Riverfront Stadium.

FIELD: AstroTurf with mound and base cutouts, newly laid after the 1996 season

DIMENSIONS (feet): left field—335, left center—375, center field—400, right center—375, right field—335

FENCES (feet): 10

LOCATION: 600 Stadium Circle, Pittsburgh, PA 15212. BOUNDED BY: First base (W): Allegheny Ave., the union of the three rivers. Third base (N): Reedsdale St. Left field (E): I-279. Right field (S): N. Shore Ave. and the Allegheny River.

CAPACITY: 47,687 (baseball). Total attendance: 1,560,950 (1998). Average attendance: 19,270 (1998).

PARKING: $7–$10

TICKETS: $6–20. BEST BANG FOR YOUR BUCK: Pittsburgh has some of the best-priced seats in baseball. Splurge on the $20 tickets, which are as close as you will get to the action and relatively easy to come by.

THE BALLPARK EXPERIENCE: Although situated in downtown Pittsburgh, Three Rivers Stadium seemed set apart from its surroundings. Like the Ballpark in Arlington, Three Rivers rose above the surrounding landscape and parking lots. As we approached the park, it seemed much larger than anything else on the north side of the Allegheny River. The beautiful backdrop of the three rivers joining and the new-age skyline of downtown Pittsburgh provided a nice setting for a park. Unfortunately though, the concrete jungle of a parking lot that surrounded the stadium prevented it from blending into this setting. This lack of cohesiveness even more than the park's apparent devotion to foot-

The home-run race was heating up and all the talk that summer was of Sammy Sosa and Mark McGwire. Pittsburgh was our first encounter with either of the stars. Unfortunately, no homers for Sammy that day.

ball was the stadium's biggest drawback. The park was the antithesis of the classic Wrigley, Fenway, Camden connection between neighborhood and park.

On top of its poor synergy, Three Rivers' theme of concrete overpowered the visitor and gave the place a dull and lifeless feel, which had been exacerbated by the lack of fans at most Pirates games over the last five years. Architecturally, the park was a mirror of its cousins in Cincinnati, Philadelphia, and New York (Shea Stadium). This did little to give the park a sense of uniqueness and instead it had the same flaws as those stadiums of impersonality and seats far from the action. Given the Steelers' hordes of fans, I imagine that this park did have quite a character during football season, but in the middle of summer it is a sleeping giant.

FANS: Pittsburgh is a football town. The Steelers won four NFL championships in the 1970s with a gritty defense that reflected the character of the city. This same blue-collar character makes baseball in Pittsburgh an afterthought at times. Come September, most fans are ready for the Steelers' opener instead of a postseason appearance by the Pirates.

Nevertheless, Pittsburgh does have a long history with baseball. From Honus Wagner at the turn of the century to Bill Mazeroski's famous home run in game seven of the 1960 World Series, the Pittsburgh residents have had many reasons to be Pirates fans. And from our run-ins in the stands, it seems that the Pirates' success in the past has created a group, albeit a small one, of very knowledgeable fans who have followed baseball year in and year out. It is too bad that since the 1994 strike these fans have had very little to watch on the field.

FACILITIES: For a park of its era, Three Rivers Stadium was in good condition with wide concourses and adequate facilities. The restrooms and concession stands were a bit dated but served their purpose fine. Also, the seats had been widened in the past several years and pushed farther apart to give more legroom, which we definitely appreciated.

FOOD: Three Rivers Stadium had one of the best food items we tasted in the major leagues. This was the Quaker Steak and Lube hot wings featured at the Headwaters River Pub at Gate C. They served the widest selection of wings in existence: hot wings, super-hot wings, atomic wings, and even ranch-style wings. We loved the ranch-style wings and the hot wings, which earn their name. If you get a chance to taste them, don't pass them up. They are expensive but worth it. LAST CALL: Alcohol was served until the middle of the seventh inning.

GREAT PLAYERS AND HISTORIC MOMENTS: The Pirates have one of the richest histories of any ball club, although most of that came from the Forbes Field days, including Mazeroski's walk-off homer in game seven of the 1960 World Series. As for Three Rivers, believe it

BAT INFO

FINAL SCORE: Pirates 6, Cubs 2

OUR SEATS: Section 22, Row D, Seats 5–6

BALLPARK: 16 of 30

DAY: 24 of 30

MILES TRAVELED: 425 (9,245 total)

NEW STATES: 4 (Delaware, New Jersey, New York, Pennsylvania; 20 total)

OUR EXPENSES: $53
McDonald's $8
programs $8
gas $37
EXPENSES TO DATE: $1,732

OUR FREEBIES: $160
game tickets and parking $40
ballpark food—wings, hot dogs, beer, soda, and ice cream sandwiches (courtesy of Aramark) $60
hotel room (courtesy of Mr. Kaval) $60
FREEBIES TO DATE: $2,694

or not, Roberto Clemente did play here. You might think an icon of pure baseball would never set foot in such an antiseptic stadium, but he played his last two seasons here and even got his three-thousandth and last hit in this park. He also led the Pirates to a World Series championship in 1971. Other great players on these championship teams included home-run-producing Willie Stargell, reliever Dave Giusti, and slugger Dave Parker. There have also been two All-Star Games here in 1974 and 1994.

BALLPARK HISTORY: Three Rivers Stadium was built to replace the aging Forbes Field as well as to provide a new home for the Steelers. A new multipurpose stadium was proposed in 1958 near the spot where the Allegheny and Monongahela Rivers join to form the Ohio and near the Pirates' old Exposition Park, where they played from 1891 to 1909. After choosing the site, numerous holdups prevented construction for ten years, then once the city broke ground on the $40 million project there were further delays that pushed the opening date into the 1970 season. The Pirates christened Three Rivers on July 16, 1970. The design of the park was in the exact mold of the other multipurpose parks of the day, including Veterans Stadium in Philadelphia, Riverfront Stadium in Cincinnati, and Fulton County Stadium. And like its sisters, this park's days are numbered. A new football facility is being built next door and a new park for the Pirates, dubbed PNC Park, opens in April 2001 on the north shore of the Allegheny River.

FUN FACTS: Part of the left field wall from Forbes Field is on display in the Allegheny Club.

THE ONE THING YOU SHOULD HAVE DONE AT THREE RIVERS STADIUM AND WHY: Visit the Roberto Clemente statue on the west side of the stadium. In our opinion, the larger-than-life statue is one of the best in the major leagues. It sits in the middle of a miniature baseball diamond with bases that mention highlights of Clemente's career.

LASTING IMPRESSION: Three Rivers did a poor job disguising its real role as the home of the Steelers.

17
jacobs
field
cleveland

IN LINE with our standard practice, we drove through the night after the Pirates game to get to Cleveland. Being that two of us were Indians fanatics, we had to go straight to the park to pay homage to the structure that single-handedly turned around baseball in Cleveland. Although I had never admitted it to Dave, I was worried that Jacobs was going to be just like all of the other new ballparks, and like Coors Field and the Ballpark in Arlington, would ultimately prove undistinguished. Granted, the tour we had just finished through Three Rivers had proved that this new wave of ballparks represents a marked improvement in many cases, and there was reason to look forward to a new park in Pittsburgh if only because it meant a chance at a contending team. But all these new stadiums were supposed to have a mystique about them that makes the game a little more magical, and I was getting a little depressed realizing that a stadium can't be built and transform the game just like that, no matter how beautiful it is. Even though the new parks are unmistakably beautiful, with each one I sense a sort of ballpark pollution. The real fans are being crowded out by those with too much disposable income and nothing better to do. The sightlines are better and you get closer to the action, but the distraction of forty thousand people getting up to buy more microbrew or chatting about their jobs makes it hard to focus on baseball in these quaint little stadiums. Not that I'm not just like the other forty thousand in my interest in good beer and casual conversation (after all, the laid-back pace and sociable atmosphere are among baseball's key attributes), but when there are so many people so close together with so little interest in baseball, the experience suffers, at least for those who come to watch the game.

More so than the distractions of the new stadiums though, coming into Cleveland I was worried about the unfailing similarity among the Camdenesque parks. Was Jacobs going to be just like Camden and Arlington? Was the notion of ballpark originality dead?

Our trip by Jacobs that night did not really paint my feelings for it either way, although one thing was obviously clear. It was not like all of the other parks, at least in one respect. This park was white. All white steel on the outside. A change at least, but it still remained to be seen if the white steel held up against the standard brown-brick motif better than the blue seats in Atlanta fared against the green standard. That would be determined when we were there in daylight, as would the conclusion about whether Jacobs had its own atmosphere or just reflected Camden's light.

The next day we awoke to a busy schedule that started with Dave's mother cooking us a huge breakfast. Dave's mom fits perfectly in the mold of a doting mother, always within earshot when you are in the house and always offering some other helpful hint as to what Dave and his friend might want to do this afternoon or tomorrow. We had no time to take any of her advice though, because immediately after we put our food down we had to head off for the offices of the *Cleveland Plain Dealer,* where we were to be interviewed by Dave's hometown paper and were surely to become local celebrities.

Our interviewer was Bill Miller, a large man with classic German features who knew absolutely nothing about baseball except that it was a sport and Cleveland had a team. How he ever decided to write an article on us, I'm not sure, but he was very interested in our trip, particularly in the human-interest angle, an angle that we didn't even know existed. He listened with rapt attention as we described our exploits to date, particularly keen on figuring out what beers we had been drinking all over the country. He was disappointed though to learn that neither of us had yet sampled his favorite brew from the motherland, Warsteiner. We promised that we would get to that as soon as possible. He pledged that he would write a nice article about us.

After that, our third newspaper interview (to go with three radio and television interviews and two television appearances), we stopped by Dave's place again to play some yard ball on the tennis courts and then headed into downtown. After a quick stop at Dave's barber so that we could get a much needed trim, we met up with Dave's dad and took a specially arranged tour of the stadium.

Jacobs Field

· ·

NEW YORK (AL) V CLEVELAND

Game Time: 7:05 P.M.

OUR TOUR of the Jake gave us a chance to experience every aspect of the stadium from the luxury boxes to the batting cages, where we saw Shawon Dunston throwing batting practice to his son. In line with my earlier expectations, the resemblances between Jacobs and all of the new ballparks are unmistakable. Of course, the obvious argument for the new stadiums would be to question why you wouldn't have all of the desired ballpark amenities if you were building a new stadium. And I would probably agree that you should, which is why Jacobs is stuck in this Catch-22. To their credit though, the Jacobs team manages to give the ballpark at least something of its own feel and capture whatever mystique a four-year-old stadium can.

As far as the white steel exterior goes, I never thought I could appreciate steel so much. It is the kind of touch to a stadium that is truly inimitable, because it is so conspicuous and original, like the Green Monster in Fenway. If anyone copied it, their derivativity would likely be mercilessly criticized. The design gets bonus points because it is additionally nice to look at. The toothbrush-shaped light standards, although Dave talks about them too much, are also a nice touch. The interior is nice and intimate, and the green seating is the part of the park that most resembles the rest of the new wave of ballparks. But even there, the decision-makers decided, for no apparent reason, to go with black dirt on the infield, which in addition to the white steel, really plays up the fact that these guys wanted something unique. And again, the dirt, although it is eye-catching and somewhat confusing, doesn't make you stop and scratch your head the way the palm trees in the outfield in San Diego or any of the other gimmicks for gimmicks' sake throughout the majors do. It deserves applause because it is distinctive, yet obviously inspired by that touch of whimsy that feels absent from the calculated design of a place like Coors Field. It just makes you take note again that Jacobs is different, and it makes you notice everything else about the park a little bit more.

All in all though, I think what I liked most about the entire park, although it was undeniably classic baseball, is that there was nothing in the whole stadium that Dave could latch onto and describe as reminding him of the rotunda at Ebbets Field.

After the tour, rather than exerting any more effort, we decided to barhop a little until the game. So we stopped at a little bar called Fishbone, just across the street from the Jake. We sat at the bar, and after we stopped staring at our bartender, who can only be described as Pamela Anderson with a winning personality, we ordered a couple of

Dave (pictured here with his dad) always spoke highly of his hometown ballpark, which ended up second only to Camden Yards in our rankings of the new ballparks.

Warsteiners and a shot of Jaegermeister. We even gave Bill Miller a call to let him know what we thought about his beer. For the record, it wasn't bad, although it seemed to be something of a paradox being a German light beer. The Fishbone experience was relaxing and noteworthy to me as the first time Dave and his dad had slowed down enough to have a relaxed conversation, but we couldn't stay at Fishbone forever.

We managed to finagle a couple of passes to the exclusive Terrace Club on the third-base side of the suite level of Jacobs. Actually, Dave's parents had finagled the passes for us at some charity auction and paid quite a pretty penny to give us such a privilege.

At the Terrace Club, which is obviously intended for people a lot richer than I will ever be, the prime rib and seafood were excellent. We had more fun with the open bar though, and much of the reason for that is that we were treated very well by our waitress, Vanessa, even though she could certainly tell that we didn't belong there. Vanessa may have pegged us as bad tippers, but I hope we surprised her.

She was very colorful herself and came up with some creative ideas about things we should try to take in on our trip but which cannot be reprinted here. She also invited us to come out with her and her friends after the game. Dave declined. Out of steadfast loyalty to his girlfriend, he was uncomfortable around Vanessa. I didn't have the heart to tell him that he wasn't the one she was hitting on.

Once again, we got around to the afterthought that was the baseball game. In this case, there is truly no better way to describe the game we saw than as an afterthought. The Tribe got spanked by their nemesis, the Yankees, 7-1. Dave assured me that the crowd's lackluster response was due only to the play on the field. I believe him, too, because when the Indians threatened to close the gap to five, you could feel that the crowd really wanted to come alive. I should also note that mustard in and of itself seems to be something of a local specialty food in Cleveland, and Stadium Mustard is a very good thing. Get your hands on it if you can.

Somewhere about the seventh inning, we gave up on the action on the field (to notice how my commitment to diligently watching the baseball on the field waned over the course of the trip, see the San Francisco, L.A., and Colorado chapters) and headed back to the Terrace Club. After the game was over though, they kicked us out of there, and we went out to a few bars in Cleveland.

Dave really wanted to show off his town, and we hadn't really relaxed and unwound since that monumental Tampa Bay–Baltimore drive, so it seemed like a good idea. Unfortunately, though, the town was pretty dead on this Tuesday night. Nonetheless, Dave would like it to be duly noted that, although Midwest women get a bad rap, there are attractive women in Cleveland. I make no promises about Pittsburgh though. They also had this good local brew, Crooked River Dortmunder something or other. And that's all I can say about Cleveland, at least in the pages of this book.

The Indians fans packed the house as the Tribe took on the Yankees, but many of them had left by the time this picture was taken amidst a 7-1 drumming by the New York squad.

Jacobs Field

CITY: Cleveland, Ohio

TENANT: Cleveland Indians

OPENED: April 4, 1994

NICKNAME/ALIASES: The Jake

DESIGN: Baseball-only stadium, asymmetric design, no movable seats. SISTER PARKS: Camden Yards, the Ballpark in Arlington, Coors Field.

FIELD: Grass. (NOTE: Jacobs Field has one of the most unique infields in baseball. Made from a combination of dirt and kitty litter, the Jake's infield is much darker than the brown dirt in traditional parks.)

DIMENSIONS (feet): left field—325, left center—370, deep left center—410, center field—405, right center—375, right field—325

FENCES (feet): left field—19, center and left field—8, right field corner—14. BOUNDED BY: Right field (NE): E. 9th St. First-base line (SE): Carnegie Ave. Third-base line (SW): Broadway and Ontario. Left field (NW): E. Huron St.

CAPACITY: 43,368. Total attendance: 3,466,399 (1998). Average attendance: 42,806 (1998).

PARKING: $7–$10. While it is an urban complex, the designers of the Gateway sports complex included a large parking structure across the street from the park. These spots along with the many smaller garages along Ninth Street are affordable and convenient.

TICKETS: $6–35. BEST BANG FOR YOUR BUCK: The best value seats are the bleachers in left field. The fans are lively and always into the game and there is a good chance of getting at least one home-run ball in your section. Also, sitting here means that you can loiter around the plaza near the foul pole in left field. (This is what Dave evidently did in high school.) That area is full of concessionaires, fans, and people leaning over the railing and watching the game. The plaza is a little like Eutaw Street at Camden Yards but closer to the field.

THE BALLPARK EXPERIENCE: As we walked up to Jacobs Field on game day, there was an energy around us that sent a tingle down our spines. Jacobs Field is a living park. More than any other, this park saved baseball in its city. The fans know it, the players know it, and the park knows it.

The park is set perfectly in downtown Cleveland with views of new skyscrapers as well as old steel mills near the Cuyahoga River and is a bridge between the blue-collar steel town that Cleveland used to be and the new immaculate city it has become. The white steel structure of the park surrounds a light-colored brick-and-granite frame that matches the new city, while the two-hundred-foot-high light standards above the upper deck hearken back to the smokestacks of the city's industrial past. The exposed steel girders throughout the park—especially the ones in crisscross design along the lower levels—mimic the many bridges that span the Cuyahoga River.

At Dave's suggestion, we entered the park near the bleachers in left field at Gate A. There is a great view of the sunken field from the plaza above the wall in left field. You can also watch the game from this perch and try to catch home-run balls. Similar to the grassy batter's eye in Arlington, this area is a flurry of activity when a home-run ball is hit in its direction. And one level above on the right, our beloved Terrace Club hangs with its large glass windows and great views of the action.

FANS: If there was one set of fans that I got to know on the trip, it was Tribe fans. I spent every day with a die-hard Tribe fan in Dave, and when you added the rest of the Kaval family, this reached an almost unbearable level of Tribe enthusiasm. From Dave's accounts, Cleveland Indians fans have gone through a roller-coaster experience throughout the century in their love for the Tribe. Overall, the city has a rich sports history with extremely loyal fans. The Indians developed such a loyalty early on with a string of early greats such as Cy Young, Tris Speaker, Lou Boudreau, and Bob Feller. But after 1954, when the fortunes of the Indians took a dramatic turn for the worse (often attributed to the "curse of Rocky Colavito," named after the Indians slugger who was traded just before the team sank into despair), attendance dropped off considerably. From 1969 to 1989 the Indians finished in the bottom half of the AL East every year (seven times dead-last), and often the club failed to pull seven thousand fans into cavernous Cleveland Stadium. But since the team's low point, which coincided with the memorialization of their futility in the movie *Major League,* their performance and the city's image have consistently improved in lock-step. This culminated with the opening of Jacobs Field, which has been filled every night for the last 454 home games by a mix of the blue-collar fans of the old city and the new white-collar transplants who have quickly taken to the team.

FACILITIES: Jacobs Field has world-class facilities. The concessions along the first-base line and in right field are set in the middle of the large concourses and are two-sided so that fans can see the action when ordering—a nice touch that we saw nowhere else. Not to be outdone by any of the other new parks, Jacobs pioneered the emphasis on pointing every seat in the park directly toward the battery.

FOOD: We enjoyed the outstanding variety of food at Jacobs Field. The park offers all the staples plus a full deli, a bakery, microbrew stands, full-scale chicken and ribs BBQ, and even a pierogi stand. Pierogies are dumplings served with virtually anything inside (meat and jelly are the top choices). We liked them though Dave boasted that his grandmother's pierogies were much better than the ones at the Jake. Spicy brown mustard is also a specialty food in Cleveland. Known simply as Stadium Mustard, as popularized at the old Cleveland Stadium, the rich brown condiment is perfect on the standard hot dog or the super pretzel. Dave swears by the mustard, and to this day whenever I go over to his place he serves contraband Stadium Mustard from the park. LAST CALL: Alcohol is served until the middle of the seventh inning.

GREAT PLAYERS AND HISTORIC MOMENTS: Great players that have called Jacobs Field home include Albert Belle, Carlos Baerga, Kenny Lofton, Dennis Martinez, Jim Thome, and Manny Ramirez. While only six years old, Jacobs Field has seen a lifetime worth of postseason play. It has seen more postseason action than Cleveland Municipal Stadium saw in over fifty years. The 1995 and 1997 World Series were played at the Jake, with the Indians dropping both series, first to the Atlanta Braves and then to the Florida Marlins in a heartbreaking extra-inning seventh game. These two losses in the World Series in 1995 and 1997 leave fans (read Dave and his family) waiting for their first championship since 1948.

BALLPARK HISTORY: After 1932 the Cleveland Indians played their games at Cleveland Municipal Stadium, a monolith of a park that was built solely with public money in the depths of the Depression to lure the 1932 Olympic Games. Of course, Cleveland never hosted an Olympics, but they did find themselves with a new ballpark. By the mid-1980s, the old park had become extremely run down (Dave talks about this all the time). This, combined with the unsuitable nature of the park for baseball (over eighty thousand seats, obstructed views, cold windy weather), prompted the city to consider building a new park. Finally, in 1990, the $362 million Gateway project was passed, which included a baseball-only park for downtown Cleveland and a new arena for the Cleveland Cavaliers. Construction began in 1992 with a design similar to the successful Camden Yards in Baltimore. The same architects, HOK Sport out of Kansas City, were used. The park opened in 1994 with much fanfare and attendance skyrocketed. The park was a representation of a new Cleveland: a successful city that had risen from the soot and ashes of its rust belt roots. Unfortunately, the strike-lockout of 1994 put a downer on the park's inaugural season. But unlike other places, attendance since the strike has been stellar in Cleveland.

FUN FACT: The home opener in 1996 was snowed out—there was so much snow that the players made a snowman on the pitcher's mound.

THE ONE THING YOU HAVE TO DO AT JACOBS FIELD AND WHY: Listen for John Adams, the Indians' drummer. For years John has been lugging his huge drum (the Indians had to remove a railing in the last row of the bleachers so that John could fit his large drum next to him) to the games first at Municipal Stadium and then at Jacobs Field. When the Tribe starts a rally or needs an out, you will hear John start the drum. Slowly then faster then a pause right before the pitch. Over and over the drum will sound, filling the Jake with its war cry.

OTHER THINGS TO REMEMBER: Although there are ramps that can take fans up and down from the upper deck, the stairs are a much faster way out of the park after a game. The ramps have a very small pitch, and it can take a solid ten minutes to navigate while the stairs are much quicker and take more like three minutes. Seven minutes may not sound like much, but it can be all the difference in beating the traffic out of town.

LASTING IMPRESSION: The most unique of Camden's successors, fitting perfectly into the Cleveland's new downtown.

BAT INFO

FINAL SCORE: Yankees 7, Indians 1

OUR SEATS: Section 163, Row FF, Seats 7–8

BALLPARK: 17 of 30

DAY: 25 of 38

MILES TRAVELED: 30 (9,275 total)

NEW STATES: 1 (Ohio; 21 total)

OUR EXPENSES: $48
Fishbone $20
programs $8
the Flats $20
EXPENSES TO DATE: $1,780

OUR FREEBIES: $160
Dave's mom's home-cooked meal (courtesy of the Kavals) $10
game tickets and ballpark food—prime rib, perogies, hot dogs with Stadium Mustard, beer, Jaegermeister (courtesy of the Kavals) $100
lodging (courtesy of the Kavals) $50
FREEBIES TO DATE: $2,854

18

Tiger stadium

Detroit

THE NEXT afternoon, we left town for Detroit. For the first time since Seattle, we were not traveling in my black Nissan Pathfinder. She had logged seventy-seven hundred miles, so we decided to give her a break and left her in the Kavals' garage. Dave and I moved instead to his mom's cozier Dodge Intrepid, which would take us on a four-day circuit through Detroit, Chicago, St. Louis, and Cincinnati. After that we planned to make a midnight swap in Cleveland to Dave's uncle's Jeep Cherokee, which would cycle us through all of the East Coast cities we'd missed the first time through. Then we would hit Cleveland for the last time and get back to my car.

The Intrepid was smaller than the Pathfinder, but Dave and I would be mostly alone through Cincy, so we didn't anticipate problems. For the time being though, we were not alone but part of a two-car caravan that added Dave's dad, uncle, and brother Junior and one of Junior's friends.

Before we left Cleveland, we made our fourth and final visit to baseball's past, this time the site of League Park, the original home of the Indians. League Park is where the Tribe played before Municipal Stadium was built in 1932, and in all honesty, although I think of myself as a baseball aficionado, I admit that I had never heard of League Park until that morning. Regardless of that, it was a pretty cool trip, because the field was the most intact of the retired parks we had visited. The concrete slabs of the original stands still stand outside a chain-link fence that houses a multiplex of Little League fields. It was a bit daunting when I realized that this park opened in 1891 and was christened by Cy Young, then a pitcher with the Cleveland Spiders. That was impressive in itself, and that's all it takes to keep a little of the magic going. It's pitiful to think, though, that the only reason the old park's foundation still stands is because the neighborhood around it is so poor that nobody feels it would be worth the cost to demolish those slabs of cement and stone. As the president of the Society for Ballpark Preservation (I just made that up), I'll take what I can get. Besides, when else might economic woe work in your favor?

We made it the rest of the way to Detroit without incident. It was a relatively quick three-hour sprint from city to city and made me appreciate how conducive to our trip the eastern half of the country was. We arrived at Tiger Stadium at 5:30 p.m. for an evening game to see the Tigers take on the Yankees.

We seemed to be traveling with the Yankees, which was good in that they were a great team and are usually fun to watch (even if you are opposed to what they stand for, economically speaking, of course) but bad because the game is more fun if the home team can win (which wouldn't happen this time either). In fact, to say that the Yankees were great in 1998 is an understatement, because as you probably already know, the '98 Yankees were about the best team in the history of baseball. They relentlessly destroyed their opponents. It was quite painful for me, as I had always fallen in with the opinion that rooting for the Yankees is like rooting for big business. On the bright side, though, at least I can say that I was there when . . . Having been there, I know that the worst thing about watching the Yankees on the road is dealing with the Derek Jeter fan club and other such groupies. In '98 especially, people followed the Yankees around as if they were on a rock tour. This evening in Detroit, as in Tampa Bay, the Yanks again had more fans than the poorly supported home team.

Tiger Stadium

. . . .

NEW YORK (AL) V DETROIT

Game Time: 7:05 P.M.

BEYOND ANY doubt, Tiger Stadium was (not is, because they don't play there anymore) one of the classic ballparks. Being there, you could throw yourself back in time thirty, sixty, eighty years; even imagine you were at one of the long-since departed classic parks like the Polo Grounds with its cavernous expanse in center field. It made you long for the days when the home-run leader wasn't the guy who had the most power, but the lefty who played in Yankee Stadium. Although the facts have been disputed as to which park was older, Fenway or Tiger, the essence was never a contest. Tiger felt twenty years older than Fenway or Wrigley or any other park.

The only problem with Tiger Stadium, at least from management's point of view—and as we all know by now that what is bad for management is ultimately bad for the fans—was that somebody forgot to tell the people of Detroit and the rest of America that such a gem of a ballpark was sitting in Middle America. As a result, economics led to the demise of an American landmark. In my opinion, this is the greatest tragedy in baseball since the Black Sox scandal. I loved Tiger Stadium (even though I've only been there once) and hate Comerica Park (even though I've never been there).

The gripes with Tiger Stadium have generally been these: it was dirty, cavernous, and colored unsightly shades of blue and orange. Ironically, these are precisely the reasons I loved the place.

First, Tiger Stadium was easily the dirtiest ballpark in the major leagues, and this was not limited to the stands or the restrooms but included the clubhouse and the field. When we were on the field before the game and got to sit in the dugout, Dave made note of this and mentioned to Luis Gonzales (whom we met on the field and likely doesn't remember us anymore, but we will idolize him forever anyway) that it felt like the spirit of Ty Cobb was still in the dugout. Gonzo's quick rejoinder was, "Yeah, it *smells* like the spirit of Ty Cobb is still in that locker room."

Watching a game at Tiger Stadium was like watching a game in the 1910s. It's not just the feeling that you get in great parks like Fenway or Dodger, that great things have happened here. It's something much deeper that can confuse perceptions of time and space. You get that feeling because Tiger Stadium is exactly what you expect ballparks were like in the '10s and '20s, before Babe Ruth transformed the game. The days when ball players were working men and owners were cutting every corner they could just to

The exterior of Tiger Stadium was a poor indicator of the ambiance inside.

make ends meet. The park wasn't pristine, but the working men out to catch a game didn't care, nor did the boys who were skipping school to sit in the bleachers. With a little imagination you can see those guys with the straw hats everywhere. The kind of hats that you see in barbershop quartets and old pictures. Old pictures of baseball parks. There's an air of authenticity at Tiger Stadium, the kind that comes only with age. The only physical evidence of that air is a grimy, yellowed, and frayed appearance, the same sort of thing you would expect to see if you looked at the yellowed parchment of the Declaration of Independence.

The field itself embodies this authenticity with patchy grass and a pronounced crown. Most groundskeepers would cringe at the sight, but the scene generates a look of authenticity. And that's why I love the dirtiness of Tiger Stadium.

Some point out that Tiger Stadium lacks the cozy layout and feel of what many consider the truly classic parks, Wrigley and Fenway. It's true. Tiger is twice the size, holds twice as many people, is shaped roughly like a square and goes 440 feet to center field. The Lions even played football here for thirty-seven years. But the fact that everyone has not jumped on this bandwagon, that the park does not feel artificially small (see Enron), that you *can* play football out here, that's where the authenticity of this park comes from. The dimensions were not cold and calculated to be quirky for popularity's sake. They are like that because that seemed like a good idea at the time, the same reason they've got that huge wall in left field in Fenway or ended up with a hill in center at Crosley Field. That's where the aura of nostalgia comes from, this glimpse into how they used to design ballparks out of necessity rather than on a whim. The parks today will never have it, because there is too much at stake.

The last time a ballpark included something on a whim was the old warehouse at Camden. That proved so successful that every ballpark designed since then has tried to include something that approaches the whimsical, and in so doing they have only showed their artifice. Only in a place like Tiger Stadium, with its many obstructed views from the stands is it obvious that the architects weren't worried about too much except putting a place together where some people could watch baseball. They figured everything else would fall into place. It did.

Then there's the blueness of the place. Everyone these days knows that the seats in a classic park are supposed to be green—everyone but Ted Turner. What saves the blue seats here, as opposed to the lifeless ones in Atlanta, is the ever-present orangeness. Blue and orange—if that is not classically uncommercial, then I don't know what is. A friend of mine describes it as an emptied-out swimming pool motif. I agree. It's the most unique color scheme in baseball.

Tiger Stadium is the ultimate paradox in baseball. It is an accidental master stroke that blends age, odor (some might prefer *aroma*), bad sightlines, poor fan support, nosebleed seats, and a color scheme that would give a decorator a coronary into one of the most fulfilling baseball experiences of the twentieth century.

Unfortunately, no one will ever see it again. If you ever witnessed a game here, you most likely remember it kindly. I hear that Comerica has none of the spirit of old Tiger Stadium. How could it?

When we were there we toured the place with a bunch of obnoxious Yankees fans. Actually, it was less of a tour than an escort onto the field. We were allowed to mingle with the players a little and hang out in the dugout. While most of the players were too preoccupied for us, we found at least one fan in Luis Gonzales, a.k.a. Gonzo. Meeting Gonzo was easily the highlight of the trip to Detroit. I had been a big fan of his since he played with the Astros, and he was really nice to us, demonstrating a genuine interest in our trip. In fact, although I was really excited to be in the dugouts made for little people who reeked of chewing tobacco, we had to feel for Gonzo's having to play in these conditions every day. It probably explains why he moved the next year to Arizona and the new ballpark. In short, he was the coolest guy we met on the whole trip. Dave says he's "huge" time. I guess that is bigger than big time.

As for the game, the Tigers got spanked. It wasn't even a contest, but that was immaterial. For us, it was our best baseball experience to that point of the trip. Period. The thought of it still gives me chills.

Tiger Stadium

CITY: Detroit, Michigan

TENANT: Detroit Tigers (1912–99), Detroit Lions of the National Football League (1938–74)

OPENED: April 20, 1912

CLOSED: September 27, 1999

NICKNAME/ALIASES: Navin Field (1912–37) for the former Tiger's owner, Briggs Stadium (1938–60) for the Tiger's owner, Walter Briggs.

DESIGN: Primarily baseball park, rectangular enclosed design, no movable seats. SISTER PARKS: Fenway Park in Boston, Forbes Field in Pittsburgh (razed), and League Park in Cleveland (razed).

FIELD: Bluegrass. The grass at Tiger Stadium is nothing like any we had been on at the parks in California or Florida. It was like something out of your backyard, very thick although nonetheless expertly maintained.

DIMENSIONS (feet): left field—340, left center—365, center field—420, right center—375, right field—325

Dave and I became lifetime fans of Detroit outfielder Luis Gonzalez due to his sincere interest in our trip and witty one-liners about baseball and Tiger Stadium.

FENCES (feet): 9; 5' concrete with 4' screen. There is a flagpole just left of dead center field. It is 125 feet high and in play.

LOCATION: 2121 Trumbull Ave., Detroit, MI. BOUNDED BY: Right field (NE): Trumbull Ave. Left field (NW): Kaline Dr. and I-75. Third base (SW): Cochrane Ave. First base (SE): Michigan Ave.

CAPACITY: 52,416 (baseball). Total attendance: 1,409,391 (1998). Average attendance: 17,399 (1998).

PARKING: $7–$15. Tiger Stadium is in an urban setting with little parking around the park. We chose a small pricey lot across the street from the stadium.

TICKETS: $4–20. NOTE: The Tiger Den seats featured padded seats and waiter service. The bleachers featured a different entrance, and a bleacher ticket did not allow admission to other parts of the park. BEST BANG FOR YOUR BUCK: Tiger Stadium was the only major league ballpark with double-deck bleachers in the outfield. These unique seats were a great bargain. Not only were the bleachers the closest bleacher seats in the major leagues, but they also provided a breathtaking view of the action and the park.

THE BALLPARK EXPERIENCE: Tiger Stadium felt like an old shoe. Well worn and comfortable, it was truly a window into baseball's past. Everything about the place felt unique in modern terms. The park's major black mark, though, was its white, hangar-esque exterior, which made Tiger Stadium look more like a warehouse than Bank One. You wouldn't know it was Tiger Stadium were it not for the big tiger coming out of a D insignia on the front. Also, the park was in a rundown neighborhood characterized by barred windows and liquor stores. But the park stood there as testament to the baseball of a forgotten era. The Soul Food Restaurant across the street stands in contrast as well as in harmony with the park. The park was as run down as the neighborhood.

Upon entering Tiger Stadium, visitors had to scurry through narrow passageways toward the stands. The concourses were exceedingly narrow, dirty, and cramped. We saw layers of paint chipping off of everything around us. The park is completely enclosed with two decks around the entire field. Ironically, this facet of its design resembled the cookie-cutter parks of the 1960s and '70s. As opposed to the distant feel of Veterans and Three Rivers, Tiger Stadium was the most intimate park in baseball. All the seats were close, and the park almost hung above the field. At any moment you could look up and see Ty Cobb racing around second or Babe Ruth hitting his seven-hundredth home run. The park was pure history. A throwback. A masterpiece.

FANS: We quickly found out that Detroit has a long, vibrant history of baseball. The Corner, as the intersection of Michigan and Trumbell is known, hosted professional baseball for more than one hundred years and built a fiercely loyal following in that time. The fans that we met were into the park and their team. Some of the die-hards in the second deck of the bleachers looked like they had been sitting there for fifty years.

FACILITIES: Terrible. There were not nearly enough restrooms and we all waited in lines. Seats were cramped and not directed toward the action with legroom almost as bad as the Seattle Kingdome. This just goes to show how insignificant facilities are in the grand scheme of things. These characteristics did not make a dent in our impressions of the park.

FOOD: Tiger Stadium had standard food options with a food court that gave us a decent number of choices. And given that the park was so old, the traditional food options went very well with it. Along this line, peanuts were served as the park's specialty food. Wherever you looked, there were peanut shells on the ground. Whether they ever actually cleaned the place or the shells accumulated over ninety years, I don't know, but the effect was nice anyway. LAST CALL: Alcohol was served until the middle of the seventh inning.

GREAT PLAYERS AND HISTORIC MOMENTS: Tiger Stadium saw some of the greatest players of all time compete on its diamond. The Tigers as an organization started to play in what is now known as the American League in 1901 and have one of the best overall records of any AL club. Their early history was dominated by the infamous Ty Cobb. He was a terror on the field, leading the league in batting almost every year and winning the Triple Crown in 1909. He even stole ninety-six bases in 1915, a record that stood for forty-seven years. Although the team played in three World Series from 1907 to 1909, they didn't get there in the new park until the 1930s. In 1984 the Tigers got off to a 35-5 start, the best of all time, and cruised to their fourth world championship, this time

Watching a game at Tiger Stadium was like watching a game in the 1910s. If you squint just a little, you can see Ty Cobb stealing second. We did.

over the San Diego Padres in five games. It was the Tigers' last championship at Tigers Stadium. Stars who have graced the field include Hank Greenberg, Denny McLain, and Cecil Fielder, whose fifty-one home runs in 1990 were the most in the AL since 1961. All-Star Games in '41, '51, and '71.

BALLPARK HISTORY: In 1910 Frank Navin, the new owner of the Tigers, commissioned the construction of a state-of-the-art steel-and-concrete park in the mold of recently christened Forbes Field in Pittsburgh. The park, known as Navin Field, opened for baseball on April 12, 1912, the same day Fenway Park in Boston opened its doors (and a certain oceanliner sank). Over the years, multiple additions and renovations to the ballpark created an eclectic baseball venue at the Corner. Among these renovations have been a second deck over the stands and a press box atop that deck that were added twelve years after the park opened. In the late 1930s the park was completely enclosed.

The Tigers are now at Comerica, and the move generated considerable controversy over taking the Tigers off the Corner. A plan was suggested by local fans to revitalize

Tiger Stadium by adding luxury boxes and refurbishing the park, but that plan was rejected and Comerica Park was built to house the Tigers after the 1999 season. Opponents of the new park and location claim that Tigers' management purposely oversaw the dilapidation of the park to force the city to build a new park. Old Tiger Stadium at the Corner saw its last game on September 27, 1999, ending more than one hundred years of baseball at the intersection of Michigan and Trumbell.

FUN FACT: A lighting system was installed in 1948, making it the last American League park to add lights.

THE ONE THING YOU SHOULD HAVE DONE AT TIGER STADIUM AND WHY: Appreciate the history: the truly old-fashioned double-deck stands with long overhangs, the peeling paint on the recessed dugouts that were small and cramped, and the heavy crown of the field that facilitated run-off when it rained. We lost ourselves in all of these little pleasures. It was a different way of looking at baseball. It was truly a moment of clarity. Maybe you would have seen the ghost of Ty Cobb. Dave and I did. But at the very least you would have known how it felt to sit where Babe Ruth and Ty Cobb and Walter Johnson once sat.

OTHER THINGS TO REMEMBER: Tiger Stadium was notorious for its obstructed views. The upper deck reserved (section 400) and lower deck reserved (section 200) were the worst, with seats behind the upper deck and roof supports.

LASTING IMPRESSION: A time machine into baseball's past with the most character of any park in baseball.

BAT INFO

FINAL SCORE: Yankees 11, Tigers 0

OUR SEATS: Section 131, Row 16, Seats 9–10

BALLPARK: 18 of 30

DAY: 26 of 38

MILES TRAVELED: 480 (9,755 total)

NEW STATES: 3 (Michigan, Indiana, Illinois by nightfall; 24 total)

OUR EXPENSES: $40
parking, programs, and food—hot dogs, pizza, peanuts, ice cream, and soda $40
EXPENSES TO DATE: $1,820

OUR FREEBIES: $90
lunch (courtesy of the Kavals) $10
game tickets $30
lodging (courtesy of Joe Hauler) $50
FREEBIES TO DATE: $2,944

19

comiskey
park
chicago

IMMEDIATELY AFTER the Tigers game we took off for Chicago. We said good-bye to the Kaval clan, as they were all heading back to Cleveland. We would see them again soon. Very soon.

We got out of Detroit at about 10:30 P.M. and had a 282-mile drive ahead of us. The road passed uneventfully as Dave and I had developed tremendous stamina for driving through the night.

We were staying with Dave's friend Joe Hauler in Evanston, a suburb on the North Side of Chicago. Joe had just graduated from Northwestern University and lived alone in a three-bedroom apartment. We pulled up to Joe's place around 1:45 in the morning. He was up, watching whatever was on television and eating from a wide assortment of bags of chips and cookies and ice cream sandwiches strewn about his living room. We hung out for a couple more hours, even though we had to get up (relatively) early for a day game at Comiskey on Thursday. Mostly Dave and Joe caught up on old times, their having been best friends since grade school. Eventually though, we all agreed that it would be wise to get some sleep. Joe had a job downtown that required him to be up before us. And despite the fact that there were two empty bedrooms, since Joe's room-mates had moved out for the summer, the place was so filthy, we couldn't even get into either room and probably wouldn't have been able to find anything to sleep on if we had. So we slept on the couch and some cushions in the floor. Not surprisingly, we had no trouble getting up the next morning.

comiskey park

· ·

TORONTO V CHICAGO (AL)

GAME TIME: 1:05 P.M.

HERE WAS the biggest loser of the new wave of ballparks. We had driven by Comiskey on the way into town, and it was immediately noticeable that, for a new stadium, Comiskey looked very traditional, a lot like the remodeled and unremarkable Yankee Stadium. In any case, Comiskey was the last park built before Camden Yards became a huge success and rewrote the book on how to build baseball parks. Ironically, Comiskey, which was under construction at the same time as Camden, was modeled to be not much more than a replica of its predecessor, now referred to as old Comiskey. Somehow, Comiskey came to represent the excesses and sterility of the pre-Camdenesque ballparks, even though its stated intent was to capture the magic of a nostalgic ballpark, namely, old Comiskey, and pair it with all of the amenities expected in today's era of spectatorship. Of course, Camden accomplished that. Comiskey didn't.

I imagine new Comiskey is what would have happened had Detroit tried to re-create Tiger Stadium. Although I had never been to old Comiskey, it seemed that the best thing it had going for it was age, authenticity, and the inherent nostalgia. But how can you re-create that? When you rebuild a park, you lose the age, and then you're left with nothing.

When we got to the ballpark, we had an incident with the parking attendant similar to the one we had in San Diego. We insisted that we were on the list; he insisted that we were not. His ingenious compromise was for us to pay for the parking and get reimbursed. So, of course, we were out ten bucks. Our tickets, however, were waiting for us at the gate. And when we made our way to the turnstiles, knowing that Comiskey didn't draw very well, we were surprised to see long lines waiting to get into the game. Inside we saw a very thin crowd and assumed that the ticket takers were just inefficient.

After seeing the park, although I thought it was a nice enough place, I realized why it has failed. There was nothing memorable about it. I don't have any real memories of the place. Most of the time, thinking about the park just causes me to think of Yankee Stadium, the two were so similar.

Still I want to stick up for the park. It was built the year before Camden and immediately became obsolete, but that shouldn't excuse White Sox fans (if any exist) for abandoning their team. The White Sox generally have among the lowest turnouts in the league—nineteen thousand when we were there—and it isn't much better when they are good. The upside though is that, as is the case with most of the frowned-upon ball-parks, the fans who do come out at Comiskey are baseball fans. We were the only tourists crazy enough to go there.

Despite its much derided impersonality, the park does have a couple of notable qualities. The first is that the concourses are directly above the top row of seats. As a result, it is easy to keep track of the game while you are moving about the park. Second, the park abstains from most of the catchy gimmicks that tend to cause annoyance and irritation in some of the new parks, such as the pool at Bank One. Thus it allows you to lose yourself in the game and the whole baseball atmosphere—whatever there is of one. In fact, the summer after the trip, while I was living in Chicago, I found it to be a great place to sit down with a pad of paper, off alone in the field boxes near the left-field foul pole, and write parts of this book.

The one gimmicky annoyance of the park is an intermittent sound effect, something like a reverberating gong, that goes off every inning or so in an attempt to motivate the crowd. The fact that most of the crowd ignores the effect, along with a fan poll to determine what song they should play between innings, helps to dampen the irritation of these nuisances.

The Sox lost our game. I dozed off a little, which I don't feel bad about for this kind of low-key ballgame in this kind of low-key ballpark. In fact I think the art of the baseball nap is being lost in this era of making ballparks into amusement centers. You don't go to the park to run around the food court and play games in the tunnel. You go to enjoy the game, and if it is a bit of a stalemate for a while, just nap or read the sports page. This was truly a flashback to my youth in Houston, where going to the ballpark

Without our entourage of family members, friends, or even concessionaires, we enjoyed a relaxing afternoon of baseball on the south side of Chicago at the new Comiskey Park.

was relaxation therapy. Watching the pitcher pitch, the runners creep off the bases, the fielders move into position, and the batter flinch just before he made that fateful decision to swing the bat or not. That was my definition of baseball. So many layers, so many things going on at once. You could choose just how deeply you wanted to get into it. The guys in Oakland who spend all of their time badgering the pitcher wouldn't know it, but there is a complex and interconnected system out there. There is always something to watch: how the pitcher grips his pitches, how the outfielders anticipate where the ball is going. At a place like Comiskey, there is truly nothing stopping you from taking in all of these little pleasures—no volcano exploding in center field, no arcade games beeping in the background, and no fans near you interjecting their opinion on whether that last pitch was a ball or a strike.

The White Sox game was our first opportunity to experience this on the trip. In the earlier stadiums we had spent much of our time on guided tours, checking out all the concessions, and fraternizing with the locals. But in Chicago we had none of these distractions. The team and concessionaires ignored our pleas for tours, and the stadium's simplicity made seeing all the sights about a fifteen-minute job. Additionally, the lack of bodies served to make concession trips brief and interpersonal contact rare. I embraced this opportunity as a low-key respite from the constant buzz of the trip. Nobody greeted us at the door. Nobody at the ballpark knew who we were or had heard about our trip. Nobody cared or wondered about why we were wearing matching shirts and toting around a big sign and a bunch of cameras. Even Dave, despite his talkative nature, seemed to appreciate this opportunity to enjoy the ballgame, or at least in this case, just enjoy a day in the sun, given that a real ballgame never materialized. We didn't even get one person to sign our map.

In general, despite the underwhelming experience, I came out as a fan of new Comiskey. I admit that it is cold and simplistic, but somehow it stands out next to all these so-called modern parks. As all of its oversized symmetrical forbearers fall under the wrecking ball, Comiskey should grow more distinct and appreciable with age. Dave, however, thinks Comiskey's an eyesore. Maybe he's right. Maybe I let Comiskey off the hook because I'd rather find the beauty in something everyone else criticizes than point out the flaws in something everyone else adores. This book is already full of the latter.

comiskey park

CITY: Chicago, Illinois

TENANT: Chicago White Sox

OPENED: April 18, 1991

NICKNAME/ALIASES: Comiskey Park, Comiskey II

DESIGN: Baseball-only stadium, symmetrical design, no movable seats. SISTER PARKS: none, although I'd suggest Yankee Stadium.

FIELD: Grass

DIMENSIONS (feet): left field—347, left center—375, center field—400, right center—375, right field—347

FENCES (feet): 8

LOCATION: 333 W. 33d St., Chicago, IL 60616. BOUNDED BY: West: Wentworth Ave. East: Dan Ryan Expressway. North: W. 35th St. South: West 36th St.

CAPACITY: 44,321. Total attendance: 1,391,146 (1998). Average attendance: 17,174 (1998).

PARKING: $7–$10 and abundant

TICKETS: $10–22. BEST BANG FOR YOUR BUCK: Catch a game on Monday because all tickets are half-price. Generally all tickets are well priced and the $22 lower-deck boxed seats are close to the action and in foul-ball territory. You can usually get there without paying for it.

THE BALLPARK EXPERIENCE: New Comiskey has all the amenities of a modern park with little of the character of a classic park. It was the last park to be built before Camden Yards in Baltimore, and although it was designed by the same firm, HOK Sport from Kansas City, it doesn't go for the charming nostalgia as Camden Yards or any of the other retro parks. The park follows none of the rules of the new classic parks—green seats, asymmetrical design, exposed steel—and makes you realize how revolutionary Camden Yards was at the time. Nevertheless, new Comiskey does have a certain charm in its simplicity and dedication to baseball. The architecture is, however, somewhat dominated by concrete and feels a little antiseptic, akin to the behemoths in Cincinnati, St. Louis, and Pittsburgh. As a result, it falls somewhere between Dodger Stadium and these multipurpose parks.

Walking through new Comiskey, you are surrounded by concrete walls, which, along with the park's blue seats, seem somewhat cold. Part of this may be because there is nobody there, but it is also attributable to the fact that the park is very spread out. We were told that the first row of the upper deck in the new park is farther from the field than the last row at old Comiskey. A bigger tragedy though is how they copied Bill Veeck's famous scoreboard from the old park in center field but made a cheap knockoff of the original. From fan accounts and pictures, old Comiskey's scoreboard had spinning wheels and fireworks that all rotated at different speeds. The new park's poor substitute relies on flashing lights and small fireworks. This disappointing copy is symbolic of a park that misses the mark on almost every aspect of modern baseball design, which ironically is the only thing that gives the park some unique charm.

FANS: White Sox fans have always been overshadowed by their cross-town rivals, Cubs fans. The Sox have a working-class fan base while the Cubbies attract not just the affluent but most everybody else. The romance of rooting for the Cubs and the friendly confines of Wrigley Field have long given the Cubs an edge in fan base as has the fact that Wrigley Field is a much more popular stadium and in a much more popular part of town than Comiskey. Regardless, while the Cubs draw a much rowdier and larger bunch of fans, true White Sox fans, where you can find them, are among the most astute and loyal fans in baseball. Although the team has not won a championship since the Black Sox scandal, they persevere.

FACILITIES: The facilities at Comiskey are nice. They are modern with adequate restrooms, concessions, and good seats. Many of the concourses are wide but have low ceilings.

Although often considered the worst new park in the major leagues, Comiskey surprised us with its uniqueness in light of the many Camden Yards look-alikes.

FOOD: At new Comiskey we sampled pretty standard food options. There was a fine selection of sausages, given that we were in the Midwest, with the full selection of condiments from sauerkraut to spicy mustard. There were not a lot of specialty foods, so we settled for the peculiar corn elotes, kernel corn topped with spicy powder. We enjoyed them, although they were a bizarre sight for a baseball park and are certainly found at no other park. LAST CALL: Alcohol is served until the middle of the seventh inning.

GREAT PLAYERS AND HISTORIC MOMENTS: New Comiskey Park opened in 1991 with the best White Sox team in a decade. Newcomers Frank Thomas and Jack "Blackjack" McDowell led the club to a close second-place finish. In 1993, the park's third year, the pitching staff of McDowell, Wilson Alvarez, and Alex Fernandez led the Sox to an AL West title. Unfortunately, the team fell to the future World Series champion Toronto Blue Jays in the ALCS. The Sox once again contended in 1994 only to see their hopes of a World Series thwarted by the strike. After moving to the AL Central in 1995, the team found itself behind the Cleveland Indians for several years before finally making it back to the playoffs in 2000.

BALLPARK HISTORY: The White Sox had played in old Comiskey Park since its construction in 1910. The park was old, small, and had none of the amenities of the modern ballparks. Jerry Reinsdorf, the owner of the Sox and Chicago Bulls, demanded in 1988 that a new stadium be constructed or the team would be off to St. Petersburg. At the last minute, the city approved the construction of a new $167-million modern park adjacent to old Comiskey on the South Side of Chicago. At the time of its construction, the park was considered a top-of-the-line ballpark. It was the first baseball-only park built

BAT Info

FINAL SCORE: White Sox 2, Blue Jays 5

OUR SEATS: Box 129, Row 28, Seats 8–9

BALLPARK: 19 of 30

DAY: 27 of 38

MILES TRAVELED: 60 (9,815 total)

NEW STATES: 0 (24 total)

OUR EXPENSES: $100
parking, programs, and food—sausages, corn elotes, pretzels, peanuts, and soda $40
Irish pub, magazine for Joe Hauler, Pizzeria Uno, Wrigleyville $60
EXPENSES TO DATE: $1,920

OUR FREEBIES: $70
game tickets $20
lodging (courtesy of Joe Hauler) $50
FREEBIES TO DATE: $3,014

since Kaufman Stadium was opened for the Kansas City Royals in 1972. Soon after Camden Yards was completed a year later, however, the shortcomings of new Comiskey became apparent. While modern, the park lacked many of the throwback features of Camden that were copied in Cleveland, Arlington, and Denver. In the course of one year, the park became dated and fell from state-of-the-art to middle-of-the-road. Everyone who had championed the park suddenly wished for the old one back.

FUN FACT: The infield dirt was transported from old Comiskey.

THE ONE THING YOU HAVE TO DO AT NEW COMISKEY PARK AND WHY: Take a shower. Inspired by the old Comiskey's outfield shower, there is a rain room behind the left-field bleachers that allows fans to cool off on muggy Chicago days.

OTHER THINGS TO REMEMBER: It is very difficult to find the entrance to the park. Two of the main entrances are reached via fan bridges over the streets below. You have to remember to take the bridge or you may end up at the base of the park with no entrances to use.

LASTING IMPRESSION: Not a terrible park but it looks so much worse in comparison to its beloved predecessor.

20

Busch
stadium
st. Louis

OUR GAME at Comiskey had been a day game, so afterward we had some time to see the sights in Chicago before we met up with Joe for dinner. We bypassed the Sears Tower and the waterfront and decided to sneak into Soldier Field.

Some way or another, after driving around the entire park, Dave and I managed to find our way down a single-lane ramp, through a gate, inside the walls of Soldier Field without leaving our car. After going through a tunnel, we seemed to be in some sort of outdated arena that had either been a part of the stadium at one time or had been a training field of some sort. Now it was apparently a parking lot. The area was reminiscent of the ruins of League Park, with the concrete foundation for stadium seating remaining, just no seats on top of it. Dave and I were lightheaded just being there and took pictures of ourselves on the steps, never knowing when we might get tossed out. The inner arena, however, beckoned, and we could see the tunnel that would take us there. We could also see about fifty maintenance people on the inside. All, we assumed, were posed to toss us out. But we had grown accustomed to taking certain liberties, and confident in our ability to talk our way out of a jam, we proceeded toward the playing field.

Walking into the playing arena from field level was a majestic experience. We had seen great football stadiums on our trip in Miami and San Diego, but Soldier Field is undoubtedly to football what Fenway Park is to baseball. The stadium feels mammoth, and in classic old-style coliseum fashion the seats fan away from the field in a perfect bowl, giving a sense of unity to the environment and providing a truly democratic opportunity for everyone to rush the field when the situation calls for it. The simplicity of the Roman facade and columns encasing the press box and the smooth, pillared exterior wall provide the finishing touches of this paradigm of football stadium perfection.

Soldier Field is, of course, the home of the Chicago Bears, but during the summer it is the home of Chicago's professional soccer team, the whatzits. And it was this realization that hit us like a ton of bricks when we walked out of the tunnel onto the playing field. We didn't immediately grasp what was wrong with the markings on the grass, or for that matter what those trapezoidal frames were that stood at each end of the vast and lush oval-shaped patch of green. It didn't take us long to realize what was going on: They were getting the stadium ready for a soccer game. We saw people watering the field, cleaning the stands, moving equipment. Dave and I were a little baffled. Not to belittle the popular sport, we weren't sure what a soccer stadium looked like. We were pretty sure that this wasn't one, however. In this state of mutual confusion, Dave and I were jarred back to reality when a very large individual politely asked us what we were doing. We wondered the same about him but kindly informed him we were just leaving. He was satisfied with that, and we left. My first trip to Soldier Field. It somehow seemed to fit perfectly into the agenda of this baseball trip.

We met up with Joe at what he claimed was the most famous restaurant in all of Chicago, the Rock 'n' Roll McDonald's. We found out later that there were actually more famous restaurants in Chicago, but Joe was in no financial condition to go to any of them, so we settled for the Rock 'n' Roll McDonald's, which I'll grant is at least the most famous McDonald's in all of Chicago.

Later that night we checked out the Chicago scene. As we'd recently been in Houston, Atlanta, Miami, and Cleveland, Dave and I were beginning to feel like connoisseurs of the nightlife around the country. Chicago, however, disappointed us. It was surprisingly dead this Thursday night. The most exciting experience was driving through Wrigleyville and seeing the outside of Wrigley Field. It was truly a beautiful sight. After finding an appreciation of the old park in Detroit, I was even more impressed seeing the outside of Wrigley; it was as classic on the outside as Detroit was on the inside. I couldn't wait to get in there, but we'd have to wait another week. This scheduling inconvenience was thanks to the schedule makers who always keep cross-town rivals on different sides of the country. Don't they know that nobody in Chicago roots for both teams?

Somehow, despite the lack of nightlife opportunities, we managed to stay out until 3 A.M., doing what I don't even remember and crashed back at the sty for one last night. We said our good-byes to Joe that night, knowing he'd be long gone by the time we woke up. How he managed to live on so little sleep I can't fathom.

We woke up sometime around noon the next day and headed off to St. Louis. A parting note on Joe: He is a great guy and was the most enthusiastic host on our trip, but I cannot emphasize enough how big a mess his place was.

Friday marked the end of the fourth week. Almost three-fourths of the way through the trip. Almost two-thirds of the way through the parks. Finally, my relationship with Dave had seemed to reach an equilibrium. It had been volatile since southern California. But by day twenty-eight, all the tension had worked itself out. We were like an old couple in a marriage that has run anything but a smooth course. We had gone through the initial euphoria that was quickly punctured by intermittent bitter resentments. We had had some very high highs and extremely low lows. At times it didn't seem that we could make it. But the fact that we had made it across the Continental Divide, survived vandalism, survived visits to the parents, survived The Drive—all of that engendered a newfound mutual appreciation.

We didn't talk much about the trip anymore. It seemed like everything had been said. We had been through a lot together, and we both knew that we were now forever bonded by the experiences of the last four weeks. No one else could understand what we had been through, and Dave and I were so thoroughly familiar with our lifestyle that we had grown detached and relented to it. Our amazement and amusement at our temporary celebrity status had mellowed, maybe because we were starting to believe we weren't really of any importance (a scary thought), maybe because we were tired of our fame (another scary thought). All of the newspaper articles had been written and clipped out. All of the great new experiences—touring ballparks, free food, free beer, going out on the field, spitting on the grass—had been done. Now we were on pure momentum. Our

We made a habit of posing in front of statues of baseball greats outside of ballparks. Unfortunately, in this photo you can't even see the foot of the huge Stan Musial statue behind us.

movements were automatic. We were just soaking it all in; we'd reached that point where our brains were so overwhelmed by new experiences that we felt compelled to capture it all on video, not just to remind us of what happened, but to inform us later as well.

We were still looking forward to the other landmarks, especially some in particular, like Fenway and Wrigley and the field in Iowa. Yet we were at a point now where, although we didn't know exactly what was going to happen or how it would feel, we could sense what it was going to feel like. We were veterans at this game. Get on the bus, hit the next town. Just like the old ball players, we had to stop and think every morning when we woke up and remind ourselves how lucky we were to be here.

Also we were accustomed to taking every step together, and neither one of us would have wanted to finish the trip alone. Even though I certainly thought it would be great if Dave would shut up about the Ebbets Field rotunda.

busch stadium

LOS ANGELES V ST. LOUIS

game Time: 7:10 P.M.

UNLESS YOU were living under a rock in 1998, you know that all over the country, and especially in St. Louis, the baseball world was talking about Mark McGwire. Big Mac was on a tear in the summer of '98, and when we came through town he was up to forty homers through ninety-four games. It didn't take a mathematician to realize that he was on a pace to challenge Roger Maris's sixty-one-home-run record. Of course, by now, everyone knows what happened. The sixty-one-home-run barrier is now arcane. If you don't give seventy a run for your money nowadays, you're nothing to talk about. But in 1998 the home-run derby was in full swing, and it was the most exciting thing about the summer.

It sure was to the people of St. Louis. So much so that when we showed up at the ballpark at 5:15 P.M., about twenty minutes after they opened the gates, we were far from the first ones there. This early-bird crowd rivaled the Beanie Baby–induced mayhem we had experienced in New York, but it was more impressive in St. Louis, given that this was an everyday occurrence. The fans at the park wanted to see Big Mac put a few more out of the yard. So they even came for batting practice.

When we showed up, we were met by a representative of SportsService, who was to take us on the customary tour of the stadium. He met us in front of the stadium by the giant Stan Musial statue, which is easily the most imposing ballpark statue in America. He also came bearing gifts in the form of Cardinals caps.

Our tour took us through the bowels of Busch Stadium, which felt pretty much like your standard multipurpose stadium from that perspective. Just like at the Astrodome and the Oakland Coliseum, the concourses of Busch are cluttered with all sorts of vendors hawking specialty items from gourmet pretzels to Busch beer that stadium architects in the 1960s obviously didn't know baseball fans needed. So the once gaping passageways become somewhat constricted at times, especially given the crowds that the Cardinals were drawing in the McGwire era.

The added amenities are nice, and the Cards have even gone so far as to add a gaming area behind left field, which was just unpopular enough so as not to annoy—as opposed to the one in Atlanta. While on the tour, we discussed the surprisingly large crowds Big Mac seemed to be drawing in and the cash windfall it must be for the team. Our guide confessed that it truly was, especially since the fans were also enticed to come early and stay late, because you never knew when Mac was going to put one out.

We actually missed McGwire at BP because we were somewhere else inside the stadium. It turned out to be not very tragic, given what happened in the game.

Two swings. Two home runs. The first pitch McGwire saw from Brian Bohanon in the bottom of the first ended up 511 feet away from home plate. After that, the Dodgers threw ten straight balls to Big Mac, which turned out to be good strategy, because the next strike he saw—in the eighth inning—went out of the ballpark, too. The McGwire legend was bigger than anything I had ever experienced (I live a sheltered life), and I had to give the guy even more credit realizing it must be near impossible to hit with that many flashbulbs popping around the stadium. Dave and I were so inspired by this superhuman feat that we both shelled out for McGwire warm-up jerseys after the game. The fans in St. Louis just love him, too.

The game was one of the more exciting ones of the trip. In addition to the fact that everybody went crazy when McGwire came up (and booed whenever he was thrown a ball), the game stayed close throughout, which just made the homers that much better.

On the whole, Busch Stadium turned out to be a pretty nice place to watch a game. In addition to throwing a bunch of amenities in the concourses, they also kicked out the football team, ripped out the ill-advised artificial turf, and removed a few thousand seats in center field to add an excellent scoreboard and what can only be described as a pennant garden. The specialty pretzel booth was also noteworthy, akin to the ones that have been popping up in malls the last few years (the only reason I ever go to malls). The Busch beer, on the other hand, was bad—like it always is.

We had heard that they had been improving the park every off-season, with some plans still in the pipelines, and it really showed. Subsequently, Busch has established itself as the class of the dying breed of multisport stadiums, if only because it is no longer a multisport stadium.

We also met some nice people in St. Louis. The nicest by far being Chris Canning, a lawyer from Boston who not only took an interest in our trip but offered to set us up with Fenway tickets. Given that we didn't have any yet and with the Baltimore experience behind us, we greatly appreciated this gesture. Not just Chris, but the locals as well took an interest in us. You could tell that the baseball enthusiasm in this town wasn't just a McGwire fad. This was an old baseball town. The nine World Series championship banners were evidence of that, and the fans in St. Louis really know the history of the team.

Speaking of Cardinals history, in between McGwire bombs, we were afforded an opportunity to meet Jack Buck, the Cardinal's Hall of Fame announcer, and got an on-air interview with the Cardinals respected play-by-play man, Mike Shannon, a former infielder for the team. Given that their radio station has a fifty-thousand-watt signal or something like that (it apparently hits thirty-eight states), I figure we're pretty famous by now—somewhere.

Busch Stadium

CITY: St. Louis, Missouri

TENANT: St. Louis Cardinals

OPENED: May 12, 1966

NICKNAME/ALIASES: Civic Center Stadium (1966), Busch Memorial Stadium (1966–83)

DESIGN: Multipurpose stadium converted for baseball-only use in 1996, symmetrical design, no movable seats. SISTER PARKS: originally at least, Veterans Stadium, Shea Stadium, Three Rivers Stadium, and Riverfront Stadium.

FIELD: Grass (1966–69, 1996–), artificial turf with mound and base cutouts (1970–95)

DIMENSIONS (feet): left field—330, left center—372, center field—402, right center—372, right field—330

FENCES (feet): 8

LOCATION: 250 Stadium Plaza, St. Louis, MO 63102. BOUNDED BY: Right field (S): Spruce St. Left field (E): Broadway and I-70. First base (W): Seventh St. Third base (N): Walnut St.

CAPACITY/ATTENDANCE: 49,676. Total attendance: 3,195,691 (1998), Average attendance: 39,452 (1998).

PARKING: $7–$10. Busch Stadium is an urban park with much of the parking in small lots. We had luck using the large multilevel lot across Walnut Street from the park, which was easily accessible and affordable.

TICKETS: $7–30. BEST BANG FOR YOUR BUCK: The bleacher seats, especially those in left field where Big Mac hits many of his home runs, have the most character in the park and are also a good value.

THE BALLPARK EXPERIENCE: Although it was one of the cookie-cutter multipurpose parks of the 1960s and '70s, Busch Stadium has almost been renovated out of this class. The park is in downtown St. Louis, just minutes from the Gateway Arch and the Mississippi River. In homage to its neighbor landmark, the top of the stadium is lined with ninety-six mini-replicas of the arch. This creates a nice symmetry with the surroundings, unlike other circular multipurpose behemoths. Busch Stadium also varies from its sister parks in that it is not set in some parking lot at the edge of town. Instead it is placed in the heart of the city amid office buildings, cleaners, and even the Bowling Hall of Fame.

On the inside there is an excitement to the park. Maybe it is the five World Series played here or the proud history of the Cardinals shining through the park's fifty thousand red seats. The park feels vibrant, alive, and intimate, even though it is characterized by the same large foul areas as its sister parks. The field is quite far from even the first row of seats, and the upper deck is even worse. This is just about the park's only flaw. The extensive renovations since 1996 have removed most of the other issues. The most significant of the changes was the conversion back to natural grass.

FANS: St. Louis has one of the most storied histories of any franchise and has used this to build a strong fan base. Our tour guides also pointed out two other key factors that have made the Cardinals popular over the years. First, until the Dodgers moved to L.A. in 1957, St. Louis was the farthest team west in major league baseball. This plus the powerful radio broadcasting of 1100 KMOX made millions of baseball fans all over the West into St. Louis Cardinal fans. Second, Branch Rickey's development of the minor leagues for the Cardinals gave the club many smaller affiliate clubs all over the country with scores of fans loyal to the Cardinals of St. Louis. Within St. Louis itself, the Cardinals also have a large fan base, but in recent years, this group has been significantly watered down at the ballpark by the swarms of tourists that have converged on the place to see McGwire's heroics. The locals within the crowd, though, are a traditionalist group of fans excited that McGwire has brought so much support for the team. St. Louis (despite the Rams' recent dominance) has never been anything but a baseball town.

FACILITIES: With the renovation in 1996, the facilities are modern, clean, and well kept. Everything seems to be covered in a new coat of red paint. There were extensive renovations to the luxury boxes that keep the high-paying customers coming back. On the downside, the concourses are narrow at times and the ramps on the exterior of the park leave you distant from the action if you are moving from deck to deck.

FOOD: We found numerous food options at Busch Stadium beyond the obvious Anheuser Busch beers. Their best food is probably the thin pretzel that comes with Parmesan cheese topping, standard salt topping, or a cinnamon coating. All three are great, and you can have them as a snack or a full meal (we did both). Consistent with our travels through the Midwest, we covered the hot dogs with St. Louis's own take on spicy brown mustard. LAST CALL: Alcohol is served until the middle of the seventh inning.

If you look closely at this picture of Mark McGwire's forty-second home run of the summer of 1998, you can see the ball (just above the second-base umpire's head) rocketing out of the park.

GREAT PLAYERS AND HISTORIC MOMENTS: From their beginnings in the 1880s as the Brown Stockings to the Cardinals' greats, such as Bob Gibson and Stan Musial, the club has enjoyed baseball success. The franchise has an NL record nine world championships, which is second only to the New York Yankees, and this success has continued throughout the team's tenure at Busch Stadium. The park opened in 1966, and in its second year the Cardinals took home their eighth world championship with a win over the Boston Red Sox in seven games. Bob Gibson won three games, including the crucial Game Seven. In 1982, led by shortstop Ozzie Smith and the bat of Willie McGee, the Cardinals captured their ninth world championship, this time over Milwaukee in seven games. Some other greats of Busch Stadium's history include Orlando Cepeda, Jack Clark, and Lee Smith. Of course, in recent memory, the park's greatest moments have been Mark McGwire's record sixty-second home run in 1998 off of Steve Trachsel of the Chicago Cubs and his seventieth and final home run that season.

BALLPARK HISTORY: When August Busch bought the Cardinals in 1953, he renamed their home from Sportsman's Park to Busch Stadium. That original Busch Stadium was a relic from the turn of the century that had already seen its best years. As part of a downtown revitalization project, the new Busch Stadium was constructed in 1966 in the new circular multipurpose style. The park initially had a grass field but in 1969 switched to AstroTurf. The field was not resodded until thirty years later. Over the years the park was refurbished once in 1987, when new seats were added, and again in 1996, when the aforementioned wholesale changes were undertaken. The park was able to be converted to a baseball-only venue that year because the Rams moved to a new stadium. Plans were just released to construct a new downtown ballpark in St. Louis that could open by the 2004 season. That park would be in the Camdenesque style and incorporate many facets of Ebbets Field in Brooklyn, Camden Yards in Baltimore, and St. Louis's own Sportsman's Park.

FUN FACT: Busch Stadium was the postseason home of the Chicago Cubs from 1986 to 1988 until Wrigley Field added lights. The Cubs, however, failed to make the postseason, and the park never had to do the honors.

THE ONE THING YOU HAVE TO DO AT BUSCH STADIUM AND WHY: Get to the park early to watch Mark McGwire take batting practice; everyone else does.

OTHER THINGS TO REMEMBER: From the upper deck you can see the Gateway Arch.

LASTING IMPRESSION: Originally a forgettable multipurpose stadium, Busch Stadium has made the best of what it has to work with, molding a classic ballpark.

BAT INFO

FINAL SCORE: Cardinals 4, Dodgers 1

OUR SEATS: Section 250, Row 9, Seats 1–2

BALLPARK: 20 of 30

DAY: 28 of 38

MILES TRAVELED: 474 (10,289 total)

NEW STATES: 1 (Missouri; 25 total)

OUR EXPENSES: $101
Subway sandwiches $10
parking $8
gas $17
hotel room (in Evanston IN) $66
EXPENSES TO DATE: $2,021

OUR FREEBIES: $120
game tickets $20
programs, memorabilia, and
    ballpark food—pretzels (4), hot dogs,
    peanuts, and soda $100
FREEBIES TO DATE: $3,134

21

cinergy field

cincinnati

WE'LL NEVER know what the nightlife was like in St. Louis, because by 3 A.M. Friday night we were pulling off of I-64 into Evansville, Indiana, at the end of another late night. Again the itinerary had us backed up against a wall, as we had to make an early afternoon stop on Saturday in Kentucky at the Louisville Slugger Bat Museum and then push through to Cincinnati for a night game. By the time we swerved off the road for the last time Friday night, one hundred or so miles outside of Louisville, not only were we exhausted, but we were having some olfactory issues due to the unexpected prevalence of skunks along the highway in southern Illinois and Indiana.

I was still wearing my McGwire jersey when we showed up in Louisville the next day. The museum—which wasn't hard to find given that the five-story-high bat that marks the entrance is about the tallest structure in the city—had been newly renovated, but somehow the cost of admission was only five dollars. This was possibly our best buy on the trip. For that five bucks we were treated to the full tour of how wooden bats are made (I'm still wondering about the metal ones) and got to check out a mini hall of fame and memorabilia display consisting mostly and predictably of bats of all sorts of baseball legends throughout the ages. We even got free mini-bats in the bargain, which made Dave ecstatic. He now had twenty-one mini-bats in his collection. In addition, I picked up a Louisville Slugger shot glass and a few postcards to drop off to some friends, most notably Sam Chiu, to whom I had promised to send a postcard from each park but had managed to come up with less than half. (I still maintain that some of those parks do not sell postcards.)

Of course, we couldn't afford to dawdle in Louisville too long because we still had another hundred miles to Cincy and just under two hours to get there.

I was beginning to get apprehensive about the evening's events. Of all the ballparks and ball teams and sports cities in America, Cincinnati was the one that I had always been most prejudiced against. I wasn't too thrilled about trekking through the town and even thought about skipping it all together. I had never heard anything good about it, and I had always hated the Reds because they usually beat the Astros when it mattered. Ditto to the Bengals with respect to their record against my once beloved Oilers. In my admittedly poorly informed mind nothing good had ever come out of Cincinnati. Validating my prejudices, I should note that Dave, from the north side of Ohio, also had a poor opinion of this city on the southern border of his state.

Don't take this personally if you're from Cincinnati. You probably feel the same way about Houston.

cinergy field

··

SAN DIEGO V CINCINNATI

Game Time: 7:05 p.m.

THE GENERAL tone of our trip to Cinergy Field can be best relayed with the story of our interactions with the parking lot attendant there—just another of the interesting parking attendants we met on the trip and apparently the *only* parking lot attendant at Cinergy. When we told him why we were at the park, he replied, "I wouldn't go in there if I were you. You might as well save your money and go to Hooters."

Dave and I were determined though and would not be fazed by this jaded ballpark employee, despite his admittedly fair assessment of the place. We even noted that we would have to give the park a little credit for keeping on the payroll employees who were honest and straightforward with the patrons.

Although we had arrived relatively late to the ballgame, we were something like the second ones there, so we got what seemed like a good parking spot. To steel our nerves for what we expected to be a disappointing experience, we downed a shot of the liquor that had been rolling around in the backseat of the car since San Francisco for just such an occasion. Finally up for the job at hand, we navigated the series of passageways and tunnels that is the Riverfront . . . er, uh, Cinergy . . . parking lot, making our way to the stadium. It turns out our parking spot actually wasn't that good, although there didn't seem to be any better ones.

The Kissmobile was the highlight of an otherwise unmemorable experience at Cinergy Field.

As I mentioned in the chapter on Pro Player, Cinergy Field's most noteworthy trait is that it has the worst name in baseball. That could have been disputed a few years back when 3Com was still in the running and Qualcomm didn't conjure up visions of radically successful technology companies (Nasdaq: QUAL); the title is pretty much a consensus now. What better ballpark to hold it than such a thoroughly unattractive stadium as this one.

If it's possible, Cinergy was less than I had expected. I had at least hoped that it would be a lot like Pittsburgh: standard, symmetrical, ugly turf, nothing flashy, nothing much exciting. Even though it bore a strong resemblance to the rest of the multipurposoids, Cinergy went below and beyond. Everything about the place made it unmistakably obvious that they just weren't trying. And even though I was walking around the park for the first time, I was certain that the only thing that had changed here in the last twenty years was the name. Given its condition, it's not too surprising that the club administration basically ignored us when we passed through. Whereas people associated with twenty-six of the thirty clubs had politely offered us just about anything we wanted when we told them what we were doing and when we were going to be in town, the Cinergy crew ignored us. Now I could maybe understand the folks at Camden, with their packed house of celebrities, not having enough time to fit us into their busy schedule. For Cinergy our trip could have easily been the PR highlight of their year. Instead, we settled for the hospitality of the concessionaires alone.

One high note of our visit was that we happened to be in town on the day that Ted Kluszewski was to have his number retired. Before you go thinking that this big occasion must have been the reason we were blithely ignored, realize that it only managed to draw a handful more than the Reds usual crowd of twenty thousand. The Big Klu experience was pretty exciting, though, if only because it is quite likely that I was present at the only ceremony where they retired a baseball number by putting a big cutout of a sleeveless baseball jersey on the outfield wall. Big Klu, not just a big hitter, was the style maven of the Reds to boot.

Among other points of note from the Cincinnati experience, we went to the game with Dave's cousin Luke, whom I had been apprehensive about meeting given that he lived in Cincinnati. But he turned out to be a cool guy and seemed normal and well adjusted, convincing me that people from Cincinnati aren't all bad just because their sports teams always beat yours.

In the end, the highlight of our Cincinnati experience was our encounter with the Hershey's Kissmobile. You've all heard the legend, and it's true: They do actually pay people to drive around the country in a truck with a big Hershey's Kiss on top and hand out candy at public gatherings. We met the people stuck with that hard job. Of course, Dave was again convinced they were hitting on him. Or was that me? In any case, we both got to thinking that our recent experiences were making us uniquely qualified for such a gig should our other career plans not work out.

Other than the Hershey's Kissmobile girls, we hardly met anybody in Cincinnati. Similar to the Comiskey experience, we barely interacted with the locals. But given our apprehension at being there, it was understandable, as if we had planned it that way to contrast with the pandemonium of St. Louis. Suffice it to say that our overinflated egos were still in check, ready to head into Canada, another region that intimidated the sheltered Texan in me.

By the way, the Reds got beat by the Padres. The local crowd didn't seem to care too much. I was secretly happy, even though Dave and I had agreed we would only root for home teams. And if you want to know something about the park, read the section below. To be honest, it was so immemorable that I can't think of anything of importance to say about the ballpark at all. You also might want to check out the Pittsburgh, Philadelphia, and San Francisco chapters to get a general feel for what Cinergy is like, although it's not quite as nice as any of those parks. If the people in Cincinnati feel slighted by our treatment of the park . . . come on, admit it, it sucks. Worse than Candlestick. You guys should be thanking God and everybody that you're getting a new park soon.

cinergy field

CITY: Cincinnati, Ohio

TENANT: Cincinnati Reds

OPENED: June 30, 1970

cinergy field

NICKNAME/ALIASES: Riverfront Stadium

DESIGN: Multipurpose stadium, circular design, movable seats. SISTER PARKS: Veterans Stadium, Shea Stadium, Three Rivers Stadium, and Busch Stadium.

FIELD: AstroTurf with mound and base cutouts

DIMENSIONS (feet): left field—330, left center—375, center field—404, right center—375, right field—330

FENCES (feet): 8 (canvas)

LOCATION: 100 Cinergy Field, Cincinnati, OH 45202. BOUNDED BY: Right field (S): Ohio River and Mehring Way. Left field (E): Broadway and Central Bridge. First base (W): I-71. Third base (N): Pete Rose Way.

CAPACITY: 52,952. Total attendance: 1,793,649 (1998). Average attendance: 22,143 (1998).

PARKING: $7–$10. There is a large parking structure beneath Cinergy Field that is reserved mostly for season-ticket holders. The rest of us have to park on the other side of a lot of construction.

TICKETS: $5–21. BEST BANG FOR YOUR BUCK: Cincinnati offers $5 seats in the last six rows of the upper deck, which is a steal to get into a game anywhere, and you don't have to sit in the top six rows, although it is pretty good exercise climbing to the top. (See Veterans.)

THE BALLPARK EXPERIENCE: Approaching Cinergy Field, casual observers would be hard-pressed to determine if they were in Cincinnati, St. Louis, or Pittsburgh. We certainly didn't know. The park is a facsimile of the other two, and the riverfront setting is similar in all cases. Unfortunately, Cinergy Field, in our estimation, is the most nondescript of the cookie-cutter bunch with neither Pittsburgh's proud football heritage nor the slight architectural pronouncements of Busch Stadium.

Uniquely, Cinergy is surrounded by a large concrete mall that is also the top of its four-story parking structure. The mall overlooks the river and was a baking inferno at our game. Regardless of the temperature, the stroll across the barren mall leaves a dry taste in your mouth and makes you want to get inside as fast as possible. It is the antithesis of the carnival atmosphere on Eutaw Street at Camden Yards. Inside, the concourses of the park's lower deck stifle you with their small size and the fact that they have no views of the field. The upper-deck concourses are at least open-air and afford views of the city and river, although they still seem crowded even though there is hardly anybody there. Like Three Rivers, Cinergy sports AstroTurf under a blue sky, and this lack of glamour on the field makes the place seem as dry as the mall outside.

In general, Cinergy has all the amenities of a 1970s park that were state-of-the-art at the time but now seem standard: a Jumbotron, electronic scoreboards, ramps to take fans to the upper reaches of the park. In 1970 visitors would have been impressed by these advancements over run-down Crosley Field, but now the place is not only outdated but lacks the character of an older park like Crosley. The only thing that makes this park unique in this day and age is that they are razing most of its sister parks or adding grass. Until they tear Cinergy down, you can still glimpse a part of baseball's past uniformity and hot AstroTurf. Not a great chapter for ballparks, but one that many fans experienced for many years.

FANS: Cincinnati's long history with the game of baseball (they had the first professional team), the dominance of the "Big Red Machine" in the mid-1970s, and some of the greatest players of all time have given Cincinnati a strong base of fans. They seemed to associate with Pete Rose and his "never give up" attitude, but something has gone wrong in Cincinnati since Rose's lifetime ban from the game. The antics of Marge Schott and poor on-field talent have hurt the fan base. Our run-ins with fans made this painfully clear. Even the signing of Ken Griffey Jr. in 2000, expected to drive up atten-

There were many empty seats at Cinergy despite the retirement of Ted Kluszewski's number, which may be one of the few occasions when a big cutout of a sleeveless jersey receives the honor.

dance and interest in the club, has been fraught with resentment due to his lack of hustle. Right now fans seem to be finding it hard to get behind the team, although everything will certainly change when the Reds get their new stadium.

FACILITIES: Cinergy shows its age and lack of refurbishment. The small concourses leave little room for restrooms, food options, or views of the field. The seats, though wide and comfortable, are not angled toward the action as a result of the fact that the park once doubled as the home of the NFL Bungles, er, Bengals.

FOOD: Cincinnati was once known as Porkopolis because of the many slaughterhouses along the river. This being the case, many varieties of sausages and hot dogs are a specialty in the city as well as the park. Our favorite was the mini-chilidog covered with melted cheese. LAST CALL: Alcohol is served until the middle of the seventh inning.

GREAT PLAYERS AND HISTORIC MOMENTS: Cinergy Field (nee Riverfront) had an exciting opening year hosting the All-Star Game and the World Series. That year marked the beginning of the Big Red Machine, the nickname given to the club throughout the 1970s. Led by Sparky Andersen as manager, the team compiled two World Series wins back to back in 1975–76 over the Red Sox and Yankees, respectively. Great players such as Joe Morgan at second base, Pete Rose at third, and Johnny Bench behind the plate propelled the club. In particular, the 1976 squad is considered one of the greatest teams of all time. In 1990 the Reds made another run for the World Series with the Nasty Boys bullpen of Rob Dibble and Randy Meyers. The club surprised the Oakland Athletics in a four-game sweep to capture their third championship at Cinergy Field. Other historic moments at the park include Hank Aaron's 714th home run, tying Babe Ruth's record, on Opening Day in 1974, and Pete Rose's 4,192d hit in 1985, putting him past Ty Cobb on the all-time list. There were also All-Star Games here in 1970 and 1988.

BALLPARK HISTORY: Prior to moving to Riverfront Stadium in 1970, the Reds had played for more than fifty years at Crosley Field. The city had long desired a new park along the Ohio River. New ownership in 1966 and the awarding of a football franchise to the city finally turned these dreams into reality. The city broke ground on the new park in February 1968. The park was rushed to completion and the press box had to be added a year later; the stadium club was never finished. At the time, circular enclosed multi-purpose parks with AstroTurf were the rage. Atlanta had put Fulton County Stadium up in 1965, St. Louis copied that style in 1966, and Cincinnati and Pittsburgh followed in 1970. The parks served the needs of the baseball and football franchises and provided all the modern conveniences of electronic scoreboards, AstroTurf, and wider seats. Only in retrospect do the parks seem to lack the character of the old-time ballparks.

Construction of a new baseball-only facility in the Camdenesque mold is scheduled to be completed in time for the 2003 season. There are inklings that the design will incorporate elements of Crosley Field. Since the park will be constructed adjacent to Cinergy Field, it will require the demolition of the outfield stands of Cinergy. Therefore, for the last year of play at Cinergy, the Reds will play in an open-ended stadium similar to Shea in New York.

FUN FACTS: There are five retired jerseys on the left field wall for Johnny Bench, Fred Hutchinson, Frank Robinson, Joe Morgan, and Ted Kluszewski (whose number was retired at our game).

THE ONE THING YOU HAVE TO DO AT CINERGY FIELD AND WHY: Can I say not go? Oh, well, then. Visit the site of the new Reds ballpark. The new stadium will be a big improvement, and you can see how it will be more integrated into the surroundings.

OTHER THINGS TO REMEMBER: If you park near the river or under the mall in the parking structure, finding the park entrance or ticket booths can be confusing. You have to take escalators or stairs to the mall level to enter the park. There are many service entrances below, plus Gates 14–17, which require tickets to enter. The only ticket booths are on the mall.

LASTING IMPRESSION: Given the park's desperate condition, it is a shock to realize that any good players or great teams ever played at Cinergy.

BAT Info

FINAL SCORE: Padres 2, Reds 1

OUR SEATS: Aisle 304, Row 26, Seats 107–108

BALLPARK: 21 of 30

DAY: 29 of 38

MILES TRAVELED: 454 (10,743 total)

NEW STATES: 1 (Kentucky; 26 total)

OUR EXPENSES: $76
Louisville Slugger Museum $22
tickets, parking, and programs $26
gas $28
EXPENSES TO DATE: $2,097

OUR FREEBIES: $70
ballpark food—mini hot dogs (2 apiece), soda, and malts $20
lodging (courtesy of the Kavals) $50
FREEBIES TO DATE: $3,204

22

skyдome
toronto

I MMEDIATELY AFTER the Reds game, Dave and I were as agreeable as we had been the whole trip. A good thing, too, because we had a big task ahead of us: more than five hundred miles to Toronto and a day game on Sunday. Not as grueling as The Drive, but we didn't have Ron around for this one. We did plan on having help for this drive though, because in the middle of the night we were stopping in Cleveland and picking up Dave's brother Junior.

We made it to Cleveland by 2 A.M., and when we got to the house, his parents were ready for us. It was like a NASCAR pit crew. They met us at the car, helped transfer our gear (to Dave's uncle Gene's Jeep Cherokee, which would carry us for the next five days), and escorted us into the house with promises of breakfast and a wake-up call at 6 A.M.

Three hours later we were abruptly awakened. As is usually the case after a night on three hours of sleep, I found myself wondering if maybe it wouldn't have been a better idea to have not slept at all. The vouchsafed breakfast also materialized, but my stomach was having none of it, despite Mrs. Kaval's pleasant tone. We piled into the car and passed out. I barely even noticed that Junior was with us, much less behind the wheel.

By 9:30 A.M. we had made our way into New York, nearing Buffalo and Niagara, where we would cross into Canada. I was by this time wide awake and anxious. As you can probably imagine, I'm a pretty sheltered Texas boy, so crossing the northern border was something new for me. I didn't have any idea of what to expect in Canada. Ironically, although I had made friends from all over the world through my four years in college, it occurred to me that I didn't know any Canadians. For all I knew they hated Americans. Or was that the French?

Crossing the border was a simple task. They just waved us through. Then I realized that I wasn't anxious about getting into Canada; I was anxious about being in Canada. It was probably this anticipation that made me feel somewhat rebellious as we passed Niagara Falls. Dave and I had never discussed this, so I was not sure how he felt about the experience, but he appeared to sense my disquietude at the border and feed off of it as well. As a result, when we came upon the falls, we were too antsy to stay in the car, wishing instead to get out, feel the water, interact with the locals, whatever.

The challenge was that the lines to get into the parking lots were already obscene, and we only had about five minutes to spare before we had to be on the road for the ballpark. No real problem for us though; Dave and I were experienced shotgun tourists. We simply directed Junior to the nearest waterfalls and jumped out of the car, heading across the lawn for some quick photo ops.

To Junior's credit he fearlessly followed our lead and raised no objections when we directed him against the flow of traffic into a bus lane and ultimately into an emergency vehicle parking lot that seemed to double as a helipad. That being as close as we could get to the falls on paved ground, Dave and I sprang out of the car and ran directly toward the falls to take a couple of pictures by a railing in the mist just seventy-five feet away.

I quickly snapped a picture of Dave and he one of me, and as we were asking some nice Canadian passersby(!) to take a picture of the both of us, we began to notice a policeman about fifty feet from Junior and heading straight at him. Junior had apparently noticed him as well and was already backing out of the lot and heading down the road and out of the park.

We were relatively awake for our day game in Toronto despite our second overnight drive of the trip (more than five hundred miles).

As Junior began his maneuvers, the policeman looked at the two of us, which we saw as our cue to grab the camera and run for the car. Fortunately for us, this officer didn't see it as worth his while to chase a couple of Americans for a few minor moving violations. That was fine by us, because we had heard what the law can do to a couple of Americans who run afoul of the law on the other side of the border. Yeah, that was usually the other border they were talking about, but we weren't going to take any chances.

skydome

....

NEW YORK (AL) V TORONTO

Game Time: 1:05 P.M.

ULTIMATELY WE made it out of Niagara and into Toronto just fine. Once we were there, however, we had a heck of a time finding the stadium. As usual, Dave and I had almost no idea where the stadium was or anything else in the city for that matter, but per our general plan of attack in cities of which we were ignorant, we relied on two valuable resources. The first was our intuitive faith that city planners had a certain reverence for baseball, such that either the stadium would be situated in a way that it could not be missed, or at the very least there would be signs leading the way. Our second resource was the Rand McNally road atlas, which, in case our first plan backfired, never failed us with the red dot indicating baseball stadiums in each major league city. Of course, our hope was always to find the stadium without consulting the atlas, and we had generally been successful in doing so to this point on the trip. Toronto, however, quickly convinced us that it would not be one of those baseball-centric cities, so we took to the atlas. Sure enough, with the help of the map, we quickly determined where we were, where the stadium was, and the shortest path from point to point. The atlas, however, did not inform us that there was an Indy car race taking place at that moment and blocking a large chunk of the city between the stadium and us.

Confronted with this obstacle, we commanded Junior through an elaborate series of right turns, left turns, and U-turns, trying to avoid this city street racetrack but with little success. It seemed that the racecourse matched every snaking turn we made, invariably causing us to back out of a number of multilane roads and begin again. At one point, the racecourse along with one of the Formula One racecars snuck up on us so quickly that we were worried we had somehow made our way onto the track before we realized that this particular car was not in the competition. Exactly what it was doing, we were not sure.

We went on like this, circumnavigating the racetrack until we eventually came upon the gargantuan gray structure that is SkyDome. We also became aware that our search for the stadium could have been made much less painful had we only done a bit of research.

The fact that SkyDome sits directly beneath the towering CN Tower, the tallest free-standing structure in the world, would have made finding the way to the stadium a bit easier had we had this tidbit of information at the time. In our case though, we only gradually came to realize that the dot representing SkyDome on our map seemed very close to that tower looming on the horizon. Had we looked at the map for another five seconds, we would have seen the dot representing the CN Tower, but we weren't that smart. So instead of lamenting the half-hour we spent bumbling about Toronto, we celebrated the fact that we had at least made it to the stadium by game time.

SkyDome is first and foremost a technological marvel. As such I was excited to see it. SkyDome is the birthplace of the retractable dome (you can't count Montreal), and when it was built in 1989 it was the first innovation in the field of ballpark design since the birth of the domed stadium (say what you will) in the form of the Astrodome in 1965. It is this standing in stadium lore that led me to have such high expectations of SkyDome. The subsequent failure of SkyDome to live up to those expectations is why SkyDome was a bit of a disappointment to us. In fact, SkyDome's impersonality and lack of character rivaled that of Cinergy for the worst venue on the trip so far.

This is not to go so far as to say that SkyDome is a blight on a par with Cinergy, because it certainly has its good characteristics, foremost among them being the already mentioned groundbreaking innovation of the retractable roof. Even though you could argue that the retractable roof adds little to the place's appeal as the stadium still has a concrete cookie-cutter feel and artificial turf, you must give credit knowing that we might never have had the domed stadium with a grass field were it not for SkyDome's trailblazing. Also the stadium's hotel in center field, although not very aesthetically pleasing, is an interesting novelty nonetheless, particularly given its colorful history of providing unexpected entertainment to the fans (see BALLPARK HISTORY).

For our inaugural experience of Canadian baseball, we were treated by the team to free tickets but not much else, which upset us more than being ignored by some other clubs. Dave and I expected that there would be a lot of interesting Canadian touches around the park that we would like to learn about. Once we got there though, we were disappointed to realize how American the place seemed. The concessions, the architecture, the people, the language—everything in SkyDome and, in fact, all of Toronto seemed very American. Most disturbing was the realization that they accept American money—and even prefer it—everywhere in the city and the stadium. Walking around the concourses of SkyDome and sampling the local hot dogs, nachos, and beer (the most distinctly Canadian aspect of the place), the three of us were continually amazed by the exchange rate.

Blissfully unaware, we saw that the prices were marked in dollars, leading us to believe that was the cost in American money. Although the prices were high, they were no higher than prices in the other twenty-one stadiums we had visited. So we willingly paid six dollars for a couple of hot dogs. Yet when the $20 bill we handed over came back in the form of $22 Canadian plus two hot dogs, we assumed something was wrong. It was like we were making money by spending it. Suddenly, we were so into the exchange rate thing that we went on a buying spree, which culminated in Dave's and Junior's buying themselves official Indians baseball jerseys for something like $45 American. In the end, we forked over roughly $250 American but walked away with $200 Canadian, which made it seem like we had spent only $50. Of course, we hadn't a clue what to do with the Canadian money.

The other thing about the Canadian experience that took us by surprise was that the fans in Toronto were pretty much on a par with American fans, showing a lot of interest in the game. To make a couple of generalizations that shouldn't be taken too seriously, they were probably not quite as knowledgeable about the game as American fans on the whole, but they made up for it with exuberance. As such, the experience was a lot like the Camden one except with a lot less people in a larger arena.

The people were also pretty nice to us in SkyDome, especially the ones sitting near us in the stands. We all rallied together as we rooted against the Yankees. Of course we were also contending with the again imposing presence of the Yankees traveling fan club. (I swore I saw a couple of people I had seen at previous Yankee games on our trip.) But for once the home crowd managed to drown them out. Thanks in no small part to the fact that the Blue Jays clubbed the Yanks.

The highlights of the game were, respectively, seeing Jose Canseco become the second Bash Brother to hit two out in a game on our tour, heckling Andy Pettitte, and witnessing the closing of the roof near the end of the game as rain clouds came in.

Unfortunately, there was one lowlight that washed out much of the joy of these experiences. In a strange token attempt to assert their Canadian-ness, they do not sing "Take Me Out to the Ballgame" in Toronto. Instead, everyone stands up in the middle of the seventh inning to sing an atrocious song called "Okay Blue Jay."

The experience of this song was easily the most disconcerting thing about the entire trip to date and tainted all of the good experiences we had beforehand. My irrational fears of Canada resurfaced with hurricane force during this experience, and subsequently, as we were trying to navigate the stadium traffic after the game, I flipped out. Confronted with an intense case of international claustrophobia, I screamed at Junior (only partly in jest) telling him not to mess with me when I was in Canada. We had all the windows rolled down at the time and subsequently scared everyone within a hundred yards. Which, in retrospect, might have been the point.

skyDome

CITY: Toronto, Ontario, Canada

TENANT: Toronto Blue Jays, Toronto Argonauts of the Canadian Football League

OPENED: June 5, 1989

NICKNAME/ALIASES: none

DESIGN: Retractable roof stadium, circular design, movable seats. SISTER PARKS: none.

FIELD: AstroTurf with mound and base cutouts

DIMENSIONS (feet): left field—328, left center—375, center field—400, right center—375, right field—328

FENCES (feet): 10

LOCATION: One Blue Jays Way, Toronto, Ontario M5V 1J1. BOUNDED BY: Outfield (N): Front St. W. Home plate (S): Gardiner Expressway. First base (E): CN Tower. Third base (W): Spadina Ave.

CAPACITY: 50,516 (baseball). Total attendance: 2,454,303 (1998). Average attendance: 30,300 (1998).

PARKING: $10–$15 (Canadian dollars). There are over seventeen thousand parking spaces within two blocks of SkyDome, many of them in lots beneath the park.

TICKETS: $7–$47 (Canadian dollars). BEST BANG FOR YOUR BUCK: Remember that all prices are in Canadian dollars, a real bonus. Our seats in the lower-deck field level were as good a value as any, near the action but also affordable.

THE BALLPARK EXPERIENCE: A lot of stadiums get a bad rap for being terribly huge and impersonal—Veterans, Cinergy, Three Rivers—but SkyDome escapes such criticisms. As the critics continue to call for the old and unsightly stadiums to be torn down, Sky-Dome remains above reproach. This tacit acceptance, however, is undeserved.

SkyDome, which was once state-of-the-art, seems old. Only a little over ten years old, the park has an outdated feel. The novelty of its retractable dome has been usurped by newer, more efficient retractable facilities in Arizona, Seattle, and Houston. On top of that, the park is not old enough to be considered classic in the same way Fenway, Tiger Stadium, or even County Stadium (Milwaukee) can inspire a visitor.

In spite of this aged, nonclassic feel, the park is unique. Approaching the facility, you cannot help being overwhelmed by its size. SkyDome is enormous. With the gigantic CN tower next door, the entire complex seems larger than life. There is a festive atmosphere outside the park with numerous vendors selling everything from sausages to trinkets. Toronto has a large immigrant population, and the food options outside the park are representative of Indian, Italian, and Caribbean cuisines. The lively carnival feel does a good job overcoming the dull concrete exterior of SkyDome, which resembles a suburban mall more than a ballpark.

Once inside, the many gimmicks start to hit you. SkyDome was the first park to go all out in integrating modern features into the park, like a hotel in center field where the rooms have views of the field. There are also two restaurants in center field, including a Hard Rock Café with tables that overlook the action. The concessions are even different, featuring McDonald's throughout the park as the basic food stand. These unusual facets of the park create a special Toronto kind of baseball that is found nowhere else. Throw in the retractable roof, the largest Jumbotron in baseball, and the blue seats and you have a unique baseball experience.

FANS: After SkyDome opened, Toronto became the first club to surpass the four million mark in attendance. This was quite a turnaround from the expansion club that finished

The scary tradition of singing "Okay Blue Jay" and not "Take Me Out to the Ballgame" during the seventh-inning stretch at SkyDome caught us off-guard.

last for its first seven seasons. SkyDome is principally responsible for this, and it still draws fans in respectable numbers. Unfortunately, being north of the border has obviously deprived these guys of a true understanding of baseball, particularly with respect to the game's anthem "Take Me Out to the Ballgame," of which they seem to be ignorant.

FACILITIES: The park has modern facilities, including large concourses with views of the action, numerous exceedingly clean restrooms, and wide seats. On a down note, there is a shortage of concession stops directly behind home plate, which can create long lines.

FOOD: McDonald's is everywhere at SkyDome. Every other stand is a McDonald's that serves the regular menu plus hot dogs, pizza, and the infamous McLobster. The McDonald's hot dog is a standard dog that is fresh and warm all the time (just like McDonald's coffee). The McLobster, on the other hand, is simply scary. In spite of the virtual McDonald's monopoly, this Canadian outpost comes through with all of the expected ballpark fare as well. Beer stands are plentiful, and Canadian macrobrews—Molson and Labatt—are available everywhere, including McDonald's. There are also upscale eateries in center field, such as a three-hundred-foot-long bar with views of the field and a restaurant that can serve more than five hundred people. LAST CALL: Alcohol is served until the middle of the seventh inning.

GREAT PLAYERS AND HISTORIC MOMENTS: Toronto received an expansion American League team in 1977, becoming the second MLB franchise in Canada and joining the Montreal Expos. In 1992, led by Jack Morris, Dave Winfield, Roberto Alomar, and Joe Carter, the team beat out the Atlanta Braves in six games to capture their first world championship and the first World Series for a non-U.S. team. The next year the Blue Jays successfully defended their title with a win over the Philadelphia Phillies in six games. Joe Carter hit a walk-off three-run home run in the bottom of the ninth of Game Six. Also worth noting, an All-Star Game was played here in 1991, and Pat Hentgen and Roger Clemens won back-to-back Cy Young awards for the Blue Jays in 1996 and 1997.

BALLPARK HISTORY: When it opened in 1989 SkyDome became the first new stadium in MLB since the Metrodome in 1982. It also was the first professional baseball park with a retractable roof. When they designed the park, architects Rod Robbie and Michael Allen patented their retractable roof system. Unfortunately for them, none of the more recent retractable domes use their design. Nevertheless, SkyDome was truly a marvel of its time. Construction for the park began in 1986, and the complex took three and a half years to complete at a cost of over $500 million (USD)! Many amenities that are standard at the newer parks, like restaurants and hotels with views of the field, were pioneered at Sky-Dome. The hotel in particular has provided ticket holders free entertainment on multiple occasions when frisky couples have neglected to close their blinds.

FUN FACT: The Blue Jays front office decides whether or not to open or close the roof for regular season games. The roof is closed during the game due to weather about five times per year. All playoff games must be played with the roof closed.

THE ONE THING YOU HAVE TO DO AT SKYDOME AND WHY: Watch the eleven-thousand-ton roof open and shut. It takes about twenty minutes to open or close (four times as long as the newer parks).

OTHER THINGS TO REMEMBER: If you are in the market for big-ticket baseball souvenirs, get them at SkyDome. The exchange rate is very favorable and you can save 15 to 20 percent by purchasing in Canada. SkyDome caters to this U.S. tourist need with many souvenir shops that have jerseys, hats, and shirts of virtually every team in the league.

LASTING IMPRESSION: While not the most appealing park, SkyDome has its own flavor of baseball that is uniquely Canadian.

BAT INFO

FINAL SCORE: Blue Jays 9, Yankees 3

OUR SEATS: Aisle 118, Row 42, Seats 6–7

BALLPARK: 22 of 30

DAY: 30 of 38

MILES TRAVELED: 655 (11,398 total)

NEW STATES: 0 (26 total); 2 Canadian provinces (Ontario, Quebec)

OUR EXPENSES: $76
  programs and ballpark food—
    McDonald's hot dogs, fries, beer, and
    ice cream cones $40
  gas ($54 Canadian) $36
  EXPENSES TO DATE: $2,173

OUR FREEBIES: $80
  game tickets $30
  lodging (courtesy of our hosts in
    Montreal, the Kivenkos) $50
  FREEBIES TO DATE: $3,284

23

olympic stadium (Le stade olympique)

montreal

july 20, 1998

WHEN I said that there wasn't much difference between Canada and the United States, perhaps I spoke too soon. We hadn't been to Montreal yet. In Montreal they are so Canadian that even the rest of Canada wants to disown them. Or more accurately, Montreal and the rest of Quebec want to disown Canada. Yep, the only state or province in North America with more separatists than Texas.

I can speak candidly about the people of Montreal in these pages without worrying too much about ruining our fan base. Only one guy in Montreal actually likes baseball, and we're already friends with him, so he won't take this personally. The rest of them don't care and will never read this book. Of course, there are people in Cincinnati who like baseball and might even read this book, but I spoke a little to the far side of candid with regard to that city. In the interest of showing a modicum of respect to the people of Cincinnati, we might as well really let Montreal have it.

After the Blue Jays game we called on some friends of Dave's family who lived in Toronto, Gary and Josh Kivenko. We didn't stay very long. We were still bummed about the seventh-inning stretch debacle at SkyDome and thinking that if we kept moving, we might get over it. We stayed long enough with the Kivenkos to get directions to their family's place in Montreal, where we were going to be sleeping over our one night in Canada. Getting these directions was somewhat frustrating, however, as they were in French, at least all of the street names. Gary had to repeat them for us several times.

It was 350 miles between the two Canadian metropolises, so we were just hoping to get there before it got too late. We hadn't known what to expect in Toronto, and for the most part it had gone all right, but heading into Quebec, we faced a whole new unknown. Even the people of Toronto seemed hesitant to vouch for their fellow Canadians. All we knew was that they spoke French there, they didn't like Americans, and they didn't really like Canadians either, at least English-speaking ones.

Above I referred to the sole baseball fan in Montreal. His name is Danny Kivenko. Danny's dad and Dave's dad were friends, and so it had been arranged that we would stay with Danny and his sister, Sharon, in Montreal. Obviously we were very lucky to have connections to the only baseball fan in Montreal. When we got to their house at 10:30 Sunday night, Danny's and Sharon's kindness made us think that maybe Montreal wasn't so bad. We visited with them for a couple of hours, drinking some beers and a Tequiza-type drink. You have to hand it to the French-Canadians, they are no bandwagon jumpers. They loved their Tequiza long before everyone else hated it.

After a couple of mellow hours socializing we headed to bed. Dave and I had spent only three of the last forty hours with pillows, and we were fortunate enough that at the Kivenkos' place we all had beds again.

The next day Dave, Junior, and I had assumed that we would have a little time to rest. Dave and I, after a solid month on the road, were pretty much perpetually tired by this point and seized any opportunity to have some mellow time. We had found that sleep was good, and sleep in a bed was better, but the most relaxing and rejuvenating experience was to sit in a chair through most of the morning and afternoon and practice inactivity. It wasn't quite meditation, but it wasn't a couch potato thing either. In any case, though, Dave and I would have no time for any of it. Danny and Sharon were intent upon showing us their city. In all honesty, they had probably sensed our general skepticism and apprehension about being in Canada, at least my skepticism and apprehension, and they wanted to prove that the city was a great place.

As this book isn't really about the cities of North America, I will make the highlights of our tour rather brief. In short, it turned out that Montreal was actually a pretty interesting place. It was the oldest city I had ever been to and had a distinctly European feel to it, complete with cobblestone roads and what a simpleton like me could only describe as some very old buildings, including a convalescent home on the top of a hill that looks like a haunted castle. Danny and Sharon also treated us to what they claimed was a local specialty food and the best food in all of Montreal: smoked meat sandwiches. It was quite good, although I didn't have the heart to tell them that we had something like that, too. We call it corned beef.

All in all, we had to give it to the Kivenkos. They had a nice town. Our interactions with the people, however, were another story. In all our travels it became evident that the rumors about the locals' feelings toward Americans were true. In general, the only American thing they liked was our money. We were lucky though to be with a couple of native Montrealers, shielding us from the brunt of anti-American prejudice. Rumors of the prevalence of the French language were true though, and in many cases you just couldn't get by with English. Some people simply would not or could not speak it. We never found out which. At one point I tried to retaliate by speaking only Spanish until people caught on that I was only saying the same three phrases over and over.

olympic stadium
(Le stade olympique)

PHILADELPHIA V MONTREAL

Game Time: 7:05 p.m.

WE HAD an exhausting day doing the tourist thing (reminding Dave and me why we had mostly skipped the nonbaseball sites on our trip). When the Kivenkos had shown us enough of the city, they took us to the ballpark. We had wanted to take two cars to the stadium so that Dave, Junior, and I could take off for New York directly afterward, but Sharon and Danny convinced us otherwise. They pointed out that the neighborhood of Olympic Stadium wasn't the safest in which to leave a car, and we deferred to their judgment. It wasn't a good start for our impressions of the stadium though.

The tour of Montreal that Danny was leading us on didn't stop when we got to the stadium. Danny is a huge baseball fan and a huge Expos fan with a uniquely Canadian view of baseball history—there is an American plot to sabotage Canadian teams in the majors. This view is based entirely upon the fact that the players' strike in 1994 happened to come in the middle of the Montreal Expos' best season ever. At the time of the strike the Expos had the best record in the majors. Not only that, but the only other Canadian team, the Toronto Blue Jays, was also the two-time defending World Series champion. So the theory goes that Americans couldn't bear to see the World Series trophy end up in Canada for a third straight year. Rather than risk the chance of Montreal's taking it all, which Danny saw as a statistical certainty, the heads of the league and the players union conspired to bag the rest of the season, let the Expos lose their best

olympic stadium (Le stade olmpique)

Dave's brother Junior brought his glove along to Le Stade hoping to catch some Canadian baseballs.

players in the off-season (which they invariably did to a bunch of American teams with bigger pockets), and come back next year.

If you believe Danny's theory, then you would agree that the plan worked out beautifully. The 1994 season was definitely the Expos' last best shot at a title, and they probably won't have another one before their team is mercifully transplanted. Of course, if you believe Danny's theory, you are also probably a Montreal Expos fan, and since we have pointed out that there is only one, this means that you are Danny. (Hi, Danny!)

Crazy and provocative theories aside, Danny was a very knowledgeable baseball fan and knew everything about anything important that happened in Montreal baseball dating back to Jackie Robinson's integration of professional baseball, not with the Brooklyn Dodgers in 1947, but with the Montreal Monarchs, the Dodger's top minor league squad, a year earlier. Being so knowledgeable about Montreal baseball, Danny was also the perfect person to explain to us the troubled history of Olympic Stadium.

Over the last twenty-five years, somewhere around a billion dollars has been spent on the building, and the locals and media around the major leagues view it as the greatest debacle in stadium lore. Economically speaking this may be true, but barring such considerations, our experience of the stadium actually turned out to be rather cool.

At the game we saw, the tarplike roof was missing, so looking out from behind home plate, which is where we sat, we saw this huge monolithic tower hanging above. From the tower hung a bunch of cables with large disks, hovering just above the top rim of the stadium cylinder. The effect was a little like aliens were about to land, and thus inadvertently drew a parallel between this park and the saucer-shaped Tropicana Field in Tampa Bay.

Weirder still than this effect is the fact that everything at the ballpark is in French. The signs are in French, the scoreboard is in French, the PA announcements are in French. So now I know that *coup de circuit* means "home run" in French. The irony of course is that 99 percent of the world's French-speaking population doesn't know what a coup de circuit is.

On top of the language issue, Olympic Stadium's coup de grâce is its touch of native cuisine. Similar to SkyDome, Olympic Stadium relies upon Canadian beers. Again, Labatt is the most popular. But in line with its general theme of pushing baseball across international boundaries, Olympic Stadium does not hesitate to serve what a traditional American baseball fan can only describe as shockingly un-American foods. Whereas the craziest food in SkyDome was the McLobster (which I will grant was McStrange), Olympic Stadium raised the bar a good three notches with poutine. If you thought the Rocky Mountain oysters in Denver were a step in the exotic direction, consider a meal of french fries, gravy, and curd cheese. (That's what poutine is.) If you don't know what curd cheese is, think that chunky stuff in milk gone bad.

By now it is quite obvious that I was a bit off my game with the whole Canadian experience, and I won't deny that at the time the whole thing bothered me a bit, particularly the scoreboard's being in French. For some reason "point marques," "coup surs," and "erreurs" instead of runs, hits, and errors just didn't seem right. I'll also admit that I didn't really care for the poutine. Looking back on it, however, the Olympic Stadium experience was at the very least the most culturally enlightening experience of the trip, and in general our trip to Montreal was one of the most interesting and unique experiences we had.

Meanwhile, the Expos lost in front of less than ten thousand fans. Despite the low turnout, the crowd proved rambunctious. This was surprising given the general aloofness of the Quebecois, but we soon figured out where all of the noise came from. The seats at Olympic Stadium were high school gymnasium-style seats with hard rounded edges and indestructible frames that served perfectly to be banged back and forth, making a louder sound than the hollow floor in Pittsburgh ever could. It was also advantageous that for every person at the park there were four empty seats to bang.

After the game, we quickly said our good-byes and drove off into the night. Junior was a little apprehensive about driving through Canada after dark (or maybe he just didn't want to leave Sharon), but we pried him away anyway.

Still in red-blooded patriotic American mode (the appreciation for Olympic Stadium's cultural infusion would not come till much later), we stopped just north of the border to set off a couple of firecrackers, specifically one designed like an army tank.

A few minutes later we reentered the United States, pulling up to the guard who simply asked, "Are you guys all Americans?" Beaming grins accompanied our answers.

All in all, the Canadian experience was pretty fun. I complain about it a lot mostly because I enjoy doing so, but the honest truth is that it is pretty cool that even though the people spoke French, they came out to the baseball game anyway. More than anything, I guess I am glad to have the Montreal experience under my belt because I know that baseball in Olympic Stadium, like baseball in Tiger Stadium or County Stadium in Milwaukee, is not long for this world. The cold, hard economics of the sport won't allow it.

olympic stadium (Le stade olympique)

CITY: Montreal, Quebec, Canada

TENANTS: Montreal Expos, Montreal Alouettes (CFL)

OPENED: April 15, 1977

NICKNAME/ALIASES: Olympic Stadium, Big O, Big Owe

DESIGN: Multipurpose retractable roof stadium, circular design, movable seats. SISTER PARKS: none.

FIELD: AstroTurf with mound and base cutouts

DIMENSIONS (feet): left field—325, left center—375, center field—404, right center—375, right field—328

FENCES (feet): 12

LOCATION: 4549 Pierre de Coubertin, Montreal, Quebec H1V 3N7. BOUNDED BY: Left field (NW): Rue Sherbrooke. Right field (NE): Boulevard Viau. First base (SE): Avenue Pierre-de-Coubertin. Third base (SW): Boulevard Pie-IX.

CAPACITY: 46,500 (baseball). Total attendance: 914,909 (1998). Average attendance: 11,295 (1998).

PARKING: $7–$10 (Canadian dollars). Focus on the two to three blocks south of Olympic Stadium for your best bet.

TICKETS: $8–$36. BEST BANG FOR YOUR BUCK: Terrace seats are midlevel and offer a good price with adequate sightlines. Consider general admission, where you can spread out and try several vantage points.

THE BALLPARK EXPERIENCE: Eclectic is the one word that sums up Le Stade Olympique. Nothing, from the prevalence of French (don't they know English is the official language of baseball) to the strange retractable roof that has never managed to retract, makes any sense at the park. As we saw all the unusual ballpark tidbits, we could not help but feel we were not watching a real major league game. Approaching the park, the distinctive feature is the large arm that towers some 550 feet above it. This was intended to house the retractable tarp roof that is generally connected to it by large steel cables. Beyond the arm and roof (which we never saw), the park is large with an expansive outer concrete shell held up by thirty-eight concrete ribs.

The place has an impersonal feel due to its size and odd shape, and on the inside, the park is generally strange with enormous concourses behind the seats that are usually empty due to the lack of fans. This makes it feel like you are at the park on an off-day. Walking through the tunnels that give access to the field, you see a sea of seats unlike any others, signs in French, and a tarplike roof above. The seats are small, uncomfortable, and alternate between blue and yellow. They seem almost temporary. Given this generally negative review, the biggest shocker is that baseball here is, at least for a one-time visitor, a memorable experience. The park's idiosyncrasies, for better or worse, give it a distinctly unique and international flavor, worth noting amid the other ballparks today rushing to imitate each other.

From the signs and announcements in French to the odd food choices like the poutine, Le Stade Olympique was the strangest ballpark experience of the entire trip.

FANS: The PR folk at Le Stade Olympique brag that every fan gets to be on the Jumbotron at every game. There are so few fans in Montreal that this may be true. Le Stade Olympique was the only park to draw under one million fans in both 1998 and 1999. That is around eleven thousand fans for each game. At a park that holds almost fifty thousand fans, this creates quite an empty feeling. This poor attendance has not always been the norm in Montreal though. Montreal was the first Canadian MLB franchise and a natural choice. Long the AAA affiliate of the Brooklyn Dodgers, Montreal had a strong fan base when it was granted an expansion team in 1969. Recently, however, the club has had a difficult time drawing fans. The bad reputation of Olympic Stadium, poor on-field talent, and bad luck have contributed to this decline. The Expos' best two seasons, 1981 and '94, were both shortened by players' strikes. All of this makes it no wonder the franchise is rumored to be in danger of relocating.

FACILITIES: The 1976 facilities have run down and are in need of renovation. The seats, although an effective noisemaker, should be replaced. They resemble the small desk chairs found in many grade schools and are of comparable size. The armrests are small and the backs don't make it very far up your spine. The restrooms are plentiful but old, and the concourses are so wide that at times you feel that you took a wrong turn and ended up in an empty convention center.

FOOD: Montreal adds to its eclectic reputation with a wide variety of unparalleled food options. The smoked meat sandwich, a Montreal favorite, is similar to a corned beef sandwich with leaner meat. Although not the best smoked meat in the city, Le Stade has a suitable sandwich served on rye bread and a pickle on the side. While it is a local specialty, the smoked meat is really unnoteworthy compared to Le Stade's signature dish, the poutine. If you only try one thing at Le Stade, it has to be this crazy Quebec invention: French fries served with turkey gravy and cheese curd. Depending on who you talk to, this is either the best food at the park or the worst. For our votes, Dave lists it as one of the best food choices in all of baseball; I couldn't stomach more than a couple bites. LAST CALL: Alcohol is served until the middle of the seventh inning.

GREAT PLAYERS AND HISTORIC MOMENTS: The Montreal Expos joined the National League in the spring of 1969 as the first Canadian team in the majors. The team has had little success since, with only one postseason appearance coming during the strike-shortened 1981 season. That year the Expos won the second half of the season and defeated the Philadelphia Phillies for the right to play in the NLCS, where they succumbed to the eventual World Series champion Dodgers in five games (3-2). The next year, Le Stade hosted its lone All-Star Game. Although not blessed with great success, the Expos have been blessed with a great farm system and numerous great players such as Gary Carter, Andre Dawson, Dennis Martinez, Larry Walker, Randy Johnson, Moises Alou, and

Pedro Martinez. Unfortunately, the Expos have never had the revenue needed to keep these stars and have lost them all to free agency or preemptive trades.

BALLPARK HISTORY: The story of Olympic Stadium is tragic, particularly to hear it from Danny. Apparently the park was originally built to have a retractable tarplike roof and was to be fully operational for the 1976 Olympic Games and then used for Montreal's new baseball team the following season, à la Turner Field. A retractable roof in 1976, now that was an idea well ahead of its time. Unfortunately though, the tower didn't make it in time for the opening of the stadium, and so the place was opened without a roof. Finally, twenty years later the tower was ready, but the first time they used it to remove the tarp, the thing got ripped to pieces. To make a long story short, they tried to fix it a couple of times, but it never worked. The tarp collected rainwater and tore under its own weight. So now the stadium has a fixed dome, although when we were there the tarp was nowhere to be found. We had an interesting view of the monolithic tower above, akin to SkyDome and the CN Tower. I guess that's a Canadian thing. All told, over the last twenty-five years, the estimate is that somewhere around one billion dollars have been spent on the building. Adding insult to injury, in 1991 the Expos were forced to play their last twenty-eight home games on the road after a nonstructural piece of exterior concrete fell from the roof.

FUN FACT: With a combined price of over one billion Canadian dollars and counting, Le Stade is the most expensive baseball park ever constructed.

THE ONE THING YOU HAVE TO DO AT LE STADE OLYMPIQUE AND WHY: Ride the Funiculare to the top of the observation deck. The tower is 552 feet high and is the world's largest

BAT INFO

FINAL SCORE: Phillies 3, Expos 1

OUR SEATS: Section 202, Rangee A, Siege 3–4

BALLPARK: 23 of 30

DAY: 31 of 38

MILES TRAVELED: 182 (11,580 total)

NEW STATES: 0 (26 total)

OUR EXPENSES: $80
lunch $4
programs and parking $16
motel room (in Saratoga Springs, NY) $60
EXPENSES TO DATE: $2,249

OUR FREEBIES: $80
game tickets $30
ballpark food—smoked meat sandwich, bear claw, beer, plus poutine $50
FREEBIES TO DATE: $3,364

Architecturally, Le Stade's quasi-retractable dome (pictured here without the tarp) was a wonder to behold despite the fact that it never worked and cost over $1 billion.

inclined structure. The views are spectacular, especially of the St. Laurence River. The observation deck also has a nice bird's-eye view of the wacky dome. It gives you a much better idea of how the retractable dome was supposed to work (basically like an inverse umbrella) and why it never has.

LASTING IMPRESSION: A quirky baseball experience north of the border in the most unusual of baseball parks.

24
yankee stadium
new york

LIKE THE day we spent blazing through Louisville, Tuesday, the thirty-second day of our trip, was going to be a whirlwind of baseball tourism. The night before we drove until 1:30 in the morning and finally arrived in Saratoga Springs, New York, ninety miles out of Cooperstown. That left us with a two-hour drive to the Hall of Fame, exactly two hours to visit the hall, four and a half hours to get to New York City, and fifteen minutes of wiggle room to make our five o'clock appointment at Yankee Stadium.

Of course, to get all of this done we had to wake up at 8 A.M., which to us was tantamount to getting no sleep at all. Had I left it to Dave, we probably would have missed the hall entirely that day. He had been there before and didn't really think that much of the place. But I was so excited about going to Cooperstown that I wouldn't let his negativity deter me. I was never really all that nostalgic about a lot of this stuff to begin with, but this was different. One entire town was created as a shrine to baseball, and all my life I had dreamed about going to this place. The fact that this dream had managed to withstand the cynicism that I had acquired with age meant that it must be a pretty big deal.

In pursuit of this childhood dream, I pushed, prodded, tugged, and kicked at Dave and Junior from 7:30 A.M. until 8, when we finally headed to Cooperstown.

Once we were on the road, with Dave and Junior a bit more awake, my enthusiasm about our next destination began to permeate the car. It was quite a role reversal. Dave had always been the cheerleader of the trip, prone to overhype every move we made, and generally boosting my excitement and anticipation at every turn. For once, Dave was slightly pessimistic about a tour stop, and I had to set the tone.

Just driving into Cooperstown I could sense that this was going to be a magical experience. The sides of the highway hardly betrayed that we were approaching this baseball landmark. A road sign here and there, a couple of countryside inns, but that was about all. The architecture it seemed had also not responded to the town's importance, other than that it was well done and elegant. The town somehow seemed to live in an older, simpler time. Granted it wasn't much different from small-town America anywhere, except that the bed-and-breakfasts were a little nicer and higher priced, but it felt different. It had a buzz of significance.

The main street in Cooperstown also had a special feel to it. It was lined with sports memorabilia shops, but what really stood out along the street were the bustling people. So many fathers and sons, old men, young women, big boys, and little girls sauntered easily about the little town. They walked up and down the central street, ducked into a store to look at some photographs, grabbed a pretzel over there, walked over to Doubleday Field to sit in the stands. Even though there wasn't a ballgame going on that day, they checked out the ball field in the little town that is the heart of baseball. None of them seemed to have anything to worry about. They all had the day entirely free, and the only thing on the agenda was to take a little time to understand a little more about the essence of baseball.

We weren't in the same boat. We only had 120 minutes in town, and the clock was ticking. We checked out most of Cooperstown the city from behind seat belts, took a quick peek at Doubleday Field, and zipped over to the hall. Our first stop was in the administrative offices. We had never called anybody in advance to drum up publicity for our visit, so we decided at the last minute that we might as well give it a shot as long as the office was open. At the very least, maybe we'd get a couple of free passes.

That is exactly what we got. Along with a couple of free programs and a few well wishes. Of course the free passes came courtesy of our plea that we would essentially be spending only a half day in town on Tuesday but would be coming back through just three days later for another half day. Presenting that case in the context of our entire trip proved quite successful, and so we were granted free tickets to cover one of our two visits. The programs were a bonus touch and a very nice one at that.

Twenty minutes into our 120-minute tour we entered the hall. It was truly magical.

Dave had been a little hard on the place because, in comparison to the NFL Hall of Fame in his home state of Ohio, the setup in Cooperstown is pretty plain. They don't have any fancy interactive displays or full busts of all the players. But they don't really need anything like that to put one in awe of the sheer history of the sport. Just seeing everything, the last one hundred years and more of baseball all in one room, is magical.

I spent over an hour just reading the plaques for each of the inductees. I could have stayed for days.

The whole Cooperstown experience was something of a turning point for me. For some time I had been becoming cynical about baseball in general: the lackluster attitude of Canadians toward the game, our forgettable experience at Cinergy, the building fear that this new wave of ballparks was not going to revolutionize the game but would actually leave it in a place not much better off than the last wave of stadiums had left it, without much distinguishing character. Cooperstown stanched that tide entirely and reinspired me. Seeing how carefree all of those kids in town with their dads were, I realized for the first time in a while that what Dave and I were doing was an unthinkable dream to everyone else in this town. We were truly fortunate to be getting closer to the essence of baseball, and we had a chance to get much closer than almost anyone else.

I may have broken the promise I made to myself when I was in San Francisco that I was going to love every second of this trip. That had obviously not been the case. We had only a week left—seven parks. And I was determined to latch on to this spirit and fall in love with the sport all over again.

yankee stadium

DETROIT V NEW YORK (AL)

Game Time: 7:35 p.m.

WE LEFT Cooperstown and made it to New York with only minimal traffic. Actually, the traffic was awful by my standards, but compared to our expectations it was not bad at all.

We were back in New York for our encore appearance. The trip began with some fanfare. We had been told over the phone to find our way to Parking Lot 14 where we were on the elusive list. So we did just that, fully expecting, as had happened to us several times already, that there would be no list to speak of. Circling the stadium we began to worry that not only were we not on the list at Lot 14, but there was no Lot 14. Almost out of options, we pulled up to one of the attendants at another lot and asked him where Lot 14 was, expecting a hearty laugh in response. (I bet they pulled this on all of the jerk kids who tried to get free parking.) But with a completely straight face he directed us around the corner. "You can't miss it," he said. "It's right next to the stadium. The players' lot."

The players' lot? Now this was an even bigger joke, right? But with no other viable option, we pulled around the corner, up to the barricade that blocked the street between Lot 14 and the stadium. A security guard standing sentinel near the front of our car walked over and politely asked how he could help us.

"This is our lot," Junior told him, beaming with arrogance from behind the wheel.

The guard didn't seem to buy it for a second. Surely he was wondering who these idiot kids were trying to get into the players' lot. He walked inside the barricade and spoke to a member of the ballpark personnel who was by the chain fence that stood at the entrance of Lot 14 itself. The two of them walked back toward our car. The second man was carrying a clipboard that I was sure would seal our fate. It was the list, and I knew there was no way we were on it.

The second man walked up to the car window. I prayed Junior would be a little more humble this time. "What's your name?" he asked simply.

"Kaval," Junior replied. "Or Null," Dave quickly added from the passenger seat. Dave spoke in a very helpful tone. We had been through this process together so many times already. He, like me, was obviously also preparing for the worst and trying to soften the blow.

It didn't take the gatekeeper long to scan his list. It was obviously a very select few who managed to make it on that sacred tablet. He looked back at Junior and pointed back through the lot. "You can park anywhere across that far fence over there." Dave and I stared at him dumbfounded. Junior, naive about the magnitude of the situation, was simply trying to follow directions. Glaring back at us, the gatekeeper continued, "Do not park within this inner fence here."

We nodded understandingly and Junior sped the car into the lot. I looked behind us to make sure that neither guard had changed his mind and was running after us. For the time being they were still, but both the gatekeeper and the guard were watching to make sure we followed directions and didn't park in any of the players' spots.

Our good friend Jim joined us for a memorable game at Yankee Stadium, where we had front-row seats courtesy of George Steinbrenner himself.

Monument Park, the shrine to Yankees greats such as Babe Ruth, Lou Gehrig, and Joe DiMaggio, is situated behind the left-center-field wall at Yankee Stadium. It once stood within the field of play.

Given our early arrival time to the game, the players were actually showing up at roughly the same time as we were. As a result, while we whipped through the lot, Junior almost hit David Cone, who was coming out from between two cars. We recovered quickly though before our watchers could censure us. We proceeded to the back of the lot and parked the car as close to the far fence as possible. The watchers seemed pleased with this and resumed their original business.

A couple of fans walking along the sidewalk outside of the gate watched us intently as we got out of the car. Upon seeing Junior duck out of the driver's seat, one said to the other, "That's Andy Pettitte." Immediately a couple of pictures flashed, and we could sense them waiting for a better glimpse so that they could take more. Was this how uncomfortable it must be as a celebrity, knowing that people were waiting to snap your picture as soon as you turned around? But as soon as Junior turned around I heard a collective sigh from the fans.

"That's not Andy." Then a pause. Then a question through the chain-link fence. "Hey kid. Are you Andy Pettitte's little brother?"

Junior turned, but it was Dave who responded, nodding affirmatively.

"Can we get your autograph?" Fame by association, the only kind we knew. Of course it was mistaken association in this case, but we'd take it nonetheless.

Walking out of the lot, we looked around just like everybody else to see if there were any other important people near us. In the process, we were walking right across the same barricaded road as all of the players, so a number of autograph seekers stared at us quizzically for a minute wondering who we might be. We just smiled and waved as if we belonged there. I could imagine our two fans spreading the word. "That's Andy

Pettitte's little brother. He's a prospect." The effect was ruined when instead of going in the players' entrance we veered into the crowd.

We had made plans to meet up with our friend Jim Graham. This time the rendezvous was to take place in front of the huge concrete baseball bat situated outside the stadium just behind home plate. As in Baltimore, our rendezvous went off without a hitch.

Jim had been friends with both of us since our sophomore year of college. He was in New York for the summer, and so we were staying with him that night in Manhattan. He had a real nice hotel room courtesy of the investment bank that had just hired him, and he didn't mind sharing the wealth.

After picking up our fourth member, we headed into the stadium without tickets. Again we were on a VIP list, and this time we were met shortly by one of the stadium's PR guys, a high school kid named Brian, who took us on the full tour. For a summer intern he was pretty cool, knowledgeable, and gave us all of the inside information.

Yankee Stadium is a historic park (see HISTORIC MOMENTS). By far the most awe-inspiring element of this history is Monument Park, a shrine behind left field filled with monuments and plaques to past Yankee greats. Several of these monuments are large standalone blocks of granite dedicated to the likes of Lou Gehrig, Babe Ruth, Miller Huggins, Mickey Mantle, and Joe DiMaggio. By far the coolest thing about Monument Park is that before the stadium was remodeled in the 1970s, these monuments stood in the field of play. As the story was told us by our guide, back in the 1960s Mickey Mantle would routinely hit deep flies into the memorial so that opposing outfielders would have to run between the stones. As we looked at the monuments to these baseball legends and listened to him spin these yarns, I could really feel the legacy of Yankee Stadium. Monument Park exudes history, and because of it the whole stadium maintains its aura as The House That Ruth Built.

Sadly though, Monument Park is now safely behind the left-field fence at Yankee Stadium, a fence that runs in an arc around the outfield in roughly the same dimensions as most of the other parks built after Fenway and before Camden. It struck me as somehow tragic that this change had been made, but it was also emblematic of the theme of the entire stadium. Outside of the park, the rest of Yankee Stadium somehow lacks character. It has been around since the 1920s, but the radical remodeling during the 1970s seems to have pretty much stripped the stadium of its nostalgia, and it felt a lot like new Comiskey. It is a crime of epic proportions, considering how much history is trapped somewhere in those walls that have been whitewashed by renovation.

We were also deprived on our trip of a bit of the true experience of Yankee Stadium. During this magical summer of '98, even discriminating Yankee fans could find little to criticize about the amazing Yankees, who were 69-25 when we came through town. They could not even bring themselves to ridicule the opposing teams that were being routinely drubbed by the Yanks. So they resorted mostly to picking on each other.

We even got a little notice given the fact that we had the best seats in the house—the first row behind the Yankees dugout. As we were directed to them, a man in a dark suit intervened and told the usher flat out that these were not our seats. As with the players' lot earlier, Dave and I exchanged glances and expected to get the boot to the nosebleed section. But when the usher showed the man our tickets, he went silent.

After the usher left, he told us, "Boys, those are George's seats."

We gave him a funny look as if to say, "George who?"

"I mean George Steinbrenner," he clarified.

"Cool," Junior shot back with a big smile.

"Who are you kids?"

"The Baseball America Tour," Dave proudly answered and went into a ten-minute monologue on our trip. The guy turned out to be Steinbrenner's personal doctor and had never seen anyone use the seats but George. We never did find out how we got those tickets. I guess George must have been a fan of the tour.

Steinbrenner wasn't our only fan in New York though, because the Tigers were in town, and that meant our good buddy Luis Gonzalez would be there, too. So when he got on deck we gave our best effort to get his attention. To be honest, we didn't expect to catch his eye, and if we did we didn't expect that he would remember us. But both happened before his trip to the plate. He gave us the two-hands-behind-the-wheel gesture to prove that he remembered us. Dave and I were awestruck that someone with so many obviously more important things on his mind would remember us and our excuse to avoid the real world. Whether he genuinely cared or not, Luis Gonzales gave us validation for our trip. If he thought it was memorable, then we must be doing something right. After all, this guy personified baseball. In the end, his gesture put both Dave and me squarely into the "Gonzo for the Hall" camp for life.

The amazing Yanks and Gonzo made an exciting experience out of it, even if our man didn't have the best game (0-4 with two strikeouts). In the end though, the Yanks manhandled the Tigers, as was expected by Dave, me, and the other thirty-eight thousand fans there with us.

One final note, though the El Niño heat wave had followed us steadfastly throughout the summer, in New York it was somehow significantly hotter. I was sweating like crazy and somewhat delirious. Maybe the heat had something to do with why, in the sixth inning, I lost a one-sided shoving match for a foul ball pop-up coming toward my seat. Maybe not. Anyway, it was my second near miss (Dave called them drops) in a little over a week. After the ball hit the ground, my foil pounced on in and came up with the souvenir, beaming with pride. I stood there stunned at his audacity and also at the Mark Wohlers's mental block that seemed to be preventing me from catching those foul balls.

Yankee Stadium

CITY: New York, New York

TENANT: New York Yankees

OPENED: April 18, 1923

NICKNAME/ALIASES: The House That Ruth Built

DESIGN: Baseball-only stadium, asymmetrical design, no movable seats. SISTER PARKS: No true sister parks although Anaheim Stadium and new Comiskey have copied some of the design elements.

FIELD: Grass

DIMENSIONS (feet): left field—318, left center (left of bullpen)—379, deep left center—399, center field—408, deep right center—385, right center—353, right field—314

FENCES (feet): Left field—7.5, left center and center field—7.3, right field—9

LOCATION: River Ave. and East 161st St., New York, NY 10451. BOUNDED BY: Right field (SE): River Ave. Home plate (W): Harlem River and I-87. First base (SW): East 157th St. Left field (NE): East 161st St. Third base (NW): Ruppert Pl.

CAPACITY: 57,545 (baseball). Total attendance: 2,955,193 (1998). Average attendance: 36,484 (1998).

PARKING: $10–$15 at ten to twelve parking lots adjacent to Yankee Stadium. The lots along River Avenue across from the park are most convenient but most expensive.

TICKETS: $8–$42. BEST BANG FOR YOUR BUCK: Yankee Stadium has an enormous backstop, which makes the seats behind home plate on all three levels far away from the action. Bleacher seats and seats along the first- and third-base lines are much closer. For a truly unique experience, try the bleachers at Yankee Stadium. Full of rowdy fans (see FANS), the bleachers are vibrant, exciting, and a little tense.

THE BALLPARK EXPERIENCE: More baseball history has occurred at Yankee Stadium than at any other park. The place is where legends are made and World Series won. There is a swagger to the park, fans, and players that gives the place a level of excitement that we found at no other baseball venue.

As we approached Yankee Stadium, we were surprised, even though the park was built in 1923, that the place did not feel old or nostalgic. The concrete exterior feels more like the cookie-cutter parks of the 1960s and '70s than the old exposed-steel neighborhood parks like Fenway and Wrigley. As we navigated the narrow concourses or looked up at the second deck, we could tell that the newer seats, stands, and supports are covering a historic past. It goes without saying that it is a huge letdown that the park has camouflaged the past that one feels at Wrigley, Tiger, or Fenway.

The developments that have brought about this sterilization were the "improvements" made to the park in the mid-1970s. To modernize the park, George Steinbrenner removed the many support beams, including the famous roof facade. A replica facade was added above the bleachers but the park forever lost its historic feel in 1976. This is truly tragic for the generations of fans who never experienced old Yankee Stadium. Although the swagger is still there and the winning tradition continues, the park is more of a 1976 park built over a 1923 classic.

FANS: Even though Yankee Stadium may be disappointingly lacking in character, New York fans are not. Whether you love them or hate them, you have to give them one

With all the renovations in the 1970s, Yankee Stadium has lost much of the historic feel that made it the "House That Ruth Built."

thing: They certainly provide for a palpable atmosphere and are largely responsible for that Yankee mystique. More so than Mets fans, Yankees fans are intense. They intimidate opposing teams, opposing fans, their own players, and even each other. When the Yankees are playing great, they make it a raucous experience. When the Yankees play poorly, they make it a riotous experience. When nothing much of interest seems to be happening, they provide their own entertainment, generally in the form of heckling. Usually they heckle opposing players. Sometimes they heckle their own players. They always seem to find one or two people in the crowd to pick on. That, as your mother might say, is how they show that they love you, and if you dare to root for the other team, they will show you a great deal of such love.

FACILITIES: Even though the park was remodeled in 1976, Yankee Stadium's facilities felt old and not up to the standards of the new wave of parks. The concourses behind the lower deck are narrow. Concession booths are crowded and were very hot in the summer of El Niño. The restrooms also needed some repair.

FOOD: At Yankee Stadium we sampled the average assortment of ballpark fare. The foot-long hot dog is a signature item that is best ordered from a roving concessionaire since the lines can last an inning. We tried a good selection of burgers and chicken sandwiches as well as the seasoned curly fries that come with most meals. As was the case at Shea, everything was somewhat predictable but of good quality. LAST CALL: Alcohol is served until the middle of the seventh inning.

GREAT PLAYERS AND HISTORIC MOMENTS: The Yankees' history of winning corresponds perfectly with their ballpark. Before Yankee Stadium was built, the New York Yankees had never won a world championship. Babe Ruth not only built the house, he stocked it with banners as well, notching four for the Yanks before he retired. The 1927 club led by Ruth and Lou Gehrig, with 110 wins, a 3.20 team era, Ruth's 60 home runs, and a World Series sweep of the Pirates, is often labeled the best team of all time. In the 1930s, a young Italian from San Francisco named Joe DiMaggio became the new Yankee Clipper, leading the club to three straight World Series wins from 1937 to 1939. Another turning point for the Yankees came in 1949, when Casey Stengel was brought on to manage the club and enjoyed the greatest success in baseball history. The Yankees won five consecutive World Series with the pitching of Whitey Ford and the hitting of Yogi Berra and DiMaggio. In 1954 the streak ended when the team's 103 wins weren't enough to top Cleveland's 111, but the championship era lasted through back-to-back wins in the 1961 and 1962 Series. After that, the Yankees did not win again until George Steinbrenner took control of the club in 1973. Taking an active role, Steinbrenner brought Reggie Jackson to the team and installed Billy Martin as manager. A loss in the World Series in 1976 against the Big Red Machine was followed by back-to-back

We were treated to a great tour of the stadium that allowed us to see many of the intricacies of the park, including Monument Park and the lush tomato plants that are diligently nurtured in the Yankees bullpen.

wins in 1977 and 1978 against the Los Angeles Dodgers. This was followed by another droop in the '80s before the Yankees' dominance in the late 1990s.

BALLPARK HISTORY: In an event that defies modern baseball economics, the New York Yankees moved out of the Polo Grounds in 1923 to a new state-of-the-art stadium just across the Harlem River. The Yankees had shared the Polo Grounds with the rival New York Giants since 1913, and the Giants, who owned the park, had grown weary of the Yankees' outdrawing their club. The owners of the Yankees, Jacob Ruppert and Tillinghast Hommedieu Huston, wanted their own park that would surpass in grandeur the Giants' Polo Grounds and the Dodgers' Ebbets Field. They wanted more than a field, they wanted a stadium, which is funny because these days most owners want a field and not a stadium. The House That Ruth Built stood unblemished for fifty years until Steinbrenner called for major renovations in 1974–75. The park was closed for two seasons, and the Yankees played at Shea Stadium as the refurbishment was undertaken. The park lost all of its obstructive steel columns as the second and third decks were cantilevered. Unfortunately, the park's distinctive copper facade along the upper deck was also lost and a reconstructed version was added to the top of the bleachers. Exterior ramps and escalators were added, and the entire feel of the park changed. It was no longer the same Yankee Stadium that the Babe had played in. Recently, there has been an initiative to build a new Yankee Stadium in Manhattan, and the recent collapse of a five-hundred-pound steel beam inside the park in 1998 drew questions as to the safety of the existing stadium. Of course, there are major obstacles to building a new stadium. Those being the legacy of The House That Ruth Built and real estate prices in Manhattan.

FUN FACT: Rows of tomato plants line the sides of the Yankee bullpen, and if you are close enough you can see relief pitchers pruning the plants during the game.

THE ONE THING YOU HAVE TO DO AT YANKEE STADIUM AND WHY: Visit Monument Park. The plaques and memorials have highlights from the players' careers plus a quote. We liked the quote for Babe Ruth: "A Great Ball Player, A Great Man, A Great American."

OTHER THINGS TO REMEMBER: Remember that Monument Park is open two hours prior to home games but closes forty-five minutes before the start of the game. Get there early to see a piece of baseball history.

LASTING IMPRESSION: Although still a classic, Yankee Stadium lost much of its luster with its 1970s renovations.

BAT INFO

FINAL SCORE: Yankees 5, Tigers 1

OUR SEATS: Section 11, Box 33, Seats 5–6

BALLPARK: 24 of 30

DAY: 32 of 38

MILES TRAVELED: 343 (11,923 total)

NEW STATES: 0 (26 total)

OUR EXPENSES: $140
Cooperstown memorabilia $16
McDonald's $8
gas $20
programs and ballpark food—chicken sandwiches, foot-long hot dogs, curly fries, beer, and peanuts $36
nightlife (Gemini club) $60
EXPENSES TO DATE: $2,389

OUR FREEBIES: $136
Cooperstown tickets and programs $36
game tickets and parking $50
lodging (courtesy of Jim Graham) $50
FREEBIES TO DATE: $3,500

25

veterans
stadium
philadelphia

After the Yankee game we went to Jim's place in Manhattan and caught a much-needed nap before we went out in the big city with some of Jim's friends from work. It was a Wednesday night, but it didn't feel like it. We went to a Brazilian club called Gemini, and it was packed. This was a big change for us since we hadn't run into much of a social scene in a while. Granted, our schedule had prevented us from giving some of the cities we went through a chance, but recently neither Chicago nor Cleveland had offered much on our weeknight visits. New York, however, proved to be on a par with our experiences over the Fourth of July weekend in Atlanta and Florida.

Of the four of us, Junior definitely enjoyed himself the most, managing to make one particular Brazilian girl much enamored of him. From our point of view, watching the whole pickup scene was comical, given that Junior was an eighteen-year-old in an over-twenty-one club. It became even more humorous when we found out that Junior's new friend was only seventeen. Junior himself didn't seem prepared for the affection either and found himself returning to our table throughout the night constantly pleading for help and mumbling, "Junior confused."

In any case, we managed to get him out of the bar safely at the end of the night (if we had lost him, there's no telling where we would have found him later), and we also managed to throw away eighty dollars on our bar tab. We wouldn't have felt we had truly had a New York experience if we hadn't overpaid. The thirty-five-dollar parking made us clearly aware of how expensive Manhattan is.

On Thursday we enjoyed a leisurely drive to Philadelphia. We tried to convince Jim to skip his afternoon training sessions and come with us, which he appeared glad to do, but he claimed to have important plans on his social calendar for the evening (more important than us?), so we left without him. The trip down the coast was uneventful. The East Coast felt like old hat to us since we had already been through once before. We were driving to Philly, two hours away, for a ballgame and then planned to hop back to New York to crash at Jim's again, where we had a free floor to sleep on and a thirty-five-dollar spot in the garage. Junior was still suffering a little confusion from his run-in with the universal language, so we were all trying to help him cope with that.

veterans stadium

ATLANTA V PHILADELPHIA

Game Time: 7:35 P.M.

Veterans Stadium, the Vet, is one of the most reviled stadiums in the majors. The park is of the multipurpose cookie-cutter variety, so driving into Philly we already pretty much knew what the stadium was going to look and feel like, because we had seen a half-dozen like it already. Nonetheless, when we saw this stadium from the road, we still felt a little thrill of excitement. In the balance, the Vet seemed a bit nicer than the other cookie cutters, with the exception of Busch. Maybe that's because they put in some new seats five years ago.

The keys to Veterans Stadium are its sheer vastness and its seemingly indifferent relationship to its industrial surroundings. It truly blights its environment. This characteristic of the Vet has often been cited as a reason why the stadium is considered by many to be the biggest eyesore in baseball. Ironically, it managed to instill a bit of awe in me. I do not deny that it presents a total incongruity to the rest of the city's architecture, but for the same reason, it is somehow worth marveling at. One thing, ugly or beautiful, must be acknowledged if it can have such a profound effect on the landscape. At least it makes itself known rather than trying to fade into the background.

Complementing this overpowering effect is the purity of the Vet's symmetry, which provides the facility with a certain mythical grace. This symmetry and vastness together give it a quality eerily reminiscent of approaching an ancient coliseum. Reminiscent, that is, in the way that anything can be reminiscent of an experience that one has never had. This simple grandeur made the Vet, to me, feel like a powerful structure, very similar to my traditional take on the Astrodome.

Junior and Brad enjoyed a great day for baseball in Philadelphia.

This may sound like a bit of a love letter to the Vet, but don't start to confuse this place with Tiger Stadium. More likely I was just riding the wave that Cooperstown had got me on of appreciating the experiences we had. It must have been a powerful wave, too, because I have since found that I am just about the only person with anything good to say about the Vet at all. Even then, I'll readily admit that I dwell on the enormity of the park because quite frankly that is just about all that this place has going for it.

Then there's the Phillie Phanatic, every kid's favorite mascot since the mysterious disappearance of the San Diego Chicken. The Phanatic is not just entertaining but enterprising as well. Take his use of AstroTurf. While critics contend that turf is utterly useless, the Phanatic has used it to his advantage. Because of its resilience, the turf allows the mascot to tool around through the outfield on his scooter between innings and shoot hot dogs into the stands. Unfortunately, at our game the hot dog gun wasn't working, so after a few failed attempts, the Phanatic had to get off the scooter and throw them into the stands by hand. This was bad news for those in the upper decks but a good save by the Phanatic.

All of these were small victories, though, and I'll readily admit that a huge building and an enterprising mascot do not constitute a great baseball experience. This is particularly true when, as has been the lot of the Phillies for the last few years, you can't manage to get more than a fraction of that structure full for any given game.

Fortunately for us, we had something other than the park's somewhat pedestrian qualities to be excited about. It was why this date had been highlighted in Dave's and my respective calendars for some time. Here was where we would resolve our animosities and cash in on perhaps our biggest publicity coup of the trip: The Extreme Games.

Dave, with a conspicuous X on his back, prepares for the bean dip–fueled Extreme Games in the upper deck of the Vet.

To understand the significance of the Extreme Games, you must understand what Dave and I went through to get them on the schedule. Since the beginning, Dave and I had devoted tremendous efforts to cajoling club and stadium reps to let us take part in memorable experiences on the trip. As quickly as we asked, the teams each took the opportunity to politely refuse us permission to throw out the first pitch or sing the national anthem. They practically begged us not to keep asking to take batting practice.

The Phillies, in the City of Brotherly Love, were the only ones to take us up on our offer to do anything we could for some cheap publicity. Thus they offered us a forum to act on our simmering animosity toward each other and resolve our grudge match in the Extreme Games. It would be our charge in the middle of the second inning to race each other from the bottom to the top of the lengthy upper deck of the stadium. If you take seriously how big I said the stadium was, you will realize that this was no small chore. We would do all of this while wearing hideous green-and-yellow Phillies jerseys to distinguish ourselves from each other. The jerseys were so hideous, in fact, that for the life of me I can't remember which color I was.

Dave and I were excited about this event to be sure, but not so much that we felt compelled to get ourselves into prime shape for the competition. Thus, to make it even more of a challenge and lower our standards of play, Dave and I, in true competitive fashion, conditioned for the race by eating oversized Fritos and bean dip. He ate a third of the can. I ate roughly half. Junior, despite not being invited to participate in the contest, partook of the training table meal only halfheartedly. He ate the balance of the bean dip while still mumbling "Junior confused," obviously not as into the rivalry as we were. Note, also, I won the bean-dip challenge.

243

As for the race itself, it was somewhat anticlimactic. By the time we took center stage in the middle of the second inning, the Phillies were already down 8-0 and half of the four-digit crowd had already left while the other half had apparently only stayed so they could get some heckling in and see if their Phillies might get no-hit. Throughout this early inning debacle, Dave and I waited interminably for our moment of glory in the mostly abandoned upper deck where we were to race up the steps in adjacent aisles. I wanted to psyche him out before the race, but I wasn't allowed to go over to his aisle as we had to be ready to start the moment the inning ended. It apparently sometimes took quite a while for some folks to get through the course, and all we had was one commercial break in which to do it.

Sitting alone in my abandoned section and trying to get my game face on, I looked over at Dave and noticed a look of worry creeping across his face. I imagined that the concern registered on Dave's countenance was either in response to the building hostility of the crowd and how they might react to us or was simply an outward betrayal of digestive issues having to do with the pregame meal. I never figured out which. For my part, the meal worried me a little bit, but I used it to my advantage and when the race actually came was able to propel myself to victory.

Said victory was promptly spoiled when we were politely informed by the Phillies front office folk that we could not keep our game jerseys. Upon hearing this news while we sat and recovered in the outer reaches of the Vet, Dave and I considered making a break for it. We had seen enough of the park and this game. Our bodies were in no condition to move anymore though, so we surrendered the jerseys. Anyway, we had to hurry back to our seats on the field level as we had been informed that Junior was having some trouble with a few ushers in the region. Apparently Dave and I had taken all of our ticket stubs with us to the upper deck, and nobody believed Junior when he told them that he was with us.

"With who?"

"Those guys on the Jumbotron. See, that's my brother."

"Yeah whatever, let's go. Besides, don't you know it's illegal to videotape a major league game?"

"Yeah, but I wasn't taping the game, just the race."

"Whatever kid. I don't want to hear it anymore. Let's go."

By the time we got involved in this discussion, it had devolved into Junior's being planted firmly in his seat, refusing to budge and chanting, "Junior confused." He had quite a crowd around him, but we managed to diffuse the situation sufficiently.

After a very rocky start on the field, the Phillies cruised in with only a mostly rocky finish. As we watched with one out in the bottom of the ninth and the Phillies only a couple of formalities away from closing out a 14-2 game, without warning, the heavens opened up. Suddenly a torrential rain fell on us. Fifty-two outs into the lousiest game of our trip, and this was our rain scare.

It was the most bizarre occurrence of my baseball spectating career and the only rain delay I have ever experienced. As the handful of fans, including Junior, who had stayed through to the pitiful conclusion, scurried for the exits, Dave and I sat there under our own cloud of disbelief. We couldn't believe that rain was going to cut into our trip at a time like this.

While Dave and I pondered the implications of this sudden deluge, which we determined were mostly inconsequential (the game still counted after all), the rain suddenly stopped as quickly as it had started. It had been a five-minute delay. Five minutes later the game was over, and we filed out of the stadium with the other twelve people who had found the justification to stay until the bitter end.

On the whole, it was at least an interesting experience in Philly. We got the full-service tour again and even got to go out on the turf, which if you have never been on, it is a strangely cool experience despite what the critics say. For the most part though the tour was the same old stuff with which Dave and I were less and less impressed each time through. No free food, but we shelled out for all the staples anyway, as we had at every park. Fortunately the food was cheap. Unfortunately, none of it was very good. The hot dogs were tiny, and the Philly cheesesteaks paled in comparison to the ones in Seattle.

As for our tour, the biggest highlight was meeting the Phanatic and hanging around in his mascot room where we shared war stories. He talked to us about how all the younger mascots in the league would write him, looking for a little guidance, and he would occasionally take them under his wing. We talked about how he was cooler than all of the other mascots we had met and generally pretended to pay attention while snapping covert footage of his lair. It never occurred to us that we might ask to get some footage of his mascot room and he would say yes. I guess that was just our gut feeling that we were really frauds on this whole trip. It seemed ironic to me that that fear would manifest itself, not at Yankee Stadium's Monument Park, but in Philadelphia of all places, after we had grown so comfortable with our pseudo-celebrity.

Before heading back to New York after the game, we finished off our Philly excursion with the consummate Philadelphia experience. Noticing the statue of Sylvester Stallone (a.k.a. Rocky) in front of the arena across the street from the Vet, we took off our shirts and ran up the steps singing the Rocky theme and pumping our fists into the air. We saw the Phanatic again, sans costume, as we danced around the statue making fools of ourselves, so we said our good-byes to him and thanked him again for all he had done for us. Fifteen minutes later we left Philly, figuring there couldn't be anything else in the city that could top that experience.

veterans stadium

CITY: Philadelphia, Pennsylvania

TENANT: Philadelphia Phillies (MLB), Philadelphia Eagles (NFL)

OPENED: April 4, 1971

NICKNAME/ALIASES: The Vet

DESIGN: multipurpose stadium, circular design, movable seats. SISTER PARKS: Fulton County, Three Rivers Stadium in Pittsburgh, Riverfront Stadium in Cincinnati, and Busch Stadium in St. Louis.

FIELD: AstroTurf with mound and base cutouts

DIMENSIONS (feet): left field—330, left center—371, center field—408, right center—371, right field—330

FENCES (feet): 12

LOCATION: 3501 S. Broad St., Philadelphia, PA 19148. BOUNDED BY: Third base (NW): Broad St. First base (SW): Pattison Ave. and Arena. Left field (NE): I-76. Right field (SE): 10th St.

CAPACITY: 62,382 (baseball). Total attendance: 1,715,722 (1998). Average attendance: 21,181 (1998). (NOTE: Veterans Stadium has the largest capacity of any National League park.)

PARKING: $6 at the general stadium lot adjacent to the park.

TICKETS: $7–$22.50. BEST BANG FOR YOUR BUCK: Tickets at Veterans Stadium are inexpensive and easy to find. The park rarely sells out and general admission and upper reserved seats are always available. You may want to splurge for the field box seats. At only $22.50 they are a good deal.

THE BALLPARK EXPERIENCE: The Vet is like Three Rivers Stadium or Riverfront without the water. Since the water is about all the other two parks have going for them, this is not good news. Veterans Stadium was the last cookie-cutter park built, and as you approach the park you feel the weight of its enormous size. The largest National League park, Veterans can hold over sixty thousand fans and feels every bit big enough to fit one hundred thousand. Although it appears at first to be cylindrical, like Cinergy and Three Rivers, the park is in fact a rounded polyhedron consisting of many narrow faces. Vertical concrete columns surround the park with horizontal ramps leading fans to all levels.

Veterans Stadium feels far more like a football stadium than a baseball park. Its defining characteristic is its size, which would be a tantalizing possibility if anyone showed up for the Phillies games. As the case is now, on the inside, the place is depressingly hollow and undistinguished. The only item that lets you know you are in Philadelphia is the bell, a huge concrete replica of the Liberty Bell (a Philadelphia thing) that sits atop the exterior wall in dead center field. You would never know how big the bell is as you drive up to the park. It looks somewhat minuscule from the outside. But it is huge. Regardless, the immense stadium seems to swallow it whole and completely marginalize it. The dark blue seats and other renovations to the stadium made in 1994, while managing to make the park feel more modern, really only manage to imbue it with an antiseptic Comiskey feel.

FANS: Fans in Philadelphia are among the harshest in baseball. This is possibly due to the fact that only once in their one-hundred-plus-year history have the Phillies captured the World Series crown. Regardless, on our trip, whenever any Phillies player struck out with men on or made an error, the stadium erupted with heckling, boos, and airborne cups of beer. Of course, the drubbing we saw was probably worse than most, but

The Phillies lackluster performance against Atlanta was roundly booed by their ruthless fans, whose numbers came nowhere close to filling the sixty-thousand-seat capacity of Veterans Stadium.

nonetheless, we hear this is a common phenomenon in Philly, albeit an unexpected one, two states removed from New York. In any case, if you are of the heckling sort, we recommend you make yourself at home in Philadelphia.

FACILITIES: Veterans saw a large renovation in 1994. New seats were added along with new restrooms and newer concession facilities, and the whole place was given a paint job. The park with these new changes is adequate for baseball and football. But only adequate.

FOOD: While the park has many specialty foods, like the city's famous cheesesteak, the best bet as far as food quality is concerned is the Krukker and Wild Thing's Foul Territory Sports Grille. The restaurant is down the first-base line and is operated by John Kruk and Mitch "Wild Thing" Williams. It affords views of the field and some tasty ribs. In the park itself all the ballpark favorites, from standard hot dogs to chicken sandwiches, are available, but most disappoint. The cheesesteak does not meet the good quality expected within the Philadelphia city limits, and the hot dogs, while tasty, are disappointingly small. LAST CALL: Alcohol is served until the end of the seventh inning.

GREAT PLAYERS AND HISTORIC MOMENTS: The Phillies entered Veterans Stadium in 1971 with almost ninety years of history and no World Series championships. Finally, in 1980, the club put it together. Backed by an MVP season from Mike Schmidt at third base and Steve Carlton's third Cy Young award, the club bested the Royals in six games for their first world championship. It had taken the Phillies an incredible ninety-seven years to accomplish that feat, the longest such streak in baseball history (although the

BAT INFO

FINAL SCORE: Braves 14, Phillies 2

OUR SEATS: Section 206, Row E,
    Seats 2–4

BALLPARK: 25 of 30

DAY: 33 of 38

MILES TRAVELED: 198 (12,121 total)

NEW STATES: 0 (26 total)

OUR EXPENSES: $88
    overnight parking $20
    lunch (really stepping out) $30
    programs $8
    ballpark food—Philly cheesesteak,
      chicken sandwiches, hot dog,
      and soda $30
      EXPENSES TO DATE: $2,477

OUR FREEBIES: $86
    game tickets and parking $36
    lodging (courtesy of Jim Graham) $50
      FREEBIES TO DATE: $3,586

Cubs are closing fast). Thirteen years later the Phillies tried to repeat the trick after a decade of poor seasons, but lost two late-inning leads in the 1993 Series against the Toronto Blue Jays and ended up losing in six games. Additionally, the Vet has hosted two All-Star Games, in 1976 and 1996.

BALLPARK HISTORY: Veterans Stadium was financed by the city of Philadelphia to house the Phillies and NFL Eagles. The multipurpose park was built at a cost of over $50 million and completed in time for the 1971 baseball season. The park initially held fifty-six thousand fans but was expanded to sixty-five thousand. It was renovated in 1994 by the Phillies, who took over management of the park from the city, but the improvements haven't done much for the ballpark's image. There is currently a plan to build a new baseball-only ballpark in downtown Philadelphia.

FUN FACT: The home plate is the same one as was used at the Phillies old ballpark, Connie Mack Stadium.

THE ONE THING YOU HAVE TO DO AT VETERANS STADIUM AND WHY: Meet the mascot. The Philadelphia Phanatic is by far the best mascot in baseball, and many standard mascot tricks of today were concocted deep within Veterans Stadium. The Phanatic especially loves kids and is easy to spot signing autographs and generally making people laugh.

OTHER THINGS TO REMEMBER: Veterans Stadium has four generic statues that surround the park on the podium level: Gate B—statue of a baseball player sliding into a fielder; Gate D—statue of a football player being tackled; Gate F—statue of a baseball player hitting; and Gate H—statue of a football player kicking. So remember not to make plans to meet your friends at "the statue."

LASTING IMPRESSION: Ironically, only the Phillies' bad fans make this place lively.

26

Fenway
Park
Boston

AFTER THE game we headed straight back to New York. On the way home, Junior received a phone call from his Brazilian friend. She wanted to see him again, but he was not prepared to deal with the confusing circumstances that might ensue. Likewise, we were in no condition to leave him behind. So we guided him through a polite deflection of all advances. He came out of it okay, and I think he has engineered some kind of long-term long-distance friendship out of it. Nevertheless, we gave him a lot of grief about it at the time and captured it all on videotape.

The next day we had lunch with Jim before we took leave of New York and our wallets. Jim is a good guy and not much for compliments, but we gave them anyway, along with a sincere invitation to join us for the Boston leg of the trip. He couldn't accept, and so we said good-bye.

The road to Boston was slick with rain. The deluge that had flirted with us in Philadelphia picked us up just outside of Manhattan and shadowed us all the way to Bean Town. We were panicked. Rain had been the one uncontrollable element to our timetable, and we feared it more than any other potential situation. It was the one thing against which we had no alternative. Our plan of going through most of these cities in less than twenty-four hours also left us with a very slim margin for error. Looking at rain-out statistics for the league, from an average of six per year in Florida to none in the domes, we figured we had roughly a 50 percent chance of making it through unscathed, or at least getting each of our games started. We had made it five-sixths of the way, so the odds were in our favor.

We had not come this far to be rained out just five parks from the finish. And in Fenway Park of all places. We scanned radio stations zealously, seeking weather updates for Boston and any prognostication as to how things looked for the evening. This concern dominated our ride up to Boston and ultimately proved unnecessary as the baseball gods answered our prayers about thirty miles outside of town. We headed in under clear skies, and with the rain having drifted out of the region, we figured the humidity and El Niño would let up on us a little bit. We were looking forward to some cool, comfortable weather for the first time since L.A. Unfortunately, it didn't turn out that way. Boston was as hot as the rest of the country.

The weather issues resolved, I had other, bigger things to worry about. To wit, we were supposed to pick up my dad at Logan Airport, the easternmost point on our trip, en route to the game. I had invited him because Dave and I had a tacit agreement that, whenever possible, we would fill the car with a third. The past thirty-four days had proved we were best off that way. I also wanted dad to share in this magical trip. After all, if it weren't for him, I wouldn't have been in this situation in the first place.

Like most every other boy (and a few girls), around age four I received my first baseball glove from my father. His face beamed when he gave it to me. I am sure of this even though I have no clear memory of it. I know how excited he must have been anticipating the opportunities we would have to play some ball together. It would be like reliving his childhood, and he could teach me all the things he never learned about the game until years later. I am sure he envisioned me starring for the Astros. And so we walked out to the backyard, and I learned to throw, catch, hit, bunt, steal, and pitch a curve ball. Granted I never did any of these things as well as he would have liked me to, but we gave it our best effort through Dad's Pitch, Little League, and into high school and beyond. Eventually that dream of playing for the Astros faded.

The Tour had transformed that dream into something no less idealistic than the first, a dream of once again living a baseball life to the bone. This time, I wasn't on the field; I was on the other side of the fence, watching, where my dad had been all these years watching me. I had reached the point where I understood what it felt like to be a spectator. Like my dad had learned before me, I was learning to appreciate others playing the game I had enjoyed playing. I wanted to share that with my dad, wishing that he could have seen me make that diving backhand in the hole, but settling for sitting next to him when Nomar Garciaparra does it.

Fenway Park

··

TRAFFIC IN Boston was as bad as it had been anywhere and twice as confusing—particularly getting through the construction that took us to the airport and back to Boston proper. Finally we made it to the ballpark, which is nestled, like everybody had said, into a quaint city block among a number of other buildings. Some of the other parks we had been to were snuggled inconspicuously among other buildings, but Fenway's aged green steel and red brick blended in so well in this old city that you would never know that it was there were it not for the Red Sox banners hanging over the sidewalks.

The four of us were plenty early to the ballpark, because we had a tour lined up with Jack Lyons of Aramark. This being our last Aramark park, we were eager for the last red-carpet experience that L.A.'s Lon Rosenberg had set up for us at each of his sister parks.

Before the tour, though, we had to pick up the tickets Chris Canning had left for us at the will-call window. Knowing that Fenway was a tough ticket, we were excited to have this issue resolved and avoid another fiasco like we had experienced in Baltimore. Talking to Chris the day before, we confirmed that he had tickets for us. He assured us that the tickets would be waiting for us when we got to the park.

The only problem was that there were no tickets waiting for us. We had an appointment to meet inside the stadium in five minutes, but no way to get in. Our worries were further compounded by the fact that we could not reach Chris to determine whether the tickets were on their way or not. This definitely was not how I wanted to reintroduce dad to the Baseball America Tour.

Maybe the tickets had just not yet arrived. (They were supposed to have been couriered to the will-call window.) It was a slim hope, but it was the only one we had. The game was sold out, and we didn't have time to solicit scalpers, few of whom were circulating with the game still hours away.

Clinging to this possibility, Dave, Junior, Dad, and I walked up to the main gate, behind home plate, and told the attendant there that we were here to see Jack Lyons of Aramark. No, we did not have tickets. We had an appointment.

In the same way it had worked at getting us into places we didn't belong countless times before, we passed through the gate into the holy grail of stadiums—Fenway Park.

Fenway truly is the holy grail. Not just because everybody says so, but because, when everybody else loves something, it usually comes as a disappointment when you finally get there. I am skeptical enough to discount the hype about anything. (See Yankee Stadium or Turner Field.) But Fenway was different.

In Boston they call it Fenway "Pahk," and its personality is ingrained in the city. Beginning with the unassuming exterior that portrays the park as just another steel-and-brick structure in a working-man's district of downtown Boston, the park just fits.

The corridors are worn with age but maintain an air of authenticity, much like Tiger Stadium but with less of a smell. These concourses are packed with vendors, making movement through them somewhat stifling. Of course, this inefficient layout was never the plan and only gradually developed as newer ballparks began adding more amenities, forcing their older relatives to pack to the gills to try to keep up. Where the result just feels sloppy in most older parks, in Fenway it contributes to a cozy atmosphere.

This atmosphere is personified by the ballpark's general design. Fenway is the park that Camden and its successors want to be, and the characteristic coziness and nostalgic atmosphere that those parks draw on are readily apparent here. Fenway's quaintness outdoes them all. First, because it is smaller than the new parks. Yes, it was a radical break for Camden to go under 50,000-seat capacity when its immediate predecessors, the multisport models, were up around 60,000. But Fenway seats 33,871, a number that the Camden dons surely never considered. Of course, at the time Fenway was built in 1912, it was considered a monster. Obviously, times have changed, and this monster is now the granddaddy of all parks and outclasses its progeny on all counts.

Speaking of monsters, there's Fenway's defining characteristic, the 37'2"-high left-field wall of green wood that stands 310 feet away from home plate. The Green Monster. It is truly the original element of baseball Americana, that one defining ballpark

Brad's dad joined us in Boston to see the splendor of baseball at Fenway Park.

monument that even nonbaseball fans recognize. That one simple architectural touch, a defining shorthand for the ballpark's personality that so many other parks from Camden with its warehouse to Pac Bell with its waterfront right-field wall have tried to imitate. The Monster surpasses them all.

Unlike the carefully contrived artifice and plea for publicity of placing the right-field wall at Pac Bell right on the water, the Monster outdoes them because it seems like an afterthought. Granted, Camden deserves credit for leaving the warehouse on the ballpark grounds. That decision implies an act of creativity as opposed to a PR move. The Monster, however, feels more special because it doesn't hint at creativity—it was a way to build the ballpark without running into the street. Thus the Monster feels organic, an integral part of the stadium. It's not like the hill at Houston's new Enron Park, which could just as easily have been leveled by the builders. The Monster, with its sense of restriction, heightens the aforementioned coziness of the ballpark. It's as if the builders of Fenway had every intention of constructing a full stadium, but they had to stop before they got to the left-field corner. Sorry, they said, we don't have room for any more. So they put up this big wall to block the rest out. In the end Fenway emerges with a unique character and a sense of exclusivity and privilege, as if you should truly feel honored to be here.

There is a certain combination of a ballpark's beauty, age, and television history prerequisite to attaining this kind of status. Although the Camdenesque ballparks are beautiful replicas of classic ballparks, the only images that pop into your head when you get there are those that unfold in front of you during that visit. Likewise, older parks such as Wrigley Field and Tiger Stadium, despite their history, seem to be short on zeitgeist to hold a place in the collective psyche. Only Dodger Stadium, Fenway Park, and, to a lesser degree, Yankee Stadium are eternally etched in the American memory. These are the rare structures that have become shrines. Before the first pitch at any game in these parks, fans can imagine Kirk Gibson pumping his fist as he rounds the bases with that game-winning home run in the 1988 World Series, or Carlton Fisk apparently willing the ball into an equally important home run over the Green Monster in 1975. Although it is politically correct (baseball politics here) to say that Wrigley Field is the epitome of all that is good about baseball, you don't think about the Cubbies getting beat up on WGN when you think of classic baseball moments. You think of Mickey Mantle or Joe DiMaggio or Carlton Fisk. You think of Yankee Stadium and Fenway Park.

These two parks are among a select stadium fraternity that every warm-blooded baseball fan walks around with every day. The difference is that at Fenway Park, when you walk into the stands, those images that before were only the size of a television screen suddenly fill your entire field of vision. You see Fisk trotting around the bases. Likewise, the old black-and-white footage of Ted Williams suddenly leaps into color.

The reason for this is that Fenway Park still looks and feels like the ballpark it was eighty years ago. At the heavily renovated Yankee Stadium, you have to squint to imagine Mantle or DiMaggio running between the monuments that now stand beyond the left-field wall. Although the newfound nostalgia Cooperstown had engendered in me had allowed me to savor the Yankee experience, there was definitely something bittersweet about it all. Those visions of the Mick and the Yankee Clipper will forever be confined to the newsreels.

To be honest though, in the first moment in which we entered Fenway, none of these romantic or nostalgic feelings jumped to mind. For the most part, I was worried about our tickets ever showing up and was trying to figure out how we could not get thrown out of the place when they didn't. This concern obviously dampened my enjoyment of the otherwise wonderful tour that Jack Lyons gave us of the stadium, making certain to point out all of the interesting tidbits of ballpark history along the way (which are documented below).

Additionally, the anxiety that had gotten hold of me was eating into the rosy outlook on the trip that Cooperstown had rekindled within me two days prior. Subsequently, I was increasingly annoyed at Dave's banter with our host. Maybe they were interesting questions, maybe they weren't. To me it registered as chatter and hindered my appreciation of this great ballpark. Truth be told, I can't see, looking back on it now, any glaring deficiencies in Dave's behavior in Boston that should have upset me. But I was agitated and accustomed to being annoyed at Dave.

As the tour carried on, I was torn between praying that this tour would continue indefinitely and wanting to find our tickets. It would be horrible if we not only lacked tickets, but upon being booted out of the park, could not find tickets to get back in.

Jack, probably sensing my distress, stopped us in the middle of our tour, just before we were going to get to the good stuff (that is, food), and suggested that we see if our tickets had arrived. Suddenly partners in panic again, Dave and I shared a fearful look. Oddly, Junior and my dad apparently had every confidence. Fortunately, their confidence was rewarded. The tickets were waiting for us.

That off of my mind, the experience was immediately transformed into great joy, and we made quick work of some Fenway Franks and Boston clam chowder and headed to our seats. Even then though, I hadn't achieved that feeling of Fenway enlightenment—probably because I kept expecting it. Regardless, the seats were awesome, and there was a lot more legroom than I had expected, given many warnings. Being 6'4", I had been warned how short Fenway was on legroom, but it was adequate for me.

The El Niño heat and humidity had not abated, despite the recent downpour, so the experience was slightly sweaty and uncomfortable. Of course, most of the last twenty games had been similarly hot, but this was Fenway—I was expecting more. The experience went on like this, an unassuming game through the early innings, while we relaxed and sat back and enjoyed it all.

In the fourth inning Jack came by to see how we were doing and if we would like to visit the upper deck for a couple of innings. Not wanting to miss the complete experience, we accepted and wandered upward, where the magic seized us. Maybe it was the breeze, maybe it was the view, maybe the walk had somehow improved my mood. Whatever it was, I got that feeling that you sometimes get at a ballgame. That feeling that this game could go on forever, and I'd have no reason or desire to leave. I could have stayed up there until dawn. It would have been a great day. That's why Fenway is the paramount park to me.

Unfortunately we only stayed up there for two innings. The magic, however, followed us, and the baseball gods blessed us with a great game.

Going into the bottom of the eighth, the Sox were down 6-1, but the fans stood by them. Hardly anybody left the stadium. To start their next at-bat, the Sox collected a couple of hits, at which point the Jays pulled their pitcher. When they did, the home fans gave their traditional standing ovation to the opposing pitcher, which is an even nicer touch than I thought it would be when I first heard about it. This good karma worked out in the Sox's favor as the next pitcher fared little better, finally serving up a bases-loaded fastball to Damon Buford, which he deposited over the Monster (we've got pictures). That closed the gap to 6-5, and in the ninth, the Sox put together a couple of hits to tie it and almost won, but pinch runner Steve Avery was gunned down at the plate. It was of no matter, because the Sox persevered and squeezed across the winner in the tenth. I would not have minded if the game hadn't ended though, because we were having way too much fun.

Fenway was a perfect experience. It matched exactly my mental image of the place. Being there was a perfect moment. I wish we could have stayed forever. That, however, is the curse of the traveler; those sublime moments are always transitory.

fenway park

CITY: Boston, Massachusetts

TENANT: Boston Red Sox, Boston (later New England) Patriots (NFL) 1963–68

OPENED: April 20, 1912

NICKNAME/ALIASES: Fenway

DESIGN: Baseball-only stadium, asymmetrical design, no movable seats. SISTER PARKS: Tiger Stadium (which opened the same day), Wrigley Field, old Comiskey, Forbes Field in Pittsburgh, Crosley Field in Cincinnati, Ebbets Field in Brooklyn, the Polo Grounds in New York, the Baker Bowl and Shibe Park in Philadelphia, Sportsman's Park in St. Louis, and League Park in Cleveland. Of these historic parks, only Wrigley Field and Fenway still host major league baseball.

FIELD: Grass

DIMENSIONS (feet): left field—310, left center—379, center field—390, deep right center—420, right center—380, right field—302

FENCES (feet): left field—37'2" (the Green Monster), left field to center field—17, bullpen fence—5, right field—3.5

LOCATION: 4 Yawkey Way, Boston, MA 02215. Right field (E): Ipswich Street. First base (S): Van Ness Street. Third base (W): 24 Jersey Street and Brookline Ave (a.k.a. Yawkey Way). Left field (N): Lansdowne St. (a.k.a. Ted Williams Way).

CAPACITY: 33,871 (baseball). A record 47,627 packed into the park on September 22, 1935, for a game with the Yankees. Total attendance: 2,310,704 (1998). Average attendance: 28,577 (1998).

PARKING: $10–$20. Although we used a $20 lot, mostly to aid our getaway, try using public transportation or parking at the Prudential Center or on the campus of Boston University.

TICKETS: $14–$45. BEST BANG FOR YOUR BUCK: Go for the right-field-roof box seats. Hopefully you will have a moment of clarity such as the one that overwhelmed us.

BALLPARK EXPERIENCE: Fenway is more than a ballpark. It is an embodiment of baseball, a classic park unspoiled by time and nurtured by the hard luck of its hometown team. Approaching the park, we sensed an electricity to the streets surrounding it. Food vendors and fans mesh together in front of an unassuming red-brick building.

Upon entering, the park hangs above you in narrow rundown aisles and sprouts up beneath on uneven concrete floors and ramps. The park is old and it shows. Upon seeing the field, we were immediately struck by its small size. Even the Green Monster in left field seems smaller than you would have thought. But the size creates intimacy and all the seats are close to the action, even in the deep bleachers. The park is only one level with a second deck that is small and features mostly loges and the press box. Fenway is the lone park in the majors with primarily one deck, which adds to the homey feel.

Everywhere small idiosyncrasies lurk for the fan: the Jimmy Fund sign in right field, the ladder that the grounds crew uses to reach balls hit in the Green Monster's net, and the retired numbers on the awning in right field. Fenway's main scoreboard on the base of the Green Monster in left field was added in 1934. One of Jack Lyons's best tidbits of info concerned the scoreboard. The initials of former Red Sox owner Tom A. Yawkey and his wife, Jean, are featured in Morse code in green dashes and dots on the

Fenway Park has a magical quality that manages to come across in just about every image of the field, day or night, rain or shine. This park is the best in all of major league baseball.

vertical white bars between the leftmost out-of-town scores. Even more so than Wrigley and Tiger, the park has a quirky charm combined with its star-crossed inhabitants that make this the best park in baseball.

FANS: Red Sox fans are some of the most die-hard and devoted fans in baseball. They have suffered since 1918 without a World Series championship and four times since have lost a World Series in Game Seven. It is a hard-luck club with a tough fan base. The intimate feel of Fenway and its historic past augment this love for the team. The fans also show some unusual traits. First, in our experience, they are the most pessimistic fans in baseball. The team could be up 7-0, and the fans are convinced that they are going to lose. From our calculations, this seems like a symptom of the Curse of the Bambino that sent Babe Ruth to New York and any hope of winning down the Charles River. Second, they are generally the most respectful fans in baseball. They have a history of giving opposing pitchers a standing ovation en route to the showers, a stark contrast to the derogatory Jumbotron visuals most stadiums employ. Red Sox fans, however, are not without their dark side, which is displayed in their deep enmity for the Yankees. The most telling anecdote about this rivalry concerns an occasion during the 1999 playoffs, when miniature Yankees caps suddenly appeared in place of the sanitary blocks in the park's urinals.

FACILITIES: We saw firsthand that the facilities at Fenway are old. Jack Lyons showed us concession stands jammed into spaces under the seat risers that made this painfully clear. Concourse space is especially limited and the rush into the park before our game created a lot of congestion. You could potentially count this against the park, if you wanted to waste your time on such a minor detail.

FOOD: Limited concession facilities don't prevent Fenway from serving some of the best food in the majors. The famous New England clam chowder with mini oyster crackers is a must. Be careful because it is served scalding hot. Hot dogs at Fenway (Fenway Franks) are also especially good and are served fresh, in a folded piece of white bread instead of a hot dog bun. LAST CALL: Alcohol is served until two hours after the start of the game or at the discretion of the stadium manager.

GREAT PLAYERS AND HISTORIC MOMENTS: Most of the historic moments at Fenway Park have revolved around George Herman "Babe" Ruth. In 1919 Ruth exploded as a slugger, hitting twenty-nine home runs, but the debt-ridden owner of the Red Sox, Harry Frazee, sold Ruth for one hundred thousand dollars (this was a lot of cash back then) to the

GAT INFO

FINAL SCORE: Red Sox 8, Blue Jays 7 (F 10)

OUR SEATS: Section 23, Box 136, Seats 5–6

BALLPARK: 26 of 30

DAY: 34 of 38

MILES TRAVELED: 437 (10,958; 12,558 total)

NEW STATES: 3 (Connecticut, Rhode Island, Massachusetts; 29 total)

OUR EXPENSES: $54
tolls (over a couple of days) $20
parking and programs $14
gas $20
EXPENSES TO DATE: $2,531

OUR FREEBIES: $150
game tickets (courtesy of Chris Channing) $50
memorabilia and ballpark food—
hot dogs, soda, peanuts, ice cream sandwiches, plus chowder (courtesy of Aramark) $50
hotel room (courtesy of my dad) $50
FREEBIES TO DATE: $3,736

rival New York Yankees. What followed for the Red Sox has been aptly called a curse. Ruth and the Yankees went on to dominate baseball and the Red Sox never won another World Series. In the post-Ruth era, the Red Sox played in four World Series where they lost in seven games in each instance (sounds like a curse to us). In the 1946 World Series, Ted Williams's poor performance led to a loss to the Cardinals. The Red Sox' next heartbreak was in 1967 when Carl Yastrzemski won the Triple Crown (the last player to do so) but the Sox lost again to the Cardinals in seven games. In 1975, the heroics of Carlton Fisk in game six, hammering a memorable home run over the Green Monster, almost propelled the team to victory. The Red Sox then lost a close 4-3 contest to the Cincinnati Reds the next day, and their World Series hopes were dashed again. Most recently and memorably, in 1986 against the New York Mets with victory almost in the bag in game six (the scoreboard at Shea Stadium said "Congratulations Red Sox"), Bob Stanley's wild pitch and Bill Buckner's error cost the Red Sox the series. The Mets went on to win Game Seven by an 8-5 margin. The Curse of the Bambino lives.

BALLPARK HISTORY: Fenway Park was built in 1912 to replace the Huntington Avenue Grounds, where the Red Sox had played since 1901. The park was constructed in the steel-and-concrete design pioneered by Forbes Field in Pittsburgh and replaced a wooden structure that was prone to fire. Renovations have kept the park playable—club seats, new restrooms, new concessions—but barely economically feasible. The city is planning on erecting a new park adjacent to the old one, introducing updated facilities and trying to retain the ambiance of Fenway. This is much easier said than done (for example, new Comiskey). To ruin a shrine to baseball such as Fenway would be a crime. A grass-roots organization—Save Fenway Park!—exists to preserve the old park through renovation.

LASTING IMPRESSION: Simply the best.

A Day of Rest

JULY 24, 1998

DAY 35

A DAY of rest. How long had it been since we had one of these? Sixteen days?

Actually, we had eight hundred miles to drive, including a return trip to Cooperstown. To top it off, it was my dad's birthday, so we were orchestrating a little surprise party for him in Cleveland, where we would arrive sometime around sundown. In Cleveland we were dropping off Junior and Dave's uncle's Cherokee, picking up my Pathfinder and pushing into Indiana by nightfall.

No baseball games on the agenda this day, but still possibly the busiest day of the trip. After the great Red Sox game, we departed and took our rest in Albany, New York, just sixty-five miles from Cooperstown. For the second time in four days, we woke up at dawn for a quick ride to and whirlwind tour of Cooperstown.

It was just as much fun the second time. Even though the mystique for me was gone, Dad seemed to enjoy it thoroughly. Also, we were there the day before the inductions of Don Sutton, Larry Doby, Bullet Rogan, Lee MacPhail, and George Davis (don't worry, I've never heard of a couple of those guys either), so the vibrancy of Cooperstown in general had picked up considerably.

In my eyes though, the trip revolved around my being with my father. Oddly, although we had shared a love of baseball for the better part of two decades, this was one of the first times I had talked with him about his baseball roots. I guess I just assumed that his history started when I was born, or at the very least when Houston received its first major league team in 1962. Imagine my surprise to learn that before all that, he had been an Indians fan.

Like our previous trip to the Hall of Fame, this one ended prematurely, given everything else we had to accomplish that day. Again I regretted having to leave but was fortunate in picking up a Bob Feller poster for Dad's imminent surprise birthday party. Good thing he liked the Indians.

Hours that felt like minutes later, we shot into Cleveland. Dave's mom, who had been the one to cook up the whole surprise party thing, greeted us and escorted us to the back patio for a light dinner. We put Dave's dad, the talkative one, on distraction duty and headed back to get the present and cake.

The whole thing took my father aback. We relaxed with the cake for about a half-hour, enjoyed the tail end of the sunset, and then left.

Our last of three trips to Cleveland was complete, and we had dropped off our penultimate companion. Back in the Pathfinder, we headed west.

BAT INFO

MILES TRAVELED: 733 (13,291 total)

NEW STATES: 0 (29 total)

OUR EXPENSES: $94
Subway subs $10
Cooperstown tickets and gifts $64
gas $20
EXPENSES TO DATE: $2625

OUR FREEBIES: $65
dinner (courtesy of the Kavals) $15
hotel room (courtesy of my dad) $50
FREEBIES TO DATE: $3801

27
wrigley field
chicago

WE DROVE until we made it to South Bend, Indiana, one hundred or so miles outside of Chicago, which left us with a morning drive that we really didn't anticipate as that challenging. We made a quick detour to check out the Notre Dame campus, which would have been a whole lot cooler if we could have gotten into the stadium there. The Soldier Field experience would not be replicated though. My dad had no interest in getting arrested. So we settled for a couple of pictures of "Touchdown Jesus" instead.

Two hours later, we were in the baseball lover's heart of Chicago, Wrigleyville.

wrigley field

NEW YORK (NL) V CHICAGO (NL)

GAME TIME: 12:15 P.M.

I HAD been looking forward to this since the first time we were through town to see the White Sox play. That drive-by of Wrigleyville and Wrigley Field had been awe-inspiring and the first time I had seen a ballpark crammed into the middle of a city. Camden and

Jacobs were downtown ballparks, but they each took up a couple of city blocks and had sprawling walkways and greenery that allowed them to demand the attention of passersby. Wrigley, however, like Fenway, was snuggled inside a single city block, and as such fit perfectly with the city and the neighborhood.

From the outside, Wrigley has a lot in common with Fenway. Both neighborhoods are pretty lively with a lot of bars and all sorts of vendors on the street corners. (For some reason Philly had a lot of vendors on the street corners too, but that is where similarities between the Vet and Wrigley end.) On the inside, Wrigley felt nostalgic. The old-time brass band that played near our seats in the sixth inning was a nice touch, too. The ivy, the neighborhood, the scoreboard, the fans—everything about Wrigleyville was as exciting as legend would have it. We again saw a great come-from-behind game.

Appropriately, we saw a day game at Wrigley, and for the first time in a month the weather was bearable. Despite the fact that everything about the game was so perfect, Wrigley still lacked something.

Perhaps that something was a favorable spot in the rotation of ballparks on our tour. Wrigley suffered in that we had come straight there from Fenway, probably the only park that measures up to Wrigley in almost every category. As a result, our visit lacked the goosebump experience that struck me at Fenway. Regardless, we appreciated Wrigley for its competitive advantages in this matchup with Fenway. So to do the two ballparks justice, rather than rehash all of the great things I said about Fenway—its feeling authentic and quaint, which are certainly true of Wrigley as well—I will dwell instead on Wrigley's superlatives. They are the beer men, the fans, and the neighborhood. I make only a passing note that my comment about the 33,871-seat Fenway being even more cozy than the new wave of ballparks holds true for the 38,902-seat Wrigley as well.

Let's begin with the beer men. It has been mentioned in these pages how certain ballparks have no beer men at all, particularly most of the ones in California. Fenway took that shortcoming one step further by limiting fans to only one beer apiece at the concessions, instead of the customary two. I don't know if that is the Puritanical influence of the region or a byproduct of a past incident. If the latter, I'd be inclined to give the ballpark and its fans a little more slack. Regardless, it makes for what is at the very least an inconvenience at the ballgame.

Wrigley is exactly opposite. The park has the most beer men per capita of any baseball park in America. Even more than Arlington. As an added bonus, half of them serve the superlative local macrobrew, Old Style.

This tremendous beer presence impinges upon the second asset of Wrigley Field, the fans. First, the fans at Wrigley are not necessarily better than Red Sox fans, just different. Both groups of fans share an amazing history of loyalty to a historically depressing team, but the Cubs get decisive points based strictly on the zealousness of their fans,

The buzz around Wrigley Field before the game was infectious. No park is better integrated into its surroundings than this one, even lending its name to the neighborhood.

which for better or worse have begun to change the way baseball is viewed in ballparks across America.

It's almost a tired story of the nostalgic feel of the new ballparks in San Francisco, Houston, Detroit, etc., but in addition to providing a copy of the nostalgic ballpark experience, these new cozy confines also seem to be breeding the sort of fans you used to expect to see only in Chicago or New York. The real hard-nosed fan who has been sitting in the same box seat for what seems like eighty years. The bleacher bum who knows bleacher etiquette. To wit, in the first exhibition game at Enron Field in Houston, two home-run balls (by the visiting team of course) were thrown back. In the inaugural regular season game at Pac Bell in San Francisco, the guy who caught the historic first home run there was attacked twice before being ejected forcibly from the stadium.

This renaissance of the fan is, in my opinion, founded upon artifice. Those fans haven't been in the same box for eighty years. Most of them never even came to support the team at the old ballpark at all, which is inexcusable. These new guys throw out a lot of money to go to the new park mostly to socialize and, to a lesser degree, see their team win. More than anything, they want to get a true baseball experience, at least as it is defined by them. This baseball experience is a parody of the Wrigley experience, basically, drink a lot of beer and throw balls back on the field.

At Wrigley, these rules are hard and fast. Even though, with the resurgence of Wrigley's popularity of late, given this ballpark renaissance and Sammy Sosa, these same caricatures of fans have crept into the Wrigley stands as well. But Wrigley Field will never be defined by these wanna-bes. It will eternally be known for the truly frustrated die-hard Cub fans who are ten times as surly as any of these trendy followers could ever hope to be. The followers talk trash to the opposing team, but only true Cubs fans can pick fights with opposing players. Likewise, only true Cubs fans can manage to get so drunk and subsequently so uncontrollable as to force the organization to rethink the decision of playing night games at all.

Already we are spilling over into the third and greatest asset of Wrigley Field: Wrigleyville. Dave and I had a history of checking out the nightlife whenever possible, but we had never checked out the "daylife." We didn't even know there was such a thing until we showed up in Wrigleyville.

On the day of our game, we arrived at noon on a Saturday to find not just activity in all of the Wrigleyville bars, but jam-packed, police-line activity. If you wanted to get a beer at Murphy's or Hi-Tops or the Cubby Bear or Yak-Zies, you could do it, but you wouldn't get to the bar and out alive in time to make the first pitch, which was ninety minutes away. If you truly wanted to preparty in Wrigleyville, you had to be there by 11 A.M.

In fact, a large number of the people at these bars don't even have tickets for the game. They just come down for the atmosphere. They sit in the bar, drink Old Style, maybe put down some buffalo wings (Yak-Zies has the best), and watch the game on television with the added benefit of a thunderous roar in surround sound whenever the Cubbies score. Then, after the game, the whole scene gets even more hectic. The crowds in the bars spill into the streets, and the parties go all night—win or lose. Numerous enterprising vendors, many of them homeless, pick up six-packs of beer at the local minimart before the game lets out, and then sell the beer to the people in the streets who can't make it into the bars. Five dollars will get you eighteen at this racket.

Sadly, we had to take off for Milwaukee without much more than an outside peek at the activity inside a couple of the bars. Fortunately, fate found me living in Chicago less than a year later, just two blocks from Wrigley Field. Being a die-hard Astros fan, I never caught Cubbie fever, but I enjoyed the atmosphere regardless. I also learned never, *ever,* to reveal my allegiances in this part of town.

In sum, Wrigley is an incredible and unique experience, and thankfully so. With the much-debated impending demise of Fenway, Wrigley seems poised to stand alone as the last remaining classical shrine to baseball. It is deserving of that role. One can only hope that Steinbrenner gets his Yankees a new stadium before Wrigley falls to old age. Such a cosmetic hodgepodge as what was once The House That Ruth Built could never do justice to the role of ballpark emeritus.

The one disappointment of the Wrigley experience: No one hit the ball out on Waverly Street. Not only that, but Sammy Sosa didn't even put a scare into the crowd. This was a bit of a disappointment for us because, like everybody else at the park, many of whom had come a long way just to see Sammy swing, we were keeping a close eye on the home-run chase. More so after the display McGwire had put on for us in

St. Louis. By now, McGwire was at forty-three and Sammy close behind at thirty-seven, and a history-making year was almost a foregone conclusion. We figured both would shatter the record, and we would have liked to have firsthand experience of both men in action doing just that. We would have to settle for our Big Mac story.

We got out of Chicago with what we thought would be plenty of time to get to Milwaukee, three and a half hours to go ninety-four miles. In the end though, we needed three hours to get there, because in getting out of Chicago, traffic was a huge pain. Three hours?! I hated the city of Chicago for a long time after that but have since learned my lesson. Do not drive to Wrigley Field if you can at all help it. If you do, don't plan on leaving anytime soon after the game is over.

wrigley field

CITY: Chicago, Illinois

TENANT: Chicago Cubs

OPENED: April 23, 1914

NICKNAME/ALIASES: Wrigley, North Side Ballpark (1914), Weeghman Park (1914–15), Cubs Park (1916–26), Whales Park (1915), Harry's House (for legendary broadcaster Harry Carry)

DESIGN: Baseball-only stadium, asymmetrical design, no movable seats. SISTER PARKS: Tiger Stadium in Detroit, old Comiskey on the South Side of Chicago, Forbes Field in Pittsburgh, Fenway Park in Boston, Crosley Field in Cincinnati, Ebbets Field in Brooklyn, the Polo Grounds in New York, the Baker Bowl and Shibe Park in Philadelphia, Sportsman's Park in St. Louis, Griffith Stadium in Washington D.C., and League Park in Cleveland. Of these historic parks, only Wrigley Field and Fenway still host major league baseball.

FIELD: Bluegrass and clover

DIMENSIONS (feet): Left field—355, deepest left center near well—357, left center—368, center field—400, right center—368, deep right center near well—363, right field—353

FENCES (feet): left field corner—15, left field to bleachers—12.5, left center to right center—11, right field corner—15. (NOTE: Bill Veeck, the legendary promoter, added the brick wall and ivy in 1937. Veeck planted 350 Japanese bittersweet plants and 200 Boston plants. He also added 8 huge Chinese Elms in the bleacher stair step that unfortunately died due to the tough winds off Lake Michigan.)

LOCATION: 1060 W. Addison St., Chicago, IL 60613. Right field (E): N. Sheffield Ave. First base (S): W. Addison St. Third base (W): Seminary Ave. Left field (N): W. Waveland Ave. Home plate (SW): N. Clark St.

Wrigley Field

CAPACITY: 38,902 (baseball). Total attendance: 2,623,194 (1998). Average attendance: 32,385 (1998).

PARKING: $10–$15. While weekday day games are a cinch, we found it difficult to find parking at our Saturday game. Do not try to use street parking or your car will be towed, since all street parking is by permit only.

TICKETS: $6–$25. Tickets are much more expensive on weekends, night games, and during the midsummer. Wrigley is the only park to have different prices depending upon the day of the game. BEST BANG FOR YOUR BUCK: At our game, the bleachers were filled with die-hard shirtless fans. The action from the bleachers is close and the environment lively and fun. The seats are also less expensive. The bleachers are the place to be, but also the hardest ticket to get.

THE BALLPARK EXPERIENCE: Even without a moment of clarity, Wrigley Field was a one-of-a-kind experience. Walking up to the famous red sign that reads "Wrigley Field: Home

With Fenway Park's days possibly numbered, Wrigley may soon be the only classic park left to give fans a window into the baseball of a bygone era.

of the Chicago Cubs" takes you back. The history is pervasive and encompasses everything about the park, from the signature ivy to the row houses that line Waveland Avenue. More than any other park, Wrigley Field is at one with its city. The neighborhood around the park is aptly named Wrigleyville, and it is the only park where you can catch the game from a friend's roof. We are still trying to find such a friend.

On the inside, the red-brick outfield wall covered in ivy and the almost nonexistent foul territory that allows fans to reach out and touch the players are the two most noticeable and talked-about characteristics of the park. They are also a big part of what makes it great and cozy. Adding to this experience is the simplicity of the stadium itself. The seats around the field are in an austere two-deck design with numerous supporting columns and obstructed views that date the park and ironically add to the intimacy. Also, the bleachers, the heart and soul of the park, are right above the ivy and always packed to the gills. Behind the bleachers are the many neighborhood row houses where fans sit on their roofs to watch games.

Other memorable features of Wrigley Field include the most popular scoreboard in the majors, which towers above the bleachers in dead center, flanked by flagpoles and keeping track of the standings in each division of the National League. It was built by Bill Veeck in 1937 at the same time he added the bleachers and ivy. The Cubbie faithful also informed us that there is always a flag that denotes if the Cubs won or lost their last game (Win = White Flag with Blue W; Lose = Blue Flag with White L). The scoreboard, intimacy, bleachers, and connection with the neighborhood give Wrigley a feel all its own that all fans should enjoy at least once.

FANS: In Chicago we met a lovable, loyal, and hard-knock group of fans. Although there are a lot of wanna-bes in and around the park, they fade away next to the true Cub fans. Without a World Series win in over ninety years, the hapless Cubs have created a cult of fans that mourn their setbacks at every game, win or lose. A group of fans in 1966 even created the "Bleacher Bums," a willy-nilly bunch dedicated to rooting for the Cubs regardless. Any fan whose team has a tradition of losing can empathize with the Cubs fans. Dave and I certainly could relate, being from Cleveland and Houston. Unlike in most underperforming cities, however, Cubs losses do not translate into quiet and unenergetic fans during the game. Cubs fans root and root loudly, even when the Cubs are down by five or six runs. The fans will pull for every batter to mount a rally.

FACILITIES: Although Wrigley was built in 1914, it has much better facilities than either Tiger Stadium or Fenway Park, which were built in the same era. The park, however, is by no means an equal of the Camdenesque venues and suffers from limited restrooms and old, rundown seats. On the bright side, the concourses are sufficiently wide to allow fans to navigate from one section to another.

FOOD: Wrigley Field was the first park to have permanent concession facilities. Being a classical Midwest park, it has a real forte in sausage and beer. Otherwise though, there is little selection, and no specialty food unless you include the Old Style, a great macro-brew. The hot dog has spicy mustard and sauerkraut as options, which was consistent with the Midwest and our taste buds. The ice cream and malt options are also great and seemingly endless. This can help on hot muggy days. LAST CALL: Alcohol is served until the middle of the seventh inning.

GREAT PLAYERS AND HISTORIC MOMENTS: The Cubs have never won a World Series at Wrigley Field despite playing six times in the fall classic. The most memorable of these series was in 1932 when Babe Ruth's called shot in Game Three at Wrigley ultimately led to the Cubs undoing. Easily the Cubbies' greatest player has been the great short-stop Ernie Banks, memorialized for saying: "What a great day for baseball. Let's play two!" Outside of the World Series futility, great games at Wrigley have included the only no-hitter thrown by both pitchers through nine innings in 1917 between Jim "Hippo" Vaughn of the Cubs and Fred Toney of the Cincinnati Reds. The Reds won in ten off a Jim Thorpe RBI. All-Star Games were played here in 1947, 1962, and 1990.

BALLPARK HISTORY: Wrigley Park was built to house the Federal League's Chicago Federals (a.k.a. Whales), who were disbanded. The park got its signature look in 1937 when Bill Veeck added the bleachers, red-brick wall, the ivy, and the scoreboard. The other largest renovation came in 1988 when lights were added to the park. The Cubs had threatened to move without lights and MLB had already barred the team from playing playoff games at the park due to the lack of lights (all playoff games in the late 1980s were to be played at Busch Stadium in St. Louis). So on August 8, 1988, Wrigley Field hosted its first night game. The baseball gods apparently disapproved: the game was rained out.

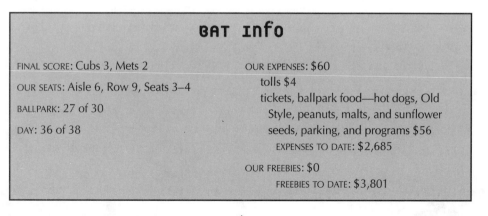

BAT INFO

FINAL SCORE: Cubs 3, Mets 2	OUR EXPENSES: $60
OUR SEATS: Aisle 6, Row 9, Seats 3–4	tolls $4
BALLPARK: 27 of 30	tickets, ballpark food—hot dogs, Old Style, peanuts, malts, and sunflower seeds, parking, and programs $56
DAY: 36 of 38	EXPENSES TO DATE: $2,685
	OUR FREEBIES: $0
	FREEBIES TO DATE: $3,801

All talk of moving the Cubs has ended, and the city and team are proud to be playing in such a historic and unique park.

FUN FACT: "The Star-Spangled Banner" was played here at the beginning of the 1918 World Series, which started the tradition of opening baseball games and sporting events with the song.

THE ONE THING YOU HAVE TO DO AT WRIGLEY FIELD AND WHY: Sing "Take Me Out to the Ballgame" during the seventh-inning stretch as loud as you can. For years, Harry Carry led fans through the song, waving his microphone and crooning into the sky. Nowhere in baseball did the seventh-inning stretch feel as perfect as at Wrigley. Too many parks speed through the song, with fans casually mumbling the lyrics. These days at Wrigley they have guest singers every day, in homage to Harry, and the fans still enthusiastically accompany them, just as they did with Harry.

LASTING IMPRESSION: The epitome of the neighborhood park still thrives on the North Side of Chicago.

28

county
stadium
milwaukee

HEADING FOR Milwaukee, I was already feeling a sense of loss. Wrigley had been such a great start to the day, and now the whole experience was going to be tainted by a trip to what I was sure would be another huge, empty, and impersonal multipurpose stadium. After seeing two great games at the two most storied parks in baseball we were heading into . . . Wisconsin.

No worry though. We had an amazing time in Milwaukee. County Stadium was filled with twenty-eight thousand screaming fans, and the place was riotous. It was probably the most fun experience of the trip, which is ironic because it was one of only three parks at which we received nothing gratis from ballpark personnel. On second thought, maybe this lack of salesmanship had something to do with the warm-blooded, true-blue American vibe we got from the ballpark.

county stadium

· ·

MONTREAL V MILWAUKEE

game time: 7:05 p.m.

FIRST OFF, I admit that I have made an effort to devote a little more space to the ballparks that are recently deceased, with the possible exception of 3Com. In all of the other chapters there is a sort of Catch-22 in that, if it is a great ballpark, I could never do it justice in words, and at best can only hope to offer some idea of what to expect there. For the lesser ballparks, I realize that it is more likely that these words may be the only image some will ever have of the stadium. In the case of County Stadium, though, by the time these words appear, the park will be lost. Thus the following is a poor substitute for the lost experience.

County Stadium is perhaps the most American major league ballpark I have ever visited. I love the old ballparks. I rave on and on about Wrigley Field and Fenway Park. Those parks have a certain quality of being from another time. Although I enjoy the bountiful amenities of the new ballparks, they have a certain imported feeling to them, as if they came out of a mail-order ballpark catalog. If the old ballparks are the personality and the new ones are the dapper clones, then County Stadium is the heart.

In my fantasies I imagine the true baseball fans in Milwaukee chaining themselves to the stadium and refusing to let the authorities shepherd the Brewers into the predictably unique Miller Park across the parking lot, thus relinquishing all the character Milwaukee has infused into this park.

I don't know exactly what gives me this impression of County Stadium. It's certainly a confluence of factors. First, there's the whole red-and-blue color scheme from the seats to the fence to the overhang. In the context of modern ballpark landscaping, this scheme (right up there with Tiger Stadium) is among the most refreshing visual experiences of any ballpark.

Also attractive to me are the unassuming bleacher seats in the outfield. They are so unincorporated into the park that they make the place feel less like a stadium and more like a place where everyone comes together to watch a ballgame. Then there is Bernie the Brewer, the life-sized puppet that slides into the big beer stein when the Brew Crew hits a home run—the park's lone gimmick. His cabin high above the outfield wall is small enough that you might not necessarily notice it were your eyes not continually drawn back to it given the relative barrenness of the rest of the park's backdrop. Bernie seems to tell a story all by himself, saying, Here it is, my ballpark, enjoy the game foremost, and if things work out, maybe you'll get to see me slide into a mug of beer.

All of these elements of County Stadium seem destined to be lost forever, but I can at least hope that Miller Park might preserve and hopefully even improve upon perhaps the most beloved feature of County Stadium: the great fans of Milwaukee. The crowd at our game was perhaps the most lively colony I have ever been a part of. I have never heard the national anthem resonate so loudly through so many voices with so much passion. Although I have lamented the dilution of real fans in the crowds at these new parks, I am very confident Milwaukee will draw a more enthusiastic, supportive, and good-hearted crowd when they move into Miller Park.

In the midst of my lavish praises upon the baseball fans of Milwaukee, I should add that we were there on hat day, and by virtue of that fact we were witness to a bit larger crowd than County was historically used to (27th in major league attendance in 2000). Certainly twenty-eight thousand fans didn't make it out for every game at County Stadium. If they did, the park would still be with us. Our experience just proved how great this stadium could have been, how great the fans in Milwaukee really are when something motivates them to go out to the ballpark. That sad testament to the economics of baseball is precisely the problem with this situation. You can go to a ballgame with thirty thousand strangers and have a great time, and despite that, only fifteen thousand will be here the next night when no one is passing out anything. Although I imagine they'll have a blast and still manage to sing the national anthem louder than most Super Bowl crowds, they won't generate the necessary revenue.

So the only way to bring in the fans is to build a whole new stadium, like the ones in those other cities. Right? Then people will come. So who gets hurt? The people of Milwaukee seem to want the new stadium. I expect they'll enjoy it, too. They are not as cynical as I am. So maybe I'm the only one who comes out upset in this deal. I can live with that. I only hope that years from now we don't suddenly realize that we made the whole cookie-cutter stadium mistake all over again.

In the end, this ballpark experience was all about attitude. My attitude. The ballpark's attitude. Where the ballpark got its attitude from I'll never know, but maybe it has something to do with the fact that *Major League* was filmed in here. Then again, maybe it was just the fans and the general level of inebriation in the ballpark on that particular day that made for such a comfortable experience.

In Milwaukee, we found the heart of baseball at a run-down ballpark in the middle of an old quarry.

Maybe it was the food, which should not go without mention. In the heart of sausage country you expect the best dogs in the country. You don't even have to ask about the bratwurst.

Regardless, it definitely helped the experience and the atmosphere even more that we saw a great game and our third consecutive come-from-behind win for the home team. Jeromy Burnitz hit two home runs, including one to win it in the bottom of the ninth, and the crowd went nuts. Maybe it was the free hats that brought them out to the ballpark, but in contrast to the Beanie Baby Shea fans, these guys definitely did not consider the game to be an afterthought.

The final element of the scenery at County was Miller Park. Right in the ballpark's backyard, it was going up. All the while we were having a perfectly swell time at the old place. That juxtaposition really made me wonder. I mean new parks are fun to go to, but this park was a blast. Sometimes it helps a ballpark's character if the place is half-empty.

county stadium

CITY: Milwaukee, Wisconsin

TENANT: Milwaukee Braves (1953–65), Chicago White Sox (nine 1968 games and eleven 1969 games), Milwaukee Brewers (1970–2000) Green Bay Packers (1953–94 for two or three home games a year)

OPENED: April 6, 1953

NICKNAME/ALIASES: County Stadium

DESIGN: Multipurpose stadium, symmetrical design, no movable seats. SISTER PARKS: Memorial Stadium in Baltimore (razed) and Cleveland Municipal Stadium in Cleveland (razed).

FIELD: Grass

DIMENSIONS (feet): left field line—315, left field—362, left center—392, center field—402, right center—392, right field—362, right field line—315

FENCES (feet): 10

LOCATION: 201 S. 46th St., Milwaukee, WI 53201. Right field (S): W. National Ave. First base (W): General Mitchell Blvd. Third base (N): I-94 and Story Pkwy. Left field (E): US 41.

CAPACITY: 53,192 (baseball). Total attendance: 1,811,593 (1998). Average attendance: 22,365 (1998).

PARKING: $6–$10 in the thirteen thousand parking spots surrounding the park.

TICKETS: $5–$28. BEST BANG FOR YOUR BUCK: The bleachers are a great value and you get to see Bernie Brewer up close as he slides into the beer stein.

THE BALLPARK EXPERIENCE: Dave and I didn't think they played games at venues like County Stadium anymore. The stands were rickety, and the exterior resembled a tin roof that six guys put up last weekend. But the true blue-collar baseball-loving fans and the tasty brats made this park a memorable experience. More than the circular cookie-cutter parks of the 1960s and '70s that we had visited, County Stadium had a unique flavor because no one park exists quite like it anymore. At our game, the fans added to this feeling and made the park feel more like a football game with tailgating, chants, and an overall intensity rarely seen on the trip.

The park was built in an old stone quarry, and concrete parking lots and cars racing on I-94 are the distinctive features around the area. We were struck by the barrenness around the park and how the old tin-can-looking structure seems to fit in so well with the location. If you imagined what a park built in a quarry would look like, you would probably come up with a pretty good image of County Stadium. The latest parks brag about how they fit into their neighborhood, but County Stadium definitely fit much more snugly into this surrounding than the new Miller Park right next door ever will. On the inside, the concourses were buried beneath steel and concrete and layers of fading paint. The seats looked and felt especially old, and the second deck was distant from the action and full of obstructed views. Despite these flaws, the lively atmosphere and intense fans made the park a winner in our book.

FANS: By now you get the trend that blue-collar towns tend to have blue-collar fans, and Milwaukee's are the bluest of the blue. These guys were a lot more like the prototypical football crowd than a bunch of George Will baseball connoisseurs. They were also the most enthusiastic bunch of the trip. We had heard about Milwaukee fans' tailgating exploits but were in awe of the thousands of people with BBQs surrounding the park. Their devotion has been born out in County Stadium's attendance numbers that, until the last couple of years, were very respectable for a small market with little history of success. In talking to the fans around us, it became obvious that their knowledge of baseball was also excellent both in terms of Milwaukee baseball history and in general. With many newer parks full of corporate seats and visitors who would be challenged to name the all-time home-run king (Henry Aaron), Milwaukee fans are a throwback to yesteryear. One can only hope that their dedication will be rewarded someday with a World Series.

FACILITIES: Very old and rundown sum up the facilities at County Stadium, and they were probably the worst overall on the trip. The seats were especially hard and uncomfortable in our reserved seats. Fans were keen to point out that the park especially saw a decline over the last few seasons as the Brewers awaited their new park.

FOOD: Our food experience in Milwaukee was all about bratwurst. This German sausage delicacy was ubiquitous at the park and sold at virtually every stand and the famous

While we enjoyed the great bratwursts at County Stadium, we also saw a great come-from-behind game and enjoyed one of the best features in all the ballparks—Bernie the Brewer and his brew house.

Klement's Sausage House. We saw fans roving the aisles with five or six brats and a couple of the local brews, Miller. Food is simple in Milwaukee but very, very good. It is probably underappreciated though, because they say that the brats grilled at the tailgates before the game are even better. With the time crunch of our drive from Chicago, we unfortunately did not have the opportunity to befriend any locals and get a home-cooked brat. Had we had the time, we are sure they would have shared. They are an all-American crowd. LAST CALL: Alcohol is served until the middle of the seventh inning.

GREAT PLAYERS AND HISTORIC MOMENTS: Hank Aaron summed up the great history of County Stadium when he said, "When they tear down County Stadium to make way for Miller Park they will take a piece of my heart with it." County Stadium has been home to two different major league franchises, three World Series, and many historic achievements. The Braves moved into the park in 1953, and the powerful Henry Aaron and Eddie Mathews powered the club to the 1957 and 1958 World Series. In 1957, behind the three wins of Lew Burdette, the Braves beat the Yankees in seven games for the world championship, the only world championship for a baseball team located in Milwaukee. In 1958 the Yankees got their revenge, topping the Braves in seven games. During the residency of the Brewers, the park had little glory to brag of. Other great moments include Nolan Ryan's three-hundredth win, the bulk of Paul Molitor's thirty-seven-game hitting streak in 1987, and many of Hank Aaron's now-historic tally of home runs. All-Star Games were played at County Stadium in 1955 and 1975.

BALLPARK HISTORY: Ground broke for County Stadium on October 19, 1950, with no tenant. The park was built with twenty-eight thousand permanent seats and eight thousand portable bleacher seats. In 1953 Milwaukee successfully lured the Boston Braves to the new park, and the park was expanded to accommodate them, increasing the capacity to over forty-three thousand by adding more grandstand seats.

The park had no baseball team from 1966, when the Braves left, until 1970, when the Seattle Pilots relocated to Milwaukee as the Brewers. The Brewers will move into Miller Park in 2001, and County Stadium will end its tradition of baseball. A portion of the field will remain as a memorial to the old ballpark.

FUN FACT: Cecil Fielder is the only player to have hit a home run out of County Stadium.

THE ONE THING YOU HAVE TO DO AT COUNTY STADIUM AND WHY: Watch Bernie Brewer. At our game, he spent most of the game in the brew house jumping around and leading cheers. When Jeromy Burnitz hit the game-winning home run, Bernie gave us what we had been waiting for, the slide into his stein of beer. Everyone went nuts.

LASTING IMPRESSION: A park full of character from a bygone era on its last legs.

BAT INFO

FINAL SCORE: Brewers 4, Expos 3

OUR SEATS: Box 22, Row 6, Seats 14–15

BALLPARK: 28 of 30

DAY: 36 OF 38

MILES TRAVELED: 447 (13,738 total)

NEW STATES: 2 (Wisconsin, Minnesota by nightfall; 31 total)

OUR EXPENSES: $78
tickets, ballpark food—bratwurst (4 each), soda, parking, and programs $60
gas $18

EXPENSES TO DATE: $2,763

OUR FREEBIES: $50
hotel room in St. Paul, MN (courtesy of my dad—some benefit has to come out of traveling with your family)

FREEBIES TO DATE: $3,851

29

The Metrodome

Minneapolis

WHEN WE left Milwaukee, Dave and I were on something of an adrenaline high. Excited about the day's many memorable experiences, we felt ready for the long drive ahead. We could almost see the end of the road. Only two parks to go.

Dad was a little more realistic. Older and wiser, he was well aware of the toll the day's activities had taken on us. He was already showing their effects. When we got into the car, he passed out before we left the parking lot.

About fifteen minutes later, as Dave was pulling onto Interstate 94, I silently acknowledged that my father had the right idea, and I fell asleep in the backseat. Dave soon reached the same point, and before we had made it outside of Milwaukee proper, Dad ended up behind the wheel and stayed there for most of the next five hours.

We hadn't intended to drive that long that night. My father was much more of a morning person and had been pushing for us to stop as soon as possible. It was 327 miles to Minneapolis though, so we knew we needed to make significant headway. What we didn't account for was the fact that Wisconsin is something of a travel destination on midsummer weekends, and there were no hotel rooms available between Madison and St. Paul, Minnesota.

Of course, we did not realize this until we pulled into an all-night diner to get a late bite (don't ask how we were hungry) and inquire about vacancies in town. We received a lot of funny looks and chortles and the unencouraging refrain, "Good luck." Over omelets we pulled out the cell phone and our travel guides and began calling ahead to all of the motels between Madison and the Minnesota state line. To no avail. We faced the fact that we might not find a room anywhere that night. Maybe in the Twin Cities area. Maybe.

We steeled ourselves for the possibility and loaded up on coffee before leaving the diner. As we departed we took a couple of quick pictures near a huge red ceramic moose outside the roadhouse. Once we started driving, we didn't stop until 3 A.M. in St. Paul, where we only got a room because somebody had already left to get an early start on the hunting season or the fishing season or the camping season or whatever season it was that was drawing this seasonal migration to the north.

The next morning, Dad woke us up entirely too early for the half-hour drive to the ballpark.

The Metrodome

TEXAS V MINNESOTA

Game Time: 1:05 P.M.

ALL GOOD things come to an end. We were on an intense emotional high coming into Minnesota, despite our lack of sleep. We had three great ballpark experiences behind us, but the Metrodome could do nothing to sustain it. My mom always said, if you can't say something nice, don't say anything at all. So I am tempted to tell you simply that the Metrodome is a clean place.

Rather than list the failures of a subpar ballpark and rehash why these things don't work at the Metrodome, I'll say simply that, like Pro Player Stadium, great football fields don't necessarily make great baseball fields. Like Cinergy Field, cavernous and empty stadiums have no atmosphere. Like Comiskey, pseudo-new, pseudo-clean parks are somewhat antiseptic. Now place all of that inside an inflatable balloon of a building. That's the Metrodome.

The inflatable balloon aspect is easily the most distinctive thing about this place, although I am sure the designers expected to get a little more mileage out of it. In actual practice, it just means that the roof looks a little softer than most domes. Fans might wonder whether they paint the thing red when the circus comes to town. The fact that the dome is inflated provides for a couple of notable experiences. Those being, first, that all entrances are airtight revolving doors, and second, after the game, that you can leave through a nonairtight sliding door, which literally propels you out of the building (see THE ONE THING TO DO AT THE METRODOME).

279

Our friends Gary and Eric joined us at the Metrodome for the most lackluster ballpark experience of the trip.

Along the same lines as Pro Player, from the looks of it, the Metrodome is a pretty good football stadium. It better be. Half the seats are pretty much useless for baseball: some face right across the outfield, others are so high and close to the field that you can't see anything behind second base, and some are almost completely obstructed.

Along with thirteen thousand other folks, we saw a game that was a bore. And we had to overpay for bad seats to do so.

On the bright side, we met up with friends Gary Colvin and Eric Harp from Minneapolis, who at least managed to warn us of the less than thrilling experience that is the Metrodome before we actually got inside. Given the fact that we were the only ones there, my dad and I were afforded the opportunity to scout out the place and experience baseball from some of the worst sightlines in the major leagues. My favorites were the seats off of the right-field foul line that hang about three feet off the line and twenty feet up in the air. Don't even try to figure out what the right fielder is doing with the ball in the corner if you are sitting in those seats.

Well, making a positive out of a negative, at least it is good to know that there is one park in the ballpark fraternity I wouldn't mind replacing. Unfortunately, the Twins don't seem to be getting a new stadium any time soon.

Bad sightlines, not much legroom, not many fans, little to see from eleven-dollar seats, no enthusiasm in the park—even though the Twins were winning big—and the food is best left not described. I hate being so negative.

If you had to have such an un-American experience though, I guess it wasn't the worst timing. There is always something therapeutic about relaxing in an empty stadium, and we needed a respite from our recent ballpark euphorias, the previous night's long drive, and the highly anticipated trip we had ahead of us to the Field of Dreams. It wasn't much of a bright side, but we were desperate.

After the Twins game, we said our good-byes to Eric and Gary, dropped my dad at the airport on our way out of town, and headed for Iowa. It was on to the Field of Dreams, just the two of us.

The Metrodome

CITY: Minneapolis, Minnesota

TENANT: Minnesota Twins, Minnesota Vikings of the National Football League

OPENED: April 3, 1982

NICKNAME/ALIASES: The Hubert H. Humphrey Metrodome (this is its official name), the HHH Dome

DESIGN: Multipurpose stadium, circular design, movable seats. SISTER PARKS: Pontiac Superdome in Detroit, the Kingdome in Seattle, and the domed stadium in Vancouver.

FIELD: AstroTurf with mound and base cutouts

DIMENSIONS (feet): left field—343, left center—385, center field—408, right center—367, right field—327'

FENCES (feet): left field—13, right field—23. The right field wall is 23' high and is covered with a blue plastic tarp. It has been nicknamed the "Hefty Bag."

LOCATION: 34 Kirby Puckett Place, Minneapolis, MN 55415. Right field (SE): 10th Ave. First base (NE): 6th St. Third base (NW): Chicago Ave. Left field (SW): 4th St.

CAPACITY: 55,883 (baseball). Total attendance: 1,165,976 (1998). Average attendance: 14,394 (1998).

PARKING: $6–$10. Go for the street parking if available (see OTHER THINGS TO REMEMBER).

TICKETS: $4–$21. BEST BANG FOR YOUR BUCK: From our experience, avoid the upper deck unless you bring binoculars or are planning to see a Vikings game.

THE BALLPARK EXPERIENCE: The Metrodome is an engineering marvel but a lousy place to see a baseball game. To start with, the financial district, where the park is built, is generally desolate by the 7:05 start time of most games. This lack of energy continues on the inside of the park. The concourses are all concrete and lighted fluorescently, giving off a strange glow. The field and seating areas are enormous, betraying the fact that they have been designed to suit football first and foremost. More so than any other park, the Metrodome has to fight to turn its football stadium into a baseball park, creating a very odd and unconventional design with a 23' wall in right field that partly hides and partly is composed of extra seats for football. These seats are basically pulled out to generate a good layout for football. During the baseball season though, they are folded under the seats used for the game and are still generally in plain view, like creating the odd image of a few hundred seats pointing straight down.

It is sad that a park built as recently as 1982 and heralded as a state-of-the-art facility is already outdated. Our experiences in the newer ballparks in Baltimore and Cleveland or the classic parks in New York or Boston or even the cookie-cutter outdoor stadiums all have this park beat. Overall, the place has little charm, was not intended for baseball, and breeds a poor AstroTurf style of baseball. We can only hope that Minnesota gets a new park that will wash away the memories of this place.

FANS: Although the Twins won World Championships in 1987 and 1991, the winning spirit by the time our tour rolled into town had all but abandoned the city. The game at the Metrodome was quiet and lacked energy. The poor quality of the team on the field and the venue, with its institutional feel, are likely the key reasons for this malady. As a result, it is hard to say much about the fans. You can hardly hold it against them for not coming out to this ballpark. At one point in time at least, this park definitely had a strong fan base—the team's glory period in the late '80s. When the Twins were winning, the Metrodome was one of the worst venues for an opposing team. It simply got so loud in the park that it was intimidating for the other team. While this was more significant for football, the Twins in 1987 postseason won all their games at home, including four in the World Series. That year the Twins also became the first team in the American League to surpass three million fans in a season. Needless to say, the situation in Minnesota has fallen off considerably.

FACILITIES: The facilities are spotless, with plenty of restrooms and concession booths. The concourses are wide and everything is clean. While this overall taintlessness is just about the park's only asset, it also contributes to the place's institutional feel.

FOOD: Like the Midwest parks, the Metrodome served us the standard baseball fare with little in the way of specialty food. Unfortunately, though, the Metrodome did not come through with the high-quality staples we had come to expect from Milwaukee and Chicago. The hot dog was okay, thanks in large part to the ample availability of sauerkraut throughout the park. Otherwise there was little of note at the concessions, and the lack of options made the experience something of a downer. LAST CALL: Alcohol is served until the middle of the seventh inning.

GREAT PLAYERS AND HISTORIC MOMENTS: The Twins have captured two World Series championships in the Metrodome. In 1987 the team led by Kirby Puckett and Frank Viola outdueled the St. Louis Cardinals for the first World Series ever for Minnesota. The 1987 series was the first time the fall classic was played indoors, and Minnesota capitalized by winning all four games at home in the seven-game series. That is home-field

Large, impersonal, and designed for football, the Metrodome, though it served up a rare Twins victory, still managed to end up rock-bottom on our list.

advantage for you. In 1991 the Twins once again were World Series bound with a veteran Puckett and the pitching of Jack Morris. The series once again went to seven games, and in the bottom of the eleventh of the last game at the Metrodome, Gene Larkin lined a shot over the left fielder for the only run of the game to win the series over Atlanta. The only All-Star Game played here was in 1985.

BALLPARK HISTORY: The Minnesota Twins moved to the Metrodome in 1982. The park was only the fourth domed stadium in baseball (the Astrodome in Houston, Olympic Stadium in Montreal, and the Kingdome in Seattle all predate the Metrodome). The dome made the short summers of very northern Minnesota easier to deal with. Attendance was expected to increase with the new facility and did over sporadic stretches. Ultimately, the place came to be reviled as a lifeless baseball stadium. In spite of the fact that the park is not even twenty years old, there are discussions to build a new baseball-only or more advanced multipurpose park. This is still at least five years off. If the Twins do not get a new place, expect them to leave Minnesota very soon.

BAT INFO

FINAL SCORE: Twins 11, Rangers 3

OUR SEATS: Section 223, Row 13,
    Seats 20–21

BALLPARK: 29 of 30

DAY: 37 of 38

MILES TRAVELED: 447 (12,138; 13,738 total)

NEW STATES: 1 (Iowa; 32 total)

OUR EXPENSES: $110
    game tickets, ballpark food—hot dogs,
    hamburgers, peanuts, and soda,
    parking, and programs $55
Subway subs $10
gas and sundries $45
    EXPENSES TO DATE: $2,873

OUR FREEBIES:
    priceless—sleeping on the Field
    FREEBIES TO DATE: $3,851

FUN FACT: Dave Kingman, who seems to hold every record in domes (see the Kingdome) hit a ball through the roof on May 4, 1984. Although it traveled farther than just about any other ball ever hit in the park, he was only given credit for a ground rule double.

THE ONE THING YOU HAVE TO DO AT THE METRODOME AND WHY: Watch people walk out of the "windy tunnel door." The Metrodome is held up by air pressure, and revolving doors for entrances and exits keep sufficient air pressure inside to support the roof. There are several regular doors, however, only used when the game is over, and these create a wind tunnel when opened. Hair gets blown forward, papers go everywhere, and sometimes people scream.

OTHER THINGS TO REMEMBER: Do not pay for parking. There is plenty of free street parking about five blocks from the park.

LASTING IMPRESSION: Very little character, very few fans, and very boring interior make this one of the worst parks.

The Field of Dreams

NEAR THE end of the Twins game, Dave and I both became noticeably antsy. We were counting the hours to the Field of Dreams, which was to be the high point of our trip, the Field having so inspired us that we put a computer-rendered likeness of it on the front of our Baseball America Tour T-shirts. Now we were just hours away from that field, and the excitement was growing at an exponential pace.

By the time we crossed into Iowa after the game, Dave and I were at a high point of the trip. We had been through so much tension, given our inevitable disagreements and general fatigue at dealing with each other. Even though most of that had faded, I know both of us still felt a lingering annoyance with each other on an hourly basis. Dave was telling the same story again. I was telling Dave what to do again.

En route to the field, those tensions had vanished. Dave recapped most of the last five weeks, and not only was I not annoyed, I was nostalgic. When I suggested that we pull over for gas, Dave complimented me on a good idea. The trip had taken an upturn ever since our first trip through Cooperstown, but this was a whole other level.

It was like Christmas Eve. I had a feeling of great excitement about the events just around the corner, but I was not too eager that I could not enjoy the moment we were in, this moment of anticipation. Still, we were both obviously ready to get there. I noticed Dave was driving a little faster without my having to hurry him.

We wanted to get there by sundown.

Unfortunately, there was no way to cover the 197 miles in the two hours before sunset, so we were destined for a late-night rendezvous with the Field of Dreams. No matter, we thought. This might even be cooler. Maybe they would leave the lights on.

Though Dave never did disappear into the corn, we had a spiritual experience at the Field of Dreams. We borrowed some uniforms and just appreciated the moment, hoping someone would come . . .

We could have played catch on that Iowa field forever.

Granted, nobody outside our inner circle had been taking much of an interest in our trip over the last few days. But this was the last night of the trip. What with the VIP treatment we had experienced from Los Angeles to Cleveland, we didn't think it was out of the question. Over the last thirty-seven days, stranger things had happened.

Alas, when we pulled up to the field at 9:30 P.M. Sunday night, it was pitch-black. We had a pretty hard time finding the field at all. Were it not for the fact that Dave had been there before and vaguely remembered the way, we might have found ourselves in somebody else's cornfield. When we arrived, we could barely make out the outlines of the diamond under the crescent moon.

The lack of photo-quality lighting made no difference to us. The force was with us on this mission, and even though we couldn't see it, we could definitely *feel* the field. We got out of the car and walked toward it, our eyes slowly adjusting to the darkness. Gradually we could distinguish the dirt of the infield, the corn, a light post. We stepped onto the damp field, and how I wished we could just flip the lights on and start up a game. I'd seen the movie. The light switch was on the porch of the house in the background. Or so the film would have us believe. I couldn't bring myself to go up there. We had gotten permission to sleep on the field but not to turn the lights on and start a ballgame. Besides, we didn't even have permission to go on the right side of the field or the property beyond it, where the house stood. I didn't want to get arrested in Iowa, not at the Field of Dreams, not the day before the end of the trip.

So we gave up on the idea of playing and instead turned our attentions to the corn. Our original giddy squawking began to die down to a stunned silence of awe. Even Dave shut up. We walked a ways into the corn and just looked up at the stars. I thought

I had seen a clear sky before, but here were more stars than I had ever seen. Even more amazing about it was that it had been raining all day until we got there. The only signs of the rain that remained were on the ground.

After what seemed like an hour in the corn, I had to break the silence, mostly because I was worried that something might have happened to my usually loquacious companion. He confirmed that he was still there, and we returned to the field and became antsy and hyper all over again. Finally we started to put the cell phone to good use, calling most everyone we knew who might care that we were actually on the field. Of course at such an exciting time, nobody seemed to be home, so we gave up on them. It wasn't their trip anyway. We were plenty overcome with our own emotions, so we pulled out our sleeping bags and lay down on the field, soaking everything in. Although things had been hectic and strained for the last two weeks, the field relaxed everything, relieved all our worries.

We were allowed to sleep in left or center field, because our benefactors only owned that half of the field. As it turns out, the field that the filmmakers envisioned building for their movie was situated across a property line between two farms. Of course, this was no problem for the filmmakers. Just compensate the owners of the two plots of land and build your field wherever you want. But it generated a number of comical difficulties after the filming of the movie was over.

For one, the year after they made the film, Al Amskamp, the owner of the land that left and center fields cut through, decided to replant it with corn. The owners of the rest of the field preserved whatever they could and built a souvenir stand around it. Apparently Al, or some entrepreneurial thinker who got in touch with him, realized that was not such a bad idea, and so the next year, the field was rebuilt and two souvenir stands were up. This is the case today. Two roads lead to the field, and at the end of each a souvenir stand hawks general paraphernalia. The owners and operators of both are also generous with their criticisms of each other and quick to claim their own superior sensitivity.

If you stop and think about it, you can generate a really cynical view about this money trap real fast. Consequently, Dave and I chose not to think about it. We put our loyalties squarely behind Al, because not only did he let us sleep on his field, but he also gave us a personal wake-up call the next morning. He was a humorous guy and seemed genuine in his excitement about the attraction in which he held such a stake. Sure, he had plowed it under, but only because he never figured anyone would want to come out to his little farm.

What refreshing modesty.

30

kauffman
stadium
kansas city

THERE'S NOTHING magical about the number thirty-eight. Although we had a couple of appointments later in the summer, Dave and I didn't have a hard and fast need to complete our trip in thirty-eight days. It didn't have to have that sense of urgency.

Of course, we knew that the faster we got it done, the more publicity we would get. But that's not the real reason (or, at least, the whole reason) why we did it in less than forty days. In fact, when a reporter specifically asked about the thirty-eight days, our response was along the lines of, "Well, they play every day, right? So why should we get a day off?" But that's not the real reason.

The truth, I guess, is that we made a decision to do something, and we realized it was a once-in-a-lifetime opportunity. We really wanted to just get down to the essence of the whole thing. If we were going to go on the ultimate road trip, to create for ourselves the ultimate baseball experience, then we were going to immerse ourselves in it as deeply as we could go. We wanted to get as close as we could to the true essence of baseball.

We are not freaks. Baseball lovers, yes, but not freaks—at least not normally. We're normal guys who like baseball, not much more than the average guy (or girl) who grew up with their dads taking them to the ballpark, buying them a pretzel, and letting them steal a sip of beer before promptly spitting it out. With this trip we were testing the bounds of that deep relationship we had with baseball. (Although, in the beginning we never realized how much we would be testing the bounds of the relationship we had with each other.)

This was the last day. We started it early because the sprinklers on the Field of Dreams woke us up at about 4 A.M. We relocated to foul territory, where they got us again about sunrise, at which point we surrendered and got up. Shortly after the sprinklers came on, Al drove up on his tractor. He stopped while mowing the field to talk to us about the trip and, although not necessarily a baseball fan, became a quick fan of ours. Likewise we became quick fans of his. We talked off and on as he mowed the field and we played catch. Shortly thereafter one of the people who runs Al's concession stand showed up, and we talked to her. She gave us some old White Sox jerseys to take a few pictures in. We had to give them back, of course.

At 9 A.M. we were allowed to take the field, so Dave and I went out for BP, to launch a few toward the corn. Soon a couple vanloads of kids showed up and it turned into a pretty big event with everyone taking their rips. I wished we didn't have to leave for Kansas City so early, because we would have hung around and got a game going. But we had plans of taking in the Negro League Hall of Fame in Kansas City before the game that evening. Prior to our leaving, we stocked up on souvenirs, this being the consummate tourist trap and our being consummate tourists.

On the whole, our fourteen hours at the Field of Dreams were amazing, and I am forever grateful that they left it there for people like us after the movie was wrapped. It only makes me a little sad that possibly the only reason the field is still intact is because someone thought they could make a little money off of it. In any case, they were right; we dropped a fair bit of change there ourselves. The saddest part is the whole dueling gift shops thing, which simply comes off in the end as sad and pathetic. I mean that's not exactly the spirit of the field is it?

Before we made it to our last game, we made a quick stop in Van Meter, Iowa, the birthplace of Bob Feller (remember the poster I gave my dad for his birthday?). We didn't want to pass up anything baseball-related on our last day. They had a small museum there, so we took some pictures, talked to the locals, bought some trinkets, and took off for a quick tour of the Negro League Hall of Fame.

The Hall of Fame in Kansas City was a late addition to our schedule, and as such we had neglected to do much preparation beforehand other than figure out roughly where it stood geographically. We had the same sort of situation with the Feller museum in Van Meter, and that went off very easily. Turns out it is not too hard to find anything in Van Meter, Iowa. But the hall was a different story. Unprepared as we were, we were totally ignorant of the fact that the hall, like most barbershops, was closed on Mondays. Even though we hadn't known that the hall existed until a couple of days prior, this was a huge blow to us.

At the Negro League Hall of Fame we met up with our friends Andy Ochsner and Charles Schoonover, who, along with Andy's brother and Charles's uncle and cousin, were going to be joining us on this historic last day of our trip. As there wasn't much to see at the hall this Monday, we decided to get the whole last-ballpark thing over with a little quicker. So we headed to Kauffman with our final entourage in tow.

Kauffman stadium

MINNESOTA V KANSAS CITY

Game Time: 7:05 p.m.

KAUFFMAN HAS often been called the most underrated park in baseball and for good reason. It's got all the class of Dodger Stadium without the hype. It's also at the middle of an amazing sports complex that houses the equally grand Arrowhead Stadium, home of the NFL's Chiefs.

Easily the most distinctive feature of Kauffman Stadium is the fountain that cascades just beyond the outfield wall. Everybody talks about it. Everybody loves it. And for exactly that reason I wasn't too thrilled about it. After thirty-eight days of ballpark appraisals, if there was one thing I was not, it was awestruck at the cool new features of various parks. It would be less than a stretch to say that I was cynical at best when confronted with all of these new features. As for the fountain, I grew to appreciate it, even though I would rather not overhype it and ruin the experience for others. All in all it is something nice to look at when the action on the field doesn't provide much of interest.

In our experience, this was very much the case. We saw a lousy game in Kansas City. The Royals didn't really put up a fight. It was the thirtieth park of our trip—the last day, the last game. We were expecting something special. The baseball gods owed us something for all we had been through. It was not to be. Instead, we got a final lesson from baseball, the ultimate display of how baseball mirrors life in that right when you expect something magical to happen, you are confronted with the mundane. Nonetheless, we appreciated every last out. We knew this was the end.

Beyond the fountain, Kauffman Stadium is a beautiful place. In particular, the field has often been proclaimed as the most beautiful in all of baseball. It definitely seemed beautifully maintained to us, although I don't know that I would single it out as the most beautiful. In all honesty, I wouldn't be able to tell the difference between the playing field at Kauffman and that of a dozen other ballparks. Throughout the trip, with the obvious exception of the turfed stadiums, the only imperfect field we noticed was Tiger Stadium. As I noted in that chapter, that field is sublime in its own way.

What Tiger Stadium has on Kauffman is indicative of what Kauffman is lacking on the whole. The entire place is very nice and clean and stocked with amenities, but there is not much of a baseball atmosphere to it. Not to say that the experience was as unmemorable as the Metrodome, but Kauffman really doesn't (or should I say didn't, given that they have remodeled the place since our visit) project itself to be a quintessential ballpark.

Of course, given the lackluster performance we got out of the Royals, the fans at our game were not inclined to make our experience anything special. Maybe if they knew that we were there, knew what a momentous occasion this was for us, then they would have given a little more effort to conclude the Baseball America Tour on the right note. Maybe the players would have helped, too.

Looking back, I realize that after all of the perks and freebies along the way, in the last four parks of our trip, all we got was a foursome of free tickets. You would have thought that this would have been upsetting to two guys with a pretty high opinion of themselves (namely, us), but in retrospect it worked out beautifully. We hardly noticed the lack of frills. We were part of a routine in which so many little things passed unnoticed in the later parks—a slightly larger foul territory, slightly more expensive or inconvenient parking. We had figured out something of consequence: We knew that those little distinctions weren't the important things. Likewise, the perks and frills weren't necessary to get what was to be gotten out of the experiences of these individual stadiums.

We knew what was important. The atmosphere. That sense of the Boys of Summer, one good bratwurst or clam chowder or fish taco or Rocky Mountain oyster or beer.

The hand signal at Kauffman Stadium says it all: thirty ballparks in thirty-eight days.

Sitting in left field with only a couple of friends around, keeping score or catching McGwire fever along with fifty thousand others. Hopelessly watching the Yanks dismantle another opponent or hoping against hope to pull at least one out for the futile Floridians. There are so many great things about so many parks. Our job was to spread the word. (This does not apply necessarily to Minnesota or Cincinnati and possibly a couple of other places.)

Subsequently, it is ironic to note that at the end of this trip, the Kauffman experience as a baseball happening fell flat. We had hoped, at times even expected, that something magical would happen on our trip—a no-hitter, an unassisted triple play, something. But the fates didn't present such to us, so we had to find our own. We did. In the little things.

The one thing I didn't expect about this trip was the realization that the more ballparks you go to, the more in common they seem to have. At the risk of undermining myself, I have to admit that the primary attraction of a baseball park is the baseball being played there. Everything else about the park is secondary. Aside from the Metrodome, there is not a ballpark in America that I wouldn't mind visiting again.

When the Royals game finally ended, there was no fanfare or recognition. Only our small group of seven knew what had been accomplished that day, at that moment. We appreciated it. Afterward we thought about celebrating in town but decided it would feel kind of weird hanging out with a bunch of people we didn't know. They also seemed aware of the gravity and significance of our situation, and as Dave and I were basking in the glow of our achievement after the game ended, they all quietly disappeared without a trace.

Subsequently, Dave and I decided that the right thing to do was to shut the door on the trip and on Kansas City. We had missed the Negro League Hall of Fame entirely, but we couldn't hang around and wait for it the next day. Our instincts said go. The trip was over. That's what we did.

We walked through the turnstiles, getting full video documentation of the occasion. The recording of events had become so second nature that we hadn't really thought about it much since L.A. and wouldn't think about it much until we realized that we had roughly eleven hours of footage.

Fittingly, although we had amassed so much memorabilia throughout our trip, so many free T-shirts and baseball hats, when we left Kansas City, we were still wearing the same Baseball America T-shirts. I again had on my lucky Stanford cap, and Dave the Cleveland Indians Chief Wahoo hat he had worn when we walked into 3Com-stick.

Our night fell somewhere across the Kansas border. We tried to party in the hotel room, but Dave passed out after about five minutes, and I wasn't far behind him. I guess that's all appropriate. This is the way the tour ends . . . with a whimper.

Kauffman stadium

CITY: Kansas City, Missouri

TENANT: Kansas City Royals

OPENED: April 10, 1973

NICKNAME/ALIASES: Royals Stadium (the park was renamed in honor of Royals owner Ewing Kauffman)

DESIGN: Baseball-only stadium, symmetrical design, no movable seats. SISTER PARKS: Some design elements of Dodger Stadium in Los Angeles.

FIELD: Grass. Kauffman Stadium is known for its superb groundskeeping. The funny thing is that the park had AstroTurf with mound and base cutouts from 1973 to 1994.

DIMENSIONS (feet): left field—320, left center—375, center field—410, right center—375, right field—320

FENCES (feet): 8

LOCATION: 1 Royal Way, Kansas City, MO 64129. Home plate (S): Arrowhead Stadium and Royal Way. First base (E): Red Coat Drive. Third base (W): Lancer Lane. Center field (N): I-70 and Spectacular Dr.

CAPACITY: 40,529. Total attendance: 1,494,875 (1998). Average attendance: 18,455 (1998).

PARKING: $6 for each of the nineteen thousand spaces around the park.

TICKETS: $7–$17. BEST BANG FOR YOUR BUCK: Tickets are unbelievably inexpensive in Kansas City. Splurge and go for the club box seats, which are on top of the action and offer great views of the fountain.

BALLPARK EXPERIENCE: Kauffman Stadium surprised us with a modern feel that few parks match. Designed with Dodger Stadium in mind, the park's two decks, large waterworks, huge scoreboard, and clean facilities make it a surprising gem of a ballpark. Walking up to the park, we were struck not only by Kauffman Stadium but also by the large football stadium (Arrowhead) next door. The two stadiums make an architecturally matching complex complete with red seats and curves and fluidity rarely seen in ballpark design. Kauffman is largely a concrete structure in two massive decks (and a third smaller deck) with a flowing design. It lacks the jagged edges of the old- and new-wave parks and the boring symmetry of the circular cookie cutters.

On the inside, we were greeted by modern facilities with a bucolic feel accented by the greenery in center field and the fountain. The fountain sets Kauffman completely

Kauffman Stadium's classic design was reminiscent of Dodger Stadium, but our experience lacked the drama with which we were hoping to end our trip.

apart from any other park. Besides being unique, the fountain is a delight to watch, and children stand transfixed by the four-story columns of water. The scoreboard at Kauffman is also unique. In dead center field, it is topped with a large gold-colored crown in the shape of the Royals emblem. The crown is so big that its top almost reaches the height of the light standards (twelve stories). With more and more parks being built in the Camden style, Kauffman is one of the only original designs left in baseball. Only the fact that the place feels somewhat dead, probably due to the Royals' poor performance of late and consequent poor support, prevent the experience from being truly memorable.

FANS: Kansas City is the smallest market of any major league city. This fact has not prevented the Royals from developing a solid base of fans over the years and from seeing a fair share of success. When we were there though, the crowds seemed to be staying away. The ones that do come out are also a more mellow bunch. In marked contrast to New York hecklers, the Royals fans we encountered were very respectful and subdued. Their resulting courtesy impressed us, but the lack of enthusiasm was disappointing.

FACILITIES: Kauffman Stadium is often compared to Dodger Stadium in terms of design, but both parks also share a level of cleanliness found at few parks. Unfortunately, the low-key nature of the fans can make this cleanliness almost too pronounced. Not as bad as the Metrodome, but without the rough edges that give a park some character.

FOOD: Kansas City is known for its barbeque, and Kauffman Stadium follows closely in this tradition. The BBQ sandwich is a delicacy of chopped beef on a kaiser roll. Our eyes were larger than our stomachs because neither of us could finish the sandwich. Maybe the gluttony of the trip had finally caught up with us. LAST CALL: Alcohol is served until the middle of the seventh inning.

GREAT PLAYERS AND HISTORIC MOMENTS: The Royals are considered the most successful of all expansion clubs. In 1980, with George Brett chasing .400 (he finished the season at .390) and Dan Quisenberry's thirty-three saves, the club beat the Yankees to capture their first pennant. In the World Series, the Royals upended the Phillies in six games. In 1985, big performances from Bret Saberhagen and Brett got the team into the playoffs again. In the ALCS they fell behind one game to three but somehow managed to rally against the Toronto Blue Jays. The story repeated itself in the World Series, with the Royals overcoming a three-games-to-one St. Louis lead to claim the world championship. The only All-Star Game at Kauffman was played in 1973.

BALLPARK HISTORY: The Royals moved into Kauffman Stadium (then known as Royals Stadium) in 1973. It was built as part of a sports complex that features the home of the

BAT INFO

FINAL SCORE: Twins 3, Royals 0

OUR SEATS: Aisle 101, Row U, Seats 8–9

BALLPARK: 30 of 30

DAY: 38 of 38

MILES TRAVELED: 485 (14,223 total)

NEW STATES: 1 (Kansas; 33 total)

OUR EXPENSES: $242
Field of Dreams memorabilia $80
Bob Feller memorabilia $10
KFC $10
ballpark food—BBQ sandwich, curly fries, soda, and ice cream, parking, memorabilia, and programs $75
gas $17
motel room (in Lawrence, Kans.) $60
EXPENSES TO DATE: $3,115

OUR FREEBIES: $40
game tickets $40
FREEBIES TO DATE: $3,891

Kansas City Chiefs (Arrowhead Stadium). Constructed as a baseball-only facility, it debuted as one of the best parks in baseball. In 1999 the Royals made major renovations to the park, which included the addition of a Crown Club and dugout seats. This enhanced the higher-price amenities and kept the park viable. All the orange seats were also removed and new dark blue, wider seats with cup holders were added. Kauffman Stadium is set to live on into the next century.

FUN FACT: There is a statue of Ewing and Muriel Kauffman at the entrance of the park that honors the couple who brought baseball to Kansas City.

THE ONE THING YOU HAVE TO DO AT KAUFFMAN STADIUM AND WHY: Watch the fountain. It encircles the entire outfield and is the largest privately funded water display in the world. It has numerous levels, waterfalls, columns of water zooming into the air, and scenic grass dividing the water. We hear it also tends to go haywire when the Royals score, but we never saw that happen.

LASTING IMPRESSION: A park with a design unto itself that is hidden in the smallest market in baseball.

final
Tally

BAT Info

· ·

BALLPARKS/DAYS: 30/38

BEST RECORD IN THE GAMES WE SAW: Atlanta Braves 3-0

WORST RECORD: Oakland A's 0-3

NUMBER OF PARKS IN WHICH WE RECEIVED FREE TICKETS: 24

NUMBER OF PARKS IN WHICH WE RECEIVED FREE FOOD: 16

NUMBER OF PARKS IN WHICH WE RECEIVED TOURS: 19

NUMBER OF PARKS IN WHICH WE GOT ON THE FIELD: 7 (Dodger, Qualcomm, Edison, Veterans, Pro Player, Jacobs Field, Tiger Stadium)

NUMBER OF PARKS WHERE THE TEAMS, CONCESSIONAIRES, AND OPERATIONS PEOPLE COLLECTIVELY IGNORED US: 3 (County Stadium [Milwaukee], Wrigley Field, and the Metrodome)

NUMBER OF HOT DOGS, BEERS, AND JAEGER SHOTS DAVE AND I CONSUMED APIECE: 49/23/18

TOTAL TRIP DAYS: 41

ADDITIONAL MILES TRAVELED: 2,224 (TOTAL: 1,600 by air; 14,847 by car; 16,447 total)

NEW STATES: 1 (Nevada; 34 total)

ADDITIONAL EXPENSES: $1,615
    moving violation $70
    gas $130
    food $90
    lodging (in Richfield, Utah, and Las Vegas, Nev.) $125
    cell phone costs $600
    film costs $600
      TOTAL EXPENSES: $4,730
      TOTAL FREEBIES: $3,891

Latest Additions

SINCE OUR trip, four new parks have popped up, with several more on the way. We didn't feel this book would be complete without addressing these new parks. Dave and I, still recovering from the trip itself, did not make it to all of these parks, so we solicited help from a couple of friends in getting informed opinions. We appreciate their assistance.

The sections that follow cover:

- Safeco Field in Seattle, Washington
- Comerica Park in Detroit, Michigan
- Enron Field in Houston, Texas
- Pacific Bell Park in San Francisco, California

The following parks should debut in 2001:

- Miller Park in Milwaukee, Wisconsin
- PNC Park in Pittsburgh, Pennsylvania

safeco field

FOR MY whole life I watched the Seattle Mariners play their home games at the Kingdome, and I always felt that there was something lacking. As a competitive baseball player growing up, I played on many of the nicer fields in the Seattle and western Washington area, many of which seemed preferable to the Kingdome and its green carpet. This always seemed peculiar to me. Logically, a major league team should have a park that surpasses all others in the surrounding area, but this was not the case in Seattle . . . until the opening of Safeco Field.

Being a spectator at Safeco Field is undeniably far more pleasurable than it was at the Kingdome. Safeco Field was designed for one reason—baseball. The multipurpose Kingdome's artificial turf, artificial lighting, and artificial environment were better served to house car shows than baseball games. These substandard attributes of the Kingdome are replaced with sunlight and natural grass in the new ballpark, where you can lean

298

back in your seat and bask in the sun amid the backdrop of the city's beautiful skyline. If it rains, as has been known to happen in Seattle from time to time, an $80 million retractable roof deploys in minutes. This innovative design never completely seals the stadium and allows both air circulation and a view of the outside world.

My favorite feature of the new stadium is the Bullpen Market. From this patio section behind the bullpens in center field you can get a great view of the game while standing at a little table and enjoying your favorite beverage. This area reminds me a little of Eutaw Street at Camden Yards. Additionally, I appreciated the open concourses. You can walk around the whole stadium searching for your favorite concessions without losing sight of the field.

There is only one advantage that the Kingdome had over Safeco: A sellout crowd of 59,166 fans packed inside the dome could create quite a lot of energy, and the decibel level could get as loud as any other stadium in the country. The open-air park and smaller seating capacity of 47,116 fans mean that Safeco will never be as loud as the Kingdome once was.

The main difference between Safeco Field and its now extinct predecessor is in the style of baseball that each park fosters. Safeco is much larger, and because it is open to the elements, baseballs don't carry very far. Balls that would have been home runs at the Kingdome now die in front of the warning track at Safeco. In contrast to Houston, Seattle went from home run central to the consummate pitcher's town. Wisely, the Mariners have built their team to suit the new ballpark, focusing on better pitching after being forced to trade Ken Griffey Jr. (It has been rumored that one of the reasons contributing to Griffey's departure was his discontent with the dimensions of Safeco.)

Safeco Field is a beautiful stadium and adds immeasurably to the baseball experience in Seattle. While it is consistent with the trend of the other new ballparks around the league in trying to re-create a historic, more old-fashioned atmosphere, Safeco provides all the comforts of a modern park, including more legroom in the seats, a wider variety of concessions, and high-tech ticket scanning, to name a few. What sets Safeco apart from the other great stadiums recently built are the unparalleled views of a beautiful city that the park provides. From different areas in the stands one can see the Space Needle, the skyline of downtown, Mount Rainier, Elliott Bay, the Olympic Mountains, and Capitol Hill.—Steve Juno

safeco field

CITY: Seattle, Washington

TENANT: Seattle Mariners

OPENED: July 15, 1999

DESIGN: Baseball-only convertible dome park, asymmetrical design, no movable seats.
SISTER PARKS: Enron Field in Houston, Bank One Ballpark in Arizona, and Miller Park in Milwaukee.

FIELD: Grass

DIMENSIONS (feet): left field—331, left center—390, center field—405, right center—387, right field—327

FENCES (feet): 8

LOCATION: 1250 First Avenue South, Seattle, WA 98134. BOUNDED BY: First Ave. and South Atlantic.

CAPACITY/ATTENDANCE: 47,116. Total attendance: 2,914,624 (2000). Average attendance: 35,983 (2000).

PARKING: $15–$20 at multiple lots near the park, especially in the business district.

TICKETS: $5–$32

BALLPARK HISTORY: Safeco Field was built to replace the Kingdome, which was only twenty years old but had become economically unviable. The park brings natural turf and open air back to Seattle baseball. The complex was a huge expense at over $400 million, split between the city and the team. As with Pacific Bell Park in San Francisco, naming rights provided a key revenue stream, and Safeco purchased the rights for $40 million.

FINAL ANALYSIS: KINGDOME V SAFECO: Safeco, running away.

comerica park

IN MY most recent visit to Detroit's Comerica Park, I experienced two of the best things about baseball: a great game between a couple of bad teams and free seats. The game was a 1-0 nail biter, courtesy of the hometown Tigers, who had finally clawed their way to .500 by the last week of the season, and the Minnesota Twins, who had been in last place since early 1992. That is possibly the greatest thing about baseball; you can see a masterpiece any day or night of the year, no matter who is pitching and who is hitting.

The second little baseball gem of that night was the phenomenon I think of as seat poaching. After the fifth inning in a half-full park, discreet fans can almost always migrate into the great seats behind home plate. Nestled securely under the overhanging upper decks, the club seats are not hard plastic fold-downs bolted into the concrete, but free-moving wooden armchairs with soft cushions, wooden end tables, and waiters and waitresses.

Even if you're not in the club seats, Comerica is a good place to watch a ballgame. It's in line with the Camden Yards–initiated trend of modern amenities in a facility designed to look and feel like an old ballpark with a unique spin. Unlike most of the Camdenesque parks, Comerica doesn't play like a bandbox. Much to the dismay of first-year Tiger and former home-run champion Juan Gonzalez, the field dimensions are quite long, and it seems to play even longer.

Aside from the actual dimensions of the playing field, Comerica is a big park. The concourses are wide all the way around, but you cannot swing a bat without hitting a food stand or souvenir shop of some type. From the outer concourses, downtown Detroit's surprisingly nice skyline is visible. Even from the seats, the view is nice because the seats behind center field are lower and the park thus opens to a downtown vista. Behind the center-field fence are bleachers, and above them is a plaza for private parties. In the area behind home plate and the infield are two sizable food courts and outdoor seating areas, an indoor sports bar–restaurant, and an amusement center, complete with a carousel and other carnival attractions for the kids.

If it seems like going to Comerica Park is something like going to the circus, it is, presumably because the imagery of the Tiger can be so readily extended in that direction. Comerica is one of the centerpieces of Detroit's admirable attempt to rescue itself from the urban decay in which it has dwelt most of the last few decades. The park has large white masonry walls around most of its facade, and there are stonework tiger statues everywhere: full-bodied tigers atop pillars next to the gates, busts of tiger heads at intervals along the top of the wall, painted tigers on signs on the gates. It's not unpleasant, but it's a little over the top. The amusement park aspects of Comerica fall into that category as well. Comerica has a lot of nonbaseball options. Even though the main concourses are open to the playing field, the game cannot be seen from the midway attractions and the food courts. If the park is only half full, the game is little more than a rumor. To their credit, though, the designers set up the park so that once the fans are in their seats, a lot of the other stuff melts away.

One thing that isn't over the top is the statue plaza of Tiger greats. It's easy to forget because they've been so bad for the last twelve years or so, but Detroit has been home to some fantastic ball players. Huge, impressive metal statues of Ty Cobb, Hank Greenberg, and Kirk Gibson line a stretch of walkway behind left center field.

As for the food, my friend Rich seemed to enjoy his pork sandwich from the Southern barbecue stand. I had a hot dog with yellow mustard, which was nothing to rave about but did at least live up to the baseball experience. My biggest disappointment with the concessions was the mustard selection. Hot dogs should always be covered in spicy brown mustard that will mask the taste of the meat and give some body to the typically lifeless buns, but CoPa only offers fluorescent yellow mustard that fulfills neither criteria. Beyond that, the place is a smorgasbord of seemingly workable options: pizza, nachos, sausages, sandwiches, barbecues, sodas (called "pop" in that cute way that Midwesterners have), ice cream, elephant ears (I have no idea what these are), beer in cups, beer in plastic bottles that look like glass bottles. The list goes on and on. The prices are absurdly high, but that's not limited to Comerica, so it's tough to hold that against it.

The natural inclination is to compare Comerica with its predecessor, Tiger Stadium. People in southeastern Michigan feel pretty nostalgic about Tiger Stadium. I saw a game there in the summer of 1998, and I fell in love with it. The place was a piece of history— a dank, rickety heap of peeling paint and poles blocking the view—a genuine set of quirks (rather than today's contrived ones) like the flagpole in center field, the porch in right field, and those amazing seats in the upper deck behind home plate. It obviously wasn't loaded with amenities, and the seats tended to be uncomfortable, but it was one of the most authentic places I'd ever been. I'm sure Comerica will make the Tigers a more economically viable franchise for the people of Detroit, but even when Rich and I drove by Tiger Stadium on our way to Comerica, we got a little misty-eyed.—Dave Halsing

comerica park

CITY: Detroit, Michigan

TENANT: Detroit Tigers

OPENED: April 11, 2000

NICKNAME/ALIASES: CoPa

DESIGN: baseball-only park, asymmetrical design, no movable seats. SISTER PARKS: Camden Yards in Baltimore, Coors Field in Denver, the Ballpark in Arlington, and Jacobs Field in Cleveland.

FIELD: Grass

DIMENSIONS (feet): left field—345, left center—398, center field—420, right center— 379, right field—330

FENCES (feet): 8

LOCATION: 2100 Woodward Ave., Detroit, MI. BOUNDED BY: Home plate: Montcalm St. Center field: Adams St. First base: Witherell St. Third base: Brush St. and site of Ford Field.

CAPACITY/ATTENDANCE: 40,000. Total attendance: 2,438,617 (2000). Average attendance: 30,106 (2000).

PARKING: $15–$20 at many spots adjacent to the park especially since it is in an urban setting.

TICKETS: $12–$30

BALLPARK HISTORY: Comerica was a controversial stadium because it replaced Tiger Stadium, which had housed the Detroit club since 1912. The park was largely financed by $60 million from Comerica for naming rights.

FINAL ANALYSIS—TIGER STADIUM V COMERICA: Not a fair comparison.

Enron Field

FINALLY THERE is a ballpark in Houston where one can watch a game on a grassy field and look out at the night sky without growing faint in the sweltering heat. At the same time, it is sad to lose the truly unique and beloved Astrodome in favor of just another copy of Camden Yards, this time with a roof that can slide over the top.

Apparently the guys in Houston heard all the nostalgic things said about what makes the old parks (and the new) great and determined not to be outdone. Thus there is a quirky outfield wall and terrain and a plethora of dining and spending opportunities throughout the stadium. Some of these features are comical (check out the little hill on *SportsCenter* sometime), but in spite of themselves, the architects of this ballpark did not manage to ruin the spirit of the park.

At least, not until they put in the train. I understand that the train is supposed to highlight the Union Station motif upon which the designers focused; Union Station being the essentially abandoned train station that abuts Enron Field and the stadium's original namesake before Enron bought the rights. But I fail to see any purpose or merit in the motif. Everybody would have been better served if the train—and the Astros' new mascot, Union Jack, who serves mostly to make all of the fans wonder what happened to the more appropriately themed mascot, Orbit—had just stayed on the drawing board.

What Enron has going in its favor is that it is an amazing feat of engineering. I was suitably amazed the first time I went to Bank One, the first retractable-roof dome with natural grass on the inside. Enron, just two years its junior, takes the retractable experience to another level. Where Bank One was something of a warehouse that had a ceiling that could pop off, Enron's design slides away both the ceiling and one of the walls. When the lid is open, it feels like an outdoor game. In fact, even when the lid is closed, the glass retractable wall lets in enough view and sunlight to give an impression of the outdoors. I understand that Safeco has a similar design, but I'd have to say Enron's engineering is more impressive, given that it is in a climate that demands a domed stadium. Thus I would side with Enron as the king of ballpark functionality.

As for the food, there is something very fishy going on at Enron. They've got the same concessionaire as the Astrodome, but somehow the food is inferior. The biggest problem here is that the best barbecue in all of baseball, courtesy of Luther's BBQ, has been inexplicably replaced by the thoroughly awful (by Texas standards) Sheriff

Blaylock's fare. Additionally, the best ballpark beer in America, Shiner Bock, which was readily available throughout the Dome, is almost impossible to find in the new park. The Enron folks managed to turn the Astrodome's greatest asset—its food—into one of Enron's greatest liabilities.

Another of the Astrodome's relative strengths was that it was just about the only pitcher's park left in the major leagues. With the opening of Enron, Houston shifted from being the consummate pitcher's town to home run central. Maybe the designers were trying to attract power hitters; maybe they were trying to attract fans who have an enthusiasm for the long ball. But they seemed to have miscalculated a bit, and what they've got is a place where you can rarely finish a game in less than three and a half hours, thus the fans get bored because the games never seem to end, players get frustrated because no lead is safe, good pitching will never come into play, and the home team quickly falls to the bottom of the rankings. In short, you've got the Colorado Rockies, but without the overzealous and undiscriminating fans. If they know what's best for them, the powers that be in the Astros organization will get the front three rows of the Crawford boxes in left field removed so they can have a more respectable ballgame and a better team.

Of course, it wouldn't hurt to lose a couple of the gimmicks, too. Like all of its new ballpark brethren, Enron is overloaded. On top of the general motif of the park, which is stolen from the Camden blueprint, Enron has a hill (reminiscent of Crosley), buildings just over the fence (reminiscent of Wrigley and Camden), a flagpole in play (reminiscent of Tiger Stadium and the old Yankee Stadium obstacle course), and replicas of both the Astrodome's old electronic fireworks show scoreboard and the Dome's more recent manually operated one on the left-field wall. They also have all of the latest amenities: a luxurious and exclusive club deck, a restaurant in center field, cocktail tables just behind the batter's eye, and so on. With all of these disparate sources, how can the fans generate any ballpark atmosphere?

Hopefully, the designers of new ballparks will learn the power of omission.

As for Enron, its one saving grace is that the technological marvel of its design, in conjunction with the necessity of air conditioning, can make this a truly great park. Until some changes are made, it will never find a soul.—Brad Null

enron field

CITY: Houston, Texas

TENANT: Houston Astros

OPENED: April 11, 2000

DESIGN: baseball-only convertible dome park, asymmetrical design, no movable seats.

SISTER PARKS: Safeco Field in Seattle, Bank One Ballpark in Arizona, and Miller Park in Milwaukee.

FIELD: Grass

DIMENSIONS: left field—315, left center—362, center field—435, right center—373, right field—326

FENCES: left field—21, center field—10, right field—7

LOCATION: BOUNDED BY: Texas, Congress, Crawford, and Hamilton Sts.

CAPACITY/ATTENDANCE: 40,950. Total attendance: 3,056,139 (2000). Average attendance: 37,730 (2000).

PARKING: $10–$15 at more than twenty-five thousand spots within a short walk of the park

TICKETS: $5–$29

BALLPARK HISTORY: Enron Field, as with many newer parks, was constructed to keep the home team from hightailing out of town. Drayton McLane, the owner of the Astros, threatened to move the club to Virginia unless a new park was built. The old Astrodome had become run-down and was not cost-effective to operate.

The city passed a measure in 1996 to build a $250 million stadium that would have a retractable roof. The extreme heat and humidity in Houston necessitated a dome so that fans would be able to enjoy the game (see Astrodome). As an interesting note, some-how the city of Houston has built a state-of-the-art facility for a fraction of the cost of other retractable domes. According to the Harris County Sports Authority, Enron's total price tag was only $248 million, compared to $342 million for Bank One in Phoenix, $352 million for Miller Park in Milwaukee, and $517 million for Safeco Field in Seattle.

FINAL ANALYSIS—ASTRODOME V ENRON: Enron, but only because of the grass.

Pacific Bell Park

PACIFIC BELL Park is not overwhelming. What does overwhelm the fans is the swarm of people around the Willy Mays statue. As an urban park, Pac Bell has all the feel of Fenway, Camden, or Jacobs Field. This energy is the best thing about the complex.

My many trips to Pac Bell in 2000 have been punctuated by the excitement of the crowd. San Francisco has truly come alive as a baseball town. The winning record of the Giants certainly doesn't hurt, but the park should get some credit as well. Many of the new fans, however, seem to be more interested in talking about business than the baseball on the field. At Pac Bell, as in many new-wave parks, the real fans have been squeezed out by the high ticket prices and corporate season-ticket holders.

Built in the Camden style, Pac Bell has all the most recent amenities plus the asymmetry of the old parks. The biggest novelty, aside from the ungodly Coke bottle in left field, is the bay. The park sits adjacent to San Francisco Bay, and balls hit over the right-field wall have a shot for the water, although only five balls made it in the first year, with four coming off the bat of Barry Bonds.

Much has been made about the park's being on the water for good reason. The plain fact remains, however, that the team chose this site and purposely created the water hazard. John Miller's comments that Pac Bell is just like Fenway, in that it is tucked into a city block, is an overstatement. Fenway was forced into a city block that required a 37'2" wall in left field out of necessity; Pac Bell's architecture was completely contrived.

This contrivance is emblematic of the park's bigger problem: It is an East Coast park on the West Coast. The park unashamedly copies the Camden design while integrating the design into the surrounding city. This was obviously the safe way to go. Camden-style parks are a clear winner, and the Giants did not want a new Comiskey on their hands. But could the park have been better if traditional design elements from San Francisco had been incorporated? San Francisco has few red-brick buildings, and as a result, the park sticks out rather than being integrated into the city, like Camden's design in Baltimore or Jacobs's white steel in Cleveland. Instead, the park tends to immediately emit a distinct Camdenesque smell and ultimately has little claim to originality.

To give credit where credit is due, Pac Bell does make use of its carbon-copy design in some arenas. Great aspects of the new park include the views of the water, the cozy feel, and the promenade in right field. The view box seats in the upper deck have a wonderful view of the action as well as the bay. Boats are always clustered in McCovey Cove, waiting for home-run balls. As for its size, the park is unavoidably cozy. The size of the park is great for ambiance but can be problematic at times, especially in the lower deck where concourses are too narrow and restrooms limited.

The signature feature of the park is the right-field promenade, where fans can sit or stand on the wall that separates the field from the cove. The openness that this area creates is a hallmark of the park. The designers could have easily added more seats in this area and closed the park in. Thankfully they did not.

The Giants have also turned over a new leaf with their food service at Pac Bell. Gone are the limited options of 3Com. Fans can choose from chowder, sausages, and the traditional Gordon Biersch garlic fries. All are served fresh and at many stands throughout the park. Beer is also much easier to come by with numerous smaller beer stands at the top of the ramps along the lower deck. This means you do not miss a half inning while getting a beer.

The biggest thing that you hear from fans is how much better Pac Bell is over 3Com. This is all too true, although not much of an accomplishment. 3Com was a nightmare for baseball. In Cleveland, Jacobs Field replaced a rundown behemoth, and similarly San Francisco is rekindling interest in its version of the American pastime.

Overall, Pacific Bell Park is a lively experience with solid facilities, a fun atmosphere, and so far a good product on the field. Giants fans should be happy that they have left 3Com to the 49ers.—Dave Kaval

pacific Bell park

CITY: San Francisco, California

TENANT: San Francisco Giants, XFL. I have to make light of the fact that the WWF XFL fake football league will be playing football games at Pac Bell. This is a disgrace. Why the Giants would build a beautiful baseball-only facility and then try to cram football into it is beyond me. It must be for the money, which makes it all the worse.

OPENED: April 11, 2000

NICKNAME/ALIASES: Pac Bell Park, The Bell

DESIGN: multipurpose facility, asymmetrical design, no movable seats. SISTER PARKS: Camden Yards in Baltimore, Coors Field in Denver, The Ballpark in Arlington, and Jacobs Field in Cleveland.

FIELD: Bluegrass hybrid turf grass

DIMENSIONS: left field—335, left center—364, center field—404, right center—420, right field—307

FENCES: left to center—8, right field—25

LOCATION: BOUNDED BY: Right field (S): McCovey's Cove (part of the San Francisco Bay). Left field (E): Second St. and Marina. First base (W): Third St. Third base (N): King St.

CAPACITY/ATTENDANCE: 42,000. Total attendance: 3,318,800 (2000). Average attendance: 40,972 (2000).

PARKING: $10–$15. Contrary to popular belief, there are always parking spaces south of the park in Lots A, B, and C even when the game sells out.

TICKETS: $10–$23

BALLPARK HISTORY: Pacific Bell Park was the first privately funded ballpark since Dodger Stadium in 1962. Its completion was instrumental in keeping the Giants in San Francisco. The team was scheduled to move to St. Petersburg in 1992, but at the last minute a new ownership group led by Peter Magowan stepped in and saved the team. The park took an extended period of time to fund due to the lack of public money. The key sponsor was Pacific Bell, which paid $50 million for the naming rights for twenty-four years. The city broke ground on the park on December 11, 1997, and the park took two and a half years to complete. The Giants moved in on April 11, 2000.

FINAL ANALYSIS—CANDLESTICK V PACIFIC BELL: Pac Bell. But is this really a fair fight?

And coming in 2001:

Miller park

CITY: Milwaukee, Wisconsin

TENANT: Milwaukee Brewers

OPENING DATE: April 6, 2001

DESIGN: Baseball-only convertible dome, asymmetrical design, no movable seats. SISTER PARKS: Safeco Field in Seattle, Enron Field in Houston, Bank One Ballpark in Phoenix.

FIELD: Grass

LOCATION: The park is adjacent to County Stadium.

CAPACITY: 43,000.

TICKETS: $5 –$50. BEST BANG FOR YOUR BUCK: We are not exactly sure but the prices have really shot up with the new park. Bud Selig will be racking it in.

BALLPARK HISTORY: Miller Park has been a long time in coming. The Brewers first discussed the possibility of a new park in 1987. After much political maneuvering, the park was finally approved in 1996 with a mix of public and private money. Built with a retractable roof, the park had a complex construction procedure that included one of the largest cranes in the world. Unfortunately, the crane collapsed on July 14, 1999, in strong winds, and three crewmen lost their lives. This incident delayed the stadium's opening until the start of the 2001 season.

PNC park

CITY: Pittsburgh, Pennsylvania

TENANT: Pittsburgh Pirates

OPENING DATE: April 9, 2001

NICKNAME/ALIASES: We hope someone comes up with one soon.

DESIGN: Baseball-only stadium, asymmetrical design, no movable seats. SISTER PARKS: Camden Yards in Baltimore, Jacobs Field in Cleveland, The Ballpark in Arlington, Coors Field in Denver, and Pacific Bell Park in San Francisco.

FIELD: Natural grass

DIMENSIONS: left field—325, left center—389, center field—399, right center—375, right field—320

FENCES: Left field—6, center field—10, right field—21

LOCATION: On the north shore of the Allegheny River near the Sixth Street (Roberto Clemente) Bridge

CAPACITY: 38,127

BALLPARK HISTORY: PNC Park will open at the beginning of the 2001 season in downtown Pittsburgh on the north shore of the Allegheny River. The park was financed through a state grant of funds and built in only fourteen months. The park will be one of the most intimate parks in baseball with only thirty-eight thousand seats on two decks. Its proximity to the river, the city skyline, and the Roberto Clemente bridge will give it an urban feel. HOK Sports of Kansas City designed the park; the firm also designed many of the newest parks (e.g., Camden Yards in Baltimore, Jacobs Field in Cleveland).

epilogue

LOOKING BACK on the parks two years later, I can only say that we were lucky. Not only was it, with McGwire and Sosa and the Yankees, the season that reestablished baseball as the American pastime, but it was a turning point in ballpark design as well. We ended up seeing parks from a lot of different eras. Eras that won't be represented in the pantheon of ballparks five years from now, such as the oft-reviled multipurposoids, which will soon be extinct as a ballpark species. At the time, I wasn't too thrilled to be at Cinergy or 3Com or some of the others, but had we come five years later, we would have missed out on that experience entirely and missed out to a large extent on the opportunity to get a good idea of what going to the ballparks has been like over the last few decades. We were and are in the midst of a wholesale conversion of baseball America. The five new-wave parks we saw have already been accompanied by four more, with at least half a dozen others on the horizon.

Obviously no one knows where this whole trend is going. Economically speaking, the new parks are sound. Across the board, they are all still making more money than their predecessors, drawing bigger crowds, and generally exciting cities (and ball club owners).

Maybe we should give a little thought to this madness. Now County Stadium, Busch, Three Rivers, and Cinergy are being replaced. While I agree that some of these parks deserve replacement, I sincerely believe that a couple of them had a shot to grow into great ballparks.

I'll admit, Dave and I are in a unique position. Most fans haven't been to more than two or three parks, much less thirty. You can look at what our friends have said about Safeco and Comerica to see what the casual fan thinks about these new parks. They love them. With each new copy of Camden Yards, however, the uniqueness of each new park fades a little. Make no mistake, every park built since Camden has been a copy.

Being in the position we are, I would like to think that Dave and I can glimpse a little of the future. From our experiences, all of these new parks have started to blur into one. They are nicer than the average, but none, except maybe Camden, are great, because greatness comes from growing into the national consciousness. From age— look at Fenway and Wrigley. Both are practically national treasures. The attendance numbers bear this out. As for the new wave of ballparks, beyond Camden, which among these parks will grow to such stature as Fenway and Wrigley? Probably only the ones that last the longest. The others will fade in popularity as the novelty of it all wears off, and in twenty to thirty years will have to be replaced by the next big thing.

But why does everybody want their park to be a commodity? At some point there is a line. Tearing down Tiger Stadium would be over the line. I'm sure Comerica is a great new park; I imagine I have a good idea of what it feels like to take in a game there. But will it be so great in ten years? They're already playing to half-empty crowds in the inaugural season. Tiger was truly original. Even though it is not much appreciated now, in this era of conformity and nostalgia, its day surely would have returned.

If you don't agree with me on Tiger, what about Fenway? Now they want to tear it down and put up a new park. It will be just like the old one they promise—only better. We've heard this story before, notably in Chicago. How many people here wish old Comiskey was still standing? Fenway is the greatest park in the country. There's some consensus on this. You tear that down, you go from number one to at best a one-in-thirty shot of getting the title back. I don't care if Fenway is old. Replace every nut and bolt. If it is not safe, do what you have to do to make it safe. But keep that ballpark there. Of all people, the folks in Boston should understand the sanctity of baseball. If you thought the Curse of the Bambino was bad, what do you think is going to come of the Curse of Fenway Park?

It's futile to try to stop stadium designers from copying the latest popular design and putting it in a new city. Ballparks are too expensive to take these major risks, and the planners won't do it until they have to. Like the last time we had a new wave of ballparks with the multipurposoids, this trend won't stop until people get sick of these new parks. Make no mistake, this will happen. Then we will muddle through failed experiments like the Metrodome, Tropicana, new Comiskey, and brief fads like SkyDome, until the whole trend begins again with the next Camden.

We accept this unobstructable course of ballpark design. But how much we would give to go back and see a game at Forbes, Crosley, and Tiger (just one more)? We only caution, argue, pray, and beg that not everyone jumps on this bandwagon. Save Fenway. Save Wrigley. Save Dodger. Save even the already bastardized Yankee. We will appreciate them, we promise.

Baseball is a game founded on history, and its rich tapestry is so much richer with these characters in it. Don't take our history from us.

As for the Baseball America Tour, by the time it was over, Dave and I experienced a huge sense of accomplishment. A lot of people had said we couldn't get it done. We did. And we rode the subsequent high to about the Missouri state line, at which point it immediately devolved into exhaustion.

We came away from the trip with some great memories, particularly of historic parks like Wrigley Field . . .

The rest of the twenty-two hundred miles we traversed across the country to our California destination was relatively uneventful, except for the fact that I got a ticket in Kansas. That really annoyed me. Dave and I had this perfect excuse to use if we ever got pulled over while we were on the trip. We would pull out The Map and the cop would be awestruck by the greater good of what we were doing and let us go. But wouldn't you know it, fourteen thousand miles on the trip without incident. The day after it's over I get busted.

After that unfortunate event, throughout that trip back across the country, we often didn't speak for hundreds of miles at a time. Not because we were bitter at each other (although we were admittedly tired of each other), but more because there was truly nothing left to say.

Life with respect to the baseball tour continued on that way for several months. Dave and I didn't see each other very much. In fact we barely even spoke.

Over time, as we began to run into each other more often, meeting up at parties or getting together for drinks or barbecues, wouldn't you know that the Baseball America Tour would keep coming up.

As far as I could tell, there are two reasons for this. First, simply because we shared the trip with so many friends; everyone we hung out with kept bringing it up or asking about it. Although I was not inclined to rehash everything ad nauseum (Dave was, of course, more eager to do so), everyone kept wanting to hear about it, so the stories just started to flow. Second, and more important, the tour kept haunting us because there were generally so many reminders of it everywhere. McGwire's home-run chase. The Yankees dominance through the World Series. Miller Lite. Jaeger shots. Attractive wait-

. . . and Fenway Park. They top our list of the best ballparks in the country.

resses (like the ones in Cleveland). Sassy kids (like the one in Miami). The trip had evolved from a series of ballparks to an agglomeration of experiences over a thirty-eight-day period. In that thirty-eight days, we had seen most everything. We'd had all the fun there was to have. It was life in a microcosm, and it seemed like everything in life afterward tied into this trip.

So when they say that baseball is life, maybe it's true. Our trip certainly mirrored life with its ups and downs. It could have been so easy to look at our experiences through a dirty window and paint them as bitter: the disagreements we'd had along the way, the frequent skepticism as to what may be happening in the world of baseball. But we didn't see it like that.

A lot of life gets eaten up waiting for things of significance to occur, but the lesson that baseball teaches us is that there are no dull moments. There are so many things going on under the surface. At any given time there are at least ten people out there on a baseball field, and they are all constantly working. This is true in baseball and in life, and it was definitely true in regards to our trip. There are so many things going on all around us, you just might have to look a little closer to see them.

Looking back on it, I see a sublime trip of so many varied experiences in a short span of time. Although there was one constant of baseball throughout, it was a rich and deeply varied canvas of experiences, and I will forever cherish it for the depth it has added to my character. (Dave says ditto.)

appendixes

The List

YOU CAN probably guess the question we get asked the most from people who heard about our trip. It is probably the first thought that formed in your head when you picked up this book. Which is the best ballpark? Or its slightly more annoying sister question: What are the top five? So to dispense with the formality quickly and easily, here's the list, all thirty ballparks, in order of preference. You will undoubtedly have some problems with it and will wonder how we came up with it, but that's part of the fun of it.

Like great ball players, great baseball parks often defy a statistical explanation of their greatness. To try to rate each park among x factors and then average the ratings for an "objective" list of the greatest parks would be folly from the start. So we won't even try. Sure, we could take the categories below and multiply the parks' respective rankings by some ratio that would make it all average out into this composite list. The objective, however, was never to prove our opinions. In the end, our rankings are roughly in order of how privileged we felt just to be there.

1. **Fenway Park** (Boston, MA), home of the Boston Red Sox
2. **Wrigley Field** (Chicago, IL), home of the Chicago Cubs
3. **Tiger Stadium** (Detroit, MI), home of the Detroit Tigers
4. **Dodger Stadium** (Los Angeles, CA), home of the Los Angeles Dodgers
5. **Oriole Park at Camden Yards** (Baltimore, MD), home of the Baltimore Orioles
6. **County Stadium** (Milwaukee, WI), home of the Milwaukee Brewers
7. **Jacobs Field** (Cleveland, OH), home of the Cleveland Indians
8. **Yankee Stadium** (New York, NY), home of the New York Yankees
9. **Coors Field** (Denver, CO), home of the Colorado Rockies

10. **Bank One Ballpark** (Phoenix, AZ), home of the Arizona Diamondbacks

11. **Kauffman Stadium** (Kansas City, MO), home of the Kansas City Royals

12. **Oakland Coliseum** (Oakland, CA), home of the Oakland Athletics

13. **The Ballpark in Arlington** (Arlington, TX), home of the Texas Rangers

14. **Edison International Field** (Anaheim, CA), home of the Anaheim Angels

15. **The Astrodome** (Houston, TX), home of the Houston Astros

16. **Qualcomm Stadium** (San Diego, CA), home of the San Diego Padres

17. **Le Stade Olympique** (Montreal, Canada), home of the Montreal Expos

18. **Comiskey Park** (Chicago, IL), home of the Chicago White Sox

19. **Busch Stadium** (St. Louis, MO), home of the St. Louis Cardinals

20. **Turner Field** (Atlanta, GA), home of the Atlanta Braves

21. **SkyDome** (Toronto, Canada), home of the Toronto Blue Jays

22. **Three Rivers Stadium** (Pittsburgh, PA), home of the Pittsburgh Pirates

23. **The Kingdome** (Seattle, WA), home of the Seattle Mariners

24. **Shea Stadium** (New York, NY), home of the New York Mets

25. **Pro Player Stadium** (Miami, FL), home of the Florida Marlins

26. **Veterans Stadium** (Philadelphia, PA), home of the Philadelphia Phillies

27. **Tropicana Field** (St. Petersburg, FL), home of the Tampa Bay Devil Rays

28. **3Com Park** (San Francisco, CA), home of the San Francisco Giants

29. **Cinergy Field** (Cincinnati, OH), home of the Cincinnati Reds

30. **The Metrodome** (Minneapolis, MN), home of the Minnesota Twins

Design

Design can generally refer to anything about the external and internal architecture of the park, but the key criteria is innovation. What has this park done toward the advancement of baseball parks on the whole?

TOP 10

1. **Fenway Park:** Perfectly nestled within a city block, Fenway is the classic old-style park complete with the signature Green Monster in left field. Its design is unique, focused on baseball, and one of the most enduring images of baseball in America.

2. **Oriole Park at Camden Yards:** Camden ushered in a renaissance in ballpark design that called upon the parks of yesteryear. This historical significance (although some argue it is not such a good thing) combined with its unmatched integration with its surroundings (the B&O Warehouse) create a memorable and unique park design.

3. **Dodger Stadium:** A masterpiece of proportional design, Dodger Stadium fits nicely into Chavez Ravine. The park's unique design amid the pressure of conformity in an era of cookie-cutter multipurpose parks merits extra points.

4. **Wrigley Field:** Even more so than Fenway, Wrigley is at one with its surroundings, where the houses in the outfield are an extension of the park. This unique feature and its charming small size make the Friendly Confines a winner.

5. **The Astrodome:** The first domed stadium was an engineering marvel and paved the way for baseball on real grass in tolerable conditions.

6. **Bank One Ballpark:** The first in a series of new-wave retractable domes, Bank One Ballpark set the stage for parks in difficult climates.

7. **The Ballpark in Arlington:** Simply the best exterior in baseball. Reminiscent of ancient Rome's Coliseum.

8. **Tiger Stadium:** The last enclosed dual-decked park had a unique interior. Unfortunately, a poor exterior keeps this classic out of the top five.

9. **Jacobs Field:** Jacobs Field has the most unique design of the newer Camdenesque parks with white steel, toothbrush-style light standards, and tan brick. This and its proximity to downtown Cleveland are hallmarks of the park's design.

10. **SkyDome:** Introduced the retractable dome. Too bad they couldn't do more with it.

THE CELLAR

1. **Tropicana Field:** This thing looks like a UFO. Who decided a dome was a good idea in Florida anyway?

2. **Cinergy Field:** The biggest and baddest, literally, of the cookie cutters.

3. **The Metrodome:** You would never guess that baseball was played here—it shouldn't be.

4. **The Kingdome:** Another totally unnecessary roof. I don't believe it actually rains in Seattle anyway.

5. **3Com Park/Veterans Stadium:** See Cinergy Field.

facilities

The best facilities include nice seats with good sightlines, wide concourses, well-organized concession stands, pristine restrooms (relatively speaking), and overall cleanliness.

TOP 10

1. **Dodger Stadium:** Has a deserved reputation as the cleanest park in baseball. Especially impressive since the park is from the 1960s. Wide concourses and ample concession stands also help the park achieve its number-one ranking.

2. **Coors Field:** One item that sets Coors apart from its prototype, Camden, is that you can walk around the entire park and still see the field. Wide, well-structured concourses, plentiful restrooms, and nice, new seats.

3. **Jacobs Field:** The best sightlines in baseball with every seat directed at the pitcher's mound. Almost all of the newer parks have copied this design.

4. **Oriole Park at Camden Yards:** Still state-of-the-art ten years after it was built.

5. **Kauffman Stadium:** New seats, club sections, and renovations have rescued Kauffman's worn facilities.

6. **Qualcomm Stadium:** Best multipurpose park in this category thanks to the major's highest percentage of in-seat concession service.

7. **The Metrodome:** The second cleanest park in baseball. Unfortunately, this leads to an institutional feel that deprives the park of even a hint of character.

8. **Bank One Ballpark:** It is all about air conditioning.

9. **Oakland Coliseum:** One good thing that came out of the renovation.

10. **Pro Player Stadium:** Another solid multipurpose park with all the required food stands, restrooms, and new seats.

THE CELLAR

1. **Tiger Stadium:** Dirty, cramped, and old. Some fans have argued that the club purposely did not keep up the park so that it could get the city to finance a new one.

2. **Le Stade Olympique:** The worst seats in baseball (small and uncomfortable) and concourses that are so wide that it takes ten minutes to reach a restroom.

3. **The Ballpark in Arlington:** Like Le Stade, the concourses are too wide, which makes it inconvenient to traverse the park.

4. **Tropicana Field:** Just look up. Many of the ceiling lights and paneling were never completed.

5. **3Com Park:** The dirtiest restrooms in the majors.

Fans

The best and worst fans in baseball based on attendance, knowledge of the game, and of course, love of the game.

TOP 10

1. **Chicago Cubs Fans:** Ninety-two years of "wait till next year" have created a cult of Cubbie fans. The Bleacher Bums generate an unrivaled energy that the new pretenders on the Sammy Sosa bandwagon have not diluted.

2. **Cleveland Indians Fans:** 454 straight sellouts over 5 years. Need we say more?

3. **Boston Red Sox Fans:** The curse of the Bambino, Bill Buckner, and numerous losses in the World Series, but these resilient fans keep coming back. That is love.

4. **Colorado Rockies Fans:** Terrible teams have not deterred Denver fans from coming out in droves. Plus the fans know their team and the game, despite having had the game in town for only just over a decade.

5. **New York Yankees Fans:** Truly the tenth man for the Yanks. The hometown crowd makes other teams shiver. WARNING: Do not root for the opposing team in Yankee Stadium. You will regret it.

6. **Milwaukee Brewers Fans:** Blue-collar fan base that zealously supports its team, at least when they come out. History with the Milwaukee Braves gives the fans a depth unlike any other expansion team.

7. **St. Louis Cardinals Fans:** The second most successful franchise after the Yankees, the Cardinal's fans are widespread and devoted. You will not find more people in one place keeping score than in St. Louis.

8. **Detroit Tigers Fans:** The many fan efforts to keep the team at old Tiger Stadium should be commended. Tiger Fans realized the special nature of Tiger Stadium even if the team (and the bulk of Detroit denizens) didn't.

9. **Texas Rangers Fans:** Anyone who sits in 100-degree heat with 96 percent humidity, day in and day out, should get written up in a book.

10. **Kansas City Royals Fans:** The smallest market keeps its stadium full and lively.

THE CELLAR

1. **Philadelphia Phillies Fans:** Ruthless heckling of the home team gives these fans a notorious reputation.

2. **Atlanta Braves Fans:** Even World Series games do not sell out. This spoiled group of fans needs a jolt of energy.

3. **San Francisco Giants Fans:** We know there are good Giants fans out there somewhere. They just don't seem to be the ones at the ballpark.

4. **Los Angeles Dodgers Fans:** Half the fans leave by the seventh inning even in a tight contest.

5. **New York Yankees Fans:** Heckling, excessive pride, and tons of bandwagon make Yankees fans the most despised in baseball.

Food

TOP 10

1. **Coors Field:** The best super dog of any park as well as the infamous Rocky Mountain oysters make Coors Field a top-five pick. In spite of your reservations and the fact that you are eating bull's testicles, the Rocky Mountain oysters are an American delicacy.

2. **County Stadium:** The bratwursts are the best food in any park. Add sauerkraut and you'll be in heaven. Even nonsausage fans should try one. We devoured five apiece. That was after we had downed three dogs at Wrigley earlier that day. That is a lot of sausage.

3. **Oakland Coliseum:** Selection is the buzzword at the Oakland Coliseum. From their famous Chicago dog that features peppers, onions, pickles, and sauerkraut, to the super nachos that could feed a family, to their wide selection of beers, Oakland has it all.

4. **Qualcomm Stadium:** Fish tacos are the highlight at Qualcomm courtesy of local fast-food chain Rubio's Mexican Grill. Pick up plenty of napkins because the special sauce drips. Also, don't forget Randy Jones BBQ with his half-pound hot dogs—the biggest in the majors.

5. **The Astrodome:** Fantastic Luther's BBQ sandwich steals the show.

6. **Jacob's Field:** The traditional Stadium Mustard, the only good thing about the food at old Cleveland Municipal Stadium, makes for great hot dogs along with other attractions in this new park.

7. **Olympic Stadium:** Le Stade Olympique wins the award for most unusual food. The poutine is a tradition in Quebec and is made of French fries covered in tasty gravy. Be warned that the poutine is hot, so give it at least five minutes to cool down before digging in.

8. **Pro Player Park:** The Cuban sandwich is a monster with three kinds of meat, provolone cheese, and plenty of oil and vinegar.

319

9. **The Ballpark in Arlington:** The turkey legs that take two innings to eat are worth every out. Also the ballpark's lemon icees are essential on those hot Texas nights.

10. **The Kingdome:** We'll admit, we might be biased toward this one just because of the novel experience we had there of eating free ballpark food for the first time. Regardless, it couldn't have been that bad if it kept us eating that long.

THE CELLAR

1. **Turner Field:** Cold hot dogs and stale beer are the lasting legacy.

2. **The Metrodome:** Poor options and the lack of condiments make this park subpar.

3. **Comiskey Park:** Average dogs and the lack of specialty foods push Comiskey into the cellar.

4. **Veterans Stadium:** The flimsy cheesesteaks fail to live up to expectations.

5. **3Com Park:** Only the garlic fries kept this park out of last place altogether.

Food Item

Simply the best single food item at any park.

TOP 10

1. **Rocky Mountain Oysters (Coors Field):** Try some bull's balls today.

2. **The Bratwurst (County Stadium):** You will not be able to stop at one.

3. **Fish Tacos (Qualcomm Stadium):** It's all about the special sauce.

4. **Parmesan Cheese Pretzel (Busch Stadium):** This thin gourmet pretzel covered in cheese is not your traditional ballpark pretzel.

5. **New England Clam Chowder (Fenway Park):** Probably not the best chowder in Boston, but pretty close.

6. **Super Nachos (Oakland Coliseum):** This is a monster with beans, cheese, salsa, sour cream, and guacamole.

7. **Garlic Fries (3Com Park and Oakland Coliseum):** Same Gordon Bierch Fries at either Bay Area ballpark. Bring some breath mints.

8. **The Poutine (Le Stade Olympique):** Poutine is a Montreal delicacy made of French fries covered in cheese curd and turkey gravy.

9. **The Turkey Leg (The Ballpark in Arlington):** A two-inning feast.

10. **Philly Cheesesteak (The Kingdome):** Large and filling. Get ready for a food coma.

THE CELLAR

1. **The Hot Dog (Turner Field):** Cold dog and crumbly bun.

2. **The Philadelphia Cheesesteak (Veterans Stadium):** Expectations are quickly dashed by this microwave-quality sandwich.

3. **The BBQ Sandwich (Turner Field):** Next time bring your own BBQ sauce. On second thought, bring your own barbecue.

4. **The Hot Dog (SkyDome):** McDonald's cannot do the dog justice, which is probably why you do not see hot dogs on the traditional McDonald's menu.

5. **The Poutine (Le Stade Olympique):** See the cheese curd comment above.

Beer

So many different beers throughout baseball America. Below the best beers, and the best places to enjoy them.

TOP 5

1. **Shiner Bock (The Astrodome):** The best beer in Texas and, in my opinion, the country.

2. **Old Style (Wrigley Field):** Yes, Old Style is a cheap macrobrew in the region, but it somehow fits perfectly with Wrigley.

3. **Gordon Biersch Marzen (3Com Park):** If only because there is little else worth consuming in the whole park.

4. **Great Lakes Dortmunder (Jacobs Field):** Dave's hometown makes a good brew.

5. **Pyramid Hefeweisen (The Kingdome):** Goes perfectly with the Philly cheesesteak.

THE WORST

1. **Tomahawk Ale (Turner Field):** This park can't seem to do anything right on the edible frontier.

Ballpark History

TOP 10

1. **Yankee Stadium:** Home of twenty-six world championships, Babe Ruth, Joe DiMaggio, and Mickey Mantle. This place seeps history even if the renovations try to hide it.

2. **Fenway Park:** Heartbreak after heartbreak has occurred here, despite the momentary giddiness that image of Carlton Fisk waving the ball over the Monster gives all baseball fans.

3. **Tiger Stadium:** A time machine that takes you back to the days of Ty Cobb.

4. **Dodger Stadium:** Has seen everything from Kurt Gibson's home run to Sandy Koufax's no-hitters.

5. **County Stadium:** The duels between the Milwaukee Braves and the Yankees in 1957 and 1958 were unparalleled. Yes, they took place here.

6. **Shea Stadium:** Site of Bill Buckner's infamous error in 1986.

7. **Wrigley Field:** Babe Ruth's infamous "called shot."

8. **Jacobs Field:** Has seen its share of postseason baseball in only five years.

9. **Kauffman Stadium:** Hosted the Royals' great teams of the late 1970s.

10. **Cinergy Field:** Home of the Big Red Machine. You would think that would make the place feel a little more romantic.

THE CELLAR

1. **Tropicana Field:** none

2. **Bank One Ballpark:** none

3. **The Ballpark in Arlington:** A couple of Yankee wins in the playoffs.

4. **Le Stade Olympique:** No park has been around longer and managed to lack distinction so completely.

5. **Comiskey Park:** Losses in the playoffs sum up this park's history.

scoreboards

This list ranks the best and worst scoreboards in baseball according to the information provided, novelty, and fit within the park.

TOP 10

1. **Wrigley Field:** Classic design with all the necessary information.

2. **The Astrodome:** Manually updated inning-by-inning scores of all away games.

3. **Jacobs Field:** Largest free-standing board with out-of-town scores on the wall in left field.

4. **Kauffman Stadium:** Giant twelve-story crown scoreboard in dead center complements the fountain.

5. **Busch Stadium:** Dancing red neon cardinal steals the show.

6. **Fenway Park:** Scoreboard on the Green Monster has both information and idiosyncrasies. It probably has more balls played off of it than any other in the majors.

7. **Coors Field:** All the necessary info augmented by small electronic boards.

8. **Oriole Park at Camden Yards:** Scores on the right-field wall would be better served as a manual and not electronic scoreboard.

9. **The Ballpark in Arlington:** Every key stat but the temperature.

10. **Dodger Stadium:** While not ornate, the scoreboards have all the necessary info.

11. **Le Stade Olympique:** I don't know why, but this baseball stuff in French is somehow kind of cool.

THE CELLAR

1. **County Stadium:** While state-of-the-art in the early 1980s, the color of the Jumbotron resembles an old *Three's Company* episode.

2. **Veterans Stadium:** Scant information and lack of unique elements place the Vet in the cellar.

3. **Cinergy Field:** Am I at a Reds game or a Bengals game?

4. **Comiskey Park:** A cheap knockoff of the original Comiskey scoreboard.

5. **Le Stade Olympique:** Parlez vouz Francais?

Nicknames

Which parks have the best nicknames that are actually used and have historical significance (or at least a good story behind them)?

TOPS

1. **The Friendly Confines (Wrigley Field):** A perfect description of a near perfect park.

2. **Camden (Oriole Park at Camden Yards):** Everyone uses this name, which is what the park should have been called to begin with.

3. **The Jake (Jacobs Field):** Gives the park a harder edge and has been widely used since the park opened.

4. **Underwear Stadium (Pro Player Stadium):** Pro Player gets what they deserve with this name, although we'll grant that it probably isn't that widespread a moniker. (NOTE: Pro Player sells underwear, hence the name.)

5. **The House That Ruth Built (Yankee Stadium):** Always a reference at Yankee Stadium, the Bambino would be proud.

6. **The Big Ed (Edison International Field):** A good nickname because the regular name is so long and hard to remember with the whole international thing.

7. **The Dome (The Astrodome):** The first park to use this moniker.

8. **The Coliseum (Oakland Coliseum):** Reminds you of ancient Rome.

9. **The 'Stick (3Com Park):** More character than the corporate name.

10. **Coors (Coors Field):** It's all about the beer.

THE CELLAR

1. **The Vet (Veterans Stadium):** Sounds like you are checking into a hospital.

2. **The Ballpark (The Ballpark in Arlington):** The full name is classy. The short one is confusing.

3. **The Bob (Bank One Ballpark):** What about Bob?

4. **The Q (Qualcomm Stadium):** What have we said about corporate names?

5. **The Ted (Turner Field):** Isn't this guy's ego big enough?

Best Mascot

TOP 10

1. **Philadelphia Phanatic** (Veterans Stadium, Philadelphia, PA): The godfather among mascots. Others call him for advice.

2. **The Moose** (The Kingdome, Seattle, WA): The Moose is a master prop mascot with an ATV routine that he could charge for.

3. **Bernie Brewer** (County Stadium, Milwaukee, WI): When the Brewers go yard, Bernie dances a jig and slides into a huge beer stein. Once again a perfect incarnation of the love.

4. **Youpie** (Le Stade Olympique, Montreal, Canada): With a name like that, how can you go wrong?

5. **Mr. Met** (Shea Stadium, New York, NY): Immortalized in a *SportsCenter* ad, also known for riding elevators (see Shea Stadium chapter).

6. **Stomper** (Oakland Coliseum, Oakland, CA): The A's were called white elephants by New York Giants manager John McGraw in the 1920s, and Connie Mack took

to the challenge by placing elephant patches on the Athletics' jersey sleeves. Stomper is a descendant of this joke.

7. **Pirate Parrot** (Three Rivers Stadium, Pittsburgh, PA): Pirates and parrots, get it? Arrgg.

8. **Slugger** (Kauffman Stadium, Kansas City, MO): Slugger the lion is the most mobile in the business, being the one mascot that visits every section of the park at virtually every game.

9. **Billy the Marlin** (Pro Player Stadium, Miami, FL): The Fish has done a good job keeping fans interested with games, giveaways, and appearances.

10. **Paws** (Tiger Stadium, Detroit, MI): Fun-loving tiger makes the people laugh.

THE CELLAR

1. **Mr. Red** (Cinergy Field, Cincinnati, OH): A low-grade replica of Mr. Met, Mr. Red's head looks like two third graders made it in their basement. We know Cincinnati is a small market, but this is ridiculous.

2. **Slider** (Jacobs Field, Cleveland, OH): A Phanatic wanna-be.

3. **Dinger** (Coors Field, Denver, CO): I guess they found dino bones at the site of Coors Field and went with the dinosaur theme. The stretch is a little too much, plus the costume has a striking similarity to Barney.

4. **Crazy Crab** (3Com Park, San Francisco, CA): A strange second-class mascot for the Giants that few even know exists.

5. **FireBird** (Busch Stadium, St. Louis, MO): Simply the scariest mascot in baseball.

Field

We wanted to rank the playing fields, but we could hardly tell the difference between any of them, except of course for Cleveland's, with its signature dirt, and Tiger, with its throwback convex drainage-enabling shape. In general, major league grounds crews do an excellent job. We defy anyone to attempt to label each of the major league ball fields just by looking at the grass and dirt alone. That said, we do have a few bones to pick with the worst fields in baseball, so we list only the cellar below. They are all turf fields.

THE CELLAR

1. **Cinergy Field:** There is simply no good reason for any outdoor stadium to have AstroTurf with mound and base cutouts.

2. **Three Rivers Stadium:** Ditto.

3. **Tropicana Field:** Yeah, we know it's under a dome, but this is Florida. We want grass.

4. **The Kingdome:** Ditto for Seattle, another city with no good reason to deprive us of the smell of grass.

5. **Veterans Stadium:** Displaces itself from Cinergy and Three Rivers by virtue of the Phanatic's pioneering use of the turf to provide ATV entertainment value.

Irrational Exuberance

ours for particular stadiums based on our experience

Five parks that we love for no good reason other than that we had a real good time there.

TOP 5

1. **County Stadium:** We just love the place. Nobody else does. We don't know why.

2. **Qualcomm Stadium:** Who says you can't buy friends? They treated us like kings, and the extra perks go a long way in making us wish we had never left.

3. **The Astrodome:** The free-flowing Shiner Bock and the many perks we experienced, along with three of our closest friends, turned the oft-reviled Astrodome, toward which I was already biased, into one of Dave's favorite places.

4. **Jacobs Field:** Dave always loved the Jake. It took the Terrace Club experience to convert me.

5. **Fenway Park:** Yeah, it probably would have been number one, but the experience we had, including baseball-induced moments of clarity for both of us, puts it in a class of its own.

Irrational Exuberance

stadium employees for us

Five parks in which we were treated entirely too well.

TOP 5

1. **Dodger Stadium:** Not only did we get all of the perks you could imagine at Dodger Stadium, but everyone involved in taking care of us really seemed interested in our trip and excited to be around us.

2. **Qualcomm Stadium:** A gaggle of free stuff, complimentary food coma, the best seats in the house, and a trip to the owner's box. Who did they think we were?

3. **The Astrodome:** We must clarify that all attention paid to us at the Dome was from Aramark personnel, not the stadium or team people. We still got great seats, full-access passes, and free reign with some of the best food in baseball—just going to show that the concessionaires are the ones with the real power.

4. **Coors Field:** Again, we were treated to all the frills, and the experience was magnified by the fact that the people showing us around were having as much fun as we were. How do I get that job?

5. **Camden Yards:** Again, all Aramark. These guys deserve special consideration for getting us into the park when there were no tickets to be had in the city.

top comments and questions that come up all the time

1. **Are Dave and you still friends?** Yes. Don't ask how that's possible. It's complicated. Suffice it to say that the bond formed between two people when they share such a substantial experience with so many indelible memories is thick enough to withstand any petty squabbles. Yes, it was a substantial experience.

2. **Did you eat a hot dog in every park?** Yes, and usually more than one. No, neither of us got sick of them. In fact, we are still organizing regular Sunday barbecues trying to re-create that magical Milwaukee brat.

3. **Did you master the attendance game?** You think you've got it figured out, but you don't. Sometimes it comes down to the middle two choices, but sometimes the widest two, and more often than not, the answer is higher rather than lower.

4. **"Take Me Out to the Ballgame"** Although they sing it everywhere (we refuse to acknowledge what happened in Toronto), the lyrics are somehow always different. Is it "to the crowd" or "with the crowd"? "ever get back" or "never get back"? "crackerjack" or "crackerjacks"? I'll tell you one thing, none of the stadium operators seem to know. All I know for sure is that it is "root, root, root for the Astros."

5. **How did you deal with the fifteen thousand miles of driving?** First, we had a lot of friends do the dirty work for us. Nonetheless, this was the most difficult part of the trip. It required motivation, many naps, and caffeine. Our similar music tastes helped out as well.

6. **Did you bring a video camera? Will there be a movie?** At times it was a huge pain, but it was worth it, just watching the eleven hours of footage we shot. Someday I hope to get it cut into something watchable. As far as a movie goes, we are thinking Ben Affleck as Brad and Ben Stiller as Dave.

7. **What do you enjoy about baseball?** The artistry. The relaxed, sociable pace. Cheering on your team. Being able to appreciate how hard it actually is to hit a baseball. And because it was always there (except during the strike of '94) when there was nowhere else to turn, as James Earl Jones says in that great movie, "The one constant through the years has been baseball."

8. **What would have been the one thing that would have made the trip even cooler?** Taking batting practice on a major league field.

10 Tips if you are thinking about touring the ballparks on your own:

1. **Find someone to go with you:** You could make this a personal journey and spend the whole summer traveling across the country and getting in touch with your true self. But unless you are at that soul-searching stage in life, you are going to get very bored trying to pull this trip off alone. Additionally, if you are working with a budget and have certain time constraints, such as a job perhaps, you need to move through the country fast. No one can or should drive that much by themselves. We know what kind of wandering the mind can do when you are stuck behind the wheel with nothing but an open road in front of you and a sleeping friend in the passenger seat. It was plenty introspective enough for us this way. We would have gone batty had we been forced to be any more alone with our thoughts than we already were when we were together.

2. **Try not to kill each other:** Now that you have found someone to go on your trip with you, you need to make sure you will both make it through the trip together. We are not entirely sure how you are supposed to do this. We still think it was mostly dumb luck that we both survived the trip intact. But we do have a number of suggestions:

   - If at all possible, recruit a few mutual friends to meet you at various points on the trip and travel with you so as to cut the inevitable tension. It is best if these are mutual friends, but even respective families can be an effective buffer.
   - Find time at regular intervals to be apart, anything from splurging on separate motel rooms to sitting in opposite corners of the stadium for a couple of games. You need time apart, and you need to use it whenever you can get it.
   - Know ahead of time what each other's musical tastes are and ensure that they are compatible. If not, abort the mission entirely. Music is the one constant on the road, and if you can't agree on anything to play, then you won't survive.

3. **Contact the teams:** They generally love people who do this, and if you can convince them you are for real, they will support you.

4. **Contact the concessionaires:** Financially speaking, contacting concessionaires is more important than contacting the teams. You will undoubtedly feel compelled to sample liberally among the ballpark's fare, and costs can run up real fast.

5. **Get a cell phone:** This is the wireless age, and you will need to be just a phone call away at all times. Without the cell, you will never be able to keep in touch with the representatives at the later ballparks who are going to be taking care of you.

6. **Get free roaming and long distance on your cell phone:** This was the biggest lesson that Dave and I learned. You are going to be using the cell phone a lot. More often than not, you will not be in a major metropolitan area. Buck-a-minute roaming fees can add up real fast. Ours totaled almost four figures.

5. **Don't sell yourself short:** What you are about to do is truly crazy. You should be well aware of that going in. Sell yourself as such when you talk to people, particularly team and ballpark representatives, about your trip. If you only see this as a chance to get some free food and notoriety, you are not truly crazy and will never make it.

6. **Understand that you are truly crazy:** We can't stress this enough. You may think that you are just an avid baseball fan and this is every fan's greatest dream. You are mistaken. Normal people think that something like this is insane. They are right because they are normal. You are not normal. Do not try to pretend that you are, because people you talk to will figure you out in a second. Simply accept that you are crazy and revel in it.

7. **Try to have fun:** This is your trip. Don't go into it thinking that you have to do certain things—like keep a detailed journal, spend a lot of time trying to weasel your way into free stuff, or stop at every National Park along the way—just because you should get everything out of such a momentous trip. Sure, we did these things, but only because we were unnecessarily paranoid and poor (although we'll grant they have helped a lot in writing this book). You don't need to do anything if it doesn't suit you. In the end, what is really going to matter to you about the trip will be the memories you share with the people who were there with you and the stories that you share with everybody else.

8. **Take a lot of pictures:** Thus ensuring that you will never forget anything important that happened on the most memorable trip of your life.

References

We would like to thank the teams for supplying general information on the ballparks. While most of the information in the book is from our trip, other supporting facts were provided by the teams. This is a list of the references used in each chapter to obtain and check public information on the ballparks. The data include dimensions, ballpark history, and attendance. Information for the appendix chapters on Safeco Field, Enron Field, Comerica Park, and Pacific Bell Park was provided by the respective teams.

The Astrodome (Houston, TX), home of the Houston Astros—all references provided by the Houston Astros and their website *www.astros.com.*

The Ballpark in Arlington (Arlington, TX), home of the Texas Rangers—all references provided by the Texas Rangers, their media guide, and their website *www.texasrangers.com.*

Bank One Ballpark (Phoenix, AZ), home of the Arizona Diamondbacks—all references provided by the Arizona Diamondbacks and their website *www.azdiamondbacks.com.*

Busch Stadium (St. Louis, MO), home of the St. Louis Cardinals—all references provided by the St. Louis Cardinals and their website *www.stlcardinals.com.*

Cinergy Field (Cincinnati, OH), home of the Cincinnati Reds—all references provided by the Cincinnati Reds and their website *www.cincinnatireds.com.*

Comiskey Park (Chicago, IL), home of the Chicago White Sox—all references provided by the Chicago White Sox and their website *www.chisox.com.*

Coors Field (Denver, CO), home of the Colorado Rockies—all references provided by the Colorado Rockies and their website *www.coloradorockies.com.*

County Stadium (Milwaukee, WI), home of the Milwaukee Brewers—all references provided by the Milwaukee Brewers and their website *www.milwaukeebrewers.com.*

Dodger Stadium (Los Angeles, CA), home of the Los Angeles Dodgers—all references provided by the Los Angeles Dodgers, their media guide, and their website *www.dodgers.com.*

Edison International Field (Anaheim, CA), home of the Anaheim Angels—all references provided by the Anaheim Angels and their website *www.angelsbaseball.com*.

Fenway Park (Boston, MA), home of the Boston Red Sox—all references provided by the Boston Red Sox and their website *www.redsox.com*.

Jacobs Field (Cleveland, OH), home of the Cleveland Indians—all references provided by the Cleveland Indians and their website *www.indians.com*.

Kaufman Stadium (Kansas City, MO), home of the Kansas City Royals—all references provided by the Kansas City Royals and their website *www.kcroyals.com*.

The Kingdome (Seattle, WA), home of the Seattle Mariners—all references provided by the Seattle Mariners and their website *www.mariners.org*.

Le Stade Olympique (Montreal, Canada), home of the Montreal Expos—all references provided by the Montreal Expos and their website *www.montrealexpos.com*.

The Metrodome (Minneapolis, MN), home of the Minnesota Twins—all references provided by the Minnesota Twins and their website *www.mntwins.com*.

Oriole Park at Camden Yards (Baltimore, MD), home of the Baltimore Orioles—all references provided by the Baltimore Orioles and their website *www.theorioles.com*.

Pro Player Stadium (Miami, FL), home of the Florida Marlins—all references provided by the Florida Marlins, their media guide, and their website *www.floridamarlins.com*.

Qualcomm Stadium (San Diego, CA), home of the San Diego Padres—all references provided by the San Diego Padres and their website *www.padres.com*.

Shea Stadium (New York, NY), home of the New York Mets—all references provided by the New York Mets and their website *www.mets.com*.

SkyDome (Toronto, Canada), home of the Toronto Blue Jays—all references provided by the Toronto Blue Jays and their website *www.bluejays.ca*.

Oakland Coliseum (Oakland, CA), home of the Oakland Athletics—all references provided by the Oakland Athletics and their website *www.oaklandathletics.com*.

3Com Park (San Francisco, CA), home of the San Francisco Giants—all references provided by the San Francisco Giants and their website *www.sfgiants.com*.

Three Rivers Stadium (Pittsburgh, PA), home of the Pittsburgh Pirates—all references provided by the Pittsburgh Pirates and their website *www.pirateball.com*.

Tiger Stadium (Detroit, MI), home of the Detroit Tigers—all references provided by the Detroit Tigers and their website *www.detroittigers.com*.

Tropicana Field (St. Petersburg, FL), home of the Tampa Bay Devil Rays—all references provided by the Tampa Bay Devil Rays and their website *www.devilray.com*.

Turner Field (Atlanta, GA), home of the Atlanta Braves—all references provided by the Atlanta Braves and their website *www.atlantabraves.com.*

Veterans Stadium (Philadelphia, PA), home of the Philadelphia Phillies—all references provided by the Philadelphia Phillies and their website *www.phillies.com.*

Wrigley Field (Chicago, IL), home of the Chicago Cubs—all references provided by the Chicago Cubs and their website *www.cubs.com.*

Yankee Stadium (New York, NY), home of the New York Yankees—all references provided by the New York Yankees, their media guide, and their website *www.yankees.com*

And we want to add a special thank-you to everyone else who helped with the facts on the ballparks, including Brendon Foster and Ira Kaufman.